THE EUROPEAN UNION SERIES

General Editors: Neill Nugent, William E. Paterson

The European Union series provides an authoritative library on the European Union, ranging from general introductory texts to definitive assessments of key institutions and actors, issues, policies and policy processes, and the role of member states.

Books in the series are written by leading scholars in their fields and reflect the most up-to-date research and debate. Particular attention is paid to accessibility and clear presentation for a wide audience of students, practitioners and interested general readers.

The series editors are **Neill Nugent**, Visiting Professor, College of Europe, Bruges and Honorary Professor, University of Salford, UK, and **William E. Paterson,** Honorary Professor in German and European Studies, University of Aston. Their co-editor until his death in July 1999, **Vincent Wright,** was a Fellow of Nuffield College, Oxford University.

Feedback on the series and book proposals are always welcome and should be sent to Steven Kennedy, Palgrave Macmillan, Houndmills, Basingstoke, Hampshire, RG21 6XS, UK, or by e-mail to **s.kennedy@palgrave.com**

General textbooks

Published

Laurie Buonanno and Neill Nugent **Policies and Policy Processes of the European Union**

Desmond Dinan **Encyclopedia of the European Union** [Rights: Europe only]

Desmond Dinan **Europe Recast: A History of the European Union** [Rights: Europe only]

Desmond Dinan **Ever Closer Union: An Introduction to European Integration (4th edn)** [Rights: Europe only]

Mette Eilstrup Sangiovanni (ed.) **Debates on European Integration: A Reader**

Simon Hix and Bjørn Høyland **The Political System of the European Union (3rd edn)**

Dirk Leuffen, Berthold Rittberger and Frank Schimmelfennig **Differentiated Integration**

Paul Magnette **What is the European Union? Nature and Prospects**

John McCormick **Understanding the European Union: A Concise Introduction (5th edn)**

Brent F. Nelsen and Alexander Stubb **The European Union: Readings on the Theory and Practice of European Integration (3rd edn)** [Rights: Europe only]

Neill Nugent (ed.) **European Union Enlargement**

Neill Nugent **The Government and Politics of the European Union (7th edn)**

John Peterson and Elizabeth Bomberg **Decision-Making in the European Union**

Ben Rosamond **Theories of European Integration**

Sabine Saurugger **Theoretical Approaches to European Integration**

Esther Versluis, Mendeltje van Keulen and Paul Stephenson **Analyzing the European Union Policy Process**

Hubert Zimmermann and Andreas Dür (eds) **Key Controversies in European Integration**

Forthcoming

Magnus Ryner and Alan Cafruny **A Critical Introduction to the European Union**

Also planned

The Political Economy of European Integration

Series Standing Order (outside North America only)
ISBN 978–0–333–71695–3 hardback
ISBN 978–0–333–69352–0 paperback
Full details from www.palgrave.com

Visit Palgrave Macmillan's EU Resource area at www.palgrave.com/politics/eu/

The Foreign Policy of the European Union

2nd edition

Stephan Keukeleire

and

Tom Delreux

First edition 2008
Second edition 2014
Published by
PALGRAVE MACMILLAN

Palgrave Macmillan in the UK is an imprint of Macmillan Publishers
Limited, registered in England, company number 785998, of Houndmills,
Basingstoke, Hampshire RG21 6XS.

Palgrave Macmillan in the US is a division of St Martin's Press LLC,
175 Fifth Avenue, New York, NY 10010.

Palgrave Macmillan is the global academic imprint of the above companies
and has companies and representatives throughout the world.

Palgrave® and Macmillan® are registered trademarks in the United States,
the United Kingdom, Europe and other countries

ISBN 978–1–137–02575–3 hardback
ISBN 978–1–137–02574–6 paperback

This book is printed on paper suitable for recycling and made from fully
managed and sustained forest sources. Logging, pulping and manufacturing
processes are expected to conform to the environmental regulations of the
country of origin.

A catalogue record for this book is available from the British Library.

A catalog record for this book is available from the Library of Congress.

Typeset by Cambrian Typesetters, Camberley, Surrey

Printed in China

Contents

List of Figures, Tables and Boxes

Figures

Tables

Boxes

Preface to the Second Edition

The second edition of *The Foreign Policy of the European Union* is a thorough revision and update of the first edition of 2008. This new edition takes into account the latest developments in EU foreign policy since the entry into force of the Lisbon Treaty and up to the enlargement of the EU to 28 member states. It extensively relies on the recent thriving academic literature analysing the EU in global politics, the external relations of the EU and foreign policy in general. As compared to the first edition, it comprises two new chapters (on key issues and on the EU and multilateral organizations) and several completely new sections (such as on the European Neighbourhood Policy and on the EU's relations with emerging powers). The current version also includes a set of boxes with case studies and explanations of theoretical concepts, meant to further strengthen its didactical approach.

This major update was only possible thanks to a number of people and institutions, who all deserve our warmest thanks. First of all, we would like to express our gratitude to Jennifer MacNaughtan, the co-author of the first edition of this book who, after finalizing that first edition, exchanged writing on foreign policy for practicing foreign policy. We thank our publisher at Palgrave, Steven Kennedy, as well as Stephen Wenham and Helen Caunce; the 'European Union Series' editors, Neill Nugent and William Paterson; and anonymous reviewers for their constructive comments and continuing confidence.

We are grateful for the intellectual input we have received over many years from colleagues at the Institute for International and European Policy, the Centre for European Studies, and the Leuven Centre for Global Governance Studies at the University of Leuven (KU Leuven, Belgium); at the Institut de sciences politiques Louvain-Europe of the University of Louvain (UC Louvain, Louvain-la-Neuve, Belgium); and at the Department of EU International Relations and Diplomacy Studies at the College of Europe in Bruges (Belgium). Stephan's work on this book has also been possible through the support of the 'Total Chair of EU Foreign Policy', which he has held at the College of Europe (2011–13).

Several colleagues closely followed the process of writing this second edition and provided support in various ways. We are particularly grateful to Edith Drieskens and Amelia Hadfield for the stimulating discussions we had on this new edition. We also thank our colleagues from other universities and research institutes across the globe, as well as the European and national diplomats and civil servants for the stimulating discussions and for contributing to our understanding (or misunderstanding?) of the EU and its foreign policy.

Through the entire writing and rewriting process, we could count on the critical comments, substantive input and practical assistance of the following very dedicated researchers and assistants: Floor Keuleers, Bas Hooijmaaijers, Dimitri Renmans, Irina Petrova and Arnout Justaert at the University of Leuven; Anahita Sabouri, Xavier Follebouckt, Bart Van Ballaert and François Randour at the University of Louvain; and Raphaël Metais, Charles Thépaut and Bohdana Dimitrovova at the College of Europe. Many thanks also go to our proofreaders, Jed Odermatt and Colleen Carroll.

We are also grateful to the students who were as always a stimulating sounding board and who provided constructive comments on the first edition of this book when following our courses on the foreign policy and external relations of the EU in the master's programmes 'EU International Relations and Diplomacy Studies' and 'European Interdisciplinary Studies' at the College of Europe in Bruges/Natolin; 'European Studies: Transnational and Global Perspectives', 'European Politics and Policies' and 'Comparative and International Politics' at the University of Leuven; and 'European Studies' and 'The Interdisciplinary Analysis of the European Construction' at the University of Louvain and the Saint-Louis University (Brussels).

In embarking on the second edition of this book, we once again want to express our gratitude to our family and friends and particularly to Klaartje, Camille and Soetkin (for Stephan) and to Marjan, Marte and Stien (for Tom), who initially shared our illusion that preparing a second edition of a book is not at all that much work.

STEPHAN KEUKELEIRE
TOM DELREUX

A range of supporting materials for this book, including an internet guide to EU foreign policy, didactical resources and suggestions for further reading for each chapter and section, is available on the comprehensive Online Resource Guide 'Exploring EU Foreign Policy': www.eufp.eu

List of Abbreviations

AA	Association Agreement
ACP	African, Caribbean and Pacific
ACTA	Anti-Counterfeiting Trade Agreement
AFET	Committee on Foreign Affairs (European Parliament)
AFSJ	Area of Freedom, Security and Justice
AMIS	African Union Mission in Darfur
AMISOM	African Union Mission in Somalia
APEC	Asia-Pacific Economic Cooperation
APF	African Peace Facility
AQIM	Al-Qaeda in the Islamic Maghreb
ARF	ASEAN Regional Forum
ASEAN	Association of Southeast Asian Nations
ASEAN+3	ASEAN + Japan, South Korea, China
ASEM	Asia–Europe Meeting
AU	African Union
BAM	Border Assistance Mission
BASIC	Brazil, South Africa, India, China
BiH	Bosnia and Herzegovina
BRIC	Brazil, Russia, India, China
BRICS	Brazil, Russia, India, China, South Africa
BUDG	Committee on Budgets (European Parliament)
CAC	Codex Alimentarius Commission
CAP	common agricultural policy
CCP	common commercial policy
CDP	Capability Development Plan
CEECs	Central and Eastern European countries
CETA	Comprehensive Economic and Trade Agreement
CFSP	Common Foreign and Security Policy
CIS	Commonwealth of Independent States
CIVCOM	Committee for Civilian Aspects of Crisis Management
CMPD	Crisis Management and Planning Directorate
CONT	Committee on Budgetary Control (European Parliament)
COREPER	*Comité des représentants permanents* (Committee of Permanent Representatives)
COREU	*Correspondance européenne* (European Correspondence)
CPCC	Civilian Planning and Conduct Capability
CPFI	Civil Protection Financial Instrument

CSCE	Conference on Security and Cooperation in Europe
CSD	UN Commission on Sustainable Development
CSDP	Common Security and Defence Policy
DCFTA	Deep and Comprehensive Free Trade Area
DCI	Development Cooperation Instrument
DDR	disarmament, demobilization and reintegration
DEVE	Committee on Development (European Parliament)
DG DEVCO	Directorate General Development and Cooperation – EuropeAid
DG	Directorate General
DRC	Democratic Republic of Congo
DROI	Committee on Human Rights (European Parliament)
EADS	European Aeronautic Defence and Space Company
EaP	Eastern Partnership
EAS	East Asia Summit
EBA	Everything but Arms
EBRD	European Bank for Reconstruction and Development
EC	European Community
ECB	European Central Bank
ECFR	European Council on Foreign Relations
ECHO	European Community Humanitarian Office
ECJ	European Court of Justice
ECOFIN	Economic and Financial Affairs Council
ECSC	European Coal and Steel Community
EDA	European Defence Agency
EDC	European Defence Community
EDEM	European Defence Equipment Market
EDF	European Development Fund
EDRT	European Defence Research and Technology
EEAS	European External Action Service
EEC	European Economic Community
EED	European Endowment for Democracy
EIB	European Investment Bank
EIDHR	European Instrument for Democracy and Human Rights
EIF	European Investment Fund
EMP	Euro-Mediterranean Partnership
EMU	European Monetary Union
ENI	European Neighbourhood Instrument
ENP	European Neighbourhood Policy
ENPI	European Neighbourhood and Partnership Instrument
EP	European Parliament
EPA	Economic Partnership Agreement
EPC	European Political Cooperation
ESA	European Space Agency

ESDP	European Security and Defence Policy
ESS	European Security Strategy
EU	European Union
EU27	European Union (with 27 member states)
EU-3	France, UK, Germany
EU-3+3	EU-3 with China, Russia and the USA
EU4	UK, France, Germany, Italy
EUAVSEC	European Union Aviation Security Mission
EU BAM	European Union Border Assistance Mission
EUCAP	European Union Capacity Building Mission
EU COPPS	European Union Coordinating Office for Palestinian Police Support
EU EOM	EU Election Observation Mission
EUISS	European Union Institute for Security Studies
EUFOR	European Union Force
EUJUST	European Union Rule of Law Mission
EULEX	European Union Rule of Law Mission
EUMC	European Union Military Committee
EUMM	European Union Monitoring Mission
EUMS	European Union Military Staff
EUNAVFOR	European Union Naval Force
EUPAT	European Union Police Advisory Team
EUPM	European Union Police Mission
EUPOL	European Union Police Mission
Euratom	European Atomic Energy Community
Eurojust	European Union Judicial Cooperation Unit
Europol	European Union Law Enforcement Agency
EUSC	European Union Satellite Centre
EUSEC	EU advisory and assistance mission for security reform
EUSR	EU Special Representative
EU SSR	European Union Security Sector Reform Mission
EUTM	EU Training Mission
EVHAD	European Volunteer Humanitarian Aid Corps
FAO	Food and Agriculture Organization
FPA	foreign policy analysis
FPIS	Foreign Policy Instrument Service
FYROM	Former Yugoslav Republic of Macedonia
G20	Group of Twenty
G7	Group of Seven
G8	Group of Eight
GDP	gross domestic product
GMES	Global Monitoring for Environment and Security
GMO	genetically modified organism
Gx	G7/8/20

HoD	Head of Delegation
HR	High Representative
HR/VP	High Representative of the Union for Foreign Affairs and Security Policy/Vice-President of the European Commission
HRC	UN Human Rights Council
IBSA	India, Brazil, South Africa
ICC	International Criminal Court
ICTY	International Criminal Tribunal for the former Yugoslavia
IFI	international financial institution
IfS	Instrument for Stability
IGC	Intergovernmental Conference
ILO	International Labour Organization
IMF	International Monetary Fund
INTA	Committee on International Trade (European Parliament)
IPA	Instrument for Pre-Accession Assistance
IR	international relations
JHA	Justice and Home Affairs
LDC	least developed countries
MDGs	Millennium Development Goals
MEA	multilateral environmental agreement
MEP	Member of the European Parliament
NATO	North Atlantic Treaty Organization
NGOs	non-governmental organizations
NPT	Non-Proliferation Treaty
ODA	official development aid
OECD	Organization for Economic Co-operation and Development
OHQ	Operational Headquarters
OJ	Official Journal of the European Union
OpsCen	EU Operations Centre
OSCE	Organization for Security and Co-operation in Europe
OTIF	Intergovernmental Organization for International Carriage by Rail
PCA	Partnership and Cooperation Agreements
PI	Partnership Instrument
PSC	Political and Security Committee
QMV	qualified majority voting
R2P	responsibility to protect
REIO	Regional Economic Integration Organization
RIC	Russia, India, China
RIO	Regional Integration Organization
SAA	Stabilization and Association Agreement

SAARC	South Asian Association for Regional Cooperation
SACEUR	Supreme Allied Commander Europe
SALW	small arms and light weapons
SAP	Stabilization and Association Process
SCIFA	Strategic Committee on Immigration, Frontiers and Asylum
SCIMF	Subcommittee on the IMF and Related Issues
SCO	Shanghai Cooperation Organization
SEA	Single European Act
SEDE	Committee on Security and Defence (European Parliament)
SFOR	Stabilization Force in Bosnia and Herzegovina
SHAPE	Supreme Headquarters Allied Powers Europe
SITCEN	Situation Centre
SSR	security sector reform
SWIFT	Society for Worldwide Interbank Financial Telecommunication
TCA	Trade and Cooperation Agreement
TEU	Treaty on European Union
TFEU	Treaty on the Functioning of the European Union
TFG	Transitional Federal Government (Somalia)
TRIPS	Agreement on Trade-Related Aspects of Intellectual Property Rights
TTIP	Transatlantic Trade and Investment Partnership
UAV	Unmanned Aerial Vehicle
UfM	Union for the Mediterranean
UN	Unites Nations
UNDP	United Nations Development Programme
UNFCCC	United Nations Framework Convention on Climate Change
UNGA	United Nations General Assembly
UNSC	United Nations Security Council
UNSCR	United Nations Security Council Resolution
WB	World Bank
WEU	Western European Union
WHO	World Health Organization
WMD	weapons of mass destruction
WTO	World Trade Organization

Introduction

Scope, Rationale and Relevance of the Book

This book is about the foreign policy of the European Union (EU). Applying a broad understanding of what EU foreign policy is, this book does not limit its analysis to foreign policy *sensu stricto*, namely the Common Foreign and Security Policy (CFSP) and the Common Security and Defence Policy (CSDP), but examines EU foreign policy *sensu lato*, which also considers areas such as trade, development, enlargement or external environmental policy as an inherent part of foreign policy.

As we will explain in detail in Chapter 1, we argue that EU foreign policy is 'multifaceted' (comprising the broad range of areas such as CFSP, CSDP, trade, enlargement, etc.), 'multi-method' (combining various policy-making methods, some with the member states and others with supranational institutions like the European Commission in the driving seat) and 'multilevel' (entailing the national and the European levels). The rationale behind taking such a broad perspective is that the whole picture of EU foreign policy can only be fully understood and explained if one takes into account these various 'facets', 'methods' and 'levels'.

We thus adopt a broad view on EU foreign policy, which we define as the area of European policies that is directed at the external environment with the objective of influencing that environment and the behaviour of other actors within it, in order to pursue interests, values and goals.

Considering the EU as a constantly evolving political system, the book discusses the opportunities and the constraints faced by the EU in developing a genuine foreign policy and becoming a fully-fledged global actor. It looks at what the EU can mean in international politics, how it aims to contribute to shaping the world order and what it actually achieves. It also opens the 'black box' of the EU: it examines how the EU functions internally when it acts internationally and what consequences this has for the EU's external performance. The book gives an overview of the main areas of the EU's foreign policy, its challenges and shortcomings, its driving forces as well as the political dynamics behind it.

When observing the foreign policy of the EU, one is often confronted with puzzling observations. They include, among others, the following questions. While the EU has established nearly 30 military and civilian crisis management operations and missions, why is it that the UK and France took the lead in a NATO operation in Libya in 2011 and that

1

France sent combat forces on its own to Mali in 2013? As the EU aims at encompassing strategic partnerships with Russia or China, why are the member states simultaneously sidelining the EU by concluding bilateral agreements with those countries, for instance on energy issues? Why does the EU not have the right to speak with a single voice in most international organizations despite the fact that the EU has a Delegation in a majority of third countries? And, while the EU has achieved remarkable success in stabilizing and restructuring Central and Eastern Europe after the end of the Cold War through its enlargement policy, why is its relevance as a foreign policy actor still so often questioned? This book offers insights that contribute to a better understanding of these puzzles.

Why should we care about EU foreign policy? There are historical, empirical and analytical reasons why it is relevant to study the foreign policy of the EU. A first reason is indeed *historical* (see also Chapter 2). From its very start, European integration *was* foreign policy. The EU and European integration more generally are in themselves the product of successful American and French foreign policy in the 1950s, launched to embed West Germany within a broader supranational European framework: the European Coal and Steel Community (ECSC), which was later complemented by the European Economic Community (EEC). The goal was to limit national sovereignty and transfer power over crucial policy domains (at first coal and steel) in order to fundamentally resolve the enmity between European nations, which had led to two world wars and to tens of millions of casualties.

Since its early days, European integration not only focused on internal policies, but it also had an important external relations dimension. External trade policy, development cooperation, and establishing international agreements with third countries and other regions in the world have been a cornerstone of the EU's track record since the Treaty of Rome (1957). However, the very concept of 'foreign policy' was only explicitly included in the EU's range of activities in the Maastricht Treaty in the early 1990s, when the EU's Common Foreign and Security Policy (CFSP) kicked off. The CFSP remained under the control of member states and it only modestly developed in the following years. After a British–French initiative at the end of the 1990s, the EU went a step further, launching its own Common Security and Defence Policy (CSDP). The entry into force of the Lisbon Treaty in 2009 included new changes to further increase – at least on paper – the coherence, effectiveness and visibility of the EU's foreign policy, including the creation of a European External Action Service (EEAS).

Six decades after six European countries began supranational integration with the establishment of the ECSC, the EU has developed into a political system with 28 member states and with powers over a broad range of policy fields. Today, European integration *is* still foreign policy, as is witnessed in the incorporation of the former communist countries from Central and Eastern Europe in the mid-2000s. That European integration is foreign policy also appears in the EU's current support for the transformation of the countries that emerged from the wars in the Western Balkans, which in mid-2013 resulted in Croatia joining the EU. However, the EU *is* no longer simply the product of foreign policy; it also *has* a foreign policy, which is conducted through various channels and toolboxes. It is also recognized by other actors as an important international player in many respects.

A second reason why examining EU foreign policy is relevant relates to the fact that there is a range of both political and economic *empirical* indications that the EU is in some cases an important and influential international actor. Brussels today ranks second – following Washington, DC – on the list of cities hosting the highest number of diplomatic representatives worldwide. The EU itself currently has diplomatic delegations in nearly 130 countries all over the world. Whereas the EU was absent on a number of major battlefields, such as Iraq or Afghanistan, it does play a role in some of the world's most dangerous and sensitive, yet often less visible crisis areas, such as in Somalia or Mali. Since 2003, the EU has deployed almost 30 EU military operations and civilian missions on three continents, ranging from involvement in the Western Balkans, to anti-piracy operations near the Somali coast, to military training missions in Mali and Niger to help these countries in countering Jihadist forces. The EU closely cooperates in these areas with other international organizations such as the North Atlantic Treaty Organization (NATO), the United Nations (UN) or African regional organizations.

Equally important, the EU is a major economic actor, being the world's largest trading bloc. The EU today accounts for almost one-fifth of world trade in goods and even more when trade in services is included. Likewise, responsible for more than half of global development aid, the EU and its member states are the world's largest providers of development aid. With an annual spending of more than €1 billion it is the world's second largest humanitarian aid donor. In many other domains such as the environment, it clearly has global leadership ambitions. In the last decades, the EU has grown considerably as international actor. Foreign policy is today a remarkable area of European integration, especially given the fact that it goes to the heart of member state sovereignty.

A third reason why it is pertinent to study EU foreign policy is an *analytical* one. As we explained, the EU is *in se* also the product of the foreign policies of its member states. This book thus studies the foreign policy of a newly emerged political system, the EU, that is in itself also the result of the foreign policy of European countries. That the EU consists of member states which have decided to share some of their foreign policy powers but which also still continue to pursue their own foreign policies makes it extremely interesting to study from an analytical point of view. The EU is not an actor that behaves autonomously from the member states, but these member states are an inherent and crucial component of the EU and its foreign policy. This, again, triggers interesting questions. To what extent are the member states, for instance, an impeding or reinforcing factor in the EU's foreign policy? Indeed, since member states can support, sideline or even undermine the EU in its external relations, the multilevel nature of the political system of the EU can in some cases hinder but in other cases also strengthen the foreign policy activities of the EU. This book will present insights about whether, when and how the multilevel nature of the EU matters for its foreign policy.

The Changing Context of EU Foreign Policy

Since the end of the Second World War and the beginning of the European integration project, the context in which the EU conducts its foreign policy has evolved considerably. Depending on the perspective one uses or the argument one aims to present, multiple milestones can be identified in the evolution of the EU's foreign policy. Here, we use three episodes to illustrate this changing context. In each of these three episodes, two crucial subjects of foreign policy came together: conflicts and structures.

Our first episode took place at the very beginning of the European integration project. Immediately after the Second World War, Western European countries were confronted with increasing tensions with the Soviet Union, leading to an arms race between the West and the East. But, simultaneously, the threat of conflict and military disputes in Western Europe declined considerably. Because of the process of European integration (institutionalized today in the EU) and the process of transatlantic cooperation and solidarity (NATO), the political, economic and societal structures of the countries in Europe that were each other's enemies in the first half of the twentieth century became so interrelated that military conflict between them is now very unlikely. Indeed, the integration of the European countries was above all a peace project for Europe.

Second, the end of the Cold War at the end of the 1980s and early 1990s put a stop to the latent East–West confrontation and the related military threats that left their mark on international politics for over four decades. This episode also meant the political reunification of the European continent, whereby the EU assisted the former communist countries from Central and Eastern Europe to reshape their political and economic structures. Step by step, those countries became modern democracies and shifted their economic structures from a planned economy to a free market one. This was largely triggered by the prospect of EU membership and was made possible by the EU's active involvement, demonstrating that the EU's enlargement policy is probably its most effective foreign policy tool. However, developments in the Western Balkans, and particularly in former Yugoslavia, were largely denied and a horrible conflict took place in the EU's backyard. Only with the help of non-EU actors, including NATO, could peace be established in the region. This allowed the EU to aim to restructure the relations between and inside the Western Balkan countries.

Covering events in the EU's southern neighbourhood, at the global level and inside the EU, a third episode occurred at the beginning of the current decade. In the southern neighbourhood, the Arab revolts and the subsequent events in countries like Libya, Syria and Mali have generated regime changes as well as armed conflicts and military interventions in the EU's neighbourhood. In addition to this military dimension, the question that is even more crucial is what political, economic and societal structures in these countries will look like when the storm of the revolts has calmed down. Will the EU be successful in supporting the creation of new legitimate structures in the Mediterranean and convince the population and elites of the EU's added value, or will the Gulf states and Islamic movements be more successful in exerting structural power in the region? Moreover, another shift in the balance of power at the global level is taking place. China and other emerging powers are assuming a stronger stance in international politics, diplomacy or even financial systems – often at the expense of the EU's position on the international scene. Finally, the financial and sovereign debt crisis in the eurozone is confronting the EU with probably the worst and most challenging crisis in its history. One of the consequences is the fact that the EU is rather increasingly focusing on solving its internal problems than on foreign policy. Hence, whereas the EU is focusing on internal crises and developments in its neighbourhood, a global shift is taking place, which is probably even more important for the EU's future aspirations as foreign policy actor.

These three episodes in European integration and international relations demonstrate the complexity and diverse character of EU foreign policy. Moreover, they show that the context in which EU foreign policy takes place has fundamentally changed. But they also make clear that (the analysis of) foreign policy always has to deal with two facets: the avoidance, management and solution of conflicts on the one hand, and the structuring of societies, states and regions on the other. Whereas the former receives much attention in scholarly analyses of foreign policy, the latter is largely overlooked. One of the aims of this book is to contribute to filling that gap.

Objectives and Approach

This book has two major objectives. The first objective is to provide an overview and analysis of EU foreign policy. For purposes of clarity, the book is organized in a rather conventional way, including a historical chapter, three chapters on actors, institutions and policy-making, one chapter on key issues in EU foreign policy, four chapters on the main facets of EU foreign policy (the CFSP; the CSDP; the EU's external action, including trade, development and humanitarian aid; and the external dimensions of internal policies, such as external energy, environment or migration policies), and finally three chapters on the EU's foreign policy towards other parts of the world and towards multilateral organizations. In every chapter, we present the formal and legal bases of the issues discussed, an analysis of how they function in practice, followed by a critical evaluation.

The second objective relates to the argument presented in the previous section. It aims to reappraise the nature of EU foreign policy and of foreign policy more generally. It looks beyond the narrow focus of foreign policy analysis (FPA) on states, crises and conflicts by focusing also on what we term structural foreign policy. This conceptual approach (elaborated in Chapter 1 and returned to in the assessment of theoretical approaches in Chapter 14) provides a vehicle for understanding how foreign policy seeks to shape and influence structures and long-term processes.

This book takes more of an 'inside-out' than an 'outside-in' approach. While we do evaluate the output of EU foreign policy, not least by taking a geographical perspective in Chapters 11 and 12, we can only provide a snapshot of the actual impact of EU foreign policy. Likewise, although the majority of relevant issues and geographical locations are discussed to some extent, we cannot consider the EU's policy with regard to every region of the world or every issue on the international agenda.

Outline of Chapters

Chapter 1 points to the main themes and questions to be tackled in this book by focusing on the particular nature of EU foreign policy. The multifaceted (comprising CFSP/CSDP, external action areas such as trade or development, and the external dimension of internal policies such as external environmental or energy policies), multi-method (using an intergovernmental and a Community policy-making method) and multilevel (based on the interaction between member states and the EU) nature of EU foreign policy is explained here in detail. The chapter also portrays the various areas of tension which influence this policy, and it presents the principles and objectives which inform the EU's foreign policy. The 'structural foreign policy versus relational foreign policy' framework is introduced as an approach to analyse the various dimensions of EU foreign policy. Finally, we situate the analysis of EU foreign policy within the context of globalization.

Chapter 2 gives a historical overview of the ambiguous relationship between European integration and foreign policy from the end of the Second World War to the present day. Analysing the various steps that have been taken, we show that considerable progress has been made in developing a foreign policy at the European level. The chapter also demonstrates how the roots of current discussions on European foreign and security policy are to be found in early debates and policy choices.

Chapter 3 provides an in-depth analysis of the actors and procedures of EU foreign policy. We explore the divergence between a single institutional framework on paper, and the practice of different policy-making methods and competences. The main actors are then analysed: the European Council (bringing together the heads of state and government of the member states); the Council (where ministers of foreign affairs or other sectoral ministers – or their representatives – of the member states meet); the Commission (playing a key role in defining and defending the common interest); the High Representative/Vice-President and the EU's diplomatic service (European External Action Service); the European Parliament (directly elected by the European citizens); and the Court of Justice of the EU (providing judicial oversight); as well as some actors beyond the traditional institutional framework (such as agencies, banks and private actors). Examining who or what is behind the façade of each of these actors, the chapter also provides an evaluation of their functioning and their contribution to EU foreign policy.

In Chapter 4, we proceed to analyse the policy-making process that takes place between the actors presented in the preceding chapter. We provide an overview of the distribution and the nature of the formal competences in the area of foreign policy. The various decision-making procedures are analysed, first from a formal point of view, in order to focus next on the broader policy-making processes as they occur in practice. Both are essential to understand the nature, opportunities and constraints of EU foreign policy as well as the complex web of intra-institutional, inter-institutional and interstate interaction and bargaining that it involves. We argue that on paper, the decision-making processes seem unworkable, but that in practice the EU's various foreign policy actors have developed ways to overcome this complexity. The chapter also discusses the issue of financing EU foreign policy. Finally, it addresses questions regarding the consistency of the EU's foreign policy.

Chapter 5 aims to analyse the national level of foreign policy-making and its relationship with the European level. National foreign policy actors indeed play an important role within each of the policy-making systems analysed in the previous chapter. The chapter examines the constitutional set-up and foreign policy-making mechanisms of the 'big three': the UK, France and Germany. In the multilevel foreign policy system, member states position themselves in terms of power, interests, world-views, role conceptions and special relationships, which has significant ramifications on policy at the EU level. This chapter offers a critical assessment of the 'Europeanization' debate as well as of arguments that are traditionally invoked to explain the limits of EU foreign policy, particularly 'the lack of common interests' and 'the lack of political will'.

Chapter 6 discusses four key issues of EU foreign policy: human rights, democracy and the rule of law; conflict prevention, crisis management and peace-building; non-proliferation and control of arms exports; and the fight against terrorism. These key issues are tackled through policies adopted in the context of CFSP, CSDP and the EU's 'external action', which are discussed in the following chapters. The chapter explains the goals and priorities set by the EU and clarifies the range of instruments available and actors responsible. It then evaluates the EU's actions in the light of its declaratory objectives and external impact.

Chapter 7 focuses on the Common Foreign and Security Policy (CFSP). A preliminary legal and political assessment of CFSP's basic principles and instruments provides the grounding for analysis. It becomes apparent that cooperation between member states is at least as important as common actions or positions and that, often, unilateral action continues to prevail. The chapter analyses the scope of CFSP, which has widened greatly in the last two decades. It also assesses the extent to which the EU's declaratory policy has been complemented with an operational foreign policy.

Chapter 8 on the Common Security and Defence Policy (CSDP) takes stock of the efforts to provide the EU with military and civilian capabilities and to strengthen its crisis management capacities. Taking into account the EU's relations with NATO, the chapter first discusses the military dimension of CSDP. We demonstrate that the EU's military capabilities are not achieved by creating permanent European forces, but that they are based on the voluntary and temporary contribution of the member states. The chapter then analyses the civilian dimension of CSDP, which is focused on the deployment of non-military actors who contribute to security outside the EU. We present an overview of the EU's record regarding CSDP military operations and civilian missions. The chapter offers analytical axes along which CSDP operations and future developments can be measured. Attempts to strengthen the industrial and technological basis of the European defence sector are also analysed.

Chapter 9 focuses on policy fields developed within the framework of the EU's 'external action': trade, association and cooperation agreements, enlargement, development cooperation, sanctions, and humanitarian aid. These are essential for the foreign policy of the EU since they provide its major instruments and have shaped the formation of EU foreign policy, yet paradoxically can hinder the achievement of some of its objectives. We demonstrate that the EU's attempt to protect strategic and trade interests in many cases prevail over and undermine its stated foreign policy goals.

Chapter 10 assesses the external dimension of some equally relevant 'internal' policy fields. We discuss how the EU acts internationally in the fields of energy, environment and climate change, and in the field of freedom, security and justice. We present the challenges the EU faces, the way it responds and the impediments it encounters. The EU's external activities in these areas have had a marked impact on its foreign policy as well as the way in which it is perceived by third countries and regions. In these policy fields, member states vary in their acceptance of common policies, despite the limited ability of individual states to tackle these inherently transnational challenges. The chapter ends by discussing two challenges for the EU on which it has no real external policy: health and demography.

Chapter 11, using the concepts developed throughout the preceding chapters, provides an overview and assessment of EU foreign policy towards its neighbourhood: the Western Balkans, Eastern Europe, the Mediterranean and the Middle East. For each region, as well as for the EU's European Neighbourhood Policy in general, we assess the extent to which the EU has moved beyond trade and contractual relations to developing a relational and structural foreign policy. We demonstrate that the EU has gradually and partially developed policies to help resolve conflicts, particularly in the Western Balkans. However, in contrast to the ambitions raised in the late 1990s and early 2000s, the EU increasingly faces problems in further developing an effective structural foreign policy. This can to some extent be explained by the rise of other structural powers, which is the subject of the next chapter.

Chapter 12 focuses on the EU's relationship with competing powers: global powers (such as the United States, Russia and China) and the group of emerging powers (such as India and Brazil). The chapter critically assesses the EU's so-called 'strategic partnerships' concluded with these states. We demonstrate that the EU is increasingly facing competition from Russia and China, particularly in regions like the Eastern neighbourhood or Africa. The EU also experiences that these powers do not always share the EU's foreign policy priorities and methods. Furthermore, the chapter turns to the increasingly influential structures under the umbrella term of 'Islamism'.

In Chapter 13, we look at the EU's self-proclaimed 'choice of effective multilateralism' and assess the great variety in the legal status, coordination and representation of the EU in international fora. A mixed picture emerges from the evaluation of the EU's policy in the UN, international financial institutions (such as the International Monetary Fund and the

World Bank), and the G7/8/20. Although the EU's participation in international organizations is often hindered by both external and internal legal constraints and by the divergences in member states' preferences on the desirability of European unity in international organizations, we also argue that the EU has established close relationships and practical working methods to engage in the global governance architecture. The usefulness of a 'single voice' and strictly coordinated EU positions in multilateral settings is also critically assessed. Furthermore, presenting the example of emerging power coalitions such as the BRICS (including Brazil, Russia, India, China and South Africa) and expanding multilateral frameworks in the Southern hemisphere and the Asia-Pacific area, the chapter discusses the rise of competing multilateral settings, in which the EU is largely absent and wherein competing conceptions of multilateralism are promoted.

Finally, in Chapter 14, we consider the implications of our findings with regard to theories of international relations, European integration and constructivism and consider the state of the art of these theoretical schools in the light of our empirical findings. We conclude by assessing the use of the 'structural foreign policy versus relational foreign policy' which is used as an overarching framework in the analyses presented in this book.

Chapter 1

The Nature of EU Foreign Policy

In the introduction, we presented a short overview of the genesis of EU foreign policy, a series of puzzling observations about the relevance of EU's foreign policy, and an assessment of three episodes in European integration and international relations. All of these elements provide both an illuminating and confusing picture of EU foreign policy. Acknowledging the sometimes contradictory nature of EU foreign policy, this chapter deals with the EU's peculiar foreign policy architecture.

In the first section, we portray EU foreign policy as multifaceted (comprising CFSP, CSDP, external action and the external dimension of internal policies), multi-method (combining an intergovernmental and a Community method) and multilevel (entailing the national, European and international levels). The next section then unveils various areas of tension to which EU foreign policy is subjected, followed by a third section on the EU foreign policy's objectives and principles. The overview of the three episodes in the introduction also exposes features of foreign policy in general. It reveals that foreign policy is not only about reacting to international crises and conflicts in relation to other international actors. It is also about structuring the behaviour and mindset of other actors in international politics. The difference between relational and structural foreign policy, as well as the globalizing context in which EU foreign policy takes place, are subject of the subsequent fourth and fifth sections of this chapter. Taken together, these five sections provide a comprehensive and clear analytical framework to analyse EU foreign policy in the remainder of the book.

Understanding EU Foreign Policy

Multifaceted foreign policy – but not all-encompassing

We understand the foreign policy of the EU as a multifaceted foreign policy. EU foreign policy can indeed not easily be pinned down or summarized. This is evident when looking at the EU treaties, which clearly differentiate between the CFSP and CSDP on the one hand and the EU's 'external action' and 'external dimension of internal policies' on the other.

First of all, the *Common Foreign and Security Policy* (CFSP) provides the main platform for developing and implementing the political and diplomatic dimension of EU foreign policy (see Chapter 7). Established in the early 1990s by the Treaty of Maastricht as a relatively weak component of the EU, with none of its own instruments and no EU actors bearing responsibility for it, the CFSP gradually gained strength in the last two decades. CFSP provides the platform to not only position the EU with regard to foreign policy issues, but also to actively pursue the EU's foreign policy interests and contribute to mediation efforts and other international diplomatic initiatives. A High Representative and a diplomatic service (the European External Action Service (EEAS)) are now responsible for putting the CFSP into operation. A major feature of CFSP is that, through the Council and its intergovernmental dynamics, member states retain control over the foreign policy positions and actions developed in the CFSP.

Second, the *Common Security and Defence Policy* (CSDP) includes various civilian and military crisis management instruments which can be used to underpin and implement the EU's foreign policy and to reinforce the potential and credibility of the CFSP (see Chapter 8). Launched in the early 2000s and formalized through the Lisbon Treaty in 2009, the CSDP provides the platform for launching military operations and civilian missions, which *de facto* take place mainly in the EU's neighbourhood and Africa. Mirroring CFSP, CSDP is fully controlled by the member states, which, particularly in case of more intrusive military actions, generally opt for other multilateral frameworks such as NATO or *ad hoc* coalitions. The EU does not possess its own military or civilian crisis management capacities, but relies on the voluntary contributions from the member states, although diplomatic and military staff in Brussels contribute to the preparation, support and conduct of CSDP initiatives.

Third, the EU's '*external action*' encompasses the EU's external trade policy, development cooperation, economic and financial cooperation with third countries, humanitarian aid, sanctions and international agreements (see Chapter 9). These policies have been gradually developed since the creation of the European Economic Community (EEC) in the late 1950s and have been further strengthened since the early 1990s with the establishment of the EU. The strengths of the various dimensions of the EU's external action lie in the EU's stronger legal competences in these fields, the availability of considerable financial and other resources and of a bureaucratic apparatus to prepare and implement policies.

Finally, there are the '*external dimensions of internal policies*' (see Chapter 10). Some of the internal policies of the EU – such as energy, environmental, and migration and asylum policy – also have an external dimension with important foreign policy relevance. These policies have been mainly developed since the establishment of the EU in the early 1990s, although some of them originate from earlier stages in the European integration process.

'External action' and 'external dimensions of internal policies' belong to the realm of foreign policy in three respects: they include policy fields and instruments that have important foreign policy dimensions; they provide the instruments and leverage (carrots and sticks) necessary for foreign policy action; and they can entail contractual and political frameworks (such as association agreements) that allow the EU to pursue foreign policy goals. However, as explained in Chapters 9 and 10, the relationship between foreign policy, external action, and external dimensions of internal policies is not always clear-cut, as interests and activities stemming from the various policy fields can also compete with each other.

In any case, a one-sided emphasis on CFSP/CSDP in assessments of EU foreign policy should be avoided. Depending on the foreign policy issue at hand and the time period under discussion, the centre of gravity will differ in terms of the site of policy elaboration. On several major issues, initiatives taken within the context of the EU's external action, not within the CFSP, are at the political and operational heart of EU foreign policy. This reflects the fact that it is the EU's trade policy and its ability to conclude international agreements that provide the EU with much of its power and leverage when dealing with third actors.

A closer reading of the Treaties shows another dimension of EU foreign policy: the importance of the *foreign policies of the member states* (see further). It reveals that coordination of and cooperation between national foreign policies is an equally important component of EU foreign policy.

Taken together, EU foreign policy thus includes the foreign policy developed across the CFSP/CSDP, the various dimensions of the EU's external action and external policies of internal dimensions, as well as through interaction with the foreign policies of member states. This also means that, in this book, EU foreign policy is not considered as being the same as:

- *European foreign policy*. The EU does not include all European states and is only one of the various 'European' multilateral frameworks through which foreign policy is developed; thus the EU cannot be equated with 'Europe'.
- *CFSP/CSDP*. As EU foreign policy is also developed through other dimensions of the EU's external action, it is untenable to narrow foreign policy down to the decisions and actions adopted within the CFSP/CSDP framework.
- *The sum of national foreign policies of EU member states*. Member states maintain their own national foreign policies, which may in part

be defined and developed with no or minimal involvement from the EU. As a result, the label 'EU foreign policy' only includes national foreign policies in so far as these are developed through a certain interaction with the EU.

It is important for understanding the nature of EU foreign policy that this policy is neither exclusive nor all-encompassing. The EU is equipped with considerable capacities to develop a foreign policy and these capacities are far-reaching with regard to some foreign policy dimensions (such as trade issues, where the EU has exclusive competence). However, EU member states never intended to transfer all national foreign policy competences to the EU and never wanted to see national foreign policies replaced by a common or single EU foreign policy (see also the section on competences in Chapter 4 and Chapter 7 on CFSP). In general, foreign policy is not covered by exclusive EU competences, as member states wanted to retain control of this policy domain that is so closely linked to national sovereignty. The EU's competence and ability to develop a foreign policy thus varies considerably, depending on the foreign policy dimension at stake.

As a result, the EU was not conceived to develop an all-encompassing foreign policy. This also implies that there is a wide variety in the extent to which a comprehensive EU foreign policy is formulated to tackle the many issues on the foreign policy agenda. This ranges from comprehensive policies towards the Western Balkans, for instance, to nearly non-existent policies towards territorial defence or changing security situations like those in East Asia and the Pacific.

This non-exclusive and not all-encompassing nature has important implications for the study of EU foreign policy. Scholars and external observers may, from a normative point of view, expect the EU to have a fully-fledged, all-encompassing and exclusive foreign policy. However, this cannot be the predominant touchstone for analysing EU foreign policy and its effectiveness, as this does not correspond with the nature of EU foreign policy that the member states had in mind.

Multi-method foreign policy

The multi-method character of EU foreign policy is a direct consequence of its multifaceted nature. 'Multi-method foreign policy' denotes that the varying facets of EU foreign policy are organized within two different treaty settings that reflect two different policy-making methods (see Chapter 4). This duality is reminiscent of the two EU treaties that provide the foundations for EU foreign policy: the Treaty on European Union (TEU) and the Treaty on the Functioning of the European Union (TFEU) (see Table 1.1). Although these are two separate treaties from a legal point of view, together they are often called 'the Treaties', or the 'Treaty of Lisbon'.

Table 1.1   CFSP/CSDP, External Action and external dimension of internal policies in the Treaties

Treaty on European Union (TEU)	
Title I	Common Provisions
Title II	Provision on democratic principles
Title III	Provisions on the institutions [see Chapters 3 & 4]*
Title IV	Provisions on enhanced cooperation
Title V	General provisions on the Unions external action and specific provisions on the Common Foreign and Security Policy
Chapter 1	General provisions on the Union's external action [see Chapter 1]*
Chapter 2	Specific provisions on the common foreign and security policy [see Chapter 7]*
Section 1	Common provisions
Section 2	Provisions on the common security and defence policy [see Chapter 8]*
Title VI	Final Provisions
Treaty on the Functioning of the European Union (TFEU)	
Part one	Principles
Part two	Non-discrimination and citizenship of the union
Part three	Union policies and internal actions *[including the following Titles]* [see Chapter 10]*
Title I	The internal market
Title III	Agriculture and fisheries
Title V	Area of freedom, security and justice
Title VIII	Economic and monetary policy
Title XIX	Research and technological development and space
	→

The *Treaty on European Union* (TEU) includes the main provisions for the CFSP and CSDP, which are organized on the basis of the *'intergovernmental method'*. This means that member states retain control over the development of foreign policy through the dominant position of the European Council and the Council of Ministers and through the predominance of unanimity in decision-making.

The *Treaty on the Functioning of the European Union* (TFEU) includes the main provisions on the EU's external action and the external dimensions of internal policies. These are principally organized through the *'Community method'*, which is based on an institutional equilibrium

---

Treaty on the Functioning of the European Union (TFEU)

Title XX	Environment
Title XXI	Energy
Part four	Association of the overseas countries and territories
Part five	The Union's external action [see Chapter 9]*
Title I	General provisions on the union's external action
Title II	Common commercial policy
Title III	Cooperation with third countries and humanitarian aid
Chapter 1	Development cooperation
Chapter 2	Economic, financial and technical cooperation with third countries
Chapter 3	Humanitarian aid
Title IV	Restrictive measures
Title V	International agreements
Title VI	The Union's relations with international organizations and third countries and Union delegations [see Chapter 13]*
Title VII	Solidarity clause
Part six	Institutional and financial provisions [see Chapter 4]*
Part seven	General and final provisions

Declarations [see Chapter 7]*

13.	Declaration concerning the common foreign and security policy
14.	Declaration concerning the common foreign and security policy

Note: * This refers to the chapter in this book where this Title, Chapter or Part of the Treaty is analysed.

Source: European Union (2010: 3–10).

between the Council of the EU (the 'Council'), the Commission, the European Parliament (EP) and the Court of Justice, and on the possibility of majority voting for most decisions in the Council.

This dual system, with two methods of policy-making and clear legal boundaries between the related policy fields, has far-reaching consequences for the nature and outcome of EU foreign policy. However, this formal division is also misleading as EU foreign policy is developed through both the interaction and symbiosis between the two methods. Also, the practice of EU foreign policy does not always follow the formal categorization of the Treaties. As explained in Chapter 4, there is a much larger complexity of – and diversity within – the EU's foreign policy mechanisms than is suggested by the simplistic categorizations 'external action and external dimension of internal policies versus CFSP/CSDP' and 'Community method versus intergovernmental method'. For instance, unanimity is required for some decisions within the EU's external action (such as trade agreements on foreign direct investments), while cooperation between member states' policies is also deemed to be an appropriate method in some of these policy fields (such as development policy).

Multilevel foreign policy

Characteristic of EU foreign policy is the interaction between the national and EU levels, with the centre of gravity and the nature of this interaction varying according to the issue at hand. The national and EU levels are not neatly separated from each other: national actors are part of some important EU institutions, and EU policies are mirrored in national policies. Moreover, EU policy-making also occurs in an international context: the EU and its member states are – partly, jointly or separately – part of regimes, organizations and institutions at the international level (see Chapter 13). To a large extent, therefore, EU foreign policy can be conceptualized as a complex *multilevel foreign policy*, reflecting the interconnectedness of multiple governance levels and policy arenas in the policy process. Depending on the policy issue and policy framework, the actors on the various levels have different competences, levels of legitimacy, obligations and resources.

EU foreign policy can in this sense be understood from a governance perspective (Justaert and Keukeleire 2012). Following the description of governance by Tömmel and Verdun (2009: 1), EU foreign policy may be characterized by 'the highly diversified EU procedures and practices, combining formalized modes of rule-setting with informal practices of negotiation, cooperation and consensus-building; the multilevel and multi-actor structure underlying these procedures and practices; and, not the least, the diverging patterns of implementation under a common umbrella'.

Understanding EU foreign policy as an example of multilevel governance also has wider dimensions. Although we may focus on the EU, we must avoid the trap of EU centrism, giving the false impression that for member states the EU is the only or the main international framework in which to develop foreign policy, promote foreign policy goals or fulfil commitments. EU foreign policy is embedded within a wider set of multilevel foreign policy networks and within the increasingly important context of global governance (see Telò 2009; Van Vooren *et al.* 2013; Wunderlich and Bailey 2011). This also includes other multilateral settings such as NATO, the Organization for Security and Co-operation in Europe (OSCE), the Council of Europe, the World Trade Organization (WTO), the International Monetary Fund (IMF), the UN, the G7/8/20, and more informal settings (see Chapter 13).

Nearly all foreign policy actions undertaken by the EU are developed either in cooperation with other international organizations (sometimes at their request) or in parallel with (and sometimes in competition with) the actions of these organizations. Following Wallace (2005: 78), it may be more accurate to speak of a *multi-location foreign policy* to avoid the notion of hierarchy often implied by the multilevel concept and to indicate that the EU is only one among the various relevant locations for foreign policy-making. Member states perpetually weigh up the pros and cons of developing foreign policy in the EU rather than in another foreign policy forum.

Mirroring national foreign policy?

Another crucial feature of EU foreign policy is that EU member states retain their national foreign policy, despite the existence of a 'common' foreign and security policy. Member states are required under the Treaty to support the EU's Common Foreign and Security Policy. However, two declarations added to the Lisbon Treaty (Declarations 13 and 14) underline the fact that the CFSP provisions do not affect the member states' powers in relation to the formulation and conduct of foreign policy (see Chapter 7). The resulting effect is an ambiguous multilevel relationship between EU foreign and security policies and member states' own initiatives in this field.

That the national level has to be taken seriously in analysing EU foreign policy raises the question whether EU foreign policy also mirrors, or should mirror, national foreign policy. Many studies of the EU's external relations or foreign policy focus on the EU's capabilities as an international actor and its capacity 'to mimic the features of a nation-state within the international system' (Rosamond 2002: 175). This becomes obvious in the plethora of publications concerning the famous 'capability–expectations gap' (Hill 1993) and the EU's '(strategic) actorness', 'presence' or 'performance' (see Bretherton and Vogler 2006; Caporaso and Jupille 1998; Jørgensen 2012; Jørgensen *et al.* 2011; Sjøstedt 1977; Toje 2008).

The tendency to evaluate EU foreign policy mainly or exclusively against the yardstick of the foreign policy of individual states can be questioned. It can be useful or even necessary for EU foreign policy to gain some of the capabilities and characteristics of states' foreign policy. However, it is questionable whether EU foreign policy must automatically – and on all levels – be seen as a substitute or as a transposition of individual member states' foreign policies to the European level. The specificity and added value of an EU foreign policy can be precisely that it emphasizes different issues, tackling different sorts of problems, pursuing different objectives through alternative methods, and ulti-mately assuming a form and content which differs from the foreign policy of its individual member states. At a time when globalization is demonstrating the limitations of nation states and conventional foreign policies, it seems odd that we would look to the EU to develop a foreign policy equivalent to that of a state.

Equally questionable is the tendency to automatically perceive the relationship between the foreign policy of the EU and that of its member states as a zero-sum game. The point of departure of this book is that the relationship between the foreign policies of the member states and the EU can be a zero-sum game (with a stronger EU foreign policy leading to weaker national foreign policies, or vice-versa), but that in other cases it can be a positive-sum game (with EU foreign policy complementing and even strengthening national foreign policies and foreign policies devel-oped in other international fora). The question of whether, and under what conditions, the relationship between EU and national foreign poli-cies is to be seen as either a zero-sum or positive-sum game is one of the most essential and sensitive aspects of EU foreign policy. The following chapter on the history of EU foreign policy demonstrates that, in general, significant steps forward in EU foreign policy were only possible when the member states perceive the relationship between EU and national foreign policy as complementary and as a positive-sum game, and not as potentially undermining national foreign policy.

Areas of Tension in EU Foreign Policy

Understanding the evolution and nature of EU foreign policy requires insight into a number of areas of tension which loom over discussions on European foreign policy and which are also recurrent themes in the book. These various areas of tension have a major impact not only on the macro-picture of treaty changes and EU foreign policy's evolution, but also on the micro-picture of responses to specific foreign policy dossiers. The areas of tension reflect the differences in the long-standing funda-mental choices made by member states with regard to sovereignty, inte-gration, power and interests. Allegiance to these choices and to their application in specific cases often prevails over the willingness to provide an effective foreign policy answer.

Presented schematically in Figure 1.1 and explained in detail below, these areas of tension are major explanatory factors in the analysis of EU foreign policy. The member states' and EU institutions' willingness and ability to overcome these areas of tension (or to at least temporarily avoid or neutralize their undermining effects) are an essential factor for allowing initiatives in EU foreign policy as well as EU foreign policy effectiveness.

Figure 1.1   Areas of tension in EU foreign policy

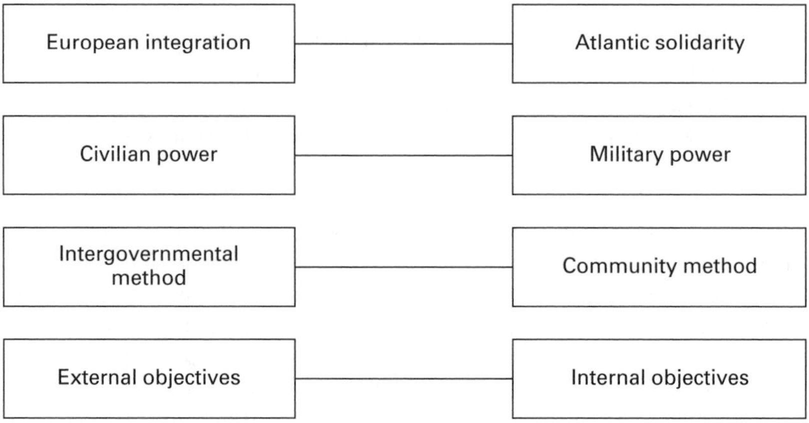

European integration	————	Atlantic solidarity
Civilian power	————	Military power
Intergovernmental method	————	Community method
External objectives	————	Internal objectives

European integration versus Atlantic solidarity

Tensions between Atlantic solidarity and European integration have had the most dominant and permanent impact on EU foreign policy, stemming from the pivotal role of NATO and the US as security providers for the majority of EU member states. The Soviet threat, the Cold War, Western European military weakness and American military superiority meant that for most member states in the second half of the twentieth century, the Atlantic Alliance and the American security guarantee were essential security conditions after the Second World War. The logic of such a choice was confirmed in the early 1950s and 1960s by the failure of French proposals to bring defence within the scope of European integration (the European Defence Community and the Fouchet Plans). It also explains why, when the member states cautiously stepped towards developing common foreign policy initiatives in the 1970s through the new European Political Cooperation (EPC), the European Community (EC) was at that time conceived and defined as a civilian actor (see Chapter 2).

Military dependence on the US not only determined defence policy, but also largely defined the parameters of member states' national foreign policies and EPC (which was the predecessor of the CFSP). As has continued to be the case after 1989, depending on an external actor for military security carries a fairly sizeable price tag since the demands of that protector must be taken into account when taking a stand on foreign policy issues. In addition to gratitude for America's security guarantee and the idea that some member states enjoy a 'special relationship' with the US, it explains why elites and public opinion in several European countries consider aligning themselves to American views and positions as a normal reflex and as being part of their identity. It explains why practically every proposal for a common foreign policy initiative was and is reviewed by several EU member states against what could be called the 'what do the Americans think?' test. The appropriateness of an EU foreign policy initiative became measured not solely, or not in the first place, in terms of the EU's potential impact on the issue at hand, but rather in terms of its impact on transatlantic relations.

The extent to which the 'Atlantic factor' had to be taken into account would prove to be one of the most divisive issues in the development of a common EU foreign policy. The end of the Cold War, which provided the necessary context to launch the CFSP and CSDP, did not make this factor irrelevant (see Chapter 8). Although the US supported the development of the CSDP (at least within certain limits), the Atlantic factor remained a powerful area of tension, particularly because the Central and Eastern European member states considered NATO and the US as their vital security guarantee with regard to Russia. Furthermore, the terrorist attacks in the early 2000s and the wars in Afghanistan and Iraq demonstrated that territorial security was not to be taken for granted and that a US-led military alliance could still be essential in view of newly emerging threats. This tension of 'Atlantic solidarity versus European integration' thus remains important and is a first recurrent theme in this book.

Civilian power versus military power

The EU's struggle with power is a second major area of tension and another recurrent theme of this book. The EU's struggle with power has two dimensions. The first is related to the question whether the EU should be merely or predominantly a civilian power or whether (and to what extent) it should also become a military power. The second dimension is related to the extent to which the EU should exert power or become a power at all.

The concept of 'civilian power' (Duchêne 1972, 1973) was one of the first and most influential attempts to conceptualize (Western) Europe's status and role in the world. It has since been widely elaborated upon. First, it refers to the transformation of interstate relations within Europe from war and indirect violence to 'civilized' politics. The EU's current (pre)accession talks with countries in the Western Balkans demonstrate this transition, which also provides an interesting formula for troubled interstate relations elsewhere (see Chapters 9 and 11). Second, the concept of civilian power focuses on the possibility of an actor being a 'power' while not possessing military instruments. It is this part of Duchêne's thesis which has received widest attention. From a normative perspective, this enables the EU's endeavours on the international stage to be conceived not in a threatening but a positive light.

The Cold War and the dominance of NATO in the military security arena left the EC/EPC in the 1970s and 1980s with little other option than to maximize its potential impact as a civilian power. However, the end of the East–West order pointed to both the constraints and challenges of civilian power. On the one hand, the EU was pressured to transform itself from a civilian power into a civilian *and* military power, as the limitations of being a civilian power in a distinctly uncivil world became painfully obvious during (and since) the conflicts in the Western Balkans in the 1990s. The EU was forced to gradually depart from the familiarity of its status as a non-military power and from 1999 complemented its CFSP with a CSDP, endowing itself with civilian and military crisis management tools (see Chapter 8). The wars in Afghanistan and Iraq and even the limited military campaign against the dictatorial regime in Libya in 2011 forced EU countries to face yet another level of military challenge, which clearly surpassed the EU's capacities and ambitions as a modest military power. Moreover, the question emerged whether the EU could still be a civilian power and profit from the advantages and attractiveness of such a role – in the second meaning of Duchêne's conceptualization – if at the same time it transformed to a, albeit modest, military power (see Orbie 2006; Telò 2006; Whitman 2010).

On the other hand, confrontation with the new world (dis)order challenged the EU to behave more as a *power*, willing to exert itself purposefully to achieve foreign policy objectives. The need to actively promote and support new political, legal and socio-economic structures in other regions of the world compelled the EU to make more active use of its non-military foreign policy tools, most of which fall under the banner of EU 'external action'. To this end, the EU quite successfully exerted power in Central and Eastern Europe states and later also in the Western Balkans, but proved reluctant to use its instruments to enforce desired changes or attitudes in other parts of the world. The EU's failure to behave as a power was particularly evident in the European Neighbourhood Policy (see Chapter 11). The EU did not manage to use its relationship with the Eastern and Southern neighbouring countries as a lever for change, which is one of the explanations for the disappointments about the EU, which were also voiced during Arab uprisings in the early 2010s.

Intergovernmental method versus Community method

The areas of tension previously discussed relate to the questions about whether the EU should be the locus of a foreign and security policy and what kind of power the EU should be. The third question is whether the EU should organize foreign policy through the 'intergovernmental method' or through the 'Community method'. As argued above, the intergovernmental method implies that member states retain control over decision-making through the dominant position of the European Council and the Council of Ministers in which they are represented and through the predominance of the unanimity rule. The Community method implies that the member states not only accept a transfer of competences to the EU, but also a sharing of power with supranational institutions such as the Commission and the European Parliament (EP), an inability to veto decision-making, and judicial oversight by the Court of Justice of the EU (see Chapters 3 and 4).

This area of tension arises from the traditional notion of foreign policy as one of the central tasks, prerogatives and even *raisons d'être* of sovereign states. This explains the reluctance of member states to lose their grasp over this major policy field. Intergovernmentalism is one of the defining features of the CFSP/CSDP, as member states want to retain full control over decision-making. The price member states paid for ensuring that the supranational institutions would not meddle in CFSP was that these policies would not be supported by established institutional mechanisms and common instruments.

This weakness of CFSP was made more explicit as its development was paralleled by the growing foreign policy relevance of other facets of EU foreign policy (in particular trade policy, development cooperation, and association and cooperation agreements) and of the Community method applicable there (with a well-elaborated institutional set-up, significant competences and extensive instruments and budgets). This explains why the Council was and is often forced to rely on other EU policy domains to flesh out or implement CFSP decisions. More fundamentally, the European Commission has gradually developed its own unspoken foreign policy dynamic through its various 'external policies'. After the Lisbon Treaty came into force, the creation of the European External Action Service and the double-hatted function of 'High Representative for Foreign Affairs and Security Policy/Vice-President of the European Commission' has only partially been able to overcome the divide between both approaches (see Chapter 3).

Member states also assess the viability of a potential EU foreign policy initiative in terms of whether it fits within their conception of European integration. Accordingly, they differ on where they envisage the appropriate balance between the intergovernmental method and the Community method to lie within the realm of foreign policy. This does not depend in the first place on considerations of efficiency or cost–benefit analysis, but rather on the member states' overarching view of the nature and *finalité* of European integration. Foreign policy debates in the EU are thus likely to focus beyond the issue at hand to broader questions centred on policy competences among the EU institutions and between the national and the EU levels. This 'intergovernmental versus Community method' tension is a third recurrent theme in this book.

External objectives versus internal objectives

The fourth area of tension is related to the nature of the objectives of EU foreign policy. These objectives hide a reality that is often disregarded by external observers. In order to understand EU foreign policy it must be appreciated that decisions on EU foreign policy are often not only steered by *external objectives* aimed at influencing the external environment, but also by various *internal objectives,* which are often not made explicit. Internal objectives can be broken into three categories: interrelational objectives aimed at managing member states' mutual relations; integration objectives aimed at affecting European integration; and identity objectives aimed at asserting the identity of the EU (Keukeleire 2003, 2008). These different kinds of objectives reflect the fact that EU foreign policy has multiple internal functionalities (Bickerton 2010; 2011: 118).

Interrelational objectives are intimately linked to the very origin and purpose of European integration. Following the harrowing experiences of two world wars, the integration process was launched as a radically new method to definitively tackle long-standing enmity between Germany and its Western European neighbours. Member states were offered a new framework to define and manage their mutual relationships and to defend and promote national interests in a less threatening way. This was gradually applied to the foreign policy domain. The EU's foreign policy framework was designed to resolve, or at least contain, the potential tensions and conflicts arising between member states when dealing with foreign policy issues, to enhance the predictability of behaviour, and to promote where feasible both mutual understanding and solidarity. The interrelational dimension of European integration implies that the EU's foreign policy or specific foreign policy actions can target the management of internal EU relations as a principal goal. Conversely, it can also imply that member states agree *not* to handle a foreign policy issue within the EU framework out of fear that doing so would revive mutual tensions and augment internal disagreement and distrust.

In addition to interrelational objectives, foreign policy initiatives can stem from two other types of internal objectives that reach beyond external goals. Member states can promote or adopt new foreign policy initiatives which primarily aim to strengthen European integration, influence the nature of the European project, or create the impression that the process of integration is progressing or regressing (*integration objectives*). The member states' main goal can also be simply to demonstrate that the EU exists, to emphasize the specificity of the European approach to international politics, to differentiate the EU from other actors (particularly the US) or to shape and strengthen European identity (*identity objectives*). The extent to which a member state will give different weight to these various objectives fluctuates over time and according to the issue at hand.

Recognizing the different types of objectives helps to gain a deeper understanding of EU foreign policy. First, it explains divergences between the levels of expectation of political leaders, the general public and the rest of the world. The general public and external actors evaluate EU foreign policy in terms of its external impact whereas political leaders may be operating according to an entirely different agenda. Second, it explains why even those member states who, in principle, may not favour a strong EU foreign policy may in some circumstances accept new initiatives if a given policy serves one or more internal objectives. Third, it explains why member states are in some cases quite uninterested in the external effectiveness of EU foreign policy action. This tension between the external objectives and the various internal objectives of EU foreign policy is a fourth recurrent theme in this book.

Back to the Treaties: Principles and Objectives

Whereas the previous discussion on the field of tension between external and internal objectives relates to the political dynamics behind EU foreign policy, we now examine the formal principles and objectives of the EU's international action that are put forward by the EU in its own treaties. The principles as well as objectives of the EU's action on the international scene are enumerated in Article 21 TEU, which is one of the only articles that cover both CFSP/CSDP and external action, thus also including trade and development policies. Article 21(1) TEU points to the core objectives and principles that guide the EU's international action:

The Union's action on the international scene shall be guided by the principles which have inspired its own creation, development and enlargement, and which it seeks to advance in the wider world: democracy, the rule of law, the universality and indivisibility of human rights and fundamental freedoms, respect for human dignity, the principles of equality and solidarity, and respect for the principles of the United Nations Charter and international law.

The EU thus takes its own principles-driven history as a point of departure for promoting these virtues to the rest of the world. One of the reasons why the EU has been labelled a 'normative power' is this focus on values as a constitutive feature of the EU and its foreign policy (Manners 2002, 2006; Nicolaïdis and Whitman 2013; Whitman 2011). This concept refers to the EU's 'ability to shape conceptions of "normal" in international relations' (Manners 2002: 239). Chapter 6 and particularly Box 6.1 analyse in more detail the EU's promotion of values and offers some critical observations about the EU as a normative power.

The subsequent paragraph – Article 21(2) TEU – includes a list of eight objectives. The first goal – safeguard the Union's values, fundamental interests, security, independence and integrity – can be seen as the overarching general objective for the EU's foreign policy. However, it provokes more questions than answers. What are the EU's 'fundamental interests', and in practice, what does it mean to safeguard the EU's security and integrity? The second objective is to pursue the principles which are set out in the first paragraph of that article: democracy, rule of law, human rights and the principles of international law.

The third to seventh objectives refer to the core goals of major components of the EU's external policy: 'preserve peace, prevent conflicts and strengthen international security' (CFSP/CSDP and external action); 'foster the sustainable development of developing countries, with the primary aim of eradicating poverty' (development policy); 'encourage the integration of all countries into the world economy' (trade policy); 'improve the quality of the environment and the sustainable management of global natural resources' (environmental policy); and 'assist populations, countries and regions confronting natural or man-made disasters' (humanitarian policy). Finally, the eighth objective reflects the overarching objective of promoting an international system based on stronger multilateral cooperation and good global governance.

How can we assess these objectives? First, rather than providing guidance for concrete foreign policy actions, the Treaty provisions are general principles to which member states could easily subscribe but that leave scope for very different views on the appropriate action to be taken in order to pursue these goals. Two examples illustrate this point. Responses to the 2011 revolt against Colonel Gaddafi in Libya are justified by the second and third objectives of Article 21(2). Member states, however, had different views on the expedience of military intervention. Another example is that the objective on eradicating poverty sounds attractive, but it hides different views on how to achieve this: primarily through development aid or through the promotion of free trade (see Chapters 7 and 9)?

Second, Article 21 TEU does not set priorities, giving the impression that all objectives are equally important to the EU. This is deceptive, though, as the legal competences, budgetary instruments and institutional set-up that the EU has at its disposal are very different for each of these objectives. They determine the importance that can *de facto* be attributed to the various Treaty objectives. The result is that a hierarchy unavoidably imposes itself. For example, the EU's exclusive competences and well-developed trade policy toolbox explain why the EU will act more firmly in this field. This contrasts to the EU's external security capacities, where its competences and instruments are much more limited.

Third, self-evident and generally accepted as the objectives may be, they are not always compatible in practice. For instance, initiatives to promote human rights and democracy in China or Russia may lead to a deterioration of relations with those countries, which can in turn impede cooperation to tackle specific international conflicts or to reach agreements on climate policies. This also explains why the goal of 'consistency between the different areas of its external action and between these and its other policies' (Art. 21(3) TEU) is in practice barely attainable (see Chapter 4).

Relational and Structural Foreign Policy

The conceptual framework used in this book to frame and analyse foreign policy was already pointed to in the introduction to this book. It reflects an understanding that, to pursue the above-mentioned objectives of EU foreign policy, this policy is not only about shaping or managing *relations* with other actors. On a more ambitious level, foreign policy is also about influencing the *structures* that determine how other actors behave. The following two subsections conceptualize both types of foreign policy using the labels of relational and structural foreign policy.

Relational foreign policy

Relational foreign policy is a foreign policy that seeks to influence the attitude and behaviour of other actors as well as the relations with and between others actors. This policy can take different forms, require different actions and employ different instruments, depending on whether these relations are conducted in a context of peace, conflict or war. In general, a considerable part of relational foreign policy is devoted to crises and conflicts.

On a declaratory level, actors continuously position themselves in relation to other actors and with regard to specific crises and conflicts – one of the main functions of diplomacy. This happens through unilateral declarations, interaction in the context of bilateral relations and the determination of positions within multilateral settings such as the UN.

On an operational level, where positions are underpinned by actions, a foreign policy actor can opt for a variety of foreign policy activities, depending on its interests and capabilities. Diplomatic efforts serve to enter into dialogue, negotiate and mediate in order to support, change or counter the position of other actors and find support for one's own position (Jönsson 2002). Diplomatic initiatives can be complemented and buttressed through economic and financial instruments (to sanction, reward or provide support) and through civilian and military crisis management instruments. These operational dimensions of relational foreign policy can be conceived and implemented in a unilateral, bilateral or multilateral mode.

Structural foreign policy

Structural foreign policy is a foreign policy which, conducted over the long-term, aims at sustainably influencing or shaping political, legal, economic, social, security or other structures in a given space (Keukeleire 2003, 2008, 2014a; Keukeleire *et al.* 2009, 2014). Structural foreign policy seeks to promote and support structural changes and structural reforms, tackle structural problems and constraints, or support and sustain existing structures. The concept of structural foreign policy resonates with the political and diplomatic usage of 'structural' by practitioners, e.g. when they refer to 'structural reforms' or 'structural change'. Furthermore, it relates to the academic conceptualization of 'structural power' (Guzzini 1993; Holden 2009; Strange 1994), which refers to the capacity to shape the organizing principles and rules of the game and to determine how others will play that game (Holsti 1995).

An example of a successful structural foreign policy is American foreign policy in the decade following the Second World War, which aimed to establish new structures in Western Europe and definitively resolve Franco-German hostility (see Chapter 2). Other examples include the EU's (enlargement) policy with regard to Central and Eastern Europe in the 1990s and toward the Western Balkans in the 2000s, designed to support the structural transformation of these regions. An example of a (largely) failed structural foreign policy is the EU's European Neighbourhood Policy, in particular towards the Mediterranean region (see Chapters 9 and 11).

Structural foreign policy and relational foreign policies are not mutually exclusive and can be complementary and mutually dependent. For example, structural foreign policy towards the Western Balkans became possible only after successful relational foreign policy actions (including military operations and diplomatic initiatives). However, that this success would be enduring was only assured through the creation of a comprehensive set of new structures to make peace sustainable in the long term (see Chapter 11).

Having defined and illustrated structural foreign policy, we turn our attention to two key aspects of the qualification 'structural': structures and sustainability. First, the purpose of a structural foreign policy is to influence or shape *structures*. These structures consist of relatively permanent organizing principles, institutions and norms that shape and order the various interrelated sectors in a society, such as the political, legal, economic, social, or security sector. Organizing principles are made operational through a complex set-up of formal and informal institutions and norms that can vary from region to region, from country to country, and from society to society, depending on the specific context and trajectories of the regions, countries and societies concerned. For example, 'democracy', 'human rights' and 'free market economy' are organizing principles that shape politics, law and economics in many states. However, the way in which they are made operational differs considerably between, for example, European countries, the US and India.

Structures can be situated on various interrelated levels: individual; societal; state; inter-societal; interstate or regional; and international, transnational or global levels. For example, human rights or the rule of law can be protected through national legislation, but also through regional organizations and international treaties. Figure 1.2 visualizes how structures can be situated in different sectors and on different levels, providing a matrix for analysing structural foreign policy of the EU as well as of other structural powers (see Chapter 12). Generally speaking, and reflecting the approach taken in this book, this matrix can help to determine which levels and sectors get most attention in the structural foreign policy of an actor and, at least as important, which of these are neglected. For example, the analyses in Chapters 11 and 12 will demonstrate that the EU mostly pays attention to the national, regional and international levels, but often neglects the societal level and the impact of policies on the individual level (see also Box 1.1). More specifically, and going beyond the scope of this book, the matrix can also be used to develop more focused, detailed and in-depth research designs, for instance to examine and explain the relationship between different sections of the matrix (see the example in Box 14.1) (Keukeleire 2014a).

Second, the objective of structural foreign policy is to produce *sustainable* effects. The purpose is not simply to shape or influence structures, but to do so in such a way that these structures develop an enduring character and become relatively permanent, including when external pressure

Figure 1.2   *Structural foreign policy: sectors, levels and internalization*

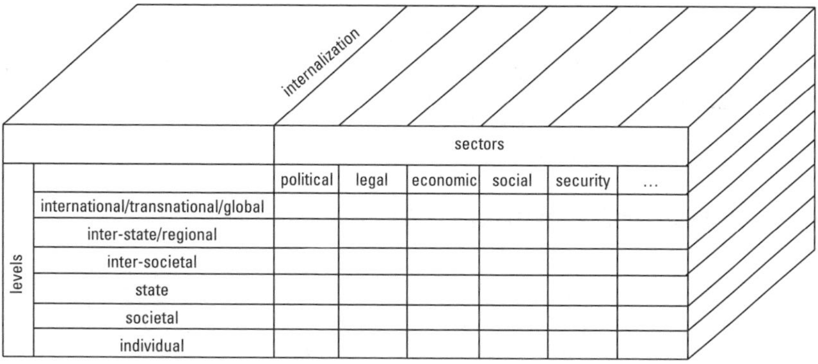

or support has disappeared. In view of their relatively permanent quality, changing the structures within which actors operate can be harder and take more time than influencing or changing the behaviour of actors. However, if successful, the impact of these efforts can be both more profound and more enduring.

Both material and immaterial factors can contribute to the sustainability of structures and thus to the long-term success of structural foreign policy (see also Box 9.1 on 'external governance' and 'diffusion'). Material factors concern the extent to which the organizing principles can be translated into functional institutions and mechanisms, able to generate the expected results. This points to the potential relevance of the EU, which through its Association and Cooperation Agreements, financial instruments, and technical and legal expertise has a major toolbox to materially support structural reforms. A structural foreign policy can generally only be effective and sustainable if it is comprehensive or at least takes into account the various relevant interrelated or 'interpenetrated' sectors and levels (see Wight 2006: 109–10, 115) (see Box 14.1). Combined with the fact that sustained effort is required over the long term, this explains why a structural foreign policy is beyond the capacity of most individual states, and consequently why the EU is a potentially interesting locus for member states to develop such a policy.

Whether changes to structures are sustainable also depends on immaterial (or ideational) factors: the extent to which the structures are seen as legitimate and are (or are becoming) part of the belief system, culture or identity of the people concerned (population as well as elites). Structures or structural changes have more chance of becoming internalized when they are perceived as desirable and legitimate, not just as the result of external pressure or of a purely rational cost–benefit calculation (acquiescing in order to avoid sanctions or gain economic support, for example) (see Wendt 1999: 266–78). The internalization process is facilitated if the structures and structural changes to some degree account for indigenous contexts, processes, preferences and sensitivities in the target country or society (see Goodin and Tilly 2006; Migdal 2001). As becomes clear in Chapters 11 and 12, these immaterial factors pose the greatest challenges to the EU's policy towards other regions in the world, for example when dealing with religious movements in the Arab world or with other 'non-Western' or 'non-modern' actors or groups that are situated on the societal level (see Box 1.1).

The Globalizing Context of EU Foreign Policy

Globalization is a major contextual factor for foreign policy in general. The increasing scope, depth, impact and velocity of globalization processes carries implications that are fundamental yet not always

---

Box 1.1   Structural foreign policy and the societal level

Most levels included in the conceptualization of structural foreign policy (see Table 1.1) are self-evident and fit within the usual typology of foreign policy (see also Wight 2006: 112). Whereas this holds true for the international or the state level, this may be less the case for the *societal level*, which is one of the often neglected dimensions in the analysis of EU foreign policy and foreign policy in general (for other 'neglected dimensions', see Keukeleire and MacNaughtan 2008: 19–25). The 'societal level' refers to the various ways in which groups of people are persistently connected on the basis of ethnicity or religion (Waever 1993:23) or on the basis of kinship or other systems to organize groups of people, ranging from extended families and clans (such as in the Western Balkans) to tribes (for example in Libya, Afghanistan or Pakistan) and large religious groups (such as the Shiites or Sunnis). These can be situated within a country, but are often of a transnational nature.

The inclusion of the societal level in the conceptualization of structural foreign policy serves to emphasize the existence of structures that do not fit within 'modern' or Western frameworks. However, these structures can – in terms of identity, legitimacy and effectiveness – be more important to the people concerned than those at the state and interstate level. Analysing the possibility of structural changes in a third country or region can thus require an understanding of the way in which societal structures can substitute or dominate over state structures, and of the way in which societies and states transform and constitute one another (see Gough *et al.* 2004; Migdal 1988, 2001). This is particularly important when analysing the foreign policy of the EU, which mainly focuses on states and regional organizations, and thereby often neglecting the societal level.

Considering the importance of the societal level also points to the lack of societal security in third countries. *Societal security* refers to the ability of a society (largely defined on an ethnic or religious basis) to persist in its essential character. Hence, it is about the sustainability, allowing for an acceptable level of evolution, of traditional patterns of language, culture, association, values, and religious, ethnic or national identity (Waever 1993: 23). Deteriorating societal security can be the result of the indirect pressure from the international system (for instance through the homogenizing impact of globalization or Westernization) (Buzan 1993; Latouche 1996). As demonstrated in Chapters 11 and 12, particularly in the sections on the southern Mediterranean and on Islamism, the lack of societal security can also have negative consequences for the EU's foreign policy if this leads to a rejection of the Western or European models and if other structural powers are seen as caring more about these societal security concerns.

---

acknowledged. Globalization refers to the expanding scale, growing magnitude, speeding up and deepening impact of patterns of social interaction and interregional flows of people, trade, capital, information, technological knowledge, ideas, values and norms. Indeed, few areas of social life escape its reach. These increasingly intensive flows are facilitated by different kinds of physical infrastructure (such as transport, communication and banking systems), but also by immaterial, normative and symbolic factors (such as trade rules, the spread of values and customs, and of English as the lingua franca) (Held and McGrew 2000: 3–4).

As globalization constrains and empowers actors, its impact is profoundly uneven, reflecting and strengthening existing patterns of inequality and hierarchy while also generating new patterns of inclusion and exclusion (Held *et al.* 1999: 27). The positive effects of globalization and increasing interdependence are matched by a growing vulnerability in a burgeoning number of interrelated policy areas. This is not only the case in the military field (proliferation of weapons of mass destruction and sensitive military technology, threat of 'low-scale' terrorist attacks with large-scale effects) and in the economic field (including energy provision or the vulnerability of information networks). It also extends to policy fields that used to receive less attention: the environment (ecological change, unsafe nuclear plants), public health (HIV/AIDS, avian influenza) and societal security (the preservation of a society's essential features). Threats are no longer solely posed by states, but increasingly by a wide range of non-state actors, anonymous and diffuse networks, and incremental developments that cannot be associated with a specific actor (see Held *et al.* 1999; Held and McGrew 2000; Turner 2010).

Exploring what globalization means for foreign policy leads to two key questions. First, has globalization 'rendered foreign policy redundant'? Second, is 'foreign policy [still] a key site of agency in international relations, or [is it] being steadily emptied of content' (Hill 2003: 13, 16)? Linking globalization to foreign policy leads to a duality. On the one hand, globalization reflects a growing predominance of economics over politics and of foreign economic relations over foreign policy. On the other hand, the implications of globalization and the vulnerabilities it causes make foreign policy more essential than ever. Hence, there is a need for more foreign policy and for a different kind of foreign policy. Yet national governments find themselves to be increasingly irrelevant in addressing the challenges of globalization, as their traditional foreign policy is impotent in the face of multiplying vulnerabilities. This not only explains the demand for 'global governance' (Held and McGrew 2002); it also provides a potential impetus for strengthening the EU's role in global governance (see Wunderlich and Bailey 2011) (see Chapter 13).

There is a rather ambiguous relationship between European integration and globalization, with the EU acting both as a shield against and an agent for globalization (Wallace 2000: 48–9; Nousios *et al.* 2012). On the one hand, the EU functions as an instrument to protect its member states and citizens from the negative consequences of globalization and tries to contain, manage and order this process. Increasingly helpless, member states' governments turn to the EU to respond to questions they are incapable of answering alone. The EU's rich cross-border legal mechanisms and the fact that an increasing number of 'internal' policy issues are now dealt with at the EU level helped member states to control some of the repercussions of globalization and to protect themselves from turbulent global events. Vulnerability in traditionally domestic or internal policy fields, such as health, the environment, energy or migration, explains the current pressure to gradually elaborate an EU foreign policy in these fields (see Chapter 10).

On the other hand, while promoting global governance in an attempt to protect itself from globalization, the EU acts as an agent of globalization. More fundamentally, the EU contributes to globalization through its trade policy and its support for a global free market economy, as well as a neo-liberal international order (including through the WTO, the IMF and the World Bank, and through its initiatives to conclude free trade agreements with other regions of the world). The EU has not always sufficiently considered the consequences of its policies: it contributes to international structures that, while positive in many ways, also reproduce and reinforce patterns of exclusion, alienation and uncertainty (see Chapter 13).

Initially perceived to not primarily affect the EU, the onset of the financial crisis in 2008 shook the EU and several European countries to their foundations and proved to be an eye-opening event (Della Posta and Talani 2011). The EU was seemingly no more successful in shielding Europe from the perils of globalization. It forcefully demonstrated that Europe could also be situated on the losing side, whereas the newly emerging countries such as the BRICS proved to move gradually to the winning side. This increasingly allows the latter to steer processes of globalization and global governance in directions that are favourable for these (re)emerging powers (see Chapters 12 and 13).

Conclusion

Today's world is a markedly different place to that of a twentieth century defined by two world wars and subsequent bipolarity. Today, the increasing impact of globalization, the rise of emerging powers and the financial crisis throw up new sets of opportunities and challenges. The context in which the EU and its foreign policy are designed and operate has thus changed. We propose a conceptual approach – relational foreign policy versus structural foreign policy – on which we base our analysis of EU foreign policy in the chapters which follow. These concepts are complementary, not contradictory – they help us understand more dimensions of foreign policy challenges and how these are being, and could be, addressed. Building on this understanding of the context and definition of foreign policy, this chapter has explored the question of what specifically constitutes EU foreign policy. We understand EU foreign policy as multifaceted (including CFSP, CSDP, external action and the external dimension of internal policies), multi-method (combining an intergovernmental and a Community method) and multilevel (embedded in an international context and also comprising the national policies of the member states). Four areas of tension characterize this policy field: between European integration and Atlantic solidarity; between civilian and military power; between the intergovernmental and the Community method; and between external en internal objectives. These ideas form the conceptual backbone on which the rest of this book is based.

Chapter 2

European Integration and Foreign Policy: Historical Overview

The relationship between European integration and the development of a European foreign policy has remained ambiguous from the end of the Second World War to the present day. Nevertheless, European integration has evolved from a primarily economic endeavour to one with a substantive political and foreign policy dimension (see overview with key dates in Table 2.1). Charting this progress, this chapter demonstrates that several obstacles that were highly problematic in the early stages of the process continue to be the stumbling blocks of EU foreign policy today.

European Integration: The Product of a Structural Foreign Policy (1945–52)

The Marshall Plan of 1947 and the Schuman Declaration of 1950 launched a highly successful structural foreign policy towards post-war Western Europe, in which the process of European integration played a crucial role. To use today's terminology, the Marshall Plan and Schuman Declaration proposed to tackle the 'root causes' of the wars and economic and political crises that had characterized Europe in the first half of the twentieth century by creating new structures to govern both the new (West) German state and its relations with its neighbours. This policy towards West Germany was one of the greatest successes of post-war American and French policy, precisely because it deviated from both the conventional concept of a foreign policy and the traditional approach to defeated nations.

The Marshall Plan

In his speech at Harvard University, the then American Secretary of State, General George Marshall, outlined the main features of a long-term American assistance programme for Europe (Hogan 1987; Marshall 1947). The US feared the further spread of communist ideology in the

Table 2.1   **Key dates in the development of European foreign policy**

Year	Treaty/document	Event/development
1947	Marshall Plan	US assistance for Western Europe
1949	Treaty of Washington	North Atlantic Treaty
1950		Creation of NATO
1952	Treaty of Paris	Creation of ECSC
		Signing of EDC Treaty
1954		Non-ratification of the EDC Treaty
	Modified Brussels Treaty	Creation of WEU
1958	Treaty of Rome	Creation of EEC
1963		Yaoundé Convention with former African colonies
1964		Failure of the Fouchet Plans
1970	Luxembourg Report	EPC
1973		Enlargement to 9 member states
1975		First Lomé Agreement with the ACP countries
		First European Council meeting
1981		Enlargement to 10 member states
1986		Enlargement to 12 member states
1987	Single European Act	EPC gains treaty basis
1988		Start of a policy towards reformist CEECs
1989		Fall of the communist regimes in CEECs
1991		Start of Western Balkan wars
1993	Treaty of Maastricht	Creation of the EU and CFSP Copenhagen criteria

$\rightarrow$

West, fuelled by the dire political, economic and humanitarian situation in Western European countries. Through the Marshall Plan, the US provided $20 billion for economic relief. It aimed to improve the socio-economic situation, to restore order and stability in Western European societies and to obtain rapid improvements in living conditions. American policy was not only elite focused, but also concentrated on the population (improving their economic situation) as well as on society (weakening the impact of communist ideology). The Marshall Plan was more than an impressive economic assistance programme. It was also an instrument to shape and/or consolidate a whole set of political, economic and societal structures in Western Europe based on the principles of democracy, rule of law and a free market economy, which affected not only individual states, but also the relationship between states.

Year	Treaty/document	Event/development
1995		Enlargement to 15 member states
		Start Euro-Mediterranean Partnership
		Strategies/partnerships towards the main regions in world
1998		End of Western Balkan wars
		Franco-British Saint Malo Declaration
1999	Treaty of Amsterdam	Creation of position of High Representative for the CFSP
		Establishment of ESDP
2000		Cotonou Agreement with ACP countries
2003	Treaty of Nice	Amendment of the Treaties (with limited foreign policy impact)
		Iraq war
		First ESDP operations
		European Security Strategy
2004		Enlargement to 25 member states
		Start of European Neighbourhood Policy
2007		Enlargement to 27 member states
2009	Treaty of Lisbon	CSDP gains treaty basis; institutional innovations
2010		Start sovereign debt crisis
2011		Establishment of the EEAS
		Arab revolts and Libya war
2013		Enlargement to 28 member states

Note: The year of the Treaties refers to their entry into force.

One of the major features of the Marshall Plan was that it was based on the principle of European 'ownership', which paved the way for future European integration. The US put pressure on Western European states to cooperate in economic reconstruction and to accept one another – including the two former enemies, West Germany and Italy – as partners. Psychologically and politically, the American approach was critical because it forced political and economic leaders, diplomats and civil servants from across Western Europe to work together. In so doing, it laid the foundations for the later European Coal and Steel Community (ECSC) negotiations, which would also be strongly supported by the US. The Marshall Plan contributed to the necessary restoration of self-confidence and responsibility in Western European countries and West

Germany in particular, as well as to the redefinition of Germany as a full partner in the West and in the Western European integration process. However, while the Marshall Plan substantially contributed to the process of *Western European* integration and reconciliation, it also caused further *European* disintegration and confrontation, as, on Soviet insistence, Central and Eastern European countries were not able to participate in the assistance programme provided to the West.

The Schuman Declaration and the ECSC

It is not coincidental that it was Jean Monnet, one of the driving forces behind the implementation of the Marshall Plan in France, who became the intellectual father of France's new policy towards West Germany. It was Monnet's preparatory work that allowed the French Minister of Foreign Affairs, Robert Schuman, to present in 1950 the first positive French policy towards its former enemy. Schuman proposed placing French and German coal and steel production under a common High Authority in an organization that was open for the participation of other European countries. Control over these two major industrial sectors (that were also the basis of the military industry) would be transferred from both France and West Germany to a supranational entity. While this proposal had a major economic component, it also went to the heart of foreign policy:

> The pooling of coal and steel production should immediately provide for the setting up of common foundations for economic development as a first step in the federation of Europe, and will change the destinies of those regions which have long been devoted to the manufacture of munitions of war, of which they have been the most constant victims. The solidarity in production thus established will make it plain that any war between France and Germany becomes not merely unthinkable, but materially impossible. (Schuman 1950)

Less than one year later, France, West Germany, Italy, the Netherlands, Belgium and Luxembourg signed the Paris Treaty establishing the European Coal and Steel Community (ECSC). Following the harrowing experiences of two World Wars, the Schuman Plan and the creation of the ECSC presented European integration as a radically new method to finally and definitively resolve hostility between states and, more generally, to organize interstate relations on the basis of equality as well as mutual solidarity and control. As Monnet noted in 1962, 'we adapted to our situation the methods which have allowed individuals to live together in society: common rules which each member is committed to respect, and common institutions to watch over the application of these rules' (Monnet 2003: 23). With the Schuman Declaration and the ECSC, the belief in a rules-based international order and multilateralism was born. This would become a constant theme in European foreign policy.

A crucial aspect of the Schuman Plan and the ECSC was that they also affected the immaterial dimension of interstate and intersocietal relations. As Duchêne (1994: 224) emphasized, the Schuman Plan was 'about turning around the psychology of relations between states and peoples'. The process of integration that it launched contributed to a gradual change in the mindset of both the elite and the people. This redefinition of the identity of the EU's founding member states contributed to the desecuritization of the Franco-German relationship, the lasting transformation of Germany from an enemy into a partner and the transformation of Western Europe into a 'security community' (see Adler and Barnett 1998; Waever 2000).

The First Decades (1952–70): A Taboo on Defence, Decisive Steps on Trade and International Agreements

In April 1949, in the face of a perceived growing threat from the Soviet Union, Western European states along with the US and Canada, signed the North Atlantic Treaty. This treaty, which would ultimately lead to the creation of the North Atlantic Treaty Organization (NATO), sealed America's commitment to providing a security guarantee for its Western European allies. However, it was not at all clear what kind of military structures would be established to organize Western Europe's collective defence and what the position of West Germany would be therein.

NATO and the transatlantic imbalance

It was not the US but the Europeans (including France) who pushed for greater American leadership and the continued presence of American soldiers to defend their territories. Initially, the US viewed the new Atlantic Alliance rather like 'a military Marshall Plan, to help the Europeans pull up their own socks and take the future in their own hands' (Cook 1989: 225). The outbreak of the Korean War in June 1950 transformed this context, and half a year later the North Atlantic Treaty was upgraded to a North Atlantic Treaty Organization (NATO). At the top of an integrated military alliance (including a heavy commitment of American troops), an American Supreme Allied Commander directed the territorial defence of Western Europe. As Calleo has underlined, with NATO, 'America's European policy moved out of its Marshall Plan phase, which had emphasized economic recovery and European initiative, and into a new phase that featured massive rearmament and direct American leadership' (1987: 28). 'Along with militarization came a different style in transatlantic political relations, a move from a "two pillars" pattern, emphasizing a European unity distinct from American ties, towards a hegemonic pattern, emphasizing America's direct role in managing European affairs' (Calleo 1983: 8).

The repercussions of transferring primary responsibility for the security and defence of Western Europe to America were to be felt for the next half a century. The parameters set by the globalization of America's military presence, by the globalization of the East–West confrontation and by the highly confrontational approach of the US, implied that in addition to structuring Western Europe's security and defence policies, the US also structured Western Europe's foreign policy. Given that the US bore the burden of the West's military efforts, it understandably expected at least a political return from its NATO allies through their active support for American foreign policy objectives and actions. Thus, the scope for Western Europe to pursue or even formulate its own foreign policy interests, to take its own foreign policy initiatives and to approach foreign policy issues in a different way was dramatically reduced. During the following decades, the US often exploited this imbalance, pulling the plug on Western European positions on matters such as improving relations with Eastern European countries, developing a balanced approach to conflict in the Middle East and particularly creating an autonomous European foreign, security and defence policy. Remarkably, this pattern of transatlantic relations survived the disappearance of the Soviet threat, as the Cold War prism was replaced by the 'war on terror' prism after 2001.

From European Defence Community to Western European Union

The US was only prepared to strengthen American forces in Europe on the condition that European countries increased their defence efforts, including using West German military potential to defend against possible attacks from the east. However, barely five years after being victims of German aggression, the idea of a new German army was a step too far for France and the rest of Western Europe.

The methods developed some months earlier in the Schuman Declaration seemed to provide the solution. Following the ECSC's example, creating a supranational European Defence Community (EDC) would mean German soldiers could operate within a European army, without having to create a new German army. In May 1952, the EDC Treaty was signed by the six ECSC states and submitted to national parliaments for ratification (Fursdon 1980; Hill and Smith 2000: 16–32). The opening article of the Treaty announced that the parties 'set up amongst themselves a European Defence Community, supranational in character, comprising common institutions, common Armed Forces, and a common budget'. On closer inspection, the Treaty was actually less 'common' or European than suggested. Under pressure from the other ECSC states and the US, the French had been forced to accept that the project become more Atlantic and intergovernmental than originally anticipated. By mid-1954, improvements in the East–West relationship had reduced the urgency and the original motivation for creating a European army. Amidst growing concerns over the loss of national sovereignty in security and defence, the French Assembly refused to ratify the EDC Treaty, effectively killing it off.

Creating the Western European Union (WEU) provided an alternative solution to the questions of German rearmament. The WEU was established by the Modified Brussels Treaty of October 1954, which allowed West Germany and Italy to enter a six-year-old military assistance pact (originally established against Germany) between France, the UK and the Benelux countries (Hill and Smith 2000: 40–1). Article IV of the Treaty stated that: 'Recognising the undesirability of duplicating the military staffs of NATO, the Council [of the WEU] and its Agency will rely on the appropriate military authorities of NATO for information and advice on military matters'. Responsibility for military affairs was de facto passed to NATO – with West Germany thus being militarily integrated into NATO through a back door opened by the WEU. Stripped of its potential as a site for European defence cooperation, the Europeans lost the opportunity to use their own military capabilities to pursue their own foreign policy choices. Forty years later, European military impotence at the outbreak of the Yugoslav war would be one of the painful consequences of this choice made in the early 1950s.

The failure of the EDC project and the subsequent creation of the WEU implied that from then on military security structures would be Atlantic not European, intergovernmental not supranational (see Duke 1999). These fault lines became more pronounced after the failure of the second French attempt to get the Six to act as one in foreign policy and defence. With the Fouchet Plans of 1960 and 1962, France proposed creating a Union with a European foreign and defence policy outside the EEC framework on the basis of purely intergovernmental cooperation. The negotiations eventually came to nothing in 1964 as most EEC partners feared that President de Gaulle's plans were aimed at undermining the Atlantic alliance, as well as the EEC and its Community method.

Overcoming these fault lines became ever more problematic when in 1965 France withdrew from the military structures of NATO after the US and the UK rejected its request to be on an equal footing with the UK in NATO's military command structure. The French withdrawal and decision to follow its own military and nuclear doctrine provoked a fundamental division between France and the other EEC countries, making cooperation or integration in security and defence virtually impossible, that is until France and the UK launched the CSDP (then ESDP) process in 1998.

The EEC's external dimension: trade and international agreements

With the Rome Treaties of 1957, the European Economic Community (EEC) and European Community for Atomic Energy (Euratom) were established. European integration was assuming a primarily economic path, with no foreign policy, security or defence dimension foreseeable. Since the EEC was conceived as a customs union with a common external tariff for its members, the EEC was also granted competences in external trade policy and for the conclusion of (association) agreements with third states. The Commission was given a leading role in these external negotiations from the beginning. These initial external competences, rooted in an economic rationale, combined with international legal personality for the EEC, allowed the latter to evolve gradually into an international actor. By 1963, the EEC had already established and organized relations with the former African colonies of its member states (particular those of France) within the framework of the Yaoundé Treaty, predecessor to the Lomé and now Cotonou Agreement with the African, Caribbean and Pacific (ACP) countries, which would become the basic foundations for the EU's development policy with these countries (see Chapter 9).

In 1964–67, in an unambiguous confirmation of a distinct European identity in terms of external trade, the European Commission acted on behalf of the six member states in the multilateral Kennedy Round negotiations of the General Agreement on Tariffs and Trade (predecessor to the WTO). Before it delved into its first multilateral trade endeavour, the EEC had already signed important bilateral trade agreements in the year before, for instance with Greece, Turkey, Israel and Lebanon, and it was engaged in the negotiation of such agreements with other Mediterranean, Asian and African countries.

The EEC's external competences forced the Europeans to define their relations with the rest of the world and created external expectations about the role of the EEC as a major power – which also entailed foreign policy related choices. The growing international 'presence' of the EEC was so significant that it was compelled to also further develop its 'actorness' (see Allen and Smith 1990; Sjøstedt 1977). This goes to the heart of the EU foreign policy problematic: the EEC gradually and quietly became a foreign policy actor despite the fact that it did not possess clear foreign policy competences. Furthermore, this had not originally been foreseen by the member states and it certainly did not have the wholehearted support of all member states.

European Political Cooperation (EPC) (1970–93): Setting the Stage

At their 1969 summit meeting in The Hague, the EEC member states relaunched the European integration process in a changing international and domestic context: détente in East–West relations; a question mark over the US commitment to Europe; a new West German Chancellor, Willy Brandt, whose foreign policy priority was rapprochement with the Eastern European countries; and the end of Charles de Gaulle's rule and thus the removal of a major obstacle to new European initiatives. In addition to decisions to strengthen the EC and to begin accession negotiations with the UK, Ireland, Denmark and Norway, the heads of state and government of the six EEC countries also instructed their ministers of foreign affairs 'to study the best way of achieving progress in the matter of political unification' (for the The Hague Summit Declaration and all EPC declarations, see Hill and Smith 2000: 71–119).

The resulting Luxembourg Report – also referred to as 'Davignon Report' – adopted in 1970 by the ministers of foreign affairs, signified the start of what was termed 'European Political Cooperation'. The report emphasized 'the need to intensify political cooperation' and, in an initial phase, to 'concentrate specifically on the co-ordination of foreign policies in order to show the whole world that Europe has a political mission'. This mission was to play a role 'in promoting the relaxation of international tension and the rapprochement among all peoples, and first and foremost among those of the entire European continent'. More precisely, the objectives of this foreign policy cooperation were defined as follows (Hill and Smith 2000: 77):

> to ensure, through regular exchanges of information and consultations, a better mutual understanding on great international problems; to strengthen their solidarity by promoting the harmonisation of their views, the co-ordination of their positions; and, where it appears possible and desirable, common action.

To meet these objectives, the following modest mechanisms were established: biannual meetings of the six ministers of foreign affairs, quarterly meetings of member states' directors of political affairs, specialist working parties, and the designation within each foreign ministry of an official to correspond with his/her counterpart.

In 1973, the heads of state and government adopted the Copenhagen Report and a Declaration on a European Identity, formalizing practices developed in the previous years, including an increase in the number of meetings. The Copenhagen Report also specified that in the foreign policy questions selected by the foreign ministers, 'each state undertakes as a general rule not to take up final positions without prior consultation with its partners'.

From these basic EPC texts a whole set of procedural and behavioural norms were incrementally developed (Smith M. E. 2001: 86–8). The London Report of 1981 and the Single European Act (SEA) of 1986, in which EPC was legally anchored in the EU Treaty, largely confirmed these foreign policy habits rather than launching major new commitments or mechanisms, and without making any attempt to solve the problems that had arisen in practice (Hill and Smith 2000: 139–45) (on EPC, see Nuttall 1992; Pijpers *et al.* 1988).

Basic features

EPC was based on purely intergovernmental arrangements between member states' Foreign Ministries, with consensus required for every decision, no transfer of competences to the European level and no formal role for Community institutions. Member states agreed to foster consultation, coordination and possibly joint action in a number of foreign policy areas. However, they retained full control over their foreign policy. EPC relied entirely on interministerial arrangements, particularly on the rotating Presidency. This became a major handicap when the number of member states and the scope of EPC activities increased. Aside from the creation of a small EPC secretariat in the 1980s, EPC's lack of common actors was not to be addressed until the creation of a High Representative for the CFSP in the Amsterdam Treaty in the late 1990s.

EPC was also rigidly separated from the legal and institutional framework of the European Community (EC). As a legacy of the Fouchet Plan debacle, France wanted to avoid any involvement of common institutions or the Community method, while the other member states wanted to avoid intergovernmental arrangements contaminating the EC. This implied that the Commission, the European Parliament and the Court of Justice had no formal role in EPC. Although the Single European Act linked EPC to the EC Treaties, the provisions on EPC were included in a separate Title III concerning 'Treaty provisions on European cooperation in the sphere of foreign policy'. This foreshadowed the development of a pillar system with the Maastricht Treaty.

In practice, the formal separation of EPC and EC was not sustainable. Although they functioned according to their own logic, interaction between EPC and the EC in both institutional and policy matters was unavoidable. As an unforeseen consequence of EPC's lack of common institutions and instruments, EPC often had to rely on the EC to give substance to its declarations and initiatives. In the 1980s, EPC needed the EC's economic instruments for sanctions (targeting Poland after the military coup, Argentina during the Falklands crisis, and South Africa in view of its Apartheid regime) and for economic support (for Central American countries' peace initiatives) (Nuttall 1997). Furthermore, the EC's successful internal market project, launched in 1985, increased external expectations about not only its economic but also its political power (see Redmond 1992).

Objectives and policies

During the first years of its existence, EPC established some basic patterns in its objectives and policies that by and large remained valid over the following decades. EPC not only aimed at pursuing *external* objectives (influencing the external environment), but also at achieving *integration* objectives, *interrelational* objectives and *identity* objectives (see Chapter 1). First, integration objectives dominated the start of EPC, which became one element of efforts to relaunch European integration. Second, interrelational objectives were prominent in the goals of cooperation defined in the Luxembourg Report: regular information and consultation was a method to ensure 'a better mutual understanding' while harmonizing views and coordinating positions was a way to 'strengthen their solidarity'. EPC provided a gentle way to keep an eye on West Germany's emerging *Ostpolitik* and to embed it in a larger European setting, while for West Germany EPC provided a tool to lever support for its new foreign policy orientation. Third, identity objectives were prominent in the 1970 Luxembourg Report, as well as in the 1973 Declaration on European Identity. More generally, EPC allowed the member states to elaborate a specific 'European' position to the world and to distance themselves from the US at a time when that country was losing international support due to the Vietnam war.

The number of issues discussed among EPC states was initially rather limited. For example, foreign policy towards the former colonies and the military dimension were both excluded from debate. However, EPC did play an important role both in the negotiations with the Eastern Bloc countries in the Conference on Security and Cooperation in Europe (CSCE or 'Helsinki Process') and in discussions on the Middle East and the Palestinian question (see Chapter 11). Experience was to prove encouraging with the CSCE, but discouraging with the Middle East – one of the determining factors being whether the US allowed the Europeans to take the lead and pursue a policy of their own. The latter was also made more difficult when three new member states entered into the EEC/EPC in 1973: the UK as the US's closest ally, the equally eurosceptic Denmark, and Ireland with its status as a neutral country.

The EEC also missed the opportunity to establish closer relations with Asia. When negotiating the 1975 Lomé Convention, France feared that the inclusion of Asian countries, particularly a large country such as India, would undermine the preferential treatment of its mainly African former colonies. As a result, Caribbean and Pacific states were included in the ACP framework, but no Asian country was permitted to join the Lomé Convention, despite the fact that some EU member states have strong ties with Asia, particularly the UK, which has a strong relationship with the Indian sub-continent. This was seen as a missed opportunity that confined 'Asian–EU relations to the lowest of priorities for the next two decades' (Holland 2002: 60).

By the early 1980s, EPC had established the general trends that European foreign policy would follow over the decades to come. There was a clear focus on promoting structural changes in other regions over the longer term. However, EPC proved ineffective in formulating a policy on the crises of the time, such as those in the Middle East, Afghanistan and Poland. From 1988 onwards, even before the fall of the Berlin Wall, the EC/EPC had increased its focus on structural changes by supporting the reforms on which some Central and Eastern European countries (CEECs) were embarking. After the fall of the communist regimes in late 1989, Central and Eastern Europe became the subject of the first comprehensive structural foreign policy of the EC/EU (see Chapter 11).

The Maastricht Treaty (1993) and the Illusory CFSP

Motivations and geostrategic context

In terms of foreign policy, the establishment of the CFSP was one of the major breakthroughs of the 1993 Maastricht Treaty. The member states' rationale in creating CFSP in the Maastricht Treaty is key to understanding its nature. Their motivations were closely linked to the geostrategic changes that had preceded and which acted as a catalyst for the Maastricht Treaty: the fall of the communist regimes in 1988–91, the reunification of Germany in 1990, military conflict in the Gulf following the Iraqi invasion of Kuwait in 1990 and the start of the Yugoslav crisis in 1991.

First, CFSP was about strengthening European integration and particularly about member states managing their interstate relations in an unstable geopolitical environment, again illustrating the importance of the interrelational objectives in the EU's foreign policy development. In conjunction with establishing the EU and Economic and Monetary Union (EMU), CFSP was part of a greater diplomatic operation and balance of power exercise in which the member states sought to firmly embed an enlarged German state in a stronger European entity while Germany gained support for its unification process.

Second, CFSP was about managing inter-institutional relations and the relations between member states and the Commission. Hence, CFSP also served an integration objective. For most member states, creating CFSP in a separate intergovernmental second pillar was deemed necessary to contain the EU as a foreign policy actor and to ensure member states' full control. Under President Delors, the Commission had become increasingly assertive in foreign affairs, taking full advantage of its potential to back up nice declarations with concrete operational measures. The foreign policy potential and aspirations of the EC needed to be curtailed, and CFSP was to serve as a filter to prevent the substance of foreign policy entering the EC machinery.

Third, CFSP was about identity and public relations management, emphasizing the identity objective of EU foreign policy. In this period of major geopolitical change, in which 'Europe' had suffered a loss of face during the Gulf and Yugoslav crises, CFSP was seen as a tool to strengthen European identity. Hence, one of the new objectives of the Treaty on European Union (TEU) was 'to assert its identity on the international scene, in particular through the implementation of a common foreign and security policy' (Art. 2 TEU).

Finally, for some of the original member states, CFSP was about creating an effective and credible European foreign policy – although for others, such as the UK and Denmark, the opposite was true. For some member states, the disappearance of the old East–West order made it imperative that the new EU become a stronger and more coherent foreign policy actor. The Gulf and Yugoslav crises demonstrated that the EU needed new tools to cope with new external challenges. However, for other member states, these crises were a stark reminder that the EU should not aim to tackle such events if only because member states differed so fundamentally on the role of the US and the use of military force.

It is clear that from CFSP's inception, interrelational, integration and identity objectives were for many member states as important, if not more important, than external objectives (see Chapter 1). Although all member states accepted CFSP for the reasons outlined above, some were firmly opposed to a CFSP that would be able to be true to its name (see Chapter 7). And for other member states, CFSP had already fulfilled its main function at the moment of its creation.

The Maastricht Treaty: debates and results

In sharp contrast to the Intergovernmental Conference (IGC) on EMU, which had been thoroughly prepared since 1988 by the Delors Committee, the parallel IGC on European Political Union, in which the CFSP was negotiated, suffered from a lack of serious preparatory discussion. This was an indication that rather than resulting from a well-considered initiative, the creation of CFSP was a panicked response to turbulent geopolitics. Foreshadowing the future of treaty negotiations, the position of foreign policy in the new treaty framework, the decision-making system and the military dimension of security all dominated the IGC (see Laursen and Vanhoonacker 1992; Nuttall 2000).

The first major issue was how to position foreign policy in the new treaty. In order to ensure efficiency and coherence of EU foreign policy, the Dutch presidency proposed establishing a unitary institutional framework, integrating the political, economic and security dimensions of foreign policy. However, this unitary system was rejected by most other member states and negotiators ultimately opted for a three-pillar approach (see Figure 2.1). The various dimensions of foreign policy were organized through distinctive policy-making methods enshrined in different titles of the Treaty, including the titles on the EC (the 'first pillar') and Title V on the CFSP (the 'second pillar'), with the latter replacing the provisions on EPC of the Single European Act. Title VI (the 'third pillar') was to deal with provisions on cooperation in the fields of justice and home affairs (JHA). The member states deprived CFSP (in the second pillar) of a direct link to either essential foreign policy instruments or the EU's strongest policy domains: trade policy, the network of trade and cooperation agreements, development cooperation, and the external dimensions of internal policy fields (all in the first pillar). This was all the more remarkable as member states did not endow the second pillar with its own policy instruments or financial resources to allow it to deliver. This pillar structure established by the Maastricht Treaty would be formally abolished 16 years later by the Lisbon Treaty (see below).

The second issue to be tackled in the run-up to Maastricht was decision-making. One of the main rationales behind the pillar system was to avoid features of the EC decision-making system being applied to CFSP. Policy-making in CFSP would be organized intergovernmentally – monopolized by the Council of Ministers with unanimous voting almost across the board and with member states also dominating the initiation and implementation stages.

Figure 2.1   EU foreign policy in the Maastricht Treaty: the EU's pillar system (to 1 December 2009)

EUROPEAN UNION		
First pillar	*Second pillar*	*Third pillar*
EC	**CFSP**	**JHA/PJCC**
External trade; EMU; cooperation and association agreements; economic sanctions; development policy; internal policies; etc.	Foreign and security policy; peace-building, crisis management; etc.	Cooperation in the field justice and home affairs (1993–99) Police and judicial cooperation in criminal matters (1999–2009)
Community method	**Intergovernmental method**	
Council (majority voting or unanimity), EP, Commission, Court of Justice	Council (unanimity)	Council (unanimity)

The third issue that dominated the IGC was the military dimension of security. It was here that divergences between member states were starkest with one group of member states led by France and Germany pleading for a 'common defence', and the neutrals and Atlantic-oriented states maintaining their opposition. They nevertheless developed two formulae to overcome this paralysing situation. By being deliberately ambiguous in its formulation and incorporating safeguards for neutral and NATO-oriented states, member states agreed that, 'the common foreign and security policy shall include all questions related to the security of the Union, including the *eventual framing* of a common defence policy, which *might in time* lead to a common defence' (Art. J.4(1) TEU, our emphasis). Furthermore, since it could serve as both the military arm of the EU and the European arm of NATO, member states agreed to use the WEU as a bridge between both camps. The major innovation, on paper, was that the Council could request the WEU 'to elaborate and implement decisions and actions of the Union which have defence implications' (Art. J.4(2) TEU).

In the aftermath of the Maastricht European Council that adopted the TEU it appeared that there was something in it for everyone. France, Germany and like-minded states achieved the grandiose phrases and symbolic changes they had asked for (i.e. 'common foreign and security policy', 'all aspects of security', 'common defence'). Yet a closer reading of the text made it clear that the UK and other member states had conceded much on words and symbols, but nothing on substance and practice (see Chapter 7). Nevertheless, this was too much for Danish public opinion. After initially rejecting the new treaty outright, Denmark obtained an opt-out from Maastricht's 'defence' provisions. This implied that Denmark could not contribute to military EU crisis management operations, either financially or in terms of military assets (see Olsen and Pilegaard 2005).

Irrespective of the member states' underlying motivations and arm-wrestling, the creation of CFSP and the very name 'common foreign and security policy' created high expectations. European leaders presented CFSP to the public as a fully-fledged foreign policy that would allow the EU to act cohesively and effectively on the international stage. In the following years, CFSP was thus tested against the standards of the conventional foreign policy it had been proclaimed to be. However, the EU was doomed to fail this test. The member states were not committed to the success of CFSP and had not provided it with the necessary instruments or institutional framework (see Chapter 7). Meanwhile, more intensive cooperation with the WEU proved elusive. In the two years between the signing and the entry into force of the Maastricht Treaty in November 1993, European impotence and disarray during the Yugoslav wars discredited the whole project from its very inception. This contributed to the further decline of member states' interest in CFSP (for the CFSP's first years, see Holland 1997; Nuttall 2000; Regelsberger *et al.* 1997).

Strategies and partnerships beyond CFSP

From 1994 onwards, member states and the EU institutions shifted their attention from elaborating CFSP to outlining general EU strategies and partnerships towards other regions in the world (Keukeleire 1998: 367–459). These strategies and partnerships encompassed the EU's three pillars, but were based essentially on the EC one. At the heart of this move lay two issues: the need to counterbalance the EU's dominant focus on the CEECs with more attention paid to the Mediterranean and other parts of the world; and the goal to apply at least partially the EU's comprehensive approach towards the CEECs, with its focus on support for structural reforms, to other regions in the world.

By the end of 1995, with the active support of the Commission, the European Council had mapped out the EU's policy towards most regions in the world. This was reflected in the extensive Conclusions of the Presidency after the European Council of Madrid in December 1995. While these Presidency Conclusions covered CFSP in barely a few lines, they dealt extensively with the strategies and partnerships that would determine EU policy for the following decade: relations with the CEECs, the Barcelona Declaration and the launch of the Euro-Mediterranean Partnership (EMP), the New Transatlantic Agenda, the EU's position for the first Euro-Asian Summit (ASEM), the EU's Strategy for Future EU/Russia Relations, and the Regional Framework Agreement with Mercosur. Breaking from the mode of the previous five years, with their quasi-exclusive focus on the CEECs and the Western Balkans, a globalization of the EU's external attentions was taking place. The EU also allocated considerable resources to developing relations with these regions, particularly the CEECs, the Mediterranean and the ACP countries. This was in stark contrast with the lack of resources allocated to CFSP objectives.

An analysis of the EU's strategic papers with regard to other regions shows that several of these were manifestations of a structural foreign policy. They aimed to promote a more favourable international environment by supporting long-term structural changes in third countries and regions. They also sought to transfer the political, societal, economic and interstate structures that characterized the EU itself: democracy, human rights, the principles of a free market economy, regional cooperation and integration, and peaceful resolutions of conflicts. The intensity, scope and success of the EU's structural foreign policy varied considerably from region to region (see Chapters 11 and 12).

In short, with its intensified partnerships towards the rest of the world and its structural foreign policy towards neighbouring regions, in the second half of the 1990s the EU did have a foreign policy. However, this was neither the foreign policy conceived by the Treaty of Maastricht through the CFSP, nor a foreign policy as might be conventionally understood.

The Amsterdam Treaty (1999) and ESDP: Moving towards Action

In the late 1990s two major attempts were made to tackle the lack of common actors and common instruments that had undermined both EPC and CFSP: the creation of the function of High Representative of the CFSP and of the ESDP (now called 'CSDP'). These qualitative changes only partially resulted from treaty reforms brought about by the Amsterdam Treaty (see also Monar and Wessels 2001). In fact, as the early development of ESDP outside the Treaties testifies, changes to the Treaties proved again to be a poor instigator or indicator of real change in EU foreign policy.

The Amsterdam Treaty

The main qualitative change of the Amsterdam Treaty was the creation of the function of 'Secretary General/High Representative of the CFSP'. The High Representative was to assist the Council and the Presidency in the formulation, preparation and implementation of policy decisions, and would be supported by a newly created 'policy planning and early warning unit'. This change was fundamental. For the first time, CFSP would be supported by a permanent actor and would also give a 'face' to EU foreign policy. The impact of this innovation was not initially clear as several member states thought a rather low-key figure would be suitable for the new job. However, following the EU's most recent Western Balkans debacle in Kosovo, the 1999 Cologne European Council opted for the high-profile political figure of Javier Solana, who as Secretary General had just led NATO through its military operations against Serbia. By appointing Solana, the member states indicated they were serious about strengthening the EU's foreign policy and security capabilities. Javier Solana successfully increased the visibility and effectiveness of the CFSP on some key occasions, including through successful mediation in Macedonia in 2001 and in Ukraine in 2004. However, his diplomatic skills alone were not sufficient to overcome all hurdles facing EU foreign policy (see Müller-Brandeck-Bocquet and Rüger 2011).

The second innovation of the Amsterdam Treaty was the creation of a new 'common strategies' instrument. In 1999–2000, three 'common strategies' were adopted – towards Russia, Ukraine and the Mediterranean. However, as they offered no real added value to the partnerships and strategies which the EU had been developing since the mid-1990s, this new instrument was quickly dropped. The third treaty change had even less effect – a slight relaxation of the voting requirements in the Council. However, voting is rare in the Council (see Chapters 3 and 4), making the new decision-making provisions as insignificant as they were complex.

Finally, the Amsterdam Treaty strengthened the relationship between the EU and the WEU. The EU gained access to the WEU's operational capability for humanitarian and rescue tasks, peacekeeping tasks and tasks of combat forces in crisis management, including peacemaking (the 'Petersberg tasks'). The EU was also to 'foster closer institutional relations with the WEU with a view to the possibility of the integration of the WEU into the EU'. However, the new provisions on EU–WEU relations were quickly overtaken by a new dynamic – the European Security and Defence Policy.

The European Security and Defence Policy (ESDP)

In the space of a few years, the military dimension, which had for decades been taboo in the European integration process (see Duke 1999) became one of the spearheads of EU foreign policy. This was made possible because for the first time in some 50 years of European integration, the member states managed to sufficiently overcome two areas of tension that had paralysed EU foreign policy: 'European integration versus Atlantic solidarity' and 'civilian power versus military power' (see Chapter 1). The first area of tension was tackled through intensive high-level negotiations among France, the UK and Germany, while the second was overcome by carefully balancing NATO states and the EU's neutral states and by complementing military with civilian crisis management tools (Howorth 2000, 2001; Ojanen 2000).

Such newly found flexibility in member sates' traditional mindsets was triggered by the Kosovo crisis which increased frustration in London, Paris and Berlin – but also in Washington, DC – over Europe's military impotence and dependence on the US. Further conflict in the Western Balkans convinced Germany that it would have to start participating in external military operations, reversing its post-Second World War doctrine. The British government, under the new Prime Minister Tony Blair, adopted a more pro-European attitude than previous British governments, for the first time seeing the strengthening of Europe's military capacities as essential to rebalance transatlantic relations and thus safeguard the future of NATO. French political leaders in turn assumed a more pro-Atlantic attitude and demonstrated a greater willingness to cooperate with NATO. For France, American military superiority in the Western Balkans was a humbling experience, while its good cooperation with British forces on the ground laid the foundations for a Franco-British entente.

These moves were sealed in several bilateral agreements, most importantly the Franco-British Saint Malo Declaration of December 1998. At Saint Malo, Jacques Chirac and Tony Blair agreed that the EU must have 'the capacity for autonomous action, backed up by credible military forces, the means to decide to use them, and a readiness to do so, in order to respond to international crises'. /The Saint Malo Declaration also referred to NATO, stating that it should contribute to 'the vitality of a modernized Atlantic Alliance which is the foundation of the collective defence of its members'. The Cologne European Council of June 1999 duly adopted the goal to establish the ESDP, repeating crucial elements of the Franco-British text. This set a pattern that would be followed in other important ESDP steps, with the UK, France and to a lesser extent also Germany effectively 'pre-cooking' decisions.

It was soon confirmed that the member states were serious about ESDP. Less than three years after their decision to establish an ESDP and to break the 45-year-old taboo, the EU had established the necessary institutional and instrumental apparatus – including the 'Berlin Plus Agreement' to provide the EU access to NATO military assets and command structures. As early as 2003, the EU had taken over the NATO operation in Macedonia, started two civilian missions in the Western Balkans and conducted a military stabilization operation in the DR Congo. Other operations followed soon after (see Chapter 8). This was rapid progress indeed for an organization infamous for its mainly declaratory nature, its slow and problematic decision-making and its paralysing internal divisions.

ESDP qualitatively changed the nature of CFSP. It allowed CFSP to move from a declaratory foreign policy focused on diplomacy to a more action-orientated foreign policy focused on more proactive crisis management. For the first time, the member states succeeded in developing a framework to effectively pool national resources within CFSP. Although still limited in scope, the EU finally had boots on the ground. This strengthened both the credibility of the EU and the potential effectiveness of CFSP in tackling conventional foreign policy issues. However, the geostrategic shock waves of the terrorist attacks against the US in September 2001 forced the EU to upgrade its foreign policy set-up with regard to objectives and approaches.

September 11 and the wars in Iraq and Afghanistan

The 2001 terrorist attacks in the US, the wars in Afghanistan (2001) and Iraq (2003), the terrorist attacks in Madrid (2004) and London (2005), and renewed fears about the proliferation of WMD all forced EU countries to focus on yet another level of military challenge. For the first time since the height of the Cold War, security threats went to the heart of the survival of a nation's population, which impacted EU foreign policy. These events had both a divisive and an invigorating effect on EU foreign policy.

The divisive element revealed itself in two ways. Initially, it further widened the gap between the three largest member states on the one hand and the rest of the member states on the other, throwing into doubt the relevance of the EU as a site for foreign policy cooperation. This resulted from member states' varying military capabilities and the American preference for only dealing with the largest states. In 2003, during the Iraq crisis, the Atlantic factor came to the fore more sharply than ever, seriously undermining the credibility of the EU as an international actor. One group of member states including the UK, Spain and Italy actively participated in the military invasion and occupation of Iraq. Meanwhile, a second group led by France and Germany actively opposed the war which they considered both illegitimate and detrimental to global and Western security. The customary area of tension between Atlantic solidarity and European integration was further strengthened as the then candidate member states joined the Atlantic camp.

These dramatic events also had a revitalizing impact on EU foreign policy – providing a new impetus to ESDP and broadening the number of issues on the EU foreign policy agenda to include strategies on the proliferation of WMD and antiterrorism. The wars in Afghanistan and Iraq painfully demonstrated the limitations of European military capabilities, leading to new commitments within ESDP to tackle these shortfalls. Moreover, with its new military engagements in Iraq and Afghanistan, it became clear that the US would be unable and unwilling to maintain its extensive military presence in the Western Balkans, implying that the Europeans should prepare to assume these responsibilities.

The European Security Strategy

External and internal shock waves forced the EU in 2003 to reconsider the basic principles and objectives of its foreign policy in order to incorporate new security threats and challenges, to formulate an approach to tackle these and to articulate a specific position within this new geostrategic context. This exercise took the form of Javier Solana's *European Security Strategy* (ESS), adopted in December 2003 by the European Council (2003a) (see also Biscop and Andersson 2007). The EU's first ever security strategy was not just important as a point of reference for future foreign policy action. It was at least as important in terms of interrelational objectives (contributing to overcoming divergence and mutual distrust) and identity objectives (highlighting the specificity of the EU foreign policy approach).

The threat-driven approach of the Strategy made it quite remarkable, particularly since actually addressing these threats was the first of three EU strategic objectives. This was indeed an innovation, as EU foreign policy texts had been traditionally filled with 'positive' approaches and concepts – the word 'threat' fitting awkwardly within the EU's civilian discourse. The second objective was to build security in the EU's neighbourhood. It aimed to 'promote a ring of well governed countries to the East of the European Union and on the borders of the Mediterranean' with whom it could 'enjoy close and cooperative relations'. The third objective was the creation of 'international order based on effective multilateralism' (see Chapter 13). The aim of developing 'well functioning international institutions and a rule-based international order' was considered to make an important distinction from American foreign policy and indeed reflected the EU's active role in promoting international organizations and treaties.

The final section of the ESS was an attempt to translate the threat assessment and objectives into policy priorities for the EU. It emphasized the role of multilateral cooperation and partnerships with key actors in achieving EU goals, which indeed reflected the reality of EU foreign policy. However, the Strategy also pointed to the need to adopt a more active approach, to undertake preventive engagement, and 'to develop a strategic culture that fosters early, rapid, and when necessary, robust intervention'.

Five years later, the *Report on the Implementation of the European Security Strategy* largely repeated the contents of the strategy, with only some small innovations: the scope of threats was expanded to include climate change, cyber security and pandemics, and a broader set of resources was listed to pursue the EU's security goals (European Council 2008). However, the general nature of the text and persisting divergences among member states about the EU's strategic interests explain why this updated version of the ESS, just as the first version, offered little guidance when the EU had to confront specific international crises.

Eastern Enlargement (2004/07), the Lisbon Treaty (2009) and New Challenges

Eastern enlargement

At the same time that it was attempting to adapt to a changing geostrategic environment, the EU concluded its most significant foreign policy act to date: the accession of 10 Central and Eastern European countries (CEECs) plus Cyprus and Malta. Enlargement in 2004 and 2007 and the prospect of further enlargement to include Turkey and the Western Balkan countries had foreign policy relevance on multiple levels (see also Chapters 9 and 11). In 2013, Croatia joined the EU and became its twenty-eighth member state. Enlargement is not likely to be over, with countries like Macedonia, Iceland, Montenegro, Serbia, Turkey, Albania, Bosnia and Herzegovina and Kosovo all at different stages of a process that might lead to accession.

The EU's enlargement process was, and is, foreign policy. The conditions set by the EU, as well as the goal of membership for the former communist countries, turned the enlargement process into the most successful structural foreign policy of the EU. Despite ambiguities and hesitations, since the first signs of reform in 1988 the EC/EU had played a crucial role in reshaping political, legal and socio-economic structures in Central and Eastern Europe. By contributing to the stabilization and transformation of this region, the EU strengthened the security situation of the entire continent. This is an achievement which is all too often underestimated but was recognized by the Nobel Committee awarding the EU the 2012 Nobel Peace Prize.

Enlargement also forced the EU to broaden and intensify its foreign policy towards its new (and prospective) neighbourhood. The 2004 enlargement turned Belarus, Ukraine and Moldova into immediate neighbours. Formerly 'distant' conflicts were suddenly very close to home, forcing the EU into more action in those regions. In response to this, the EU appointed EU Special Representatives for the South Caucasus, Central Asia and Moldova; became an active player during the political revolution in Ukraine; and launched the European Neighbourhood Policy (ENP). The ENP became the framework for strengthening the EU's relations with the former Soviet republics as well as the countries of the Mediterranean (see Chapter 11). It was designed to prevent the emergence of new dividing lines between the enlarged EU and its neighbours and to emphasize the EU's vital interest in economic development, stability and governance in its neighbourhood. In relation to the Eastern European countries, it also serves as a surrogate for full membership (Lannon 2012; Whitman and Wolff 2012a). The effects of the ENP have so far been disappointing, however. This could only be remedied to a limited extent through the 2008 Union for the Mediterranean (Bicchi and Gillespie 2011) and 2009 Eastern Partnership (Korosteleva 2011).

The new member states also had an impact on the debate on EU policy towards Russia and other Eastern European countries and on the importance of democracy and human rights considerations in the EU's policy stance. As the Iraq crisis already suggested, the accession of 10 CEECs affected the 'European integration versus Atlantic solidarity' tension, with the balance in crucial debates tilting more towards the Atlantic solidarity end of the spectrum. For the new EU member states that had also joined NATO, the security guarantee provided by that organization, and particularly by the US, was essential in light of what they considered to be Russia's unpredictable future behaviour (on the effects of enlargement for EU foreign policy, see Baun and Marek 2013; Müller-Brandeck-Bocquet 2006).

The Lisbon Treaty

As had been the norm with previous enlargements, the 2004 enlargement was preceded by negotiations on adapting the EU treaties in order to first strengthen the institutional architecture of the EU before new member states joined the club. The shock waves caused by September 11 and the Iraq and Afghanistan wars provided a further incentive to strengthen the EU's foreign policy capacities, and the European project generally. However, reflecting the growing political malaise in the EU, it was not until December 2009 when a new treaty, the Lisbon Treaty, could enter into force – two years after being signed by the member states and five years after a more ambitious treaty (the Treaty establishing a Constitution for Europe) was rejected by referendums in France and the Netherlands (Griller and Ziller 2008).

A major innovation of the Lisbon Treaty was that the EU's pillar system was formally abolished. It achieved what Maastricht had deemed impossible: bringing all dimensions of EU foreign policy under one treaty title. At the same time, the EU as a whole was granted legal personality (which had previously only been granted to the EC, which is now replaced by the EU). But, old habits die hard, and although the Lisbon Treaty abolished the pillar system in terms of presentation, it retained the division between the policy-making methods for CFSP/CSDP on the one hand and the EU's external action and Union policies on the other (see Chapters 3 and 4). Moreover, declarations in annexes to the Treaty also underlined that member states' capacity to conduct national foreign policies would not be curtailed (see Chapter 7).

A second innovation was the creation of the function of 'High Representative of the Union for Foreign Affairs and Security Policy/Vice-President of the European Commission' (HR/VP), combining the former positions of the High Representative for the CFSP and the Commissioner for External Relations. The Lisbon Treaty also created the European External Action Service (EEAS), designed to assist the HR/VP and made up of officials who were previously at the Council's Secretariat, the Commission and who are seconded from member states' diplomatic services. A new President of the European Council would not only chair European Council meetings, but also, at his or her level, ensure the external representation of the EU on issues concerning CFSP (see Chapter 3).

A third set of innovations was to be found in the chapter on the Common Security and Defence Policy (CSDP). The Lisbon Treaty not only changed its name from ESDP to CSDP, but it also formalized its existing setup which until that time had been established and developed outside the framework of the Treaties. The Lisbon Treaty broadened the original Petersberg tasks, introduced provisions allowing for flexibility as well as a solidarity clause, and formalized the European Defence Agency (EDA) (see Chapters 3 and 8). Paradoxically, at the moment that CSDP entered the Treaty framework, it also lost part of its dynamism, as its most staunch supporter – France – demonstrated less interest in CSDP. This was related to President Sarkozy's decision to return France to NATO's integrated military command structures, decreasing the significance of the long-standing tension between European integration and Atlantic solidarity (see Chapter 1) (Irondelle and Mérand 2010).

The Lisbon Treaty was less innovative in the other (formerly first pillar) chapters with an impact on the EU's foreign policy. It did not, for instance, strengthen the EU's capacity to act as a coherent force in international organizations and other fora, such as the UN, IMF or the World Bank, thereby disregarding one of the major weaknesses of the EU's international actorness (see Chapter 13). However, it did include provisions on some 'internal' policy matters with potentially important foreign policy implications. For instance, ensuring security of supply became one of the three objectives of energy policy. Furthermore, as part of the EU's research and technological development policy, the EU gained competence to develop a European space policy.

By the time the Lisbon Treaty entered into force expectations about its potential dynamizing impact on the EU's foreign policy were already lowered (see Mahncke and Gstöhl 2012; Missiroli 2010; Petrov *et al.* 2012). Some expected that EU member states would appoint internationally renowned figures – such as Tony Blair or Carl Bildt – as the first European Council President or HR/VP. However, they opted for rather low profile politicians with limited international experience, which was interpreted as an indication of the EU's limited international ambitions: Herman Van Rompuy (Belgian Prime Minister and former Minister of Budget) and Catherine Ashton (Trade Commissioner and former Leader of the UK's House of Lords). Whereas the former managed to use his expertise in financial matters to gradually find his place between the heads of state and government in the context of the sovereign debt crisis, HR/VP Ashton could not rely on similar relevant expertise to enforce a position for herself on the European and international scene (Howorth 2011) (see Chapter 3).

New challenges: withering Europe, withering West?

The laborious process of negotiating and agreeing upon a new treaty illustrated a political crisis in the EU. Once that crisis was finally tackled by the signing of the Lisbon Treaty in 2007, the EU was immediately confronted with new challenges – all of which raised challenges for its foreign policy. These included the financial crisis, which had a profound impact on the eurozone, the Arab uprising, global international economic and political developments, as well as negative attitudes towards Europe in third countries (see Allen and Smith 2012; Whitman and Juncos 2012). These not only undermined the EU and its position in the world, but also some of the principles which the EU promotes and stands for in its foreign policy (see Chapter 6).

First, the financial and sovereign debt crisis in Europe, which followed the global financial crisis that started with the bankruptcy of Lehman Brothers, generated a perception of a failing European political and socio-economic model (see Della Posta and Talani 2011; Nousios *et al.* 2012). The slow and often insufficient policy responses to the crisis, as well as the external help provided by the IMF for what the EU was not able to solve itself, added to this perception. This seriously undermined the legitimacy and the credibility of the EU, both with its own European citizens and with the outside world. The crisis in Europe pointed to a faulty design of the economic and political structures that are not only used by the EU internally, but also promoted externally. In turn, this destabilized the basis of the EU's structural foreign policy towards other regions and provided opportunities for competing structural powers (see Chapters 12 and 13). The crisis distracted the EU from its external relations, including relations with the EU's 'strategic partners', as was demonstrated by last minute cancellations of EU–India and EU–China summits due to emergency meetings of the European Council (Jain 2012; Chen 2012). The crisis also sapped the political energy as well as the economic and financial basis required to allow the EU to provide a forceful answer to the Arab uprisings and to present itself as a credible and relevant actor to the population in the Arab world.

Second, during the Arab revolutions and uprising that in 2011 led to the removal of dictators in Tunisia, Egypt, Libya and Yemen, the EU sent mixed messages regarding its foreign policy in the region (see Peters 2012a). The popular uprisings showed that the Arab population shared and longed for many of the very principles and values promoted by the EU such as democracy, freedom and welfare. However, it was also clearly evident that the democratic revolts occurred despite, rather than because of the actions of European countries. For example, through the EU's EMP and ENP, the Europeans had either supported or at least cooperated with authoritarian regimes for decades. The popularity of Islamic parties in the first democratic elections demonstrated to the Europeans that a competing political and societal model was gaining strength at its southern border (see Chapters 11 and 12).

Third, the structures promoted and embodied by the EU and the West also appeared to come under pressure on a more global scale. The almost exclusively Western-dominated international economic and political architecture was increasingly challenged by countries in the 'Global South' and in Asia in particular (Mahbubani 2008, 2013). These countries are gradually finding their voice and are increasingly dismissing what they see as European patronizing and 'neo-colonial' behaviour. The EU has so far struggled to devise a policy to deal with the shift of power that is taking place, including the rise of Asia and the emergence of new structural powers such as China (see Christiansen *et al.* 2013). Furthermore, the EU's 'strategic partnerships' with major powers were in this context little more than a fig leaf for the lack of a genuine EU strategy (Renard and Biscop 2012) (see Chapters 12 and 13).

Fourth, and equally worrying for the EU's international position is the gap between the EU's self-perception as a 'positive power' and the way it is perceived in other parts of the world (Chaban and Holland 2008, 2013; Lucarelli and Fioramonti 2010; Mayer and Zielonka 2012). A sobering picture is offered in global attitude surveys. The EU receives a positive rating from only a slim majority of respondents in the US. More dramatically for the EU, a favourable view is expressed by only one-third or less of the respondents in the Mediterranean (such as in Turkey, Egypt and Jordan) and in the two major powers in Asia (India and China) (Pew Research Center 2011: 63). Developing a policy to counter the increasingly negative image of the EU in the world may therefore appear to be one of the main challenges of the EU's foreign policy.

Conclusion

This historical overview demonstrates the remarkable progress that has been made in developing EU foreign policy. It also shows how the roots of today's discussions on European foreign policy, as well as its basic features, are to be found in the earliest debates and policy choices. First, in the first two decades after the Second World War, foreign policy was at the heart of European integration. Yet from 1954 onwards, it was also one of its principal taboos, except for the areas that would later become the EU's external action, such as trade and development policy, based on international agreements started to be concluded in that period. Since the early 1970s, incorporating foreign policy in European integration has been an incremental process of trial and error to avoid this taboo. Second, foreign policy cooperation and integration have largely focused on structural foreign policy objectives. Yet it has been generally presented and perceived through the conceptual lens of a relational foreign policy, although it has only been since the late 1990s that this foreign policy component has received more substantial attention from the member states, including through the development of the CSDP. Third, the gradual development of cooperation and integration in foreign and security policy has been as much aimed at pursuing interrelational objectives, integration objectives and identity objectives internally than pursuing external objectives.

Chapter 3

The EU's Foreign Policy System: Actors

Single in name, dual in policy-making method, multiple in nature – this is the Union's institutional framework in a nutshell. An overarching 'single institutional framework' exists on paper, but in practice, the powers and responsibilities of the EU's foreign policy actors are determined through different policy-making methods (see Chapter 1). Painting the actors and procedures in broad strokes is quite easy. In CFSP/CSDP, the Council, under the strategic leadership of the European Council, dominates all stages of policy-making, supported by the High Representative and the European External Action Service (EEAS). On the EU's external action (such as trade policy and development cooperation) and the external dimension of internal policies (such as environment and energy), the Commission proposes, the Council decides (alone, in co-decision with the European Parliament (EP), or after consultation with the EP) and the Commission implements, controls and manages budgets. In this case, acts are legally binding on the member states, and the Court of Justice (ECJ) provides judicial oversight. This chapter focuses mainly on the political actors, whereas Chapter 4 analyses how the actors interact in foreign policy-making. It examines who or what is behind the façade of each of these actors as well as their varying strengths and weaknesses in delivering and coordinating policy. The member states, also principal actors in EU foreign policy, are analysed in more detail in Chapter 5.

One Framework, Two Policy-making Methods, or a Continuum?

The Treaties emphasize that the Union is to be served by a single institutional framework. The same institutional framework is used to make and coordinate all aspects of the EU's foreign policy, irrespective of the area of action or the degree of competences in these areas, in order to ensure consistency and continuity (Arts. 13 and 21(3) TEU). However, despite this single institutional framework, the Union's foreign policy system is governed by two different policy-making methods: the 'Community method' and the 'intergovernmental method'. Figure 3.1 presents the

Figure 3.1   Institutional framework of EU foreign policy-making (basic version)

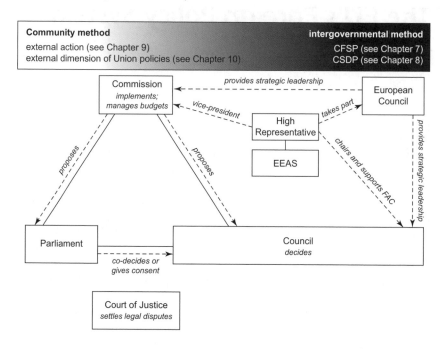

institutional framework and the main actors involved in both methods of EU foreign policy-making. In the conclusion of this chapter, Figure 3.2 will further elaborate this basic overview by including more details and complexities.

The first policy-making method is the '*Community method*'. This functions on the principle of a common interest, which actors define, defend, promote and represent. The Community method is not synonymous with supranationalism, which would imply that member states lose complete control over policy-making. Rather, it is operationalized through a system designed to maintain institutional equilibrium between four institutions: the supranational Commission with a key role in defining and defending common interests; the Council of the EU, in which ministers (or their representatives) from each of the 28 member states decide by qualified majority voting on many but not all decisions (see Chapter 4); the directly elected EP; and the ECJ, also supranational in character. The Community method applies to the EU's external action (trade, development cooperation, humanitarian aid – see Chapter 9) and the external dimension of internal policies (see Chapter 10). The term 'Community method' refers to the method used in the European Community (EC) which existed until the entry into force of the Lisbon Treaty. The term is generally still used, although the EC has now formally ceased to exist (see Chapter 2).

The second policy-making method is the '*intergovernmental method*'. The basic principle of this method is that national governments retain control over policy-making. This is achieved in two ways. Through *intergovernmental cooperation,* governments do not transfer competences to the EU, but within the EU framework, cooperate in the elaboration of foreign policy and coordinate their national foreign policies. *Intergovernmental integration*, on the other hand, implies that member states transfer competences to the EU, but that within the Union's institutional framework, governments retain strict control over policy-making through the dominant position of the Council and the application of the unanimity rule in its decision-making. The intergovernmental method is predominant in CFSP and CSDP.

The Community method and the intergovernmental method are ideal types. Many instances of EU foreign policy share characteristics of both methods. In areas of external action (e.g. trade policy) and of the external dimension of internal policies (e.g. external environmental policy), intergovernmental dynamics can often also be observed, as is the case when member states coordinate their national viewpoints or national policies. Indeed, the Council is not only an institution where policies are made; it is also a 'policy co-ordination forum' (Puetter 2011: 92). This does not necessarily result in common positions, but rather in a shared understanding of other member states' viewpoints and concerns.

Likewise, the Commission sometimes plays a more prominent role in CFSP/CSDP than one would expect from a mere intergovernmental perspective. Hence, in many foreign policy dossiers, both policy-making methods are involved, employing the competences, actors, procedures and instruments from both methods. There are also gradations within each policy-making method in terms of the role of the various institutions and of the member states, the decision-making procedures, the available instruments, and so on. Reality proves that there is a whole range of methods on the continuum between the Community method and the intergovernmental method (visualized in Figures 3.1 and 3.2 in the grey area between the two policy-making methods).

The European Council

The European Council plays a pivotal role in the strategic direction, scope and main decisions of the Union's foreign policy. It brings together the heads of state and government of the member states and the President of the European Commission. The High Representative takes part in its work. The European Council is thus the locus of power within the European Union – if not legally, at least politically and symbolically – with policy-making lines from all policy areas and from national foreign policies coming together in this forum. It is important not to mix up the

European Council and the Council of the EU, which are two different institutions. Whereas the former is made up of the heads of state and government, the latter is the institution in which the sectoral ministers (such as foreign affairs ministers, agriculture ministers or environment ministers) meet. The role of the Council of the EU in foreign policy-making will be discussed in the next section.

A President whose two-and-a-half-year term is renewable one time chairs the European Council. The President of the European Council ensures, at his/her level and in that capacity, the external representation of the Union on issues concerning its common foreign and security policy (Art. 15 TEU). In practice, this means that the President represents the EU in international gatherings on CFSP topics organized at the level of heads of state and government. Herman Van Rompuy (who until the end of 2009 served as Belgian prime minister) was appointed the first permanent President of the European Council, taking office in January 2010 (his mandate was renewed in early 2012 for a second term up to the end of 2015). During his first years as President, Van Rompuy mainly had to focus on the EU's internal policy challenges – most notably the financial and sovereign debt crises – and did not concentrate his work on foreign policy. When representing the EU internationally, Van Rompuy mostly presented himself in tandem with Commission President Barroso, as he did during the high-level G8/G20 meetings (see Chapter 13) and during the EU–US Summits (Howorth 2011; Missiroli 2010).

The European Council is to 'provide the Union with the necessary impetus for its development' and to 'define the general political directions and priorities thereof' (Art. 15 TEU). With regard to CFSP/CSDP, the European Council identifies 'the Union's strategic interests' and defines 'the general guidelines' and 'strategic lines' (Art. 26 TEU), in addition to 'the strategic interests and objectives' with regard to the EU's external action in general (Art. 22 TEU) (see also Devuyst 2012). Although it does not have a formal role in the foreign policy legislative process, it is clear that no strategic decision can be adopted in areas of EU competences without the (at least tacit) consent of the European Council. Moreover, when sectoral Council configurations are not able to find an agreement, the file is often forwarded to the European Council, where the politicians with the highest political authority then attempt to come to a decision.

Decisions by the European Council has led EU foreign policy in new directions, such as adopting new strategies towards other regions or establishing CSDP from 1999 onwards (see Chapter 8). It also decides on the direction to follow after major international developments, such as the 2011 revolts in the Arab world. However, it is its role as an '*organe d'impulsion*' (Cloos *et al.* 1993: 486) rather than as a formal decision-making actor that is most important. As can be read in the Conclusions which are adopted at each of its meetings, for most issues on its agenda the European Council 'confirms', 'welcomes' or 'endorses' decisions and documents that have either been previously agreed upon by the Council, or have been developed by the High Representative or the Commission – with the European Council subsequently 'inviting' or 'asking' other actors to further elaborate on these measures. These European Council meetings are important: they push decision-making forward from the highest political level; they make crucial intergovernmental and inter-institutional bargains on the most sensitive issues; and they confer legitimacy and visibility on decisions and policy documents essential for both internal and external audiences.

Paradoxically, the concentration of the highest authorities from all member states in the European Council is also its Achilles heel. Heads of state and government first and foremost defend their national foreign policy and act according to domestic concerns. Moreover, the EU's foreign policy is certainly not the only topic discussed in the European Council. Its agenda is primarily filled with internal policies and 'crisis management', leaving insufficient time for strategic foreign policy leadership. Even when meeting more than the four times foreseen in the Treaty – as is usually the case – it cannot provide the permanent strategic leadership needed for the most sensitive and urgent foreign policy dossiers.

The creation of the European Council's 'permanent' President by the Lisbon Treaty did not solve the European Council's capacity to provide strategic leadership, largely because no additional competences or powers were attached to this function. Moreover, the first to take up this office, Herman Van Rompuy, was considered a rather low-profile figure, certainly compared to other potential candidates mentioned in the press like former British prime minister Tony Blair. A choice for Blair would have resulted in greater international visibility, probably opened more doors in foreign capitals such as Washington, DC and Beijing, and had the potential to increase the chance of the EU being seen as a relevant international actor (Howorth 2011). However, it would also have increased the chance of internal disputes within the European Council between an outspoken and forceful president and other powerful members, such as the French president, the German chancellor and the British prime minister, who preferred a chairman to remain in their shadow. Herman Van Rompuy was however able to prove the usefulness of his new function by actively mediating between the member states in the European Council in the context of the sovereign debt crisis.

Given the high external visibility of European Council meetings, a major purpose of these meetings and of the activity of its president often relates to interrelational and identity objectives in addition to external objectives (see Chapter 1). Even where member states are divided on an issue, being *seen* to have a united and 'European' approach is often at least as important as formulating guidelines that actually provide a basis for action. There is considerable distance between defining general foreign policy principles and guidelines and putting these principles and guidelines into practice. The majority of European Council decisions require further political follow-up, operational implementation and/or legal translation by the Council, Commission, High Representative, EEAS and/or member states, implying that subsequent hurdles must be overcome before the European Council's deliberations take effect. Hence, the effectiveness of (decisions by) the European Council mostly depends on the other actors in the institutional architecture of the EU.

The Council

One Council, meeting in multiple Council configurations

Its composition, competences and frequent meetings make the Council of the European Union (or briefly 'the Council') the main foreign policy decision-making body in the EU, both in political and legal terms. The Council meets in 10 configurations, depending on the policy area at stake and the ministers attending. The primary Council configuration for foreign policy is the Foreign Affairs Council (see below), which deals with external trade, development cooperation, humanitarian aid, international agreements, CFSP and CSDP. It brings together member states' foreign ministers and the High Representative. The latter chairs Foreign Affairs Council meetings except when it discusses trade policy (Art. 2(5) Council Rules of Procedure) (see below). Depending on the issues on the agenda, ministers of defence, of development or of trade also participate as do the responsible members of the European Commission. In addition to the monthly meetings, foreign ministers also meet in the margins of international conferences and where urgent international developments necessitate an unforeseen meeting. Moreover, each rotating Council Presidency usually organizes an informal Council meeting for the foreign affairs ministers, called a 'Gymnich' meeting, named after the German castle where the first meeting of that type took place in 1974. Defence, development and trade ministers also hold their own informal or formal meetings.

Additional relevant Council configurations include the Economic and Financial Affairs Council (ECOFIN), the Justice and Home Affairs Council (JHA), the General Affairs Council and other sectoral Council configurations. When the EU participates in international environmental and transport negotiations, for example, it conducts those international relations on the basis of Council conclusions adopted in the relevant Council configuration (in this case, the Environment and Transport Council) without the involvement of the Foreign Affairs Council.

The Presidency of these Council configurations – in contrast to the Foreign Affairs Council, except when discussing trade policies – rotates between member states on a six-month basis and can directly or indirectly impact EU foreign policy (see Helwig *et al.* 2013: 23–9; Szabo 2011). The rotating Presidency chairs not only the ministerial meetings, but also some preparatory meetings held at lower diplomatic and bureaucratic levels (see below). In practice, it also often represents the EU in external, international negotiations that deal with external dimensions of internal policies (Delreux 2012a). In many environmental negotiations, for instance, it is the environment minister from the member state holding the Presidency who speaks for the EU, although such a negotiation arrangement is the subject of often tense debates in the EU (see also Chapter 13).

Ministers discuss and adopt decisions on external relations and foreign policy based on both external action/external dimension of internal policies and CFSP/CSDP procedures. The agenda does not differentiate between policy-making methods or competences, reflecting the Council's responsibility for ensuring the unity and consistency of the Union's action (Art. 26 TEU). However, although the Council is the Union's key decision-making institution for all foreign policy issues and these issues are lumped together in Council meetings, its role and power are quite different for CFSP/CDSP and for external action and internal policies with an external dimension (see Chapter 7).

The Council is the main decision-making body for *CFSP/CSDP* and formally reigns over all stages of policy-making: from issue definition to decision-making, implementation and control. In conjunction with the European Council, this ensures that the evolution and actions of CFSP and CSDP remain under member state control and supervision. The Council also plays a central role in strengthening systematic cooperation and coordination between member states' foreign policies: member states must consult one another within the Council on any matter of foreign and security policy of general interest (Art. 32 TEU). The Council is responsible for ensuring that the member states comply with the principles of CFSP and support the Union's policy (Art. 24 TEU).

The Council plays also an important role with regard to *external action* and the *external dimension of internal policies*, but it is embedded in a broader institutional set-up that incorporates the Commission, the EP and the ECJ. The Council can ask the Commission to take initiatives and propose legislation, but cannot legislate without a formal Commission proposal. The Council is involved in the adoption of all decisions, but in some major fields – such as budgetary decisions and association agreements – can only decide together with, or with the consent of, the Parliament. For non-legislative instruments, the Council can act with more leeway vis-à-vis the Parliament and the Commission, for instance by adopting Council conclusions which are not based on a Commission proposal. While the Council can make major decisions about the EU's relations with other regions and countries, it depends on the Commission to implement these decisions.

The Foreign Affairs Council

One of the paradoxes of the Foreign Affairs Council's position is that, as an *institution* involved in the full spectrum of EU foreign policy initiatives, it is at the heart of EU foreign policy-making. However, as a *meeting of foreign ministers*, it is struggling to live up to the expectations associated with being the EU's main foreign policy decision-making forum. In fact, most decisions are not actually taken by the foreign affairs ministers themselves but are taken at a lower level in the Council's substructures before reaching the ministerial meeting (see below).

The expansion of the EU's foreign policy competences, activities and instruments mean that foreign ministers often face an impossibly overloaded agenda. The agenda of the Foreign Affairs Council meeting of 23 January 2012 is illustrative of this (Council 2012a). The ministers debated the Iranian nuclear programme, the reforms in Burma/Myanmar, the situation in Syria, the EU's relations with Serbia and Kosovo, the Middle East Peace Process, the situation in Belarus, and the state of play in Sudan and South Sudan. At the start of their formal session and without discussion, they also approved a long list of (often quite important) A-points: these are the 'Agreed Points' or issues agreed upon at a lower level in the Committee of Permanent Representatives (COREPER), in the Political and Security Committee (PSC) or in the working parties (see below). Obviously, even with a system of A-points, too many important issues remain on the agenda, making it impossible to tackle them seriously. In practice, this often implies that debates focus only on the most pressing or controversial themes, with no time left for equally significant but less urgent or media-attractive issues.

Debate is not only hampered by the number of issues on the agenda, but also by the high number of participants: ministers, senior diplomats and advisers from 28 member states, the HR/VP, and another commissioner with a foreign policy portfolio (such as development or neighbourhood), EEAS officials etc. attend the meetings. Debates have become a succession of short interventions, ministers barely receive the time to explain national positions, and a genuine exchange of views and arguments is quite rare. Like in other Council configurations, the informal lunch meetings attended by ministers have become particularly important insofar as they provide a restricted 'safe' setting to debate sensitive issues and openly discuss disagreements. However, with 28 ministers sitting at the table, even the lunch format and informal Gymnich meetings no longer permit a sufficiently intimate gathering to allow for decision-making and problem-solving on issues that demand the capacity to cut through the diverging views.

However, none of the above is to suggest that Council meetings are unimportant for EU foreign policy-making. They are important, but in most cases not only for what is decided or confirmed by ministers during the meeting, but because (like European Council meetings) they lead to a monthly culmination point of consultations, meetings and decisions on lower, diplomatic and bureaucratic levels. Preparing for monthly Council meetings necessitates an intensive negotiation process that in turn pushes EU foreign policy-making forward.

The Council's substructure

Various diplomatic, bureaucratic and military actors within the Council's system prepare, support and ensure the follow-up of the ministerial meetings of the Council (see Dijkstra 2011). As we have mentioned, the meetings of the Foreign Affairs Council at ministerial level do not make a strict division between CFSP/CDSP policies and external action/internal policies with an external dimension. This is not the case, however, for the committees preparing the work of the Foreign Affairs Council – COREPER and PSC – which do make this distinction.

COREPER (*Committee of Permanent Representatives*) is the most senior preparatory body of the Council. COREPER convenes in two formations. The first formation, 'COREPER II' is composed of the member states' Permanent Representatives to the EU (at ambassador level) plus a representative from the Commission and when foreign policy is discussed also a representative of the EEAS and the chairman of the Political and Security Committee (see further). Meetings are chaired by the rotating Presidency. If necessary, the chairman of the PSC also participates in the meetings. COREPER II meets at least once a week to prepare Foreign Affairs, General Affairs, ECOFIN and JHA Council meetings. As the central clearing house for all preparatory work for the Foreign Affairs Council meetings, COREPER II also determines its final agenda and oversees the work of all other preparatory committees. However, COREPER II in principle does not change positions adopted by the PSC on security and defence policy (see below). The second formation, 'COREPER I', composed of the member states' Deputy Permanent Representatives, prepares the other Council configurations. In this way, it also plays an important role in the decision-making on the external dimension of internal policies.

The PSC (*Political and Security Committee*) (or 'COPS' from the French acronym) is a key preparatory committee in the Council for CFSP/CSDP (see Howorth 2012: 443–448). The PSC is composed of one ambassador per member state as well as a representative of the Commission, of the EU Military Committee (EUMC) and of the Committee for Civilian Aspects of Crisis Management (CIVCOM) (see below). A diplomat appointed by and falling under the authority of the High Representative chairs the PSC, which, in principle, meets twice a week with extra meetings if required. It monitors and discusses the international situation in areas covered by CFSP/CSDP, contributes to the definition of policies by the Council, and monitors the implementation of agreed policies. It also exercises, under the responsibility of the Council and of the High Representative, the 'political control and strategic direction' of the EU's military and civilian crisis management operations (Art. 38 TEU). The PSC provides guidelines to and is supported by the EUMC and the CIVCOM, and also supervises and monitors the work of the various Council working parties responsible for CFSP/CSDP issues (see below). The EUMC, composed of the Chiefs of Defence of the member states, is responsible for giving advice and recommendations to the PSC. The CIVCOM serves as the civilian equivalent of the EUMC, as it gives advice and recommendations to the PSC on the civilian aspects of CSDP operations.

Several additional high-level committees prepare Council deliberations, including the Economic and Financial Committee (Economic and Monetary Union); the Special Committee on Agriculture (common agricultural policy); the Trade Policy Committee (common commercial policy); and the Standing Committee on Operational Cooperation on Internal Security (area of freedom, security and justice). These policies also affect the EU's position in the world and can have an indirect impact on its foreign policy (see Chapters 8 and 9).

Below the level of the committees, a large network of working parties (also sometimes called 'working groups') shapes and prepares the EU's foreign policy (see Table 3.1) (Council 2012b). Experts from the member states' Permanent Representations or the national capitals, from the EEAS and/or from the Commission attend these working parties. Around 35 working parties deal explicitly with foreign policy (Council 2012b; Wouters *et al.* 2013a: 40–4). The working parties with a geographic (such as the Working Party on the Western Balkans Region or on Latin America) and those with a thematic focus on CFSP/CSDP (such as non-proliferation and human rights) are chaired by EEAS staff. In contrast, those with a thematic external action focus (including trade, development and humanitarian aid) fall under the rotating Presidency system.

Although they do not have authority to take decisions in their own right, a great amount of work is done in these working parties. They exchange views; ensure mutual consultation; further the cooperation between specialized national diplomats, EEAS and Commission staff; and identify options for consideration and decision at a higher level. However, particularly when operational action is required, this system of working parties with nearly 30 actors around the negotiating table has its limits.

In addition to the working parties that deal explicitly with foreign policy, a whole range of other working parties are important for the EU's external action and internal policies with an external dimension (and thus provide support for COREPER I and II). The names of some of these

Table 3.1 Working parties – 'Foreign Affairs'*

EEAS chair *(geographic focus + thematic* *focus on CFSP/CSDP)*	*Chaired by the rotating Presidency* *(thematic focus on external action)*
Eastern Europe and Central Asia (COEST)	Foreign Relations Counsellors (incl. sanctions)
Western Balkans Region (COWEB)	CFSP Administrative Affairs and Protocol
Middle East/Gulf (MOG)	Consular Affairs
Mashreq/Maghreb (MAMA)	Dual-Use Goods
Africa (COAFR)	European Arms Policy
Asia-Oceania (COASI)	EFTA
Latin America (COLAT)	Trade
Transatlantic Relations (COTRA)	Generalized System of Preferences
OSCE and the Council of Europe (COSCE)	Development Cooperation
	International Development Conferences
United Nations (CONUN)	Humanitarian Aid and Food Aid
Human Rights (COHOM)	Commodities
Non-Proliferation (CONOP)	Public International Law (incl. ICC)
Conventional Arms Exports (COARM)	Law of the Sea
	Ad hoc Working Party on MEPP (COMEP)
Global Disarmament & Arms Control (CODUN)	ACP Working Party
Politico-Military Group (PMG)	Terrorism
Nicolaidis Group**	Application of specific measures to combat terrorism
	Antici Group/Mertens Group**

Notes: * The EU Military Committee Working Group (EUMCWG) is chaired by an elected/appointed chair.
    ** The Nicolaidis, Antici and Mertens Groups prepare, respectively, the PSC, COREPER I and II meetings.

Source: Council (2012b).

can illustrate their potential direct or indirect impact on the EU's foreign policy: the 'Strategic Committee on Immigration, Frontiers and Asylum' (SCIFA); the working parties on 'Enlargement and Countries Negotiating Accessions to the EU'; on 'Terrorism'; on 'Space'; on 'International Environment Issues'; and on 'External Fisheries Policy' (for the relevance of these issues, see Chapters 6, 9 and 10) (Council 2012b).

Taken together, the diplomatic (COREPER and PSC) and bureaucratic substructures (the working parties) of the Council play a crucial role in the continuous process of information exchange and consultation, coordination of national policies, intergovernmental bargaining and developing common approaches. In the preparation of decisions by the Council of Ministers, each level plays its part in identifying points of special interest, highlighting in advance the main issues of contention and concern, and detecting the windows of opportunity and the bottlenecks. Dossiers that are ripe for formal decision-making, as well as those that are important but need further high-level deliberation, move up the organizational hierarchy. The rationale behind these substructures is that the ministers can limit their discussions to the most salient and politically sensitive issues.

However, several issues hamper the effectiveness of this system. The dual character of EU foreign policy has been strengthened by the coexistence of the PSC and COREPER. Even though there is no differentiation between CFSP and the external action/external dimension of internal policies issues by the time they reach the Council agenda, the limited interaction between COREPER and the PSC and between the various working parties results in parallel policy-making processes which does not facilitate a comprehensive approach towards the issue at hand.

Further, these structures are staffed by national representatives, whose primary commitment and responsibility naturally lies in promoting the national interest, despite whatever socialization effects may occur (see Chapter 5). As such, policy-making can be more about striking a balance between competing national interests in the short term than developing long-term approaches better suited to achieving 'European goals' or actually meeting the challenges of a specific dossier.

The Commission

The European Commission finds itself awkwardly positioned in EU foreign policy. On the one hand, it plays a critical role in defining, defending, promoting and representing the common interests in the EU's external action and in the external dimension of internal policies. Here, the Commission can rely on a robust administrative and budgetary apparatus. On the other hand, however, the Commission is largely sidelined in the CFSP and CSDP.

More than any other actor, the Commission has struggled with the major boundary problem between CFSP/CSDP and non-CFSP/CSDP competences, and thus also between being centre stage, backstage or not on the stage at all. This issue is closely related to other 'boundary problems' (Smith M. 1997): between external economic relations and external political relations; between 'development' and 'foreign policy' or 'security' issues; between 'domestic/internal' policy issues and 'external' policy issues. These boundary problems have led to a succession of 'border conflicts' or outright 'wars' or stalemates, not only between the Commission and the Council or between the Commission and the EEAS, but also within the Commission's own internal structures.

Internal organization

The increase in the Commission's external policy responsibilities and its difficult quest since 1993 to find a way to align itself with CFSP has made the division of labour within both the College of Commissioners and its administration problematic. The policy portfolios of the commissioners responsible for external relations, as well as their Directorates General (DGs), have been regularly reshuffled, each bringing their own turf wars (Nugent and Saurugger 2002). From 2010, the Barroso II Commission divided the main portfolios with foreign policy relevance as follows: Development; Trade; International Cooperation, Humanitarian Aid and Crisis Response; Enlargement and European Neighbourhood Policy. Additionally, the Vice-President serves as the High Representative of the Union for Foreign Affairs and Security Policy. However, other portfolios also increasingly have an external dimension such as Fisheries, Energy or Climate Action.

Besides relying on the EEAS (see further), the commissioners most directly involved in foreign policy rely on four DGs and one 'Service'. These structures play an essential role in the EU's foreign policy-making system. They each have their own working culture, set of objectives, legal bases for policy initiatives, and different types of instruments. This explains why, beyond the normal turf battles, coherent action is not always straightforward. The policies that these entities deal with are discussed in Chapter 9.

- *DG Trade (TRADE)* is in a very strong position given the EU's exclusive competences in many trade issues and its central role in representing the largest trade bloc in international trade negotiations. Despite the gradual introduction of political conditionality in trade and other agreements, the basic philosophy and overarching goals of DG Trade are the defence of EU trade interests and the liberalization of world trade, which do not always coincide with foreign policy and development goals.
- *DG Development and Cooperation – EuropeAid (DEVCO)* is responsible both for development policy in the framework of the Cotonou Agreement with the 77 ACP countries and for cooperation

with and/or development support for countries in the EU's Eastern neighbourhood, the Mediterranean, the Gulf region, Latin America, Asia and South Africa. Although EU development competences are shared with the member states, DG DEVCO gains its strength from its two main instruments: contractual relations through the Cotonou framework, and the considerable development aid budget (including the European Development Fund). Its goals focus on poverty reduction and development, with the latter incorporating a range of conditionalities such as good governance and respect for human rights. Similarly, DG DEVCO's strength with regard to other regions of the world is based on its management of the vast network of bilateral and inter-regional agreements and of two major financial instruments: the European Neighbourhood (and Partnership) Instrument and the Development Co-operation Instrument (see Chapter 4).

- *DG Enlargement (ELARG)* seemed to have lost much of its importance following the large enlargement wave (2004–7). However, the debate surrounding the accession of Turkey and the Western Balkan countries and the EU's decision to be firmer in terms of compliance with all conditions indicate that DG Enlargement's role is far from redundant.
- *DG Humanitarian Aid & Civil Protection (ECHO)* manages the EU's humanitarian aid and coordinates the EU's disaster response inside and outside Europe. With an annual budget of approximately €1.1 billion, it is one of the largest humanitarian aid donors and supports people in more than 80 countries worldwide.
- The *Foreign Policy Instruments Service (FPIS)* is responsible for the 'Instrument for Stability' (which finances crisis response projects); for election observation missions; public diplomacy; the management of civilian CSDP operations; and the financial and inter-institutional dimension of CFSP (see Chapters 6, 8 and 7). It is staffed by Commission officials, but is housed in the building of the EEAS – and is therefore a 'Commission service within the EEAS'.

Other sectoral DGs can also play an important role in specific dimensions of foreign policy. DGs Environment, Climate Action, Agriculture and Rural Development, Competition, Research and Innovation, Mobility and Transport, or Energy are directly or indirectly involved in key strategic areas of the EU's development into a global actor. High levels of interaction between external and internal policy issues imply that today, almost every DG has some relevance for external policy. Most DGs have directorates or units dealing with the EU's external relations in the area of that DG. However, coordination in the European Commission on foreign policy related issues remains a challenge (Marangoni 2013).

The Commission and the EU's external action/external dimension of internal policies

The Commission is at the heart of the EU's external action and the external dimension of the EU's internal policies, and is involved in all stages of policy-making. As the Council and EP can only adopt legislative acts and conclude international agreements on the basis of a formal proposal from the Commission, its exclusive right of initiative is powerful. However, the Commission does have to take into account the specific interests of member states if it wants to see its proposals accepted in the Council. Beyond this strictly legislative task, the Commission plays a broader role in furthering EU policy through non-binding communications, opinions or other forms of 'soft law'. The Commission has made efficient use of this competence to assert itself as a relevant foreign policy actor and, sometimes, to voice an opinion on issues over which it had no direct authority.

As far as EU competences are concerned, the Commission conducts negotiations with third states and international organizations on behalf of the EU (Art. 218 TFEU). The best-known examples are trade agreements (Art. 207 TFEU) and the various kinds of association and cooperation agreements. However also for issues that are not explicitly foreseen in the Treaties, the Commission can act as the EU negotiator. Following the ERTA principle, established by case law of the Court of Justice, the EU has the competence to act externally for all issues on which it has competences to act internally ('*in foro interno, in foro externo*'). Indeed, there exists a parallelism between internal and external competences. A consequence of this principle is that the Commission also represents the EU in negotiations touching upon issues on which the EU has adopted internal legislation. It has to be noted, however, that the Commission can only represent the EU if it is authorized to do so by the Council, which may grant the Commission a negotiation mandate and which establishes a special committee that the Commission has to consult during its negotiation task. Since the Council can only authorize the Commission as the Union's negotiator on the basis of a recommendation by the Commission, the relationship between the Commission and the Council is interdependent. The Commission not only negotiates agreements, but is also the main implementing body. The foreign policy relevance of this role of the Commission has gradually broadened as agreements have incorporated more foreign policy elements such as political dialogue and conditionality clauses regarding democracy, human rights, and so on (see Chapters 6 and 9).

The Commission also has an important budgetary function, drawing up the draft budget of the EU and implementing this budget in accordance with the provisions of the financial regulations made by the Council (Arts. 314 and 317 TFEU). This gives significant power to the

Commission, as it administers, as part of the general EU budget, an external relations budget of (in 2013) €9 billion and as other decisions with implications for the EU budget cannot be implemented in practice without the Commission's involvement (see Chapter 4).

How can we evaluate the Commission's foreign policy actions within the external action area and the external dimension of internal policies? On the positive side, the Commission has been highly active in developing and implementing long-term policies and strategies with regard to third countries/regions, which has been particularly important for the EU's structural foreign policy. Several of the Commission's communications, in addition to other documents, have been important in developing the EU's foreign policy. As a stream of often thorough conceptual and operational preparatory work, these documents have regularly allowed the Commission to quickly deliver at those moments when the policy context was ripe for concrete policy actions. They have also contributed in terms of agenda setting, and have put external action policies in a clear, strategic 'foreign policy' context. Examples include the following communications: *A New Response to a Changing Neighbourhood* (on the ENP, published jointly with the High Representative); and *A Strategy for Competitive, Sustainable and Secure Energy* (Commission 2010a; High Representative and Commission 2011) (see Chapters 8, 9 and 10).

On the negative side, the Commission too often 'administers' its various external programmes, losing sight of their foreign policy dimension. The Commission (and the EU) depends to a large extent on other actors (such as third countries, NGOs and UN agencies) to implement its policies on the ground. It risks being more focused on disbursing funds and supervising the adherence to budgetary and other procedures than on actual foreign policy output (see below) (see Thépaut 2011).

The Commission and CFSP/CSDP

After having explored the Commission's significant role in the EU's external action and internal policies with an external dimension, the question arises as to the role of the Commission in the intergovernmental CFSP/CSDP. When reading the Treaty provisions on CFSP/CSDP, one gets the impression that the Commission is almost completely excluded from the CFSP/CSDP framework. The Commission is indeed barely mentioned except in the context of the composition of the EEAS and in the provision indicating that the HR, 'with the Commission's support', may refer any question relating to the CFSP to the Council. And to avoid any misunderstanding, one of the declarations added to the Treaty of Lisbon explicitly indicates that the provisions covering the CFSP, 'do not give new powers to the Commission to initiate decisions' (Declaration 14).

Although the Commission's role in CFSP is quite distinct from its role in external action (no exclusive right of initiative, no representation task, etc.), it is not as powerless as CFSP's intergovernmental method might at first suggest. The Commission enters the CFSP game when the implementation of CFSP decisions requires the use of instruments in the field of external action (such as sanctions or the provision of aid) or when financing is required through the CFSP budget, which is part of the general EU budget and thus managed by the Commission (see Chapter 4). The Council also often relies on the Commission's expertise, e.g. on thematic issues, which also empowers the Commission. However, the question about the Commission's foreign policy impact will mainly depend on how the division of labour and power relations between the EEAS and the Commission will evolve (see Furness 2013; Helwig *et al.* 2013: 38–49; Wouters *et al.* 2013a: 46–57).

The High Representative/Vice-President and the EEAS

As prescribed by the Lisbon Treaty, the EU's institutional system provides quite an ingenious system to merge the responsibilities, instruments and approaches of the Commission, Council and member states into a multifaceted – but nevertheless common, coherent and effective – EU foreign policy. On the one hand, the 'High Representative of the Union for Foreign Affairs and Security Policy/Vice-President of the European Commission' (HR/VP) function is designed to bridge the Council and the Commission at the political level. On the other hand, the European External Action Service (EEAS) and the EU Delegations have to play the same role at the diplomatic and operational levels. However, this ingenious system suffers from some structural defects that hamper the potential of the HR/VP and EEAS as binding agents, with personal and transition-related factors further undermining their potential to serve as linchpins of the EU's foreign policy system (see Mahncke and Gstöhl 2012).

The High Representative/Vice-President

Functions
Leadership and bridging activities are expected from the HR/VP. In fact, this position bestows on one individual three functions (Art. 18 TEU):

- being High Representative for Foreign Affairs and Security Policy, responsible for conducting the CFSP and CSDP and for contributing to the development of these policies as mandated by the Council,
- presiding over the EU's Foreign Affairs Council (except when trade policy is discussed, then the rotating Presidency chairs), and

- serving as one of the Vice-Presidents of the European Commission, with responsibility for the Commission's external relations and for coordinating other aspects of the EU's external action.

By performing these three functions in two institutions – the Commission and the Council – the HR/VP is double-hatted, which emphasizes the rationale of having a bridging actor in the EU foreign policy architecture. The HR/VP not only bridges two institutions (the Commission and the Council), but also bridges two different types of interests ('European' and national ones), policy-making methods (Community and intergovernmental method) and centres of gravity of EU foreign policy (external action/external dimension of internal policies and CFSP/CSDP).

The function of the High Representative (HR) is described extensively in various other treaty provisions relating to CFSP and CSDP. This stands in stark contrast to vague descriptions of its role in the Commission: to 'ensure the consistency of the Union's external action' and to be 'responsible within the Commission for responsibilities incumbent on it in external relations and for coordinating other aspects of the Union's external action' (Art. 18(4) TEU).

The tasks of the HR can be placed under four umbrellas: decision-making, implementation, representation and consistency.

- Concerning *decision-making*, the HR not only presides over the Foreign Affairs Council (Art. 27 TEU), but can also submit initiatives and proposals to the Council with regard to the CFSP and CSDP (Arts. 30 and 42(2) TEU). As part of the HR's responsibility for relations with the EP, the HR has to regularly consult and inform the EP and ensure that the views of the EP are duly taken into consideration (Art. 36 TEU). Moreover, the HR also takes part in the work of the European Council (Art. 15(2) TEU).
- The HR is responsible for ensuring *implementation* of the CFSP decisions adopted by the Council and the European Council (Arts. 26(3) and 27(1) TEU). When a common approach of the EU is defined, the HR has to coordinate activities together with the national ministers of foreign affairs (Art. 32 TEU). The HR also ensures coordination of the civilian and military aspects of CSDP missions, in contact with the Political and Security Committee (PSC) (Art. 43 TEU) – the latter exercising political control and strategic direction of the missions under the responsibility of the HR (and the Council) (Art. 38 TEU).
- With regard to *external representation*, the HR represents the EU in matters related to CFSP, conducts political dialogue with third parties on the EU's behalf, and expresses the EU's position in international organizations and at international conferences (Art. 27(2) TEU). As noted above, the President of the European Council ensures the Union's representation on CFSP issues at the level of heads of state

and governments. The HR organizes the coordination of the member states' action in these organizations and conferences (Art. 34 TEU).

- The HR assists the Council and Commission in ensuring *consistency* between the different areas of the EU's external action (Art. 21(3) TEU). The HR, together with the Council, ensures the unity, consistency and effectiveness of the EU's action as well as member states' compliance with the principles of the CFSP (Arts. 26(2) and 24(3) TEU). One of the tools to ensure consistency is the formulation, when appropriate, of proposals together with the Commission (with the HR also acting as Vice-President in these circumstances (Art. 18(4) TEU)) (Arts. 21(3), 26(2) TEU).

Evaluation

Taken together, this multitude of tasks allows the incumbent to shape and propel EU foreign policy. This accumulation of positions creates real potential to strengthen EU foreign policy, as it breaks down institutional barriers, provides oversight of the different decision-making methods, and allows for the employment of the whole range of EU instruments. However, the HR/VP design suffers from some structural flaws.

First, it is unclear how the different institutional logics of the Council and Commission can be combined and how the intergovernmental and Community method can be embodied by one person. When chairing the Foreign Affairs Council, the HR/VP runs the risk of schizophrenia in accountability and loyalty to the Council, which he/she chairs, and to the Commission, of which he/she is Vice President (Crowe 2005: 2). The HR/VP carries out CFSP/CSDP as mandated by the Council (and thus the member states), but as a member of the Commission, he/she acts independently in the general interest of the EU and is not allowed to take any instruction from any other actor (including the member states).

Ultimately, though, the Council logic seems to dominate. In exercising the responsibilities as Vice-President responsible for the EU's external action, the HR/VP shall be bound by the Commission procedures *to the extent* that this is consistent with the HR/VP's responsibility to preside over the Foreign Affairs Council and carry out CFSP/CSDP as mandated by the Council (Art. 18 TEU). In other words: 'the High Representative may well be "double-hatted" – but his/her Council hat will sit on top of the Commission one at the final stage of decision-making by the Foreign Affairs Council' (Dashwood *et al.* 2011: 55). This points to a fundamental issue: the HR/VP, as Vice-President of the Commission, has less freedom of manoeuvre than other commissioners with external relations in their portfolio (such as trade or development). This can also explain why the role of Vice-President is under-utilized (Wouters *et al.* 2013a: 32).

Second, the HR/VP's capacity to act still hinges on the go-ahead he or she receives from the Council, on the ability of the Council to adopt decisions, and the availability of instruments to shore up diplomatic activities.

The HR/VP is not able to take positions, to negotiate with third actors or to undertake action if the member states in the Council are not able to agree on the position of the EU or on the actions this should entail. Even where the HR/VP is fully backed by the member states, success also depends on whether diplomatic activities are supported by the necessary economic, financial, military or other instruments that are not under his or her control. However, as seen before, the decision-making capacities of the Council remain problematic (see also Chapter 4), whereas the rather limited CFSP/CSDP toolbox and budget puts constraints on the leeway of the HR/VP.

Third, the HR/VP is not the only EU actor with foreign policy cards in his/her hand. This can hamper the HR/VP in fulfilling each of the four aforementioned tasks. Other relevant actors are the Presidents of the European Council and of the European Commission, other commissioners with external relations portfolios, the rotating Presidency of the Council, and obviously, national ministers and heads of state or government – each with their own priorities, bureaucracies, and desire for influence and political visibility. Even when these other actors do not act as rivals but as partners, it complicates the work of the HR/VP, increases the challenge of coordination, and limits his or her own freedom of manoeuvre. In any case, former US Secretary of State Henry Kissinger's request that there be one single telephone number to call 'Europe' remains as elusive as ever.

Rather than strengthening the potential of the function, the appointment of the rather unknown and inexperienced Catherine Ashton as first HR/VP amplified the limitations and structural defects of this function. In late 2009, the European Council appointed Catherine Ashton of the UK as the first High Representative (in agreement with Commission President Barroso), who was then appointed Vice-President of the Commission in early 2010 through the Commission's normal appointment process (including a hearing before the Foreign Affairs Committee of the EP). The choice of Ashton came as a surprise to Europe and the world – and also allegedly to Ashton herself – and was interpreted as both a sign of the EU's lack of ambition for the new position of HR/VP and for the EU's foreign policy in general (Howorth 2011: 305–9). The profile of Ashton (a former Leader of the House of Lords with merely one year of international experience as EU Commissioner for Trade) indeed contrasted sharply with that of various experienced foreign policy heavyweights whose names had also been mentioned for this position.

Ashton's wings were further clipped following the distribution of portfolios by Commission President Barroso. As the Commission's Vice-President with responsibility for external relations, Ashton paradoxically did not receive competence over any of the Commission's main foreign policy assets, which all fall under the authority of other commissioners:

enlargement, ENP, development, trade, humanitarian aid and crisis response. The leverage that comes with those portfolios – formal competences, a DG to implement policies, and substantial financial instruments to fund activities – thus remained outside the direct reach of the HR/VP, and with it of the EEAS.

How, then, does one evaluate the EU's first HR/VP? Most assessments of Ashton and of post-Lisbon EU foreign policy in general have been rather negative, with the HR/VP blamed for many of the EU foreign policy problems and with many references to her allegedly unenergetic and uninspiring actions, limited leadership qualities, absence or late reaction to several crises, etc. (see Howorth 2011). Even if these personality related arguments are partially or largely true, the structural and institutional impediments previously mentioned are at least or even more important in explaining her performance. Hence, dependent upon permissions from the Council, upon the availability of well-functioning diplomatic services, and upon instruments that support diplomatic activities, the HR/VP's credibility hinges on a host of others within the institutional set-up. This, in turn, placed Ashton in an unenviable position where her lack of established authority and inexperience further eroded her standing. This does not, however, mean that during her first years as HR/VP no CFSP successes were achieved (see Box 7.2).

The structural impediments together with her background and personality can explain why Ashton opted for an interpretation of the HR/VP function in which her role (and that of the EEAS) was to strictly work on behalf of the EU member states and to 'serve' the Council. This stands in contrast to another possible interpretation in which the HR/VP also shapes the EU's foreign policy, mediates between member states and actively contributes to defining EU lines on specific issues. Her reluctance to act as a policy entrepreneur resulted in a critical assessment from 12 foreign ministers (including from France and Germany) two years after she took office as HR/VP (Foreign Ministers 2011a, 2011b). However, Ashton's interpretation coincided perfectly with the UK's minimalist interpretation, the country that nominated her for this function. Nevertheless, it may be too early to make definitive judgements about the role of HR/VP, which was only recently created and may yet evolve in the longer term.

The EEAS and the EU Delegations

Internal organization and functions

The EEAS and the EU Delegations are the two additional links in the EU's ingenious system that bring various foreign policy actors and instruments together in what is meant to be a coherent and effective foreign policy. The Treaty explains why they can serve as cornerstone in the EU's foreign policy system:

In fulfilling his mandate, the High Representative shall be assisted by a European External Action Service. This service shall work in cooperation with the diplomatic services of the Member States and shall comprise officials from relevant departments of the General Secretariat of the Council and of the Commission as well as staff seconded from national diplomatic services of the Member States. (Art. 27(3) TEU)

A crucial component of the EEAS is the network of EU Delegations. The approximately 140 Delegations, which represent the EU in third countries and at international organizations and conferences, are placed under the authority of the HR/VP and are to act in close cooperation with member states' diplomatic and consular missions (Art. 221 TFEU). Other tasks of the Delegations include 'exchanging information and carrying out joint assessments' (Art. 35 TEU), contributing to 'formulating and implementing the common approach' of the EU (Art. 32 TEU), and 'ensuring that decisions defining Union positions and actions ... are complied with and implemented' (Art. 35 TEU) (see Chapter 4). They also contribute to the protection of EU citizens in the territory of third countries (Art. 35 TEU).

To make its CSDP policies (see Chapter 8) operational, the EU has established permanent crisis management structures (see Dijkstra 2013; Ginsberg and Penksa 2012; Vanhoonacker *et al.* 2010). These are mostly divided in separate military and civilian structures and also have a separate position in the EEAS hierarchy where they fall under the direct responsibility of the HR/VP.

- The *EU Military Staff* (EUMS) provides expertise for the CSDP, particularly in the conduct of a military crisis management operation. Working under the military direction of the EUMC, it is responsible for early warning, evaluation and strategic planning for CSDP missions.
- The *Civilian Planning and Conduct Capability* (CPCC) is responsible for the planning, deployment, conduct and review of civilian CSDP crisis management missions. It is located within the EEAS and reports directly to the HR/VP.
- The *Crisis Management and Planning Directorate* (CMPD) is tasked with the political–strategic planning and coordination of CSDP civilian missions and military operations actions.

The two institutional divides – between the military and civilian components; and between the actors in CFSP/CSDP and in other external action/external dimension of internal policies – are main challenges for the EU's crisis management policy. These are analysed in more detail in Chapters 6 (section on crisis management) and 8 (CSDP).

A last set of actors linked to the HR/VP are the EU Special Representatives (EUSRs). They receive mandates in relation to particular policy issues (often crises encompassing several countries) and they carry out their mandate under the authority of the HR/VP (Art. 33 TEU). In early 2013, the EUSRs covered the following countries or regions: the African Union, the Horn of Africa, the Sahel region, Kosovo, the Middle East peace process, Afghanistan, Bosnia and Herzegovina, Central Asia, the South Caucasus and the crisis in Georgia, the southern Mediterranean region and Sudan (see also Chapter 11). One EUSR is responsible for Human Rights. They allow the EU to take a more active stance in some important foreign policy domains (see Adebahr 2009). However, their relationship to the relevant EU Delegations, and to the crisis management structures and geographic desks in the EEAS is not always clear. Significant differences also exist in terms of mandates, staff and importance (see EEAS 2013a: 16–18).

Evaluation
Created by the Lisbon Treaty, the EEAS and EU Delegations were established in 2010 through a process of difficult inter- and intra-institutional negotiations (Blockmans and Hillion 2013; Council 2010a; Drieskens 2011, 2012; Erkelens and Blockmans 2012; Missiroli 2010). The Delegations were established on the basis of the existing network of 140 Commission Delegations in third countries and at international organizations, with the Heads of Delegation (HoDs) appointed by the HR/VP and with a creation or reinforcement of political sections in the delegations. The EEAS headquarters in Brussels, however, had to be developed from scratch. The HR/VP had the daunting task of creating a new service comprising staff from very different institutional and administrative cultures and sometimes opposite mindsets and loyalties (see Bátora 2013; Carta 2012; Dijkstra 2011; Juncos and Pomorska 2013; Smith M. E. 2013a; Spence 2012).

The difficult negotiations, institutional rivalries and, in some cases, outright obstruction from member states or institutional actors was not abnormal: the design of the EEAS and EU Delegations not only had an impact on the EU's effectiveness and consistency as a foreign policy actor, but also on the balance of power between and within EU institutions and member states (Van Vooren 2011). Moreover, the institutional rivalries were also 'conceptually underpinned by demarcation disputes: those who wish to see "development", "peace-building" and "humanitarian aid" demarcated from "foreign policy"; and others who advocate closer interaction between them, based on a foreign and security policy logic' (Spence 2012: 132).

The EEAS and the EU Delegations became operational on 1 December 2010. However, originally spread out over different locations in Brussels, the EEAS staff only moved in early 2012 to the EEAS's own

'*Triangle*' building in Brussels, located near the Commission and Council. The EEAS by then comprised a staff of around 3,600, including 1,550 in the Brussels headquarters and 2,050 in Delegations. Although it was originally foreseen that one-third of the EEAS management and administrator level staff would come from national diplomatic services, this goal was not at all reached. National diplomats are well represented in senior positions, but the vast majority of staff joined from Commission services (EEAS 2011a, 2013a: 32–4).

Not surprisingly, the EEAS had a very difficult start after becoming operational, due to turf wars and practical problems inevitable in such complex institutional reforms. The uncooperative behaviour of some member states proved an additional complicating factor. The EEAS is indeed assessed rather critically, despite recognition of some of its achievements within a quite difficult context (see Balfour 2012; Blockmans 2012; Cameron 2012: 63–82; Duke 2012; Helwig *et al.* 2013; Smith M. E. 2013b; Spence 2012; Telò and Ponjaert 2013; Vanhoonacker and Pomorska 2013; Wouters *et al.* 2013a). In her first-year report, the HR/VP correctly underlined that the creation of the EAAS is 'a long-term challenge that will take several years to reach maturity', which also implies that it is too soon to make definitive judgements' (EEAS 2011a).

It is already clear that the same structural impediments hampering the HR/VP's functioning also set hurdles that impede the EEAS's and EU Delegations' capacity to realize their role as potential cornerstones in the EU's foreign policy architecture. A major obstacle for the EEAS and for the Heads of Delegation is their lack of direct control over major parts of the EU's foreign policy toolbox. The EEAS organogram shows a rather traditional structure of a diplomatic service, organized around geographical desks and thematic desks (such as 'Human rights and democracy') (EEAS 2013b). However, as noted earlier, most of the strategically important financial instruments (such as the European Neighbourhood Instrument), as well as competences with regard to contractual agreements with third countries, fall under the responsibility of the Commission, particularly in DG DEVCO.

According to the working arrangements, the EEAS is responsible for the strategic planning and programming of most of the financial instruments (see Chapter 4), and the Commission takes care of the preparation and implementation (Council 2010a). While the EEAS is dependent on the expertise of the Commission, the Commission staff appears eager to retain control over policies and avoid being reduced to a kind of executive agency for the EEAS. A similar story applies to the EU Delegations: although both EEAS staff and Commission officials work under the authority of the Heads of Delegation, financial and staff regulations explain why Commission staff is de facto primarily accountable to their DGs in Brussels.

This leads to a related structural problem: the choices which have been made regarding staff and budgets make it difficult for the EEAS and the EU Delegation to act at the vanguard of EU foreign policy and to sufficiently feed pertinent substance into the EU's policy-making process. The percentage of staff with a predominantly CFSP/CSDP-oriented function remains rather small. In the majority of Delegations, most of the staff is linked to the Commission, with responsibility for development or trade related activities and the related operational budgets. This also implies that the context is not yet conducive to the structural change hoped for: to complement the outspoken development orientation or trade orientation (characteristic of the former Commission delegations) with a genuine foreign policy orientation. Illustrative in this context is the EU Delegation in Egypt, a country with a key position in the ongoing changes in the Arab world and the Middle East. With around 100 staff it is among the largest EU Delegations, but its political section has barely five people that fall directly under the authority of the HR/VP. Moreover, the officials and diplomats working on CFSP are often also hampered in their effectiveness as a result of a limited operational budget, often limited local language skills and limited support from the member states.

The European Parliament

As is the case for many member states' national parliaments in foreign policy, the role of the EP in EU foreign policy is generally quite limited, the exception being its budgetary powers and its major powers relating to the adoption of international agreements (see also Benedetto 2011: 86–7; Corbett *et al.* 2011). The EP has organized itself in such a way as to maximize its involvement in foreign policy affairs. The main actors are the EP's Committee on Foreign Affairs (AFET), its subcommittees on Human Rights (DROI) and on Security and Defence (SEDE); the Committee on Development (DEVE); and the Committee on International Trade (INTA). For reasons that will become clear later, the Budgets Committee (BUDG) and Budgetary Control Committee (CONT), as well as various sectoral committees, also play an increasingly important role, adding potential leverage to the EP's involvement in EU foreign policy, but simultaneously complicating EU foreign policy-making.

In addition to these Committees, the EP has more than 40 Interparliamentary Delegations for relations with parliamentary assemblies from third countries, regions or international organizations. Interparliamentary dialogue is foreseen in, for instance, the Association Agreements and the Partnership and Cooperation Agreements. These Interparliamentary Delegations are useful tools in the EP's parliamentary diplomacy as they provide the EP with the potential to influence the views and attitudes of parliamentarians from third countries and, particularly, to advance its position on human rights and democracy issues. They also give the EP an insight into specific foreign policy dossiers, which in turn strengthens its position in dialogue with the Council and Commission.

The limited power of the EP in EU foreign policy is particularly apparent in the CFSP/CSDP framework. Here, it has been granted only a very limited, consultative role. The High Representative shall 'regularly consult the European Parliament on the main aspects and the basic choices' of the CFSP and CSDP, 'inform it of how those policies evolve', and ensure that its views are 'duly taken into consideration'. The Parliament may 'address questions or make recommendations to the Council or the High Representative', and twice a year holds a debate on progress in the implementation of CFSP and CSDP (Art. 36 TEU). Since the HR/VP is also a member of the European Commission, the HR/VP undergoes a parliamentary hearing before taking office. This also holds true for the other commissioners with a foreign policy portfolio (trade, development, enlargement, etc.).

The EP voices its position on foreign policy issues through a constant stream of own-initiative reports, resolutions and parliamentary questions. It has managed to obtain regular formal and informal dialogue with the High Representative, the EEAS and the Commission (see overview in Council 2011a: 84–6). Through successive inter-institutional agreements, the EP has gradually managed to earn concessions from the Council and Commission that allow it a slightly more significant position in foreign policy affairs (see Stacey 2010).

A concrete example of the EP gaining such concessions took place during the establishment of the EEAS in 2010. Although the Council formally only had to consult the EP to set up the EEAS (Art. 27 TEU), the EP increased its leverage by linking the establishment of the EEAS to two other issues on which it had co-legislative powers: the staff regulation and the financial regulation of the EEAS (European Parliament and Council 2010a, 2010b) (see Wisniewski 2013). This resulted in some concessions from the High Representative (included in the 'Declaration on Political Accountability') with regard to informing and consulting the EP, providing more parliamentary budgetary oversights, and ensuring more systematic attention to human rights and democracy promotion within the EEAS's and EU Delegations' set-up. The EP, though, had to accept concessions, too. For instance, whereas it had initially asked to be heard before the appointment of EU Special Representatives and Heads of Delegations, the EP had to accept that it would only be allowed to exchange views with these senior officials after their appointment (but before they are sent abroad) (European Parliament 2010; Raube 2012: 71–9). Generally speaking, High Representative Ashton managed to develop a rather positive relationship with the EP, which was at least as much down to her constructive attitude towards the EP as to the substance of the EU's foreign policy (see Helwig *et al.* 2013: 50–61).

Within the framework of the external action and the internal policies with an external dimension, the EP has two major instruments to influence EU foreign policy: the consent procedure, which gives it veto power over the ratification of international agreements; and its position in the budgetary process.

The EP must consent to international agreements. The EP not only holds a veto power over association and cooperation agreements with third countries and regions, but also over the financial protocols with third countries, over trade agreements and – importantly – over the ratification of international agreements on issues that are internally regulated via the ordinary legislative procedure, such as environmental issues.

The major limitation of the consent procedure is that it is a rather blunt tool, as the EP can only accept or reject an agreement that is already negotiated with one or more third countries or organizations. In most cases the threat of actually rejecting an agreement is simply not credible, or it leads to an undermining of the EU as a credible international negotiator. A further limitation to the consent procedure is that it does not foresee formal parliamentary involvement in either the definition of the Commission's negotiation mandate or the conduct of negotiations, although through inter-institutional agreements it has been agreed that MEPs can ask to be observers during negotiations. The Treaties, though, require that the EP is 'immediately and fully informed' at all stages of international negotiation processes in which the EU participates (Art. 218(10) TFEU), including in trade negotiations (Art. 207(3) TFEU). This means that the EP can immediately make its concerns known so that it does not get confronted with a *fait accompli*. Although a parliamentary veto of international agreements is not very likely, the EP's powers are more hidden, since the Commission, Council and/or the High Representative are likely to anticipate the EP's possible reaction and, consequently, take into account its position in order to ensure parliamentary consent (Passos 2011; see also Tsebelis 1994).

Despite the limitations of the consent procedure, the EP has on a limited number of occasions refused or delayed its consent, or threatened to refuse or delay its consent. Examples from the more distant past include the Partnership and Cooperation Agreements with Kazakhstan and Uzbekistan, where the EP protested against specific (mostly human rights) problems in these countries (Corbett *et al.* 2005: 152, 227–8). Recent examples are the EP's rejection of the draft texts regarding the 'SWIFT' Agreement with the US, the Protocol linked to the Fisheries Partnership Agreement with Morocco or the multilateral 'ACTA' treaty on intellectual property rights enforcement and anti-counterfeit (see Monar 2010; Passos 2011: 52–5; Servent and MacKenzie 2012).

The EP's second major foreign policy instrument is its role as one of the two budgetary arms of the EU (together with the Council). The EP has used this budgetary power to gain indirect leverage over the EU's foreign policy. The most obvious example of this was the EP's initiative, dating back to 1994, to create a chapter in the EU budget currently entitled the 'European Instrument for Democracy and Human Rights' (EIDHR) and the subsequent gradual increase in funds under this chapter (see Chapter 6). The EP has also sought to counter the Council's propensity to enter into new political (and thus often also financial) engagements without having a priori identified a financial basis for this. The Council and member states have been critical of the EP for improperly using its budgetary powers to try to gain a foothold in CFSP. The funding of EU foreign policy has become a main arena of struggle between the EP and the Council, with the former trying to compensate for the absence of formal influence in CFSP/CSDP issues, and the latter remaining adamant that the EP should not use (or, in the Council's view, abuse) its budgetary powers (Thym 2006: 113–17).

What has been the impact of the EP's foreign policy actions? It has clearly been successful in pressuring the other institutions to take human rights and democracy dimensions more seriously. The EP has achieved this by creating and promoting the EIDHR and by consistently focusing on these dimensions in resolutions and questions to the Council, in its Annual Report on Human Rights in the World, and its yearly Sakharov Prize. In broader terms, the EP has played a role in pushing forward the boundaries of debate on EU foreign policy and bringing neglected dimensions to the fore. It has also scored some goals in specific foreign policy dossiers. However, cumulatively, its impact has been rather limited and on the whole and it remains a marginal player in shaping EU foreign policy.

This brings us to the question of whether EU foreign policy is indeed suffering from a 'democratic deficit' (see also Bickerton 2011: 99–117; Lord 2011; Peters *et al.* 2010; Sjursen 2011). Barbé presents several reasons why, for many governments, the limited role of the EP is part of the game (2004: 49, 54–5): too much parliamentary involvement would damage the need for secrecy, speed, coherence and efficiency in foreign policy; it would mean that the EP's strong emphasis on human rights and democracy would interfere in their foreign policy goals; and ministers feel primarily politically accountable to their national parliaments. Following this third reason, there is no argument for EP involvement, since national parliaments should be the locus of democratic control. However, this argument disregards the fact that national parliaments are no longer in a position to closely follow developments in all domains of EU foreign policy. Moreover, particularly with regard to CSDP, the EP and national parliaments have different views on who is responsible for parliamentary scrutiny (Wouters and Raube 2012).

The Court of Justice

The Court of Justice of the EU (ECJ) has a key position in the institutional system of the EU, as it is to 'ensure that in the interpretation and application of the Treaties the law is observed' (Art. 19 TEU). The ECJ settles legal disputes between member state governments and EU institutions, for instance about the correct interpretation of the EU's competences in the various policy areas. Individuals and organizations can bring cases before the Court if they feel their rights have been infringed by an EU institution or decision.

The ECJ has a quasi-general jurisdiction over all policy areas of the EU, including trade, development policy, environment, the area of freedom, security and justice, etc. Over the last decades, the Court has developed an extensive jurisprudence with regard to the EU's competences in the areas of external action and the external dimension of internal policies (see Dashwood *et al.* 2011; Lenaerts and Van Nuffel 2011). Several of its judgments became landmark cases, such as the *ERTA* case, which contributed to establishing the external competences of the EU (see above and see Chapter 4).

There is one major exception on the Court's quasi-general jurisdiction: CFSP/CSDP. Reflecting member states' choice to safeguard its strictly intergovernmental character, the Court has no jurisdiction with regard to provisions relating to the CFSP and acts adopted on the basis of those provisions (Art. 24(1) TEU and 275 TFEU). This means that the Court has no general jurisdiction to review the legality of CFSP acts. Nor can it judge whether member states fulfil their obligations, for instance whether they comply with the EU's action in the field of the CFSP and CSDP or refrain from any action which is contrary to the interests of the EU (see Chapter 7).

The Treaties foresee two exceptions to the rule that the ECJ has no powers over CFSP matters. The first is that the ECJ has jurisdiction to monitor compliance with the principle that implementation of the CFSP should not affect the exercise of the EU's competences in other policy fields, and vice versa (Art. 40 TEU). Given the many grey areas between CFSP and external policies such as trade and development, this equal protection against mutual encroachment (Dashwood *et al.* 2011: 908) does not simplify the work of the Court. As emphasized by Dashwood *et al.*, the cases of real or perceived overlap and of competition between CFSP competences and the EU's external action/external dimension of internal policies competences are liable to occur more frequently in view of the common list of objectives of the EU's external activities in Article 21(2) (see Chapter 1).

The second exception is that the ECJ can rule on proceedings reviewing the legality of decisions adopted by the Council that provide for economic or financial sanctions against natural or legal persons (Art. 275

TFEU), which are based on a CFSP decision (on sanctions, see Chapter 9). Important in this context are the *Kadi I and II* cases (Court of Justice 2008, 2010), in which the ECJ challenged Council decisions imposing sanctions on persons associated with Osama bin Laden, Al-Qaeda and the Taliban, in implementation of UN Security Council resolutions. The Council had adopted a common position on sanctions within the framework of the CFSP, followed by a regulation that provided for the freezing of funds and other economic resources of individuals. Mr Kadi, a Saudi resident targeted by the sanctions, brought actions for annulment before the Court, claiming *inter alia* that the regulation breached several fundamental rights. The ECJ declared the Council's regulation invalid because it found a breach of the fundamental rights (including the right of defence) that form an integral part of the general principles of EU law (see also Harpaz 2009). The judgment of the ECJ in *Kadi* thus represented a strong commitment to the protection of European fundamental rights standards and the rule of law (Posch 2009; De Baere 2012) – rights and rules which the EU is eager to promote in its foreign policy but which risk to be brushed aside in the fight against terrorism (see Chapter 6).

Other Actors

The preceding discussion of the actors in the traditional institutional framework is not to suggest that *only* those actors need to be taken into account when analysing EU foreign policy. The European Council, the Council, the HR/VP, the Commission, the Parliament and the Court also need other actors for conducting foreign policy.

A first set of actors consists of agencies that are active in the area of foreign policy. The main agency in this realm is the European Defence Agency (EDA), a major actor in the context of the industrial and technological dimension of CSDP (see Chapter 8). Established in 2004, EDA is formally included in the EU's institutional framework since the entry into force of the Lisbon Treaty (Art. 45 TEU). Its mission is to support the Council and member states in their effort to improve the EU's defence capabilities for the CSDP (Council 2011b: 17). With 27 participating countries (all EU member states except Denmark), the EDA is responsible for the implementation of different comprehensive strategies related, for instance, to research and technology or armaments cooperation. The logic is that by providing one agency with an overview of these different agendas, it should be able to realize the potential synergies between the different areas. However, the Agency's small operational budget and minimal personnel, the member states' lack of consensus about the purpose of EDA, their reluctance to adhere to common rules and procedures, and their preference for voluntary cooperation make it nearly impossible for the EDA to perform its ambitious tasks (Biscop and Coelmont 2012: 62–4, 70–1; Chang 2011).

Other agencies operating in support of the CFSP are the European Union Satellite Centre (EUSC) and the European Union Institute for Security Studies (EUISS). The EUSC is dedicated to the exploitation and production of information derived from analysing earth observation data. However, in contrast to what its name suggests, the EUSC does not own satellites, but instead depends on obtaining satellite information from other actors. The EUISS is a think-tank focused on security issues relevant for EU foreign policy, and it also provides analyses and forecasting to the HR/VP. Beyond CFSP, agencies are active in domains with foreign policy relevance, such as Frontex, Eurojust or Europol in the Area of Freedom, Security and Justice (see Chapter 10).

The European Investment Bank (EIB) and the European Bank for Reconstruction and Development (EBRD), a second set of non-traditional foreign policy actors, play an important role in financing projects outside the EU and thus also in foreign policy. The EIB was founded for the purpose of providing long-term finance in support of investment projects. Outside the EU, the EIB is active in over 150 countries, making it the largest international non-sovereign lender and borrower. The European Investment Fund (EIF) can be considered a subsidiary of the EIB. The EIB's total financing was €61 billion in 2011, of which 10 per cent went to projects outside the EU.

The EBRD is the world's only transition bank. It finances projects in approximately 30 Central and Eastern European and Central Asian countries that contribute to the transition to market economies, pluralistic democratic societies and the integration of these countries in the global market. The EBRD differs from other development banks as it operates under a politically defined mandate that prescribes a focus on states 'committed to and applying the principles of multi-party democracy [and] pluralism' (Article 1 of the Agreement Establishing the Bank). A significant part of the EBRD projects is situated in Central and Eastern European countries.

A third set of actors that are important in the conduct of EU foreign policy are actors outside the EU: other multilateral organizations (such as NATO, the IMF and many specialized UN agencies and programmes – see Chapter 13) or specialized international organizations that are in some cases closely linked to the EU (such as the European Space Agency (ESA), which gets 20 per cent of its funds from the EU budget and which link with the EU is institutionalized in the EU–ESA Framework Agreement, see Chapter 8).

Fourth, EU foreign policy is shaped by a variety of non-state actors, including interest groups, civil society organizations, private companies, consultancies and international service providers. NGOs and private actors play a crucial role in implementing projects and activities of the

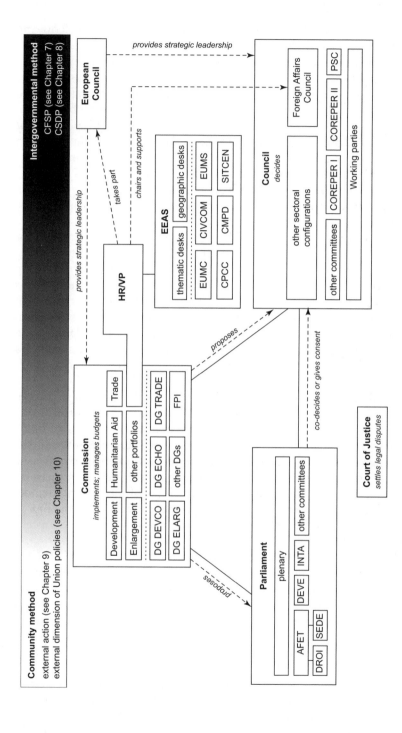

Figure 3.2   Institutional framework of EU foreign policy-making (elaborated version)

EU's external action. A major part of activities that are launched in the framework of the geographic and thematic financial instruments of the EU (see Chapter 4) – such as technical assistance, capacity-building projects, or democracy promotion initiatives – can indeed not be put in practice by the EU itself, leading to 'foreign policy by substitution'. This can also be the case in sensitive domains of foreign and security policy, such as support for security sector reform in third countries (see Justaert 2012). The EU's heavily bureaucratic approach, with complex contracting procedures and highly demanding administrative, legal and financial requirements, also explains the partial commercialization of its external policies (see Commission 2013a). As a result, mainly specialized Western private or private–public actors as well as specialized NGOs are eligible to implement EU programmes, with actors and civil society organizations from partner countries in other parts of the world often de facto being excluded. This not only limits the possibility of interaction and dialogue between the EU and the partner countries, but also implies that considerable parts of the budgetary transfers that are designated for activities in third countries in fact end up in European bank accounts. The bureaucratic nature of the EU's 'foreign policy by substitution' also explains a criticism already mentioned above: a major part of the Commission's administration in Brussels and staff in EU Delegations is too much involved in managing projects and in interacting with the various implementation actors, thereby forgetting what foreign policy is all about: realizing foreign policy goals.

Conclusion

It is clear from this chapter that the overarching idea of a 'single institutional framework' belies a much more complex reality. Further elaborating on Figure 3.1, Figure 3.2 presents a more encompassing overview of the main actors in the EU's foreign policy-making.

The structure of the EU's foreign policy system has been determined by the extent to which member states were prepared to hand over control of this policy area to other actors. However, as the number of member states sitting around the policy-making table has grown, so too has the sheer breadth of issues to be debated. These two developments have meant that even in those areas in which member states wished to retain full control, they have been forced to delegate responsibilities to common actors and smaller configurations of member states. Considering the complexity of the system – the different roles each actor plays depending on the policy area in question and the institutions' competing agendas and turf wars – it is quite impressive that the EU manages to develop any foreign policy at all. The methods developed to circumvent this complexity are the subject of the next chapter.

Chapter 4

The EU's Foreign Policy System: Policy-making

The Treaties set the boundaries and framework for the EU's foreign policy actors by conferring upon the institutions specific powers and by detailing the decision-making process. This chapter first reveals the utter complexity of formal competences, decision-making processes, voting procedures and the limits of intervention under which the institutions labour. Viewed in this light, it is remarkable that the EU manages to achieve the foreign policy output that it does. Then, a policy-making perspective is adopted – a view from the ground as it were – exposing the dynamics which drive EU foreign policy and revealing how the EU manages to overcome its institutional and procedural hurdles. Next, we go on to assess an additional layer of complexity in shaping and implementing policy – the financing of EU foreign policy – before finally turning to the difficulties of ensuring consistency between the various policy-making methods and institutions.

Competences

The distribution of formal competences is crucial to explain the nature of the EU's foreign policy and the relationship between EU foreign policy and that of the member states (for a detailed analysis, see Eeckhout 2011; Lenaerts and Van Nuffel 2011). External policy competences have evolved considerably, moving from a rather clear-cut distribution prescribed by the 1957 Treaty of Rome to a very complex distribution of competences today. According to the principle of *conferral of powers*, the EU must act within the limits of the competences conferred upon it by the member states in the Treaties in order to attain the objectives set out within the Treaties. This implies that competences not conferred upon the EU remain with the member states, and that competences are conferred upon the EU solely to meet objectives stated within the Treaties. This principle is crucial to understanding the nature of EU foreign policy. It indicates that the Union has no general, legal basis authorizing it to act with regard to the external environment. However, this does not mean that the EU has no specific external competences, since various treaty provisions allow the EU to act internationally in a large range of policy fields. Hence, when we evaluate EU foreign policy, we should never expect the EU to have an exclusive or all-encompassing foreign policy. Given its restricted competences, the expectation should rather be that the EU would not act in certain aspects of foreign, security and defence policy. This often runs counter to expectations of the public, press and politicians.

The distribution of competences between the EU and the member states varies depending on the policy field, but three general categories of competence can be discerned: exclusive, shared and supporting competences (Arts. 3, 4 and 6 TFEU). The EU's competences in the area of CFSP are laid down in Article 24 TEU. The following paragraphs focus first on the competences in the EU's external action and in the external dimension of internal policies before evaluating how CFSP and CSDP fit within this categorization.

In areas of *exclusive competence* (Art. 3 TFEU), only the EU has the power to legislate and adopt legally binding acts. The common commercial policy (also referred to as 'trade policy'), highly relevant to foreign policy, is one of the very few areas of exclusive competence. Another area of exclusive competence is monetary policy for member states in the eurozone. Moreover, the Court of Justice has established the competence to act externally on issues on which the EU has adopted legislative measures internally, even if this is not explicitly mentioned in the Treaties. Notably in the *ERTA* case (or *AETR* case; when using the French acronym), the Court established the 'parallelism principle' between internal and external competences, which means that by exercising its internal law-making powers, the EU is taken to have the power to conclude international agreements in the same area, even if this capacity is not explicitly foreseen by the Treaties. This principle is also called the '*in foro interno, in foro externo* principle'. These competences, called 'implied powers', contrast with the explicitly mentioned powers of the EU treaties, called 'express powers' (Eeckhout 2011: 120–64).

In areas of *shared competence* between the EU and the member states (Art. 4 TFEU), the exercise of competence by the member states is subject to what is called the pre-emption principle (Lenaerts and Van Nuffel 2011: 96–7). This implies that both the EU and the member states can legislate and adopt legally binding acts in a specific area, but the member states can only exercise their competence to the extent that the EU has not yet exercised its competence. Member states can thus only act where the Union's own action has left them space to do so. This category applies to a whole range of policy areas, including some that are relevant for the EU's foreign policy (such as environment or agriculture). The *ERTA* principle also applies to shared competences, albeit only to those competences that are exercised by the Union. In some areas of shared competence, the pre-emption principle does not come into play: the EU is competent to carry out activities and conduct a common policy, but in so doing it does not prevent member states from also carrying out activities and conducting a national policy. This category applies to several domains of importance to EU foreign policy, including development cooperation, humanitarian aid, research and technology.

In other policy areas, the EU has competence merely to carry out actions to *support, coordinate or supplement* the actions of the member states and cannot supersede their competence in these areas (Art. 6 TFEU). This includes various fields that can be part of the EU's contractual relations with third parties, such as culture and education.

The distribution of competences is, in practice, even more complex than the explanations above would indicate. Within one policy field there can be further variations and gradations in the competences attributed to the EU and thus, also in the scope of action which rests under member state control. In more complex policy initiatives, the use of multiple legal bases is nearly always necessary (see below), which adds to the complexity of policy-making. However, the delineation of competences – and with it the different legal bases – within the Treaties is not as rigid as it may first appear. Article 352 TFEU is a flexibility clause under which the EU can undertake action in areas not included explicitly in the Treaties (see below).

How do CFSP and CSDP fit within this categorization? The CFSP competences are not exclusive, shared or used to support, coordinate, or supplement policies. Rather they are defined according to specific provisions in the TEU (Art. 24 TEU). Generally speaking, member states have always rejected the idea of drawing up a list of foreign policy matters that would fall under exclusive (or shared) EU competence, not least because in so doing they could be prohibited from acting when a foreign policy decision had been adopted at the EU level. This is not to imply that CFSP decisions do not commit the member states in terms of the positions they adopt and the conduct of their activity (see Chapter 7).

The availability and choice of legal basis for a particular action or decision is crucial as it determines the extent to which the EU can act and because it has major implications for the actors involved, the decision-making and voting procedures used, the budgetary consequences and the possibility of recourse to the ECJ. This also explains why specific policy actions and their legal bases do not always meet the requirements of the foreign policy issue, but instead reflect the repercussions for the inter-institutional balance of power. Member states may prefer to rely on a specific treaty article because it ensures, for instance, that the Union's budget can be used or that the EP can be excluded from policy-making, not because it is seen as the most effective way to tackle the problem at hand.

The fact that the distribution of competences is not particularly clear and that foreign policy matters can often be tackled from different policy perspectives results in inconsistencies and 'turf battles' between the EU's actors. This is particularly true for the many grey areas that fall between CFSP and areas like trade, development or research and technological development, which are part of the EU's external action.

Decision-making

This section first gives an overview of the various formal *decision*-making procedures in order to focus on the broader *policy*-making process in the next section. Both are essential to understand the nature, possibilities and constraints of EU foreign policy as well as the complex web of intra-institutional, inter-institutional and interstate interaction it involves.

Before analysing decision-making with regard to the EU's external action, the external dimension of internal policies and the CFSP/CSDP, we focus on Article 22(1) TEU that deals with decisions of the European Council on the strategic interests and objectives of the Union, which not only relate to the CFSP but also to other areas of the foreign policy of the EU. These decisions may concern the EU's relations with a specific country or region, or may be thematic in approach and define their duration and the means to be made available by the EU and the member states. The procedure foreseen is as follows:

> The European Council shall act unanimously on a recommendation from the Council, adopted by the latter under the arrangements laid down for each area. These decisions are implemented in accordance with the procedures provided for in the Treaties.

Article 22(2) TEU also indicates that the High Representative (for the CFSP) and the Commission (for other areas of external action) may submit joint proposals to the Council. Taken together, Article 22 demonstrates nicely how the EU's different decision-making methods can be sewn together within European Council decisions, and subsequently again implemented through the EU's different decision-making methods. It thus allows the possibility to bring together the EU's and member states' range of instruments.

Decision-making on external action and on the external dimension of internal policies

Most decision-making on the legislative framework of non-CFSP issues follows the ordinary legislative procedure. Here, the EP decides together with the Council, acting by qualified majority voting (QMV), on the basis of a proposal from the Commission. Until 2014 (or 2017 in case the European Council decides so), each member state had a particular number of votes with the larger ones having more votes than the smaller ones, ranging from 29 for Germany, the UK, France and Italy to 3 votes for Malta. In this system within an EU with 28 member states, a QMV is obtained when 260 of the available 352 votes are reached. The new post-2014 (or 2017) system will be based on a double majority rationale, with a QMV decision requiring the support of 55 per cent of the member states representing 65 per cent of the overall EU population. The QMV rule is applied for decision-making in trade policy (Art. 207 TFEU), development cooperation (Art. 209 TFEU) and in economic, financial and technical cooperation with third countries (Art. 212 TFEU).

The main procedures for the negotiation and conclusion of international agreements are less straightforward.

- *Decision-making on trade agreements* (Arts. 207 and 218 TFEU): on the Commission's recommendation, the Council authorizes the Commission to open negotiations. The Commission then negotiates the agreement in constant coordination with the special committee appointed by the Council (the 'Trade Policy Committee', previously the 'Article 133 Committee') and in line with the negotiation mandate (or 'directives') issued by the Council. After a trade agreement has been signed, it is the prerogative of the Council to conclude the agreement. The consent of the EP is also required to conclude an agreement, but the EP is not formally involved in the authorization of the opening of the negotiations. During negotiations, the EP needs to be kept informed although the EP cannot assist – as can the Trade Policy Committee – the Commission in its negotiation work. The Council decides by QMV in general to conclude on trade agreements, except in certain circumstances enumerated in Articles 207 and 218 TFEU.
- *Decision-making on international agreements with regard to development cooperation and economic, financial and technical cooperation* (Arts. 211, 212, 218 TFEU): the conclusion (i.e. ratification) of cooperation agreements follows the decision-making process for trade agreements outlined above. Again, the Council acts by QMV, unless the agreement covers a field for which unanimity is mandated for the adoption of internal policies. To conclude such an agreement, the consent of the EP is obligatory.
- *Decision-making on association agreements* (Arts. 217, 218 TFEU): the process largely follows the principles outlined above for the negotiation of trade and cooperation agreements. However, the main difference is that the Council acts unanimously instead of by QMV.
- *Decision-making on agreements in other policy fields*: the EU has the international legal personality to enter into agreements with third parties in specific policy fields (such as environment or research). The legal basis for the agreement will then be the article on the specific policy area (which provides the substantive legal basis) combined

with Art. 218 TFEU, which deals with decision-making procedures for international agreements. For example, if the agreement relates to environmental policy, Art. 192 TFEU (on environmental policy) in combination with Art. 218 TFEU will provide the legal basis and determine the decision-making process (see Delreux 2011a: 18–23).

Two additional factors further complicate decision-making. First, agreements can have several legal bases. For instance, if an agreement includes trade issues and elements of environmental policy, Articles 207, 192 and 218 TFEU will be the legal bases. In some instances, for example the Cartagena Protocol on Biosafety, the Council and the Commission did not agree on the legal basis, and the final decision could only be taken after a ruling by the ECJ. In the case of the Cartagena Protocol, the ECJ agreed with the Council that the appropriate legal basis was an environmental article and not a trade article, as the Commission wanted. Association agreements in particular are based on several treaty articles, as they tend to cover a broader range of policy areas. This also implies that the decision-making procedures of various treaty bases can differ. In these cases, a complex set of implicit and explicit rules (including ECJ judgments) then determine what decision-making procedure will be used.

The second complicating factor is that most agreements are 'mixed agreements'. These are agreements which cover policy areas that fall under competences shared by the EU and the member states and to which the EU and the member states become a party (see Eeckhout 2011; Hillion and Koutrakos 2010; Wessel 2011a). The decision-making rules already outlined are also valid for mixed agreements. But, in addition to being concluded by the EU, the agreement is also subject to national ratification processes. Most international agreements currently concluded by the EU are mixed agreements. This is logical because the number of exclusive EU competences is actually rather limited. That most agreements are mixed also explains why, independent of whether unanimity or QMV is foreseen in the formal procedures, there is significant pressure to adopt agreements by consensus, or else endanger national ratification processes. Moreover, when mixed agreements are negotiated, the EU is formally represented at the international level through 'dual representation' (Damro 2006; Delreux 2012b) where the Commission represents the EU and another representative (usually the rotating Presidency of the Council) represents the member states. Hence, there is a logical connection between *shared competences, mixed agreements* and *dual representation*. Though in theory the EU and the member states could negotiate separately, such an arrangement is often not used in practice (see Chapter 13 and Box 13.1).

Two further procedures deserve special mention. Art. 215 TFEU touches upon decision-making with regard to the *interruption or reduction*

	Commission	Council	European Parliament	Treaty basis
Trade policy	Proposal	QMV	co-decision	Art. 207 TFEU
Development cooperation	Proposal	QMV	co-decision	Art. 209 TFEU
Cooperation with third countries	Proposal	QMV	co-decision	Art. 212 TFEU
Trade agreements	Recommendation to open negotiation; proposal for signing and concluding an agreement	QMV (with exceptions)	consent	Arts 207, 218 TFEU
International (development and cooperation) agreements		QMV (with exceptions)	consent	Arts 211, 212, 218 TFEU
Association agreements		Unanimity	consent	Arts 217, 218 TFEU
Interruption or reduction of economic and financial relations	Proposal (on basis of a CFSP decision), jointly with the High Representative	QMV	no role	Art. 215 TFEU
Action when treaty does not provide powers	Proposal	Unanimity	consent	Art. 352 TFEU

Table 4.1   Decision-making procedures on external action

of economic and financial relations with one or more third countries (i.e. sanctions, see Chapter 9). This is the only article in the TFEU that includes an explicit link to decision-making in CFSP and makes a decision on economic or financial sanctions subject to a preliminary decision in the CFSP framework. According to this article, if a CFSP decision states that the EU should interrupt or reduce economic or financial relations with a third country, a joint proposal from the High Representative and the Commission is sent to the Council and decided by QMV (see Portela 2010: 19–34). Consequently, the Commission's exclusive right of initiative – one of the basic features of the Community method – is undermined since it is pre-empted by the preceding decision of the Council in the CFSP framework.

Finally, Article 352 TFEU outlines the procedure for *actions where the Treaty does not provide the necessary powers.* If action is required to attain one of the objectives of the Union but the Treaty has not provided for the necessary powers, the Council can take the 'appropriate measures' acting unanimously on a Commission proposal and after having obtained the consent of the EP. The main decision-making procedures on external action are summarized in Table 4.1.

Decision-making in CFSP/CSDP

CFSP/CSDP decision-making follows the intergovernmental method: the Council is at the centre and decision-making is by unanimity. Member states, the High Representative or the High Representative with the Commission's support share the right of initiative; any member state or the High Representative may refer any questions and submit initiatives or proposals regarding the CFSP to the Council (Art. 30 TEU). The Treaty institutes several procedures for decision-making within CFSP. The overriding characteristic of these is that all decision-making power is concentrated in the European Council, the Council and with the High Representative (Arts. 26, 27 and 31 TEU). It is important to bear in mind from the outset that the provisions of treaty texts can be misleading, and that the provisions on majority voting (QMV) and enhanced cooperation, in particular, are not reflected in practice.

The main procedures provided for in the Treaty are:

- *Decisions on the strategic interests, strategic lines, objectives and general guidelines for the CFSP,* including for matters with defence implications, are defined by the European Council by unanimity.
- *Decisions necessary for defining and implementing the CFSP,* including decisions on *actions* and *positions,* are taken by the Council on the basis of the European Council's general guidelines and strategic lines (see Chapter 7). The basic rule is that the Council acts unanimously, with abstentions not preventing the adoption of decisions. By

way of derogation, QMV applies in the following, limited cases: when adopting a decision defining a Union action or position on the basis of either a decision of the European Council relating to the EU's strategic interests and objectives, or of a proposal of the High Representative following a specific request from the European Council; when adopting a decision implementing another decision that defines a Union action or position; and when appointing a Special Representative. The normal rules with regard to QMV apply, except when the Council is taking a decision not proposed by the High Representative. In such a case, a super-qualified majority, consisting of 72 per cent of the member states and 65 per cent of the population applies (Art. 238 TFEU).

- *International agreements* with one or more states or international organizations under the CFSP rubric (Arts. 37 TEU and 218 TFEU): the High Representative submits a recommendation to the Council, which authorizes the opening of negotiations and which nominates a Union negotiator or the head of the Union's negotiating team. Except for agreements related to CFSP decisions where majority voting is employed, the Council decides by unanimity (see above). The Council adopts the decisions to sign and conclude the agreement on proposals issued by the negotiator without the involvement of the EP.
- *Procedural questions*: the Council acts by a simple majority.

Whereas the responsibility for taking decisions is clear-cut (the European Council and Council decide), the Treaty provisions on voting procedures in the Council are more complex (Art. 31 TEU). Some additional issues complicate the already intricate voting arrangements of basic rule (unanimity) and derogation (QMV) beyond those situations outlined above:

- *Constructive abstention*: when the Council acts unanimously, abstentions by member states do not prevent the adoption of decisions. However, if a member state qualifies its abstention by making a formal declaration, it is not obliged to apply the decision which otherwise binds the Union, although, 'in a spirit of mutual solidarity, the member state concerned shall refrain from any action likely to conflict with or impede Union action'. However, if the members of the Council qualifying their abstention in this way represent more than one-third of the votes, the decision cannot be adopted.
- *Limitations to QMV derogations*: QMV does not apply to decisions with military or defence implications. Furthermore, when QMV applies but a member state declares that, 'for vital and stated reasons of national policy', it intends to oppose the adoption of a decision taken by a qualified majority, the Council does not vote. In such cases, the High Representative must seek a solution. The Council may

refer the matter to the European Council for a decision by unanimity if that does not succeed.

This overview illustrates the highly constrained nature of CFSP and CSDP decision-making. The limitations on the use of QMV imply that member states can block any decision, regardless of the gradually broadened scope for majority voting.

This is also one of the reasons why additional procedural devices, designed to allow policy-making in cases where the EU cannot proceed as a whole, are established in the Treaties. *Enhanced cooperation* (Art. 20 TEU) provides for a cooperation of nine or more member states to make use of the institutions, procedures and mechanisms laid down by the TEU and the TFEU. As of early 2013, this procedure has not been applied to foreign policy issues. Enhanced cooperation may also be applied to CSDP, but it must contribute to furthering the objectives of the Union and has to be open at any time to all member states. The Treaty of Lisbon also allows for the possibility of *permanent structured cooperation* in the area of defence policies (Arts. 42(6) and 46 TEU). This is open to those member states, 'whose military capabilities fulfil higher criteria and which have made more binding commitments to one another in this area with a view to the most demanding missions'. However, member states seem reluctant to use this option. At their informal meeting of the defence ministers in Bruges in 2010, the member states agreed not to launch permanent structured cooperation for the time being (see Biscop 2008; Piris 2012: 75) (see Chapter 8).

Treaty provisions can thus be misleading and, in some cases, quite irrelevant. Enhanced cooperation and permanent structured cooperation are effective examples since they have not yet been applied to foreign, security and defence policy situations. In a similar vein, the Treaty provisions on the use of QMV are also de facto irrelevant. Practice shows consensual decision-making has remained the norm in CFSP. And, since the Council in fact does not vote on CFSP issues, the provisions on constructive abstention are not used either. Although these various procedures are yet to be used, they may still serve their purpose by potentially deterring member states to systematically block decision-making if a relevant group of member states wants to proceed.

One procedure provided for by the Treaties in Article 12 of the Council's internal 'Rules of Procedure' plays a pivotal role in EU decision-making. The Council can use the *simplified written procedure* (or *silence procedure*) under which a proposal is deemed adopted at the end of a specified time period, unless a member of the Council objects. The silence procedure through the COREU network (the *COREU silence procedure*), which can delimit reactions to 24 or 48 hours, allows the EU to take urgent or less important decisions without having to convene a meeting (see Bicchi 2011). In practice, this procedure is also of crucial importance in overcoming, or at least putting to one side, divergent views. Major divisions cannot be overcome in this way, but the silence procedure can help overcome less significant disagreements or allow isolated member states to 'silently' drop their resistance without losing face publicly. Countries can thus clearly formulate their critical remarks and objections to a proposed decision during a Council meeting without having either to block the decision or to be seen as publicly 'climbing down'.

This reflects a general tendency to avoid formal voting. During meetings (and in the corridors of *Justus Lipsius*), the High Representative as the chair of the Foreign Affairs Council, or the rotating Presidency in the other Council configurations are expected to sense when key member states, despite remaining critical or even opposed, will no longer formally object to the proposed initiative, document or decision. In such circumstances, at the end of the debate, the High Representative will formulate conclusions and announce to participants that a consensus is presumed to be crystallizing, indicating that the initiative, document or decision can be deemed to be adopted (with the absence of a formal vote allowing member states to disagree without explicitly having to block a decision).

The absence of formal voting, the large number of issues on the agenda and the fact that many member states are not particularly interested in a considerable number of these issues begins to explain why EU foreign policy-making, in contrast to what is often asserted, is not necessarily subject to the lowest common denominator, even in unanimity-ruled CFSP. The following section provides some additional arguments for this conclusion.

Policy-making in Practice

What do we learn about EU foreign policy if we adopt a *policy*-making perspective rather than a *decision*-making perspective? How can it be explained that the EU manages to develop foreign policy at all given the many potential blockages built into its decision-making systems? This section sheds light on some basic features of EU foreign policy and on the underlying dynamics that push EU foreign policy forward.

Basic features

EU foreign policy towards most issues is *multifaceted* and includes the whole range of instruments on the EU menu. When ministers, diplomats and civil servants really want to deliver action with regard to a specific country or crisis, their priority is not whether procedures or instruments from the CFSP/CSDP or from the EU's external action or internal policies with an external dimension are used. Although on paper the CFSP would seem to be the locus for EU foreign policy, in practice the greater availability of instruments, useful budget lines in other areas (such as development or ENP), and the relative autonomy and flexibility of the Commission in implementing EU policies and budgets mean the external action areas are more involved in foreign policy actions than one would expect from a purely institutional standpoint.

EU foreign policy-making is not only based on EU decisions, but also on *systematic cooperation between member states*, on their active support and on member states adopting complementary actions (see Chapter 7). In addition to defining general guidelines and adopting decisions, 'strengthening systematic cooperation between Member States in the conduct of policy' (Art. 25 TEU) is one of the central instruments of EU foreign policy-making. The statement that 'Member states shall support the Union's external and security policy actively' (Art. 24 TEU) is more than an optimistic treaty article. Support, particularly from those member states that can make a difference on specific policy dossiers, is often essential for EU action and success. And a lack of support can also explain the lack of success of EU foreign policy initiatives. Cooperation and coordination are also important components in non-CFSP policy domains such as development cooperation. Provisions on development cooperation explicitly state that the Union and member states shall coordinate their policies, shall consult each other on their aid programmes and may undertake joint action (Art. 210 TFEU).

As explained in Chapter 1, EU foreign policy-making is also part of a broader *multilevel and multi-locational foreign policy-making process*. Involvement in EU foreign policy-making entails numerous policy-making processes within the member states. These involve different sets of national actors and different procedures, leading to the usual tug of wars, requirements to coordinate, discussions about responsibilities and budgetary consequences of policy-making. At the same time, EU policy-making is also part of policy-making processes within a wider set of interlocking international organizations. A narrow focus on the EU's decision-making process might lead an observer to conclude that EU actors take the initiative, set the agenda and implement decisions. A governance perspective demonstrates, on the other hand, that other actors (governmental and non-governmental, international organizations and third states) are often at the root of the EU's policy actions and sometimes also take responsibility for the implementation of its policies. Moreover, to be effective, EU action will often require support or complementary actions from international organizations. Within this multilevel and multi-locational foreign policy-making process, the dividing lines between the national level, EU level and other international organizations are not always evident, because political leaders, diplomats and civil servants take part in the processes in different institutional settings (see Chapter 13).

Underlying dynamics

Given the complexity of decision-making procedures, the unanimity requirement in CFSP/CSDP, and the problems of a Council weighed down by too many participants, the real question is how the EU manages to make any foreign policy at all. The argument presented here is that three different political dynamics and related operational mechanisms provide the necessary steering to allow the EU to translate declaratory policy into action. Foreign policy is steered by the Commission, the EEAS, and forms of informal division of labour between the member states. Because of these complementary and often mutually reinforcing mechanisms, the EU has been able to develop a substantive foreign policy on certain concrete issues. Some explanation of these three dynamics and mechanisms is useful:

- *Commission-steered foreign policy*: the Commission has become increasingly involved in foreign policy issues through budgetary instruments, international agreements and partnerships, and horizontal foreign policy initiatives (like human rights and democracy, conflict prevention or institution-building). The Commission's position in EU foreign policy came under pressure with the rise of new CFSP/CSDP actors and instruments. Nevertheless, competences for the external action and the external dimension of internal policy's comprehensive foreign policy toolbox, together with the activism and relative autonomy of the Commission, explain the importance of Commission-steered foreign policy.
- *EEAS-steered foreign policy*: the gradual qualitative and quantitative reinforcement of common CFSP actors (mainly the EEAS, and with it also the High Representative, Special Representatives, EU Delegations and CSDP actors – see Chapter 3) has generated mechanisms for providing political steering and operational action in foreign policy dossiers. These actors are presumed to contribute and promote the definition of a common European interest and policy.
- *Foreign policy steered by informal division of labour*: on many foreign policy issues, political steering and operational action are provided by an informal, self-selected group of member states that take the lead in EU policy-making towards specific issues, typically where they have a particular interest or added value. They provide both the necessary impetus to EU policy and essential complementary actions, for instance, in other international organizations or with regard to dimensions that fall outside the realm of EU foreign policy. The role of informal core groups, contact groups or lead countries mirrors a broader process of specialization and division of labour between member states in an EU of 28. The result is a partial segmentation of EU foreign policy, with some member states, in conjunction

with the Commission and/or High Representative, in the driver's seat of specific EU foreign policy issues. Certain member states take more permanent leading roles, as is the case of the EU-3 on Iran, where the UK, France, Germany and the High Representative assume the reins for directing policy action. Other states fill this role in a rather temporary manner, as during the Orange Revolution in Ukraine in 2004, with the High Representative and the Polish and Lithuanian presidents taking the lead (see Hill 2011, Sepos 2010). Similar dynamics spur informal division of labour in the EU in the context of the EU's external environmental policy-making. Here, so-called 'lead negotiators' or 'lead countries' informally take up representation and coordination tasks under the umbrella of the rotating Presidency, the rationale being to get the right people (instead of member states or institutions) at the right place (Delreux and Van den Brande 2013) (see Chapter 13 and Box 13.1).

The dynamic provided by the three policy-steering mechanisms further supports the conclusion that, despite the unanimity rule, EU foreign policy-making is not necessarily subject to the lowest common denominator; instead, it has developed ways to overcome divergent views and interests. These 'coping mechanisms' also help overcome a hurdle that all too often hampers the development of a more active EU policy: the lack of interest of member states towards a specific issue (see Chapter 5).

Financing EU Foreign Policy

The complex system of competences, procedures and policy processes with regard to the *substance* of EU foreign policy is interrelated with an equally complex system of competences, procedures and processes with regard to the *funding* of EU foreign policy. Analysing these financial arrangements explains some of the restrictions the EU faces as a global actor and sheds light on the nature, scope and priorities of EU foreign policy.

The difficult debate on financing EU foreign policy is closely related to tensions between the institutions and between the different policy areas having an impact on foreign policy. In certain fields, member states do want an EU foreign policy financially underpinned by the EU budget. Yet they also want to retain control and protect the intergovernmental method from unwanted interference from the Commission and the EP. The latter attempts to use budgetary powers on non-CFSP issues as a lever to gain influence on the CFSP/CSDP and on the EU's external policies in general. Thus, it is not necessarily the effectiveness of the EU's foreign policy but the ramifications on the actors' power positions which often prevail in decisions on financing EU foreign policy.

This was most obvious in the preparatory stage of the set-up of the EEAS and the appointment of the High Representative. The EP used its budgetary authority to gain influence over an entity and an actor on which it otherwise had very little impact. And within his Commission, Commission President Barroso reshuffled responsibilities and budget lines from the newly appointed HR/VP to the commissioners and DGs responsible for Enlargement, ENP and Development in order to avoid a negative change in Commission control over certain substantial parts of the EU budget. Budgetary arm wrestling also occurs during the yearly budgetary negotiations as well as during the Multiannual Financial Framework negotiations, where the budget is set for a seven-year period.

The financing of EU foreign policy extends beyond the budgetary provisions analysed below. It is part of a complex multilevel and multi-location system. This implies that the funding of EU foreign policy activities not only occurs through the EU budget but also through national budgets, through common arrangements outside the EU budget (such as the European Development Fund for the ACP countries, or the Athena mechanism for CSDP operations with a military dimension), and through funding for other international organizations (such as the UN, the World Bank and NGOs).

Multiannual Financial Framework

Funding for the various strands of the EU's external action is brought together in Heading 4 of the EU's Financial Framework, the framework for 2014–20 entitled 'Global Europe'. Appropriations under other headings can also have potential foreign policy significance, such as those foreseen for the Galileo satellite system (€6 billion for 2014–20). For the 2014–20 period, €58.7 billion, or 6.1 per cent of the committed EU budget, has been devoted to the 'Global Europe' financing package, implying an increase for this heading of 3.3 per cent compared to the 2007–13 Financial Framework. This limited increase points to the future limitations of the EU to address the new foreign policy challenges it is facing, particularly in its southern neighbourhood (see Chapter 11).

Table 4.2 presents the Multiannual Financial Framework's provisions for a set of geographic and thematic instruments. With the exception of the CFSP budget, all of these financial instruments are aimed at supporting external action policies. This clearly indicates that the power of the purse lies with the EU's external action and not in the CFSP.

The following three geographic instruments constitute the financial basis of the EU's structural foreign policy and receive the lion's share of funds: more than €40 billion of the €58.7 billion in the 2014–20 Financial Framework:

- *The Instrument for Pre-Accession (IPA)* covers candidate countries for EU membership and potential candidate countries. It provides wide-ranging economic and financial assistance, and supports these countries in fulfilling the political and economic requirements of accession. In the Western Balkans, it also supports confidence-building programmes, stabilization, regional cooperation and institution-building (see Chapters 9 and 11). This instrument receives €10.5 billion in the 2014–20 period.

- *The European Neighbourhood Instrument (ENI)* – previously called the 'European Neighbourhood and Partnership Instrument' (ENPI) – covers countries targeted by the European Neighbourhood Policy: Eastern Europe, the South Caucasus and the Mediterranean. The ENI provides the financial backing for activities under the EU's bilateral agreements with these countries, and more specifically, focuses on supporting the implementation of the Action Plans adopted in the context of the European Neighbourhood Policy (see Chapter 11). This Instrument receives €13.6 billion in 2014–20.
- *The Development Cooperation Instrument (DCI)* covers developing countries and regions that are not eligible for assistance under the two previous instruments and that do not fall under the Cotonou Agreement. Accordingly, assistance to Asia, Central Asia, the Middle East, Latin America and South Africa is provided for under the DCI (see Chapter 9). It supports development cooperation, economic and financial cooperation and its main objectives are poverty reduction in the context of sustained development, democracy, good governance and support for human rights. Besides bilateral and regional cooperation, this instrument finances thematic programmes related to global public goods and challenges such as climate change, energy, migration and food security, as well as support for civil society organizations. The DCI receives 17.3 billion for the period 2014–20.

It is important to note that cooperation under the Cotonou Agreement with the ACP countries (sub-Sahara Africa, Caribbean and Pacific) is funded mainly through the European Development Fund (EDF), which does not fall under the Multiannual Financial Framework (see Chapter 9). The EDF is funded through separate contributions by member states; the eleventh EDF (for the period 2014–20) amounted to €29.1 billion. This is more than the IPA and the ENI combined and much more than the DCI, the EU's financial instrument for development aid for the rest of the world. The inclusion of the EDF in the Financial Framework would have contributed to the coherence of the EU's external action and would have partially removed a historically defined discrimination between developing countries. However, its 'budgetization' was rejected by the member states wanting to keep control of the EDF's purse strings.

The major thematic financial instruments foreseen in the Financial Framework receive almost one-third of funds for 2014–20 and have a global reach. These main instruments, primarily designed to respond to crisis situations, whether political, humanitarian or financial, are the Humanitarian Aid instrument, the European Instrument for Democracy and Human Rights (EIDHR), the Instrument for Stability (IfS), and the CFSP. As analysed in Chapter 6, the EIDHR and the Instrument for Stability, in particular, are used for foreign policy activities closely related to, or overlapping with, CFSP actions.

The main hurdle for the implementation of the EU's financial instruments are their limited operational flexibility and the difficulties of translating these financial instruments into considerable leverage and influence (see European Parliament 2011: 14). The flexibility problem is twofold. First, the rigidity, complexity and length of the financial programming processes, as well as the cumbersome procedures to implement policy measures, run counter to the flexibility and rapidity needed in foreign policy to respond to an external environment in constant fluctuation. Second, the EU has neither a financial reserve nor efficient flexibility mechanisms that allow it to respond adequately to major unforeseen international events or crises which require the deployment of substantial financial resources. The problem to exert real influence is, among other factors, related to the EU's dependency on other actors to implement policies and translate financial resources into action.

Though the EU pursues policies by funding other international organizations such as UN agencies or the World Bank, the EU generally does not retain the legal status, political leverage or the unity of voice to proportionately exert political steering of the implementation of the activities in these fora. Such is the case even when the EU is one of the main sponsors (see Chapter 13). Moreover, the EU's high standards for project management and financial reporting implies that, in general, only established international organizations, Western agencies, and NGOs and consultancies are able to implement EU programmes. When implementation in authoritarian countries is vital, the EU often de facto depends on government-controlled NGOs and agencies. Grass-roots organizations in third countries in most cases are not able to comply with the EU's sophisticated standards and procedures, which exclude them from EU funding and which runs counter to the EU goal of promoting and interacting with civil society (see Thépaut 2011).

In practice, a major part of the EU's funding under the IPA and ENI goes to private companies and consultancies paid to provide 'technical assistance' (i.e. expert advice to the third country concerned). This 'consultancy based foreign policy' means that the often substantial financial resources for third countries regularly end up in Western bank accounts and do not always lead to direct positive and visible effects in the target country. The dependency on other actors also leads to 'foreign policy by substitution' and 'foreign policy by subvention, subsidizing or funding', which further hampers the EU's ability to directly steer operational action and influence developments on the ground.

Table 4.2   Multiannual Financial Framework 2014–20 – 'Heading 4: Global Europe' (in € million)

Financial Instruments	2014	2015	2016	2017	2018	2019	2020	Total 2014–2020
Instrument for Pre-Accession (IPA)	1,511	1,511	1,511	1,511	1,511	1,511	1,510	10,576
European Neighbourhood Instrument (ENI)	1,991	1,873	1,888	1,918	1,953	2,013	2,047	13,683
Development Cooperation Instrument (DCI)	2,176	2,280	2,388	2,491	2,601	2,714	2,740	17,390
Partnership Instrument (PI)	107	110	114	119	125	132	136	844
European Instrument for Democracy and Human Rights (EIDHR)	169	169	169	169	169	169	169	1,183
Instrument for Stability (IfS)	296	296	296	297	297	297	297	2,075
Instrument for Nuclear Safety Cooperation	29	29	29	29	29	29	28	200
Humanitarian Aid	853	849	845	840	835	835	821	5,878
Macro-Financial Assistance	72	72	72	72	72	72	70	501
EVHAC	12	14	16	20	23	23	23	130
Common Foreign and Security Policy (CFSP)	296	296	296	297	297	297	297	2,075
Civil Protection Financial Instrument (CPFI)	18	18	18	18	18	18	18	128
Guarantee fund for external actions	55	222	247	177	155	136	71	1,063
Agencies	20	20	20	20	20	20	20	137
Other	114	114	160	114	114	114	112	841
Margin	135	211	211	286	336	386	436	2,000
Total	7,854	8,083	8,281	8,375	8,553	8,764	8,794	58,704

Source: European Commission (2013d).

The CFSP budget

CFSP and CSDP policies are funded through two different mechanisms, depending on whether they are civilian or military in nature (Art. 41 TEU). CFSP actions and CSDP operations of a civilian nature are generally financed through the CFSP budget, with the exception of the salaries of personnel seconded by member states to the operation, which are borne by those member states. The Financial Framework for 2014–20 foresees €2.0 billion for the CFSP, which amounts to merely 3.5 per cent of appropriations for Heading 4 ('Global Europe') and 0.2 per cent of the total EU budget. Compared to the other allocations in the Financial Framework, this sum looks paltry.

A closer look at the appropriations during one budgetary year is useful to gain more insight into the budgetary restrictions of the CFSP. In 2012, for example, the CFSP expenses were organized under four headings: crisis management operations, conflict prevention, resolution and stabilization, monitoring and security processes (€290 million); non-proliferation and disarmament (€17 million); preparatory and follow-up measures (€0.6 million); and EU Special Representatives (€28 million). The budgetary constraints are severe. For example, with the €290 million, 11 civilian CSDP missions are to be financed. Thus, the financial basis of many of these missions is extremely limited and their scope and impact will probably be likewise. The missions in Kosovo and Afghanistan have somewhat more breathing space with a budget of €111 million and €57 respectively, although the latter pales in significance beside both the Western military spending in Afghanistan and the immense security challenges in that country (Council 2013).

The limited budgetary allocation for CFSP points to one of the main paradoxes in member states' attitudes towards EU foreign policy. They prefer CFSP/CSDP as an arena through which to develop EU foreign policy, yet they are reluctant to endow the CFSP budget with the necessary resources for serious action. One explanation for this paradox relates to the fact that the CFSP budget is subject to the general budgetary procedures of the EU. Hence, political decisions on CFSP actions and civilian CSDP operations are adopted by the Council, but their budgetary dimension is determined through the Union's normal budgetary procedure in which the Council takes heed of the budgetary powers of the Commission and EP. This also implies that if appropriations in the CFSP budget are insufficient to finance Council decisions – which proves to be a recurrent problem – the EP's consent is required to obtain a supplementary budget or to transfer appropriations from other sections of the EU budget (on a Commission proposal). As member states try to avoid what they consider inappropriate parliamentary interference in CFSP, they generally opt for ad hoc solutions to finance CFSP actions or launch these actions with insufficient funding. That the normal budgetary procedures apply to CFSP/CSDP decisions also makes CFSP/CSDP subject to rather burdensome procedures and ill-equipped for crisis management operations that require rapid and flexible action (see also Sautter 2012).

A different financial mechanism applies to CSDP operations with military or defence implications. These are completely financed by member states, with the main burden falling on those countries participating in the military operation in question. Participating member states pay the costs of their operational contribution to a CSDP mission, though a limited number of common costs are financed through the Athena Mechanism (see EEAS 2012a). This mechanism is separate from the EU budget and is under the authority of a Special Committee composed of member state representatives. Although this system allows for swift funding once an agreement is reached, its major disadvantage is that each operation requires new ad hoc arrangements between participating member states. The EU's capacity to act thus hinges on whether a sufficient number of member states are willing to provide operational support (see Chapter 8).

Consistency

The EU's complex system of competences, institutions, decision-making procedures, policy-making processes and funding mechanisms cannot but lead to significant problems with regard to consistency. A lack of consistency in EU external policies is detrimental to the EU's capacity to present a coherent message in international politics and undermines its credibility as an international actor as well as its ability to achieve specific foreign policy goals. In fact, the issue of consistency does not relate to one problem, but a series of problems (see Cremona 2011; Duke 2011a; Gebhard 2011; Mayer 2013; Portela and Raube 2012):

- *Horizontal inconsistency*: refers to a lack of consistency between policies formulated across the EU's policy-making machine. Horizontal inconsistency can occur between the policies elaborated in CFSP/CSDP, external action policies (European Neighbourhood Policy, trade, development, human rights and democracy promotion, etc.) and the external dimension of internal policies (e.g. external energy policy).
- *Institutional inconsistency*: refers to areas of inconsistency in the different sites of elaboration of external policies, that is, the Council, the Commission and the EEAS. Based on the Treaty provisions, it is difficult to delineate the boundaries between the different components of the EU's external action/external dimension of internal policy and the corresponding responsibilities of the different institutions (Van Elsuwege 2010). Institutional inconsistency can also occur intra-institutionally: within institutions, policy-making communities work towards different goals, under different mandates and with different philosophies (cf. DG Trade and DG DEVCO in the Commission).
- *Vertical inconsistency*: refers to inconsistencies arising between policies agreed at the EU level and those pursued by member states nationally. The EU's foreign policy capabilities depend on member states' adherence to agreed foreign policy positions, and on the question whether they give substance to those positions. Hence, it requires member states' active support (diplomatically and operationally).

- *Interstate inconsistency*: this refers to inconsistency between the member states' different national foreign policies, irrespective of whether a policy line has been agreed a priori at the EU level. This not only undermines the effectiveness of foreign policy actions, but is also damaging to the EU's credibility as an international actor.

Remedying this multidimensional consistency issue is complicated by the fact that solving one part of the problem often aggravates the other. The EU has, however, taken some measures. Beginning with legal instruments and practices, Article 21(3) TEU contains a general prescription for consistency:

> The Union shall ensure consistency between the different areas of its external action and between these and its other policies. The Council and the Commission, assisted by the High Representative of the Union for Foreign Affairs and Security Policy, shall ensure that consistency and shall cooperate to that effect.

In Article 26(2) TEU, falling under the provisions on CFSP, we learn that 'the Council and the High Representative of the Union for Foreign Affairs and Security Policy shall ensure the unity, consistency and effectiveness of action by the Union'. Article 7 TFEU adds that 'the Union shall ensure consistency between its policies and activities, taking all of its objectives into account and in accordance with the principle of conferral of powers'. There is, however, a lack of systematic mechanisms to translate these provisions into practice, with inter-institutional turf battles still at play. The need for more consistency has been partially addressed by the promotion of a 'comprehensive approach' (see Chapter 6) and the introduction of 'Crisis Platforms'. These Crisis Platforms bring together all actors that are relevant for a specific crisis (including relevant EEAS bodies, CSDP actors and Commission DGs). However, they are only established on an ad hoc basis for specific crises (such as the crises in Syria, Mali/Sahel or Guinea-Bissau) and are indeed more a 'platform' to allow for bottom-up cooperation than a mechanism that fosters the development of an integrated policy in a systematic way (Blockmans 2012: 29–31).

Two caveats are often neglected in the political and academic discussion on consistency. First, consistency is in practice simply impossible. The EU, just like the member states, have to pursue a wide range of policy goals that are not always compatible, such as the objectives to pursue trade or energy interests and to promote human rights (see also Chapter 1). Second, consistency does not automatically translate into enhanced influence or effectiveness. The EU can have an increasingly consistent foreign policy, but the impact may be limited if the EU's consistent position is not followed by other major international actors, as has been the case with regard to human rights issues in the UN and the Human Rights Council (Gowan and Brantner 2008, 2010; Smith K. 2010a) (see also Chapter 13). Moreover, the EU can have a very consistent policy but nevertheless be completely ineffective if it has no bearing at all on the actual situation in the target country or region.

This last caveat is related to a widely neglected dimension of consistency: consistency between the EU and between the target country. Here, the principle of 'alignment' comes into play. Alignment proves to be a major principle in the field of development cooperation, but it is also relevant in foreign policy (OECD/DAC High Level Forum 2005). Transposed into the field of foreign policy, it implies that the effectiveness of foreign policy can increase when the EU takes into account the existing priorities, needs and contexts of the target country and when it – as best as possible – fits its measures within existing policies and institutional frameworks of the third country. This has to avoid a complete misfit between the actual situation on the ground and the EU's actions and priorities (Keukeleire and Justaert 2012).

Conclusion

Foreign policy is a highly complex policy field and it is not easy to subdivide its facets. Nevertheless, the EU has sought to do precisely this by distinguishing between CFSP, CSDP, external action and the external dimension of internal policies. Understanding the distribution of competences between the different institutions in the EU's foreign policy-making system is crucial to understanding both the processes at play in any particular foreign policy dossier and the broader foreign policy themes. These include repeated battles between different policy fields with an external dimension and between the EU level and the member state level. On paper, the decision-making processes appear unworkable. In practice, the EU's various foreign policy actors have developed ways to overcome the complexity and the bottlenecks. This also means that in practice foreign policy-making is rather different to that which might appear from reading the Treaties.

Chapter 5

EU Foreign Policy and National Foreign Policy

EU and member states' national foreign policies are interconnected and mutually influencing. EU foreign policy is not only developed within and across the CFSP/CSDP, the EU's external action and external dimension of internal policies, but also through interaction with the foreign policies of member states (see Chapter 1). National foreign policy actors also play an important and varying role in the EU's policy-making methods (see Chapters 3 and 4). Hence, to understand EU foreign policy, national foreign policies and national foreign policy actors must be examined too.

In the framework of this book, it is not possible to analyse the foreign policies of every member state (see Aggestam 2013; Baun and Marek 2013; Hadfield *et al.* 2014; Merlingen 2012: 98–114; Wong and Hill 2011). Rather, the focus here is on patterns, categories, problems and issues. We also give more attention to the 'Big 3' – France, the UK and Germany – since, as will become clear, these countries play a special role in EU foreign policy. This chapter is divided into three sections. First, we consider the impact of the nature of member state foreign policy-making systems on the EU level. Second, we discuss the constitutive elements of national foreign policy: power, interests and identity. This provides a more sophisticated understanding of the issues often considered to be major obstacles for EU foreign policy: member states' different interests and 'lack of political will', as well as differences in power, world-views and role definitions. Finally, we evaluate the various dimensions of the 'Europeanization' of national foreign policies.

Foreign Policy-making in the Member States

This section examines the design and functioning of member states' foreign policy-making systems and considers how this influences policy-making at the EU level.

The political level: member states' constitutional design

The constitutional design of member states influences the foreign policy process in the EU (Manners and Whitman 2000a: 252–7). Constitutional design determines the nature of government, the relationship between the head of state or government and other governmental actors (particularly the minister of foreign affairs), and the role of parliaments and subnational entities.

With the exception of the UK and France (at least in terms of presidential elections), all member states have a governmental system based on proportional representation electoral systems. The majority of member states also have coalition governments. As such, two, three or more political parties concurrently share power. In these countries, policy formation will be more complex, particularly when the head of state or government and foreign minister (and other relevant ministers) belong to different parties. Coordination and consultation between the various members of government is difficult enough. In coalition governments, this is further complicated by the fact that the different political parties might not only have diverging views on foreign policy, but are also in continuous competition to strengthen their positions vis-à-vis their coalition partners. This can have a negative impact on the effectiveness of national foreign policy-making and on the position and consistency of that member state within the EU.

The way in which the relationship between the head of state or government, the foreign minister and other members of government is organized in the various member states is very diverse. The distinctive position of the UK and France deserves special attention. Although the constitutional set-up in both countries is very different, they have similar patterns of strong leadership and clear hierarchy, with the French president and British prime minister (supported by their own cabinets and diplomatic advisers) reigning over foreign policy. Combined with the extensive foreign policy instruments and capabilities of both countries, this strong hierarchical pattern explains why the UK and France are key players in the EU's foreign policy process.

In the British system, the prime minister holds the foreign policy reins, with the prime minister's Cabinet Office rather than the Foreign Office functioning as the lead institution to coordinate foreign policy. As Forster (2000) argues, British foreign policy-making is characterized by a very informal but highly effective system of coordination between ministries and officials, which generates a unity of purpose in terms of objectives, and which is capable of rapid decision-making. The coordination system ensures that 'on routine matters, whenever the UK needs a policy on a foreign policy issue it has one, and that the policy is advanced consistently by ministers and officials in the various fora of the Union' as well as in NATO, the UN, bilateral relations and other contexts. Further, 'the speed with which officials operate also ensures the British are one of the first to set out a position', which delivers important negotiating benefits by establishing 'a posture which other member states must accommodate if an EU policy is to be acceptable to London' (Forster 2000: 50–1).

In the French presidential system, the President exercises a hierarchical form of authority, particularly pronounced when French vital interests are perceived to be at stake. There is a close and permanent interaction between all relevant foreign policy actors. As Blunden (2000: 28) puts it:

> Foreign policy is defined and conducted in almost permanent symbiosis between the Elysée and the Quai d'Orsay [the residences of the President and the Minister of Foreign Affairs]. It is not accurate to see the Presidency, the Prime Minister's Office, the Quai d'Orsay, the Ministry of Defence, the Ministry of Finance, as separate entities … In practice, the leaders of these institutions – ministers, secretaries general, directeurs de cabinet, counsellors, in all twenty or thirty people – are in uninterrupted contact between themselves.

Such levels of interaction combined with its extensive and strong administration allow France to be nearly always among the first member states to define its position in EU negotiations in detail.

This pattern of a highly centralized system and 'tightly focused horizontal coordination' distinguishes France and the UK from the other EU member states, including Germany (Manners and Whitman 2000a: 259). Although the overall coordination of German foreign policy is in the hands of the chancellor (Aggestam 2000: 68), German foreign and security policy is characterized by a more fragmented, less hierarchical system in which the chancellor does not wield the same power as his or her counterparts in London and Paris. The foreign minister generally comes from another political party, implying that he or she has both the opportunity and inclination to take a slightly more autonomous path. The relatively high autonomy of the German Foreign Ministry combined with the absence of characteristically strict coordination mechanisms of the Franco-British system explains why German diplomats often appear to have less elaborated positions in EU meetings than their British and French colleagues.

In most member states, the foreign minister is squeezed between a dominant head of state and an increasingly important set of 'internal' foreign policy actors. On the one hand, the president, chancellor or prime minister is increasingly involved in the EU framework, since the European Council now meets on average every two months (see Chapter 3), increasing their exposure to EU foreign policy decision-making. On the other hand, the foreign minister relies on specialized ministers to implement (and gradually also to adopt) EU foreign policy decisions. For example, the growing number of CSDP operations has made EU foreign policy more relevant on the international stage. However, for a foreign minister, this has the drawback of increasing his or her dependence on other ministers and ministries at home to implement and plan the operational components of these foreign policies: the Minister of Defence for military crisis management operations; of Internal Affairs and of Justice for civilian crisis management operations (where the intervention of police officers or lawyers is needed); and of Finance and/or Budget for both military and civilian missions (see Chapter 8). A foreign minister can promise a national contribution in the EU context, but to deliver, he or she requires the cooperation of colleagues in government. This can become problematic if these colleagues are not from the same party, if they have different priorities or approaches (not only in terms of substance, but also on the question of whether to use the EU framework) and particularly when the inevitable discussion arises as to who will foot the bill.

Finally, the constitutional set-up of a country also determines whether and to what extent other actors, such as sub-national governments and parliaments, play a role in foreign policy-making. Sub-national government in those countries with a federal state system (i.e. Germany, Belgium and Austria) can play a role in specific dossiers where the regions have clear economic interests to defend, or where there are different sensitivities and approaches in the regions. However, although the foreign policy competences of their sub-national entities may vary, the federal government remains the central actor in national foreign policy-making even in these countries.

Parliamentary oversight of foreign policy is rather weak in most member states, as the formal role foreseen for parliaments is constitutionally limited and as government whips and party headquarters seek to maintain tight control. The main exception to this rule is the case of the Nordic member states (Sweden, Denmark and Finland), where specialized parliamentary committees on foreign policy and EU affairs have a considerable impact. In other member states such as the UK, parliament becomes important where foreign policy decisions touch upon fundamental issues of geostrategic positioning and identity in the world (for example, whether or not to use power, or whether the Atlantic, UN or EU framework is preferable).

The diplomatic and bureaucratic level

There are major differences in the structure of foreign policy-making bureaucracies across member states. These cleavages include: centralization or autonomy in decision-making/implementation; levels of efficiency in functioning of lines of command; the role of presidential and/or ministerial staff and their cabinets; efficiency of horizontal coordination; and the amount of autonomy of ministries and of representatives in institutions (Manners and Whitman 2000a: 258–60). Additionally, there are the substantial differences in staff sizes and budgets available to national diplomacies (Emerson *et al.* 2011: 141–2). The divisions within Foreign Ministries between 'Europe', 'Bilateral relations' and 'Multilateral relations' departments can directly affect a member state's input into the EU foreign policy system. The division between CFSP/CSDP on the one hand and the EU's external action and external dimension of internal policies on the other hand is reflected in national bureaucratic systems. CFSP/CSDP issues are often tackled by 'Multilateral relations' departments, whereas external action and external dimension of internal policy issues are dealt with by 'Europe' departments or even other sectoral ministries. This complicates the capacity for a member state to develop a coherent or consistent position to represent at the EU level. Such divisions also have an influence on the extent to which decisions and consultations within EU meetings penetrate the member state's bureaucratic system. For example, it may influence whether national diplomats' interventions in the PSC or COREPER reflect the general views and commitments of all departments in a ministry, or mainly of those specifically dealing with the EU dossier.

While foreign ministers are becoming less prominent in EU foreign policy, their Foreign Ministries are being crowded out by the growing role of other ministries in foreign policy-making. The Foreign Ministry is no longer the 'gatekeeper' controlling information flows and preferences between the domestic and the European arena, but it is more like a 'boundary spanner', managing coordination or facilitating policy-making over permeable issue boundaries and multilayered policy arenas. Increasingly, even this role is being challenged (Hocking 2005: 9–11, 285).

Quantitative and organizational differences have a substantial impact on the contribution member states make to EU policy-making, with the large countries (particularly France and the UK) having a major advantage over other member states. The sheer number of issues discussed in EU meetings, as well as their increasingly operational character, prevents the bureaucracies of many member states from keeping up. Particularly in the case of intensive negotiations on a specific foreign policy decision with major operational implications, meetings are called in rapid succession and national delegations are expected to react quickly to new proposals. In these cases, it is often only the diplomatic services of the largest member states that can scrutinize all documents completely and prepare concrete amendments to these texts, providing them with a major advantage in the ensuing debate. Member states regularly have to choose which foreign policy issues they actively follow, as not all member states have an interest or the organizational capabilities to be active on all issues. This reinforces the tendency towards foreign policy-making steered by an informal division of labour in which not all member states actively participate (see Chapter 4).

Power, Interests and Identity of Member States

The constitutional set-up and foreign policy-making mechanisms of member states are a first set of factors determining a member state's position and input into the EU's foreign policy-making system. A second set of factors are the constituent parts of national foreign policy: power, interests, identity, strategic culture and political will.

Power and capabilities

The basic ingredients of power are geography, demography, economic power, military power and diplomatic power (Cline 1980). These factors are further qualified by less tangible components such as will and strategic culture. Table 5.1 provides a general overview of some of the basic ingredients of power of the member states.

One of the most interesting characteristics of the EU is the enormous diversity in terms of the power of the 28 member states and, particularly, the cleavage between the UK and France on the one hand and the rest of the member states on the other with regard to military power. This has major implications for foreign policy-making in the EU. To put it bluntly, member states that have nuclear weapons, hundreds of combat-capable aircraft, a fleet with strategic submarines, aircraft carriers, destroyers, frigates, military bases and personnel on other continents, veto power in the UN Security Council, and a major share in the world economy behave in a different way in international relations and react differently to international crises than member states that cannot rely on such components of power (see details in International Institute for Strategic Studies 2012). These differences in power and capabilities give rise to a different status in the world and, in the EU, to different foreign policy interests, objectives and ambitions, to different possible routes of intervention and to different 'responsibilities' and expectations both within the country in question and in third countries. Combined, these differences constitute a major obstacle to developing a common foreign policy within the EU.

Member states' diplomatic representations in third countries (for an overview, see Council 2012c: 10–19) are a further example of member states' diverging capabilities. As Table 5.2 demonstrates, the number of embassies a member state has varies from fewer than 10 (Malta and Luxembourg) to around 50 (countries like Hungary, Denmark and Portugal) and more than 110 (the UK, Germany and France). Member states' levels of representation in countries where the EU deploys CSDP operations illustrates quite well the challenges facing 'common' foreign policy: only three member states are represented in Niger, only six in the new state of South Sudan, and only 10 in DR Congo. Other countries with major relevance for EU foreign policy (such as Iraq), also have less

Table 5.1 Ingredients of power of the member states

Country (in order of population size)	Population (millions, 2011)[1]	GDP (€ billion, 2012)[1]	Exports (€ billion, 2013)[1]	Official Development Aid (€ million, 2011)[2]	Defence expenditure ($ million, 2012)[3]	Total active armed forces (2013)[3]
Germany	81.844	2,593	1,057.7	10,452	40,356	196,000
France	65.398	1,997	428.2	9,345	48,121	229,000
UK	62.990	1,750	361.3	9,881	64,080	166,000
Italy	60.821	1,580	375.9	3,050	23,631	181,000
Spain	46.196	1,063	220.1	3,067	11,782	136,000
Poland	38.538	370	134.6	300	8,640	96,000
Romania	21.356	136	45.0	118	2,176	71,000
Netherlands	16.730	602	474.9	4,698	10,439	37,000
Greece	11.291	209	22.8	238	7,616	144,000
Portugal	10.542	171	42.4	481	2,599	43,000
Belgium	11.041	370	342.4	2,014	4,771	33,000
Czech Republic	10.505	156	116.6	184	2,177	24,000
Hungary	9.958	100	80.6	101	1,029	27,000
Sweden	9.483	388	134.5	4,032	5,788	21,000
Austria	8.443	301	127.8	796	3,160	23,000
Bulgaria	7.327	38	20.2	35	666	31,000
Denmark	5.581	239	81.5	2,144	4,371	16,000
Slovakia	5.404	69	57.0	62	1,012	16,000
Finland	5.401	189	56.7	1,013	3,596	22,000
Ireland	4.583	159	91.2	650	1,131	9,000
Croatia	4.398	45	–	–	816	19,000
Lithuania	3.008	31	20.2	38	322	12,000
Latvia	2.042	20	5.5	14	259	5,000
Slovenia	2.055	36	25.0	45	568	8,000
Estonia	1.341	16	12.0	18	434	6,000
Cyprus	0.862	18	0.9	28	258	12,000
Luxembourg	0.525	43	15.6	297	258	1,000
Malta	0.416	6	3.2	14	52	2,000
TOTAL	503.680	12,650	4,353.8	53,115	250,108	1,586,000

Sources: [1] Eurostat (2012a); [2] Commission (2012a: 58); [3] International Institute for Strategic Studies (2013)

Table 5.2   Member states' embassies and Union Delegations in third countries (2012)

France	134	Portugal	53
EU delegation	128	Denmark	51
Germany	125	Hungary	50
UK	114	Finland	48
Italy	97	Croatia	40
Spain	93	Slovakia	39
Netherlands	83	Ireland	32
Romania	68	Cyprus	25
Sweden	64	Slovenia	22
Belgium	63	Lithuania	20
Poland	63	Latvia	15
Czech Rep.	58	Estonia	13
Greece	57	Malta	9
Austria	56	Luxembourg	7
Bulgaria	53		

Source: Council (2012c).

than half of the EU member states represented in their capitals. Thus, most EU member states do not have the extensive diplomatic network necessary to actively support EU foreign policy action in all relevant third countries, nor to feed deliberations in Brussels with input and expertise from diplomats in the field.

The variation in the number of embassies and the absence of many member states in a major part of the world emphasizes the potential importance of EU Delegations (see Chapter 3). The EU belongs to the 110+ league, emerging as one of the rare (nearly) omnipresent European actors. Yet, in a limited number of countries, the EU must rely on the member states. It has no delegation in North Korea, for example, nor in Iran and various Gulf states. In these cases, the EU's diplomatic representation is ensured by member states that represent the EU following a rotation principle (Council 2012c: 1–9).

Cleavages in power and capabilities partially explain why the EU is not a natural arena for foreign policy-making for the member states. The smaller and medium-sized member states fear that they will be dragged along in the largest member states' power games. Meanwhile, the largest states doubt the relevance of an EU composed of powerless member states with little capabilities to offer, yet which expect to have their say in the decision-making process. This is one of the reasons why the largest member states have a tendency to act bilaterally, trilaterally or in other restricted settings, in addition to or instead of actions undertaken within the EU context (see Chafer and Cumming 2011; Sepos 2010). The power position of the largest member states also implies that they have different interests to defend than other member states. These include, inter alia, permanent seats in the UN Security Council (UNSC, see Chapter 13) and nuclear status (for the UK and France); privileged political, economic and military relationships with third countries; and access to energy sources and raw materials in third markets. Larger member states' interest in maintaining or maximizing their power can make it more difficult and sometimes impossible to develop a common EU policy on related issues.

The impact of the difference in power of the member states on EU foreign policy-making should however be qualified. First, the EU sometimes relies on this greater power of its largest member states to act on the international scene. In the case of the CSDP, the largest member states are even indispensable. The UK and France are the only member states with military bases and a considerable number of troops in overseas territories or third countries in the framework of bilateral agreements (outside the context of UN, EU or NATO operations). Their external military reach proved essential for the EU to launch several crisis management operations. However, this military presence also facilitates autonomous French and British foreign policy action, and it explains why France and the UK do not always share the opinion of other member states that a multilateral framework and legitimation is necessary for military action.

Second, while the power gap between the largest and smallest EU member states may be glaring, the power gap between on the one hand the UK, France and Germany and on the other the US, Russia and increasingly China is equally glaring. Even the largest member states are not sufficiently powerful to unilaterally exert major influence. Even the largest EU member states need partnership and support from other international or European actors to overcome their limitations. Furthermore, even if the largest member states shoulder most of the burden, they sometimes need the wider label of EU foreign policy and the partnership of other EU countries to make foreign policy actions acceptable domestically and internationally.

Third, less powerful member states may nonetheless have specific assets to offer. For geographical or historical reasons, some member states have privileged contacts (political, economic and/or military) with specific countries in the world, which can be essential for EU initiatives. For example, the mediatory role played by the Polish and Lithuanian Presidents, in tandem with the High Representative, was pivotal in the peaceful resolution of the 2004 Ukrainian Orange Revolution. Likewise, for countries such as Spain, the Netherlands, Portugal or Belgium privileged relations with former colonies can be a major component of their power. Some smaller or medium-sized countries rely on less visible but equally important immaterial power assets. These can include a country's reputation as a mediator in peace negotiations, its position as a major donor of development aid, or its role as a provider of peacekeepers. The power of Sweden and Finland, for example, is in part built on such power assets. Despite their small populations of barely nine and five million respectively, these countries can punch above their weight on some foreign policy dossiers.

Interests

Interests, like power, shape member states' foreign policy. They also determine the input and position of a member state in the EU's foreign policy system. The divergence between member states' interests and the limited number of 'common interests' are often portrayed as major obstacles for EU foreign policy. However, these arguments frequently mask a more complex pattern of converging and diverging interests, as the following categorization demonstrates:

- *Collective interests*: member states share a set of fundamental and overarching interests, such as their interest in peace and welfare in Europe and its environs, the development of a rule-based international order, and the fight against global warming. There are two main characteristics of collective interests: no single country can pursue them alone and a country can profit from their realization without actively contributing or sharing the costs (the free-rider problem). Both features explain why working through the EU can be useful, or even necessary, for member states.
- *Common interests*: member states' interests converge with regard to specific issues, such as strengthening stability or promoting good governance in a specific country or region. An example is the common interest of all member states to stabilize the Western Balkans.
- *Interests converge but member states are competitors*: member states have the same interests, such as developing privileged political relations with third countries or obtaining contracts for national businesses, but compete for a limited number of opportunities. For example, one member state obtaining a contract to supply military aircraft to China might come at the expense of the commercial and geostrategic interests of other member states.
- *Interests diverge and are incompatible*: examples include the promotion of human rights and democracy in a third country such as Russia (combined with the willingness to put pressure on that country and to use sanctions) versus the economic interest of obtaining energy contracts in Russia and the geostrategic interest of obtaining its support in the UN Security Council.
- *Absence of interest*: although largely underestimated, in many cases it is not that member states' interests are opposed, but rather that they

simply lack interest in the foreign policy priorities of other member states. This may impede the development of the EU's foreign policy, but it can also stimulate the development of a foreign policy steered by an informal division of labour (see Chapter 4). The vast majority of member states is only interested in a limited range of countries, regions or issues, and is simply not interested in the rest of the world or the rest of the issues. Consequently, they do not feel the need for an EU foreign policy vis-à-vis those regions or aspects, but they neither strongly oppose an active EU policy when most member states are in favour.

Finally, in many cases where member states' positions diverge on a specific foreign policy issue, the main obstacle is not a divergence in interests per se. Rather, it is often a divergence in issues such as timing, prioritization of interests, choice of the most appropriate organizational setting (EU and/or NATO, for example), choice of methods and instruments to pursue interests, and determining acceptable costs and risks in pursuing interests.

World-view, role conception and identity

In addition to power and interests, a country's world-view and role conception also play a role in determining its input and position in the EU's foreign policy system. These issues are more difficult to grasp and define, but are closely tied up in a state's identity.

A *world-view* is the specific conception of 'how the world is or should be' which a state holds. It incorporates all the general assumptions about the nature of the international system and inter-human relations that act as a set of lenses through which the external environment is perceived. World-views are shaped by a variety of factors, such as historical experience, geographic position and the state's security situation. World-views provide a key to answering a range of fundamental questions: for example, the use of violence in international relations (and the conditions under which this is legitimate), the preferred world order and security architecture, or the relative importance of values such as human rights and democracy compared to the pursuit of economic profit and geostrategic gain. A member state's specific world-view also has an impact on where it will stand with regard to the main areas of tension in the development of EU foreign policy: Atlantic versus European integration, civilian versus military power, intergovernmental versus Community method (see Chapter 1).

Closely linked to a country's world-view is its understanding of its particular role within this context: its *role conception*. Role conceptions are self-defined by policy-makers and, more generally, by a nation or population. They refer to 'the general kinds of decisions, commitments, rules and actions suitable to their state, and of the functions, if any, their state should perform on a continuing basis in the international system or in subordinate regional systems' (Holsti 1970: 245–6). In conjunction with its world-view, a country's role conception indicates whether it identifies with specific values and objectives and whether it sees itself playing a particular role. Role conceptions define whether a country sees itself as, for example: a promoter of human rights and democracy; as a promoter of the free market economy; as an actor that accepts the use of violence and the risks of casualties; as a privileged partner of the US or as a 'friend' of Israel, of the Arab world, or of other countries or regions in the world.

World-views and role conceptions play an important function in providing a member state with the conceptual lenses through which foreign policy issues on the international and EU table are framed (see also Aggestam 2013). They also provide a general orientation through which to define a national position even if a member state is not interested in the specific matter and has no interests to defend. It is because they are closely related to a country's *identity* that differences in world-views and role conceptions can be considered obstacles that are more difficult to overcome in defining EU foreign policy than differences in interests. They are related to the core country characteristics by which political leaders and the public identify themselves, and they are difficult to compromise. This points to one of the crucial weaknesses of EU foreign policy: the lack of a sufficiently developed common European identity. As Hill and Wallace (1996: 8) remark: 'Effective foreign policy rests upon a shared sense of national identity, of a nation-state's "place in the world", its friends and enemies, its interests and aspirations. These underlying assumptions are embedded in national history and myths, changing slowly over time as political leaders reinterpret them and external and internal developments reshape them.' However, as changes in, for instance, France, Spain, Italy and Central and Eastern European countries over the last two decades demonstrate, a national role conception and world-view can vary over time and can also depend on the political leaders and parties in power.

Strategic culture and political will

Two further immaterial components, 'strategy' and 'will', play a role in shaping the foreign policy and the actual power of EU member states. *Strategy* is 'a plan of action designed in order to achieve some end; a purpose together with a system of measures for its accomplishment' (Baylis and Wirtz 2007: 5). A major obstacle for EU foreign policy is that many member states lack the strategic culture necessary to resolutely pursue a long-term foreign policy, to determine foreign policy and security goals, to develop and deploy policy instruments, and to accept the related costs. Meyer's (2004) study of European strategic culture looks at this issue from yet another angle: the problem is not the lack of strategic culture; the problem is one of too many different national strategic cultures and the absence of a 'common' strategic culture. However, national strategic cultures have been subject to several learning mechanisms (including changing threat perceptions and institutional socialization), which has given rise to opportunities for deeper cooperation in the field of crisis management (Meyer 2007, 2013).

Encouraged by the post-Lisbon institutional set-up, it seems that a strategic culture is gradually emerging in EU foreign policy, based on the quest for international legitimacy, local ownership, multilateralism, comprehensiveness, and increasingly integrated civilian and military instruments (Biava 2011; Biava *et al.* 2011). EU foreign policy towards the Western Balkans as well as more recent EU strategies such as towards the Horn of Africa and the Sahel region (see Chapters 6 and 8) indeed reveal that the EU member states are able to agree on plans of actions and measures to accomplish objectives (see also Schmidt and Zyla 2013).

Will refers to the degree of determination of the population as well as the political elite to implement a strategy and to accept the costs of this policy (Cline 1980: 22). The 'lack of political will' of member states is one of the most popular explanations for the failure of EU foreign policy. However, 'political will' is too often prescribed as the 'magic cure' to all the EU's foreign policy ills, while the 'lack of political will' has become a convenient excuse for practitioners and analysts not to further explore what actually lies behind the EU's problems.

Member states' 'lack of political will' might actually mean that they have different interests, or are, quite simply, just not interested. It can also reflect the different power positions of the member states and, as a result, their preference for non-EU venues to realize foreign policy goals. It can also point to the different world views or role conceptions which make action on the EU level difficult, even where there are no real disagreements about a specific foreign policy issue per se. In this latter case, the so-called 'lack of political will' can be broken down into several dimensions, each of which refers to other obstacles in creating a common foreign policy:

- *A general lack of will to strengthen the EU as an international actor*: the 'lack of political will' is not related to the issue at hand, but is the result of member states' reluctance or refusal to allow the EU to play a more active role on a particular issue and in foreign policy generally.
- *A lack of political will to play a more active role in foreign policy and to take the lead*: the problem is not the attitude of the member states towards the EU as such, but the fact that member states are unwilling or not used to taking the lead in international politics.
- *A lack of political will to accept costs and risks*: the problem is

member states' reluctance to accept the political, moral, budgetary and other costs linked to a more active and assertive EU foreign policy. In most member states, there is a particularly limited willingness to accept the risk of casualties in exchange for influence.

- *A lack of 'common' political will*: even where the will for the EU to undertake assertive external action does exist, it might be focused on different aspects of international politics or different courses of action. The problem is not the lack of political will, but the fact that there are too many *different* political wills.
- *A lack of 'public' will*: the amount of political will reflects public attitudes in the member states. Opinion polls point to EU-wide public support for a common foreign policy (61 per cent in favour and 28 per cent against) and, particularly, common security and defence policy (71 per cent in favour and 20 per cent against) (Commission 2012b: 72–4). Nonetheless, this common public support disappears when less abstract and more specific foreign policy issues are polled.

There are yet more dimensions to the 'political will' problem (Keukeleire 2006), but the conclusion is clear: the 'lack of political will', often considered as one of the main obstacles for an effective and active European foreign policy, actually refers to several kinds of obstacles. This also implies that solving the 'lack of political will' problem will be more challenging than just convincing the member states to make EU foreign policy more of a priority.

Europeanization

The relationship and interacting processes of foreign policy on the national level and foreign policy on the EU level are often labelled as 'Europeanization' – although 'EU-ization' would be a more correct term, given that 'Europe' is not synonymous with the 'EU' (see Chapter 1). Europeanization means different things to different people and can be conceptualized in various ways (see Alecu De Flers and Müller 2012; Moumoutzis 2011; Olsen 2002; Radaelli and Exadaktylos 2010; Wong 2011; Wong and Hill 2011). It can have a rational or a social understanding, with the former emphasizing interests, veto points and formal institutions, and the latter pointing to the importance of norms, rules and beliefs (see Börzel 2005). Generally, Europeanization refers to the following interrelated processes:

- *national adaptation* to the EU level, implying changes in national institutions, policy-making mechanisms, policies, values and identity;
- *national projection* of domestic foreign policy objectives and approaches onto the EU level;

- increasingly *pursuing foreign policy on the EU level* (in general or on specific issues);
- *EU export* of its institutions, norms and values beyond its territory and *embedding third countries* within these.

This last dimension is relevant for the analysis of the EU's structural foreign policy, its enlargement process and its relationships with its neighbours (see Chapters 9 and 11 and Box 9.1) (see also Börzel and Risse 2012b; Schimmelfennig and Sedelmeier 2005).

In the rest of this section we will focus on the first three 'Europeanization' processes outlined above as well as the related phenomenon of 'socialization'. Each of these processes demonstrates that Europeanization varies across member states and foreign policy issues. The nature and extent of Europeanization is different in each member state, depending on the nature of the member state, its size and its tradition of neutrality (Aggestam 2013; Alecu de Flers 2012; Jokela 2011a). Europeanization is also different for the Central and Eastern European member states (Baun and Marek 2013). Furthermore, Europeanization will be different when the foreign policy issue at stake is at the heart of international politics – such as the Middle East conflict (Müller 2012) or relations with Russia (David *et al.* 2013) – or considered less essential or interesting only to a small number of member states – such as the policies towards Latin America (Ruano 2012).

Important, too, is that, in addition to Europeanization processes, EU member states can also influence each other. Member states can project their foreign policy objectives onto other member states, or feel the need to adapt to the national foreign policies of other member states, independent of interactions at the EU level (see Wong and Hill 2011).

National adaptation – or modernization?

The process of national adaptation to the EU level involves several changes: first in national policy-making structures and processes; second in the world-view and identity which lie at the core of these national policies; and third in national foreign policies themselves.

National foreign policy structures and processes adapt to the EU context on both a political and bureaucratic level. Formal procedures, organizational practices and coordination mechanisms grow out of the need to continuously formulate 'national' positions as input into EU meetings and to react to the endless stream of policy documents. The balance of power and interaction between national players change as a result of the EU foreign policy context and the political opportunity structure created by this context. Examples of this include the growing role of heads of state and government and sectoral ministers and ministries for civilian crisis management operations, as discussed above.

Europeanization implies gradual changes in a national actor's world view, values and norms, role conception and identity. We should not overestimate this process as such immaterial dimensions are deeply rooted in a member state's domestic context. Nevertheless, gradual changes have been induced as well as facilitated by EU membership. This has been clear, for example, in the development of CSDP, which could only come about because of gradual rapprochement of the world views and role conceptions of the three largest member states and the neutral countries (see Chapter 8).

The actual contents of national policies change as a result of consultation, coordination and joint policy-making at the EU level. To a greater or lesser extent, member states do take common views and policies into account in domestic foreign policy positioning. Europeanization also leads to member states developing foreign policy on issues or countries on which they previously had no policy. This is true in terms of both geographical coverage and specific foreign policy issues or approaches. For example, in the vast majority of EU member states, the Horn of Africa would normally not figure on the foreign policy agenda, but most are now involved in the EU's policy towards that region (see Chapter 6). At the time of their accession, most member states that joined the EU in 2004 and 2007 had no real development policy. But, as a result of membership and their incorporation within the broad context of EU development policy, they have explored and developed this new policy domain (Horký and Lightfoot 2012). Another illustration is civilian crisis management, which is a relatively new foreign policy domain for most member states. This example also points, though, to the limitations of Europeanization processes, as CSDP did not lead to a Europeanization of crisis management in general (Gross 2009) (see also Chapter 8).

Europeanization has offered a way for former colonial powers, traditionally neutral countries and countries which historically have had to take into account specific sensitivities (such as Germany in view of the two world wars and the Holocaust) to overcome the legacy of constraining national foreign policies. Europeanization has helped governments overcome both domestic and external resistance to change. It has allowed member states to transport problematic topics from the national arena to the European arena in order to play down a particular national line or set of bilateral relations (for example, with former colonies). It has also given member states an opportunity to either hide or adopt policies that do not fit within the traditional contours of national foreign policy, such as the military dimensions of CSDP for the neutral countries. It is in this sense that Europeanization can often be understood as modernization, allowing or forcing member states to update their foreign policy.

National projection

The EU foreign policy context also strengthens national foreign policies, as it allows member states to project or 'upload' national foreign policy objectives, priorities and approaches to the EU level. Europeanization allows member states to pursue and even expand foreign policy objectives (in specific regions or with regard to specific themes) beyond those attainable with domestic capabilities. In so doing, a state has the added bonus of obtaining support (budgetary, diplomatically and economically) from the EU institutions and from other member states to pursue objectives more intensively and with a heightened potential impact.

Using the EU as a conduit for national foreign policy has also meant member states could develop a structural foreign policy which would have otherwise been beyond national reach. Germany, Poland and the Baltic countries (in relation to Eastern Europe) and Spain and France (in relation to the Mediterranean) are examples: the EU's policy has allowed these member states to punch above their weight in these regions. Other examples include: the UK and Italy successfully uploading their foreign policy towards Somalia and the Horn of Africa; France and Belgium with regard to the DR Congo and other African countries; Spain and Portugal's foreign policies towards Latin America; and Sweden and Finland with regard to civilian crisis management (see Chapters 6, 8 and 11). In 2004, the EU's new member states also lobbied for the countries of the South Caucasus to be included in the nascent European Neighbourhood Policy, reflecting their specific concerns about stability in their region. However, member states are not always successful in projecting their foreign policy objectives to the EU level or in obtaining a fully-fledged operational EU foreign policy instead of a merely declaratory policy. This also explains the frequent frustration of member states, and their subsequent attempts to find other fora or networks through which to project their foreign policy goals.

In short, Europeanization can amplify national power and national foreign policy. Hence, national foreign policy is not in retreat, but, rather, has found new opportunities through the EU. This explains one of the basic arguments discussed in Chapter 1: that the relationship between national and EU foreign policy can be a positive-sum game, with EU foreign policy complementing and even strengthening national foreign policies.

Europeanization and multilateralization

'Europeanization' is also used as a concept to label the process in which foreign policy is increasingly pursued at the EU level and not, or not only, at a national level. Manners and Whitman (2000b: 243) argued that it seems 'appropriate to suggest that the Member States conduct all but the most limited foreign policies objectives inside an EU context'. However, this statement needs some qualification.

Crucial issues, such as the coercive use of military force, are not at all Europeanized (see Chapters 6, 7 and 8). Moreover, while most foreign policy objectives may be pursued in an EU context, the subsequent policy achieved within this framework often does not go beyond the level of declaratory foreign policy or of contractual relations. In these cases, operational foreign policies are conducted in other international fora.

EU foreign policy is only one part of a broader multilevel and multi-location foreign policy, as foreign policy objectives are also pursued in other fora (see Chapter 1). Understood from this perspective, Europeanization is one dimension of a broader process of *multilateral-ization*, which today characterizes member state foreign policies. National foreign policy structures and mechanisms have not adapted to EU procedures, practices and norms alone. These same processes have occurred with regard to other international organizations and fora such as NATO, the UN or the G7/8/20.

As Chapter 13 explains, the EU is also subject to this process of multi-lateralization. The EU often aims to project its foreign policy objectives and approaches to other international organizations (see Jørgensen and Laatikainen 2013; Jørgensen *et al.* 2011); but it also has to adapt itself to and feels the impact of these international organizations (see Costa and Jørgensen 2012). Moreover, EU member states use other multilateral fora – and their sometimes relatively strong position within these fora – to indirectly influence the EU's foreign policy or to promote their own policy preferences.

Europeanization and socialization

Often associated with the Europeanization of national foreign policies is the phenomenon of socialization. Socialization refers to a process through which national officials attached to EU institutions in Brussels or that are closely involved in EU policy-making increasingly think in European rather than (solely) in national terms (see Beyers 2010). Socialization between ministers, diplomats and civil servants has been seen as playing a major role in shaping and changing not only the prac-tices and perceptions, but also the interests, values and identity of policy-makers. Socialization processes are also linked to the 'logic of appropriateness'. As a result of their involvement in the EU's foreign policy frameworks, national actors increasingly base their actions on an assessment of what is considered appropriate, legitimate or correct in a given context, and not uniquely on the realization of their national inter-est (see March and Olsen 1989; Breuer 2012).

However, the 'socialization effect' of Europeanization must be quali-fied. First, the impact of socialization is different in the various member states. With their larger administrations, their elaborate network of bilateral relations and their more active role in other international organizations, the impact of socialization is felt less strongly in France, the UK and Germany. Second, there is a clear difference in the socialization effect on, on the one hand, diplomats and civil servants whose business is closely related to EU policy-making, and, on the other hand, those with more limited or no involvement in EU networks and with a dominant focus on bilateral relations or on other multilateral fora. Moreover, each multilateral department in a Foreign Ministry is 'emotionally as well as bureaucratically attached to its multilateral client. Each serve[s] to feed back the views and interests of the client organization and of the nations which composed it into the national bureaucracy where they [compete] with the views and interests of the unilateralists and of other multilateralists' (Jørgensen 1997: 176). In other words, a part of national diplomacy and administration may be very well socialized within the EU context (such as the diplomats and officials at the Permanent Representations to the EU, or those from the capitals who frequently participate in Council working parties), but other actors involved in foreign policy making may be subject to other socialization processes and other logics of appropriateness – for example, within NATO, the UN or special bilateral relationships.

Conclusion

Within each of the policy-making methods analysed in Chapters 3 and 4, national foreign policy actors play an important but varied role, constituting one level of the EU's multilevel foreign policy system. The policy-making systems within member states and their power, interests and identity are important indicators of their overall importance and position in EU foreign policy-making. Particularly the UK, France and, to a lesser extent, Germany, play a dominant role. This goes in two directions: the largest member states provide crucial apparatus and relationships to make EU foreign policy operational, but if they do not agree upon a particular course of action, it is unlikely that this will ever see the light of day. The smaller member states can play a more prominent role when they can draw upon specific areas of expertise and relationships with third countries. The increasing segmentation of EU foreign policy – itself a pragmatic response to managing member states' different interests – provides space for smaller member states to have an impact in specific dossiers. This also indicates that the Europeanization process is interactive, with the member states 'uploading' their policies to the EU level, and the EU influencing member states' foreign policies.

Chapter 6

Key Issues in EU Foreign Policy

This chapter discusses four key issues of EU foreign policy: human rights, democracy and rule of law; conflict prevention, crisis management and peace-building; non-proliferation and control of arms exports; and the fight against terrorism. These four issues do not provide an exhaustive list of key priorities of EU foreign policy. However, by analysing these key issues, this chapter aims to clarify the scope and the substance of a range of EU's foreign policy actions in the areas of CFSP/CSDP, external action and the external dimension of internal policies. The foreign policy objectives of, for instance, trade policy, the EU's objective of sustainable development or its choice for multilateralism are discussed in other chapters (see respectively Chapters 9, 10 and 13). With regard to the four key issues discussed here, the chapter clarifies the range of instruments available and actors responsible and it assesses the EU's actions in the light of its declaratory objectives and external relevance.

Human Rights, Democracy, Rule of Law

The promotion of human rights, democracy and rule of law is both one of the main self-declared objectives of EU foreign policy and a constitutive element of the EU as a self-declared value-driven international actor. The very first provision devoted to the EU's external action and CFSP/CSDP in the EU Treaty (Art. 21 TEU) not only lists the consolidation and support of 'democracy, the rule of law, human rights and the principles of international law' as one of its main goals; it also identifies these as principles which have inspired the EU's own creation and development and which shall guide the Union's action on the international scene (see also Chapter 1).

Instruments

The EU has created four sets of instruments (toolboxes) for promoting the principles of democracy, human rights and rule of law in its foreign policy (see also Cardwell 2011).

The CFSP offers a first important toolbox (see Chapter 7). The bulk of CFSP declarations and diplomatic activities (both formal and informal demarches) are devoted to democracy, rule of law and, particularly, human rights issues. Specific human rights dialogues and consultations have been established with third countries, including major powers such as China, Russia and, less obviously, the US (in relation to the continued use of the death penalty in certain US states). Human rights and democracy are also prominent in CFSP positions that lead to sanctions against authoritarian regimes (see Chapter 9). Civilian crisis management operations increasingly focus on actively supporting the rule of law (see Chapter 8). In addition to actions aimed at third states, the EU also promotes the rule of law on a global scale through its actions in support of the International Criminal Court (ICC) and other international criminal tribunals (Alter 2012; Bekou and Chadwick 2011).

As the backbone of a more targeted EU human rights diplomacy within CFSP, the Council has adopted specific 'EU human rights guidelines' for a limited number of priority areas: the death penalty; torture and other cruel, inhuman or degrading treatment or punishment; rights of the child; children and armed conflict; the violence against and discrimination of women and girls; the protection of human-rights defenders in third countries; and the promotion of international humanitarian law. These guidelines provide EU representatives in the field with operational goals and tools to intensify initiatives in multilateral fora and in bilateral contacts, resulting in some intensive lobbying campaigns to promote specific human rights goals (Council 2009a; EEAS 2012b: 32–60). In addition to these priority areas, the EU has also developed policies treating other dimensions of democracy and human rights, including 'new' fields of concern such as the fight against prosecution based on sexual orientation (see overview in: EEAS 2012b: 61–118).

A second important toolbox consists of the political framework agreements with third countries, such as Association Agreements and Partnership and Cooperation Agreements, and the related geographic financial instruments (the ENPI/ENI, DCI and EDF) (see Chapters 4 and 9). These agreements generally include political conditionality in the form of human rights clauses as an 'essential element'. Non-compliance can lead to the suspension or termination of an agreement and of the related financial assistance. The agreements also provide for regular political dialogue in which human rights, rule of law and democracy feature on the agenda (Devuyst and Men 2012). In the framework of support for institution building and good governance, the ENPI and – to a lesser degree – the EDF and DCI include considerable funding for long-term structural political and legal reforms as well as for more targeted projects to promote human rights, rule of law and democracy.

Support through these large funding programmes has the disadvantage of lacking flexibility. They are also dependent on the consent of the third country's government regarding funded programmes. Whereas the latter may be positive in terms of ownership, it equally implies that the promotion of human rights and democracy becomes difficult or impossible in precisely those countries where it is most needed. Human rights clauses and political dialogue are similarly problematic; human rights clauses are rarely used to confront partners with violations of this 'essential element', and political dialogue is in some cases little more than a ritual (or is simply cancelled by the partner, as China did several times).

A third toolbox is more focused and flexible, allowing the EU to work directly with NGOs and international organizations rather than with governmental actors (see also the next section for the 'Instrument for Stability'). The *European Instrument for Democracy and Human Rights* (EIDHR), with an annual allocation of approximately €150 million, finances 'EU Election Observation Missions' (EU EOM) and smaller 'Election Expert Missions'. It equally supports international regimes that work on the protection of human rights, democracy and the rule of law (such as international criminal tribunals) as well as hundreds of (generally) small-scale projects aimed at strengthening civil society's role in promoting human rights and democratic reform (Commission 2010b, 2012c; EEAS 2012b: 26–9). Adopting such a 'grass-roots' approach has been understood to be valuable in terms of strengthening the indigenous basis for democracy and human rights in third countries. However, the limited scope and political relevance of most projects have at times made EU policy look more symbolic than substantive. This also explains why the degree of spill-over from EU-supported NGOs to broader human rights and democratic reform has in many cases been more limited than hoped (IMD 2005; Bicchi 2010).

As the EIDHR in principle does not support NGOs or opposition groups that adopt a confrontational approach, it could not be used as a lever to support people-power revolutions in Ukraine and Georgia in the early 2000s or more recently in the Mediterranean during the Arab uprising. The awareness of these limitations of EIDHR prompted the creation of two additional instruments to allow the EU to more actively support progress towards 'deep democracy' in the EU's neighbourhood: the *Civil Society Facility* and the *European Endowment for Democracy* (EED) (see also Chapter 11) (EEAS 2012b; HR/VP and Commission 2011: 2–5). The former is designed to provide funding to civil society in the EU's neighbourhood, including in countries where existing EU instruments cannot be used (such as Belarus). The latter is to advance political pluralism by supporting political parties and non-registered NGOs striving for democratic change, including in countries 'where repressive political regimes continue to stifle pluralism and diversity' (HR/VP and Commission 2011: 4). Notwithstanding this, questions remain on the EED's long-term financing and status as an independent foundation, leading to doubts about its potential to support pro-democracy actors more quickly, flexibly and audaciously (Richter and Leininger 2012: 1).

Certain internal policies with an external dimension constitute a fourth toolbox to support efforts towards improved human rights and democracy (see also Chapter 10). An example is the fight against the trafficking of human beings. For the period 2012 to 2016, the Commission's DG Home Affairs has taken the lead through legislative initiatives, operational action and the development of an *EU Strategy towards the Eradication of Trafficking in Human Beings* (EU 2012: 103–7; Commission 2012c).

Recognizing the need to use the various toolboxes more coherently and effectively and to adequately respond to the EU's mixed performance during the Arab uprising, in mid-2012 the Council adopted the *EU Strategic Framework and Action Plan on Human Rights and Democracy*, which incorporates nearly 100 actions in this field. The Council took up the commitment to promote human rights 'in all areas of its external action without exception', including trade and investment, development, energy, social policy, and the area of freedom, security and justice (Council 2012d). It nominated an EU Special Representative on Human Rights to increase visibility and effectiveness and to provide strategic oversight. Moreover, to complement this top-down approach with a bottom-up approach, a human rights specialist was appointed in each of the EU Delegations worldwide and tailor-made human rights strategies were developed for each country. Their aim was to account for realities on the ground and to overcome the EU's traditional 'one size fits all' approach (Council 2012d, 2012e).

From declarations to actions

Looking at the EU's extensive toolbox, the EU emerges as a foreign policy actor that is clearly able to exceed the declaratory level. In its relations with third countries, the EU possesses the instruments to use both rewards and coercion in order to induce third countries to uphold human rights, democracy and rule of law. As a major added-value to what most of the EU member states can provide for in their national foreign policy (see Chapter 5), the EU equally has the instruments to pursue an active structural foreign policy to promote these values and principles human rights, democracy and rule of law. Financial and technical assistance in the framework of association and other agreements, EIDHR funding, CSDP missions and other instruments allow the EU to provide tangible assistance on an operational level. This is quite essential in light of the complexity and practical hurdles that have to be overcome when pursuing protracted political, legal, institutional and other structural reforms (see Chapter 1).

Given the EU's comprehensive toolboxes for promoting the human rights, democracy and rule-of-law principles and objectives, the next question is to what extent the EU has also matched its actual commitments and attained tangible results. The annual reports on EU action in the field of human rights and democracy, which are hundreds of pages

---

Box 6.1   Normative power Europe

In an attempt to move the debate on the EU's international identity beyond the 'civilian power versus military power' opposition (see Chapter 1), Ian Manners in 2002 suggested that attention should be paid to the EU as a 'normative power'. First, this normative power refers to the EU's 'ability to shape conceptions of "normal" in international relations' (2002: 239). Second, because of its origin in the post-Second World War period, its hybrid political system and its constitutional focus on fundamental human rights, the EU is also predisposed to act in a normative way and to put a particular set of norms at the centre of its relations with other parts of the world. These norms include five 'core norms' (peace, liberty, democracy, rule of law, and human rights and fundamental freedoms) as well as four more contested 'minor norms' (social solidarity, anti-discrimination, sustainable development and good governance). Manners differentiates between various factors which, directly or indirectly, contribute to the EU's diffusion of norms. Based on a case study on the EU's role in the campaign for the abolition of the death penalty, he demonstrates how the EU increasingly exercises normative power 'as it seeks to redefine international norms in its own image' (2002: 252) and concludes that 'the ability to define what passes for "normal" in the world politics is, ultimately, the greatest power of all' (2002: 253).

The concept of normative power has become a central theme in the analysis of EU foreign policy. A considerable body of work has applied the concept to the EU's stance towards a multitude of geographic regions and thematic issues, with findings varying widely over regions and issues (see, among others, Aggestam 2008; Brummer 2009; Falkner 2007; Laïdi 2008; Nicolaïdis and Whitman 2013; Noutcheva 2009; Scheipers and Sicurelli 2008; Storey 2006; Whitman 2011). The concept has also been criticized: for being too ambiguous to serve as a basis for rigorous analysis (Forsberg 2011); for being a specific dimension of 'civilian power' rather than a truly separate concept (Diez 2005); for focusing too strongly on ideational factors and neglecting material factors and the impact of changing power relations on the global level (Hyde-Price 2006; Pollack 2012); or for taking too easily European or Western norms as a basis of the analysis (Cavatorta and Pace 2010a).

---

long, testify to the wide range of initiatives and activities in which the EU is engaged and where it actively promotes the values and goals defined in the Treaty (EEAS 2012b). It demonstrates that the EU in any case attempts to systematically present itself as a normative power, i.e. as a power that promotes adherence to values as 'normal' in international relations and that is also predisposed to act in a normative way (Manners 2002: 242, 2012; Whitman 2011; Nicolaïdis and Whitman 2013) (see Box 6.1).

A more detailed analysis, however, raises doubts about labelling the EU as a normative power. The EU's approach, actions and successes vary substantially across countries in the world, across different dimensions of human rights and rule-of-law policy, and across democracy promotion policies.

First, there is a great variation in the extent to which a third country's respect for human rights, democracy and rule of law is a defining factor for the EU's relationship with that country. For instance, failure to respect human rights and democracy resulted in sanctions and a refusal to maintain normal political and economic relations with Belarus, Cuba and – until 2012 – Myanmar. Similar failures temporarily affected relations with China and Uzbekistan, but contradictorily, it constituted no fundamental obstacle for the EU's relations with Saudi Arabia and other oil-exporting Gulf states, despite their very bad performance in the majority of human rights and democracy indicators (see Schumacher 2012). As Chapter 11 will show, the extent to which the EU actively provides support for structural reforms in the field of democracy, rule of law and human rights also differs greatly from region to region and country to country.

Second, when looking at the promotion of human rights and rule of law, it appears that the EU has been at the vanguard of several campaigns. Examples are the campaigns against the death penalty (Kissack 2012; Manners 2002) and against impunity of political leaders through the political and operational support for the ICC and other international criminal tribunals (Alter 2012; Bekou and Chadwick 2011). This reflects the EU's general activism in elaborating comprehensive international and UN human rights governance structures (see Wetzel 2011; Wouters *et al.* 2012a). The EU obtained some remarkable successes in these respects, though it has not always been able to gain support for its campaigns from some of its most important partners (such as the US), nor to effectively use the UN human rights governance system to actually promote greater human rights (Basu 2012; Brantner and Gowan 2008; Gowan and Brantner 2008, 2010; Smith K. 2010a) (see Chapter 13).

EU foreign policy does not show the same kind of activism with regard to all human rights issues. The fight against human trafficking and forced labour is an issue that has not received a high level of attention from most of the EU's foreign policy actors, even though DG Home Affairs in the Commission has been quite active in this field. However, with estimations of more than 20 million victims worldwide (including around 5 million victims of forced sexual exploitation), this 'slavery of our times' affects much more people than, for instance, the death penalty (Commission 2012c; ILO 2012). Moreover, the EU generally attaches greater importance to civil and political rights than to economic and social rights. Following the predominant Western perception on human rights, the EU considers poverty, including the resulting malnutrition, as well as maternal and infant mortality as a development problem – and not as 'the world's worst human rights crisis' (Khan 2009). This also explains why the EU barely recognizes, for instance, China's major achievements in the socio-economic field in comparison to the situation in other large countries like India (see Sen 2011; UN 2012a; Zhang C. 2012).

Third, the EU's approach also varies with regard to democracy promotion policies, which, in general, receives less attention than human rights policies. This reflects the fact that democracy – in contrast to human rights – is not enshrined as a principle of international law, which makes it harder to legitimize intervening in third countries to promote the democracy cause (Smith K. 2003: 123). A comparative study of the substance of the EU's democracy promotion illustrates that the EU not only focuses such efforts on elections in third countries, but it also adopts a rather broad perspective in promoting 'embedded democracy', which includes other aspects, such as civil and political rights, separation of powers, a functioning bureaucracy, an active civil society and socio-economic conditions conducive to democracy (Wetzel and Orbie 2011).

When looking at the results of democracy promotion, the conclusions are rather mixed. What is labelled democracy promotion in practice mostly aims at governance changes rather than democratization (Youngs 2010a: 12). The EU often prefers to highlight the goal of 'good governance' and 'rule of law'; these terms are often politically more acceptable to partner countries and they also further the EU's economic interests, creating a stable legal administrative and legal framework for trade relations and investments (see also Magen *et al.* 2009; Pech 2012). More fundamentally, case studies on the EU's global stance on democracy illuminate 'the lack of strong European commitment to supporting democracy as part of foreign policy ... and a growing disappointment on the part of reformers in nondemocratic states with the paucity of support they are offered by the EU' (Youngs 2010a: 5–6).

The EU's support for democratization processes was and is outspoken in its (enlargement) policy towards the (potential) candidate member states in Central Europe and the Western Balkans (see Chapters 9 and 11). However, the lack of genuine commitment and success is clear in the EU neighbourhood, where the positive spill-over expected from cooperation and assistance to human rights, rule of law and democratic reforms did not materialize, despite the multiplicity of instruments, funds and initiatives deployed. Even when third countries adopt rules with regard to democratic governance, compliance is often a problem (Freyburg *et al.* 2009). The EU has not marked many successes in its southern and eastern neighbourhoods. The situation in some of these countries remained as problematic as before (i.e. Belarus), and in other countries, the EU was not capable of helping consolidate democratic revolutions (i.e. Georgia and Ukraine). Moreover, the structural changes in some North African and Middle East countries have occurred not thanks to, but rather

despite the EU. The EU also proved to be reluctant to accept the consequences of democratic elections in its southern Mediterranean neighbourhood when these do not fit the EU's interests. This was the case with
the democratic election of Hamas in the Palestinian Territories in 2006
(which was not recognized by the EU) and other Islamic parties in the
Arab world in recent years (which only receive limited enthusiasm in the
EU) (for case studies, see Al-Fattal Eeckelaert 2013; Balfour 2012;
Cavatorta and Pace 2010a; Morlino and Sadurski 2010; Pace 2010; Pace
and Seeberg 2009; Peters 2012a; Youngs 2010b) (see also Chapter 11).

Challenges

The initiatives adopted to react to disappointing results (see above) may
increase the EU's focus and effectiveness on some points, but these initiatives can also contain the seeds of inevitable disillusionment, as they do
not change some of the basic parameters and conditions that contributed
to earlier failures. The EU faces several challenges in this regard.

First, promoting human rights, democracy and the rule of law is for
many member states not a high priority as an external policy objective,
but is primarily an identity or interrelational objective, where the goal is
to shape a distinct international identity for the EU as a values-driven
normative power (see Chapter 1). The mantra-like referral to these
consensus-generating values not only serves to underscore the EU's self-
comfortingly superior moral identity, it often also serves to mask deeper
disagreements on concrete foreign policy actions and interests among EU
member states and institutions.

Second, an important hurdle remains balancing the promotion of
human rights, rule of law and democracy and the pursuit of other important foreign policy objectives (see also Chapter 1). This explains why, for
instance, the promises to promote human rights 'in all areas of its external action without exception' and to achieve '360 degree' policy coherence (EU 2012: 30) is simply not feasible.

Third, in order to successfully promote structural transformations, the
EU also depends on governments in third countries. However, these
governments may become less inclined to follow the EU's recipes and
conditions, particularly in light of alternatives provided by other rising
powers in international politics (see Chapter 12). The EU's attempt to
concentrate more efforts on civil society in these countries is also plagued
with problems. EU support for civil society organizations (and for opposition forces) may be counterproductive, as these groups can either be
discredited in the eyes of the public or punished by the authoritarian
regimes (Richter and Leininger 2012). Moreover, the EU's definition and
ideal of 'civil society organizations' is not always concomitant with the
dominant societal groups or movements, which may be more nationalis-
tic (such as in the Western Balkans) or religion based (such as in the Arab

world) than the EU would hope for. This has been a problem particularly in the context of the EU's democracy promotion in the Middle East and North Africa, where the EU's focus on secular/liberal political parties and civil society and its inability to deal with the much more popular Islamic parties and movements in fact functioned as an obstacle to democratic reforms (Cavatorta 2009: 137; Pace 2010; Pace and Seeberg 2009).

Fourth, perhaps the most daunting challenge relates to the weakening legitimacy of democracy, rule of law and human rights as universal values – or, at least, of their predominance over other values. The legitimacy of the EU as a promoter of these values is also in decline. Both dimensions of legitimacy have been undermined by the involvement of EU member states in what has been labelled 'gun-point democracy' (the promotion of democracy through the use of military force, such as in Iraq or Libya) (Lokongo 2012). They were also weakened by the EU's and individual member states' 'double standards' or inconsistent applications of human rights and democracy standards (see Magen *et al.* 2009; Wetzel 2011). These 'double standards' take many shapes, including:

- different application of human rights, democracy and rule-of-law principles and objectives in the EU's relations with various countries;
- more importance attached to certain principles and objectives than to others, like the greater attention given to civil rights issues than to socio-economic rights and dignity;
- a reluctance to accept the consequences of these principles and objectives when it does not fit the EU's interests or concepts;
- a reluctance to also accept democracy in international organizations and accept the privileged positions of the Europeans being turned down (see Chapters 12 and 13).

It is in this context that the *EU Strategic Framework and Action Plan on Human Rights and Democracy*, even if it includes laudable measures, may be insufficient to tackle the EU's legitimacy problems and to provide the seeds for a human rights and democracy strategy for a 'post-Western world' (Dennison and Dworkin 2010).

Conflict Prevention, Crisis Management and Peace-building

European integration can itself be conceptualized as a long-term conflict prevention and peace-building project. Finding a structural solution for the long-standing enmity between European countries was at the heart of European integration from the start; and this is still evident in the ongoing accession talks with the Western Balkan countries (see Chapters 2 and 11).

The goal to 'preserve peace, prevent conflicts and strengthen international security' is one of the EU's formal foreign policy objectives (Art. 21(2) TEU). The EU has developed a policy to deal with various overlapping stages of the conflict cycle: conflict prevention, crisis management, peacemaking, peacekeeping, post-conflict stabilization and peacebuilding, with the latter essential for preventing a conflict from re-emerging. The toolbox available to the EU is spread over various policy domains, financial instruments and institutional actors. It allows the EU to adopt a comprehensive approach towards crises and conflicts, but it equally explains the complexity and (sometimes) the inconsistency of the EU's actions.

CFSP and CSDP

The diplomatic capacities provided by the CFSP are the EU's first major tool (see Chapter 7). A considerable part of the declarations and activities developed within the CFSP is related to defining the EU's position towards an actual or potential crisis and – to a lesser extent – undertaking concrete actions, actively contributing to the solution, and following up post-crisis. The HR/VP, EU Special Representatives and senior EEAS officials, often in close interaction with the member states, have been involved in crisis mediations, or have provided an EU contribution to international mediation efforts. Examples include crises in Georgia, Ukraine, Iran, the Middle East and, particularly, the Western Balkans. As is explained in Chapter 7, though, the EU is criticized for not being active enough in conflict prevention and crisis management, not only in other parts of the world but also in its neighbourhood (as was the case during the crises in Libya and Syria).

The EU's diplomatic activities can be underpinned via military and civilian crisis management operations conducted through the CSDP, involving the deployment of soldiers, police officers and judges from EU member states (see Chapter 8). CSDP missions can fulfil a variety of tasks: 'joint disarmament operations, humanitarian and rescue tasks, military advice and assistance tasks, conflict prevention and peace-keeping tasks, tasks of combat forces in crisis management, including peace-making and post-conflict stabilisation' (Art. 43(1) TEU). Through its CSDP operations, the EU is or was involved in crises in the Western Balkans, the South Caucasus, the Middle East, sub-Saharan Africa and Asia (see case studies in Blockmans *et al.* 2010; Gross and Juncos 2011). In view of the number, size and relevance of the missions, the EU prioritized crisis areas in Europe (particularly the Western Balkans) and Africa (initially mainly the DR Congo, later on, the Horn of Africa and the Sahel region).

The nature of the CSDP operations is assessed in more detail in Chapter 8, but two remarks are already useful in this context. First, only a limited number of missions were effective at short-term crisis management or conflict prevention. In these instances, the EU helped prevent further escalation of a conflict. Examples include Operations Artemis and EUFOR in DR Congo or the EU Monitoring Mission (EUMM) in Georgia. CSDP operations are rarely involved in high-risk crises or in active military interventions of combat forces in violent conflicts. Also CSDP's military crisis management operations in the Western Balkans began after peace agreements were signed and NATO forces stabilized the situation. The ongoing anti-piracy operation Atalanta in the Horn of Africa includes some limited use of force, but in a context in which European forces are clearly superior over the so-called pirates.

Second, a major part of the CSDP missions correspond to structural foreign policy. The EU aims to contribute to establishing security and rule-of-law structures over a longer term through several rule-of-law, security sector reform and capacity-building missions (see case studies in Dursun-Ozkanca and Vandemoortele 2012; Ekengren and Simons 2011). Examples include: the large EULEX Kosovo mission, which plays a leading role in establishing a justice, police and customs administration in Kosovo; the EUSEC DR Congo mission, which contributes to the army's structural reforms by aiding the census of troops and helping to set up a chain of payments; and EUCAP NESTOR, which assists states in the Horn of Africa to develop the capacity to control their territorial seas and enhance maritime security by improving the judiciary and coastal police forces.

Instrument for Stability (IfS) and African Peace Facility (APF)

Whereas the CSDP enables the EU to be involved directly in crises or conflicts, the Instrument for Stability (IfS) and the African Peace Facility (APF) allow the EU to support the intervention or mediation of other actors in crises and conflicts.

The IfS, launched in 2007, is considered complementary to geographically oriented instruments such as the EDF, ENPI and DCI, providing a financial basis for interventions when circumstances in a third country make normal cooperation and assistance impossible (Commission 2012d, 2012e; EEAS 2012c). The IfS is to strengthen the EU's capacity in two respects. First, with its short-term 'crisis response and preparedness' component, the IfS aims to contribute to conflict prevention and to post-conflict political stabilization. Three specific examples illustrate how the EU utilizes the IfS to reach this end: it deploys financial assistance for elections and civil society participation in the transition processes in Tunisia, Egypt and Libya; it made available financing for the reintegration of ex-militants in Nigeria; and the EU financially supported the establishment of a truth-and-reconciliation process in Colombia. Second, the IfS's long-term component provides a tool to handle global and trans-regional challenges with a security or stability dimension. It provided capacity-building support for fighting organized crime on cocaine routes in West Africa; it also supported capacity-building initiatives in the Sahel countries to respond to terrorist threats and to countries in the West Indian Ocean for countering piracy.

The IfS's budget for 2007–13 was around €2 billion, including around €1.5 billion for over 200 actions responding to crises and conflicts worldwide. A major feature of the IfS is that it finances activities of non-EU actors, such as UN agencies, other international organizations and NGOs. Foreign policy through IfS is thus foreign policy by substitution, and, essentially, the EU acts via its chequebook. This can reflect a lack of agreement or capacities within the EU to take up a more direct, active role. However, it can also indicate a sound assessment of other actors' legitimacy, which holds great potential in effectively dealing with some aspects of a crisis.

The wide range of (often) small projects scattered around the world leads to the criticism that the financial means are not really used strategically. However, more positively, it may also indicate that the EU is willing to contribute to 'preserve peace, prevent conflicts and strengthen international security' beyond the EU's immediate interest. Moreover, relatively small financial contributions can also provide the lever needed to allow relevant third parties to intervene and make a difference (see Gänzle 2012; Ricci 2010). A clearer strategic prioritization has emerged from the geographic pattern of IfS spending since 2011, and currently the Middle East, Northern Africa and sub-Saharan Africa are prioritized, taking up around three-quarters of the budget for crisis response.

The African Peace Facility (APF) is a key instrument for implementing the Africa–EU Partnership on Peace and Security (see also Chapter 11). It is designed to provide the African Union (AU) and other African regional organizations with resources to mediate crises and to mount effective peacemaking and peacekeeping operations. Since its creation in 2004, more than €1 billion has been channelled through this instrument, with the largest part devoted to financial support for African-led peace operations (mainly in Somalia). Funding is also provided for developing management capacities of the AU and other subregional organizations in the context of the African Peace and Security Architecture, which fits within the APF's focus on empowerment and long-term capacity-building (Commission 2012f; see Brosig 2011; Mangala 2013).

Mainstream long-term instruments

Finally, the EU's mainstream long-term development and cooperation programmes – and the related financial instruments – are employed for crisis management and peace-building. They can underpin diplomatic

initiatives to defuse a crisis or can foster stability during periods of political transition. The EU's sanctions and conditionality instruments can be
employed to discourage or encourage actors in crisis or post-crisis situations (see Chapter 9). The advantage of instruments such as the ENP and
the EDF are the significant means at their disposal. The disadvantages are
their limited flexibility, which explains why more flexible tools such as
the IfS and the APF have been created.

More importantly, the array of association agreements, partnerships
and other agreements as well as the related budgets allow the EU to
contribute to long-term peace-building processes and to structural
reforms in conflict-prone regions (see Chapter 9). Nonetheless, as will be
explained in more detail in Chapter 11, such a structural foreign policy
and peace-building process has only been successful in a limited number
of regions. Positive changes were registered in the Western Balkans, for
example, but were not achieved in other parts of the EU neighbourhood
and beyond. Furthermore, the EU may have relied excessively on positive
spillover from cooperation programmes, development policy and democracy promotion efforts to achieve the conditions necessary for peace and
structural reforms.

The EU's comprehensive approach

Taken together, the EU has quite an impressive toolbox to deal with
crisis management and peace-building, even though this toolbox is less
impressive for conflict prevention. Practice has proved the EU to be capable of using a variety of instruments to deal with crises and conflicts. One
policy instrument and approach, though, remains outside the reach of
the EU: the use of unilateral coercive military force without the consent
of the actors involved in the conflict area. This also explains why EU
actions, even if relevant and effective, may be doomed to remain outside
the public eye, as, in general, it is not actively involved in forceful military
actions such as those in Libya, Iraq or Afghanistan that garner extreme
media attention.

The added value of the EU was described in a UK House of Lords'
report: its strength lays in operating smaller-scale, complex interventions
where a mix of political weight, economic know-how, development,
security sector training and sometimes a military capacity is needed. This
is identified in the report as the 'right niche' or 'niche role' for the EU,
accepted by all member states and other international actors. The report
equally points to the EU's complementarity to NATO: through its
comprehensive approach, the EU can 'tackle problems by providing for
the overall requirements of a situation in a way that NATO could not'.
Moreover, it can operate 'in geographical areas where NATO involvement was not welcome, or not appropriate' (House of Lords 2012:
36–7).

Recalling the analysis in Chapters 3 and 4, it is clear that a coordinated and consistent use of the various policy instruments is not all easy. The institutional fragmentation becomes obvious if considering CSDP, IfS and APF: CSDP missions are managed by the EEAS, but depend on contributions from and coordination with member states; IFS projects are politically steered through the EEAS, but managed by the Commission's Foreign Policy Instrument Service; and APF-supported missions are decided on and managed by the Commission's DG DEVCO.

Box 6.2   The EU Strategy on the Sahel Region

In order to coherently address a whole range of challenges – including weak governance systems, systemic poverty, food shortage, the rise of Jihadist movements, organized crime, drugs and weapon trafficking – that plagues the Sahel region and indirectly also threatens the EU's security, the EU endorsed in 2011 the 'Strategy for Security and Development in the Sahel' which focuses primarily on Mauritania, Mali and Niger (Council 2011c; EEAS 2013d). The Strategy aims at developing a comprehensive EU engagement around the key objectives of development and good governance, political action, security and rule of law and the fight against extremism and radicalization.

The comprehensive approach implies the use of the various tools at the EU's disposal. A wide range of programs is managed by the Commission under various financial instruments, such as development aid through the EDF, humanitarian aid, IfS financed capacity-building projects to counter terrorism and organized crime, and APF funding for the African-led military mission in Mali. Taken together, the EU's financial support to the Sahel region amounted to 1.2 billion up to 2013 (Helly 2013: 72). However, counterbalanced against the achievements of the EU in the region, this raises questions about the effective use of these sources.

Both civilian and military CSDP instruments are used in the Sahel region. The civilian CSDP mission EUCAP Sahel Niger – with 500 staff, including mainly civilian but also some military experts – was launched in 2012 to improve the capacities of the Nigerien Security Forces to fight terrorism and organized crime. Following the collapse of the security structures in neighbouring Mali and in the wake of military intervention by France in early 2013 (see Chapter 8), the EU launched its military training mission EUTM Mali, to help the Malian authorities to restore state authority and fight against terrorism and organized crime. In 2013, the EU decided to launch a third CSDP action in the region: a capacity-building mission in Libya in the field of border management (EUBAM Libya), in order to tackle the negative consequences of the porous Libyan southern borders after the collapse of the Gaddafi regime, with arms smuggling and other illegal trafficking having a negative impact on the security situation in the Sahel, Northern Africa and in this way also Europe (EEAS 2013c).

Negotiations before and after the entry into force of the Lisbon Treaty demonstrated that member states and EU institutions considered central-ized authority and management under control of the HR/VP and EEAS to be neither acceptable nor feasible. To compensate for the lack of such centralized authority, a 'comprehensive approach' is put forward by the EU as an attempt to find synergies and overcome both fragmentation and uncoordinated action (see also Johannsen 2011). Rather than through a grand strategy with explicit top-down interventions or decisions, syner-gies are to be found between the various policy actors and instruments on a case-by-case basis and through a bottom-up approach, with the system of 'Crisis Platforms' contributing to finding such synergies (see Chapter 4) (Blockmans 2012: 29–31; Keukeleire and Raube 2013). Examples of how this comprehensive approach can work in practice are the EU Strategy on the Sahel Region (see Box 6.2) and the EU's Strategy for the Horn of Africa (see also Box 8.1).

Non-Proliferation and Control of Arms Export

Since the establishment of CFSP, the EU has had in place a non-prolifer-ation policy with both a structural foreign policy component that bolsters the various international non-proliferation regimes, and a rela-tional foreign policy component that deals with countries that pose a threat in terms of nuclear proliferation. However, the EU's policy suffered from the outset due to member states' widely diverging views about the role of nuclear deterrence, with the UK and France as nuclear powers on one side and the rest of the member states on the other. Particularly the EU's northern and 'neutral' member states actively promoted nuclear disarmament, thereby countering the UK and France. This cleavage within the EU explains why, during Nuclear Non-Proliferation Treaty (NPT) Review Conferences, the EU adopted a common position and exerted some influence on a major part of the agenda, but remained divided on the high-profile issue of nuclear disar-mament in general (see Dee 2012).

The questions of how to tackle concrete nuclear proliferation chal-lenges – mainly the nuclear capabilities and ambitions of Iraq, Iran and North Korea – and the necessary mix of diplomacy, sanctions and use of force sparked varying answers within the EU (Cottey 2013: 186–91; Rhode 2010: 162–75; Quille 2013). The 2003 pre-emptive military oper-ation against the regime of Saddam Hussein in Iraq led to the deepest crisis CFSP has ever suffered, with the UK and the France–Germany duo having led the two antagonist camps within the EU. In contrast, the three countries together with the High Representative are working closely together in their intensive, yet unsuccessful diplomatic efforts to deal with Iran's nuclear ambitions in the E3+3 talks with that country.

Nonetheless, cleavages may again appear when the military option returns to the fore (Posch 2013) (see also Chapters 7 and 11). Although the EU participates in the international sanctions against North Korea, it is a rather marginal diplomatic player on this issue. Neither the EU nor individual European member states participate in the Six-Party Talks with North Korea. Beyond those three major non-proliferation cases, the EU remains silent on the possession of nuclear weapons by other states such as Israel and Pakistan, despite their clear impact on regional conflicts.

The EU faces a serious credibility problem as it pressures third countries to sign and respect the NPT, to renounce their nuclear ambitions and to accept non-proliferation provisions in contractual relations with the EU, while the UK and France refuse to forfeit their own nuclear privileges. This reinforces criticism of EU double standards. But perhaps the most important weakness the EU and its nuclear powers face in terms of power politics is that, unlike the US, they are unable to provide credible security guarantees to third countries, which often pursue nuclear capability as an answer to their precarious security situation.

In addition to nuclear-specific security concerns, the EU has also developed a wider *EU Strategy against the Proliferation of Weapons of Mass Destruction* in the wake of the various terrorist attacks in the early 2000s (European Council 2003b). This strategy incorporated an awareness of threats beyond nuclear weapons, including the proliferation of biological, toxin, radiological and chemical weapons and ballistic missiles, acknowledging the various concrete threats these weapons pose to European security (see Cottey 2013: 176–81). The strategy is implemented through the same kinds of tools discussed in previous sections: decisions and instruments of the CFSP, of the EU's external action as well as of other internal policies with an external dimension. These include addressing non-proliferation through political dialogue meetings and informal contacts with third countries, support through the IfS, economic sanctions, and financial and technical assistance to comply with international non-proliferation agreements (Council 2010b, 2012f; Cottey 2013: 175–201; Zwolski 2011). Another instrument the EU introduced is the inclusion of non-proliferation clauses as 'essential elements' of bilateral agreements, which commit the EU and its partner to fully comply with all existing non-proliferation obligations (Grip 2009: 3; Quille 2013) (see also Chapter 9).

The EU's *Strategy to Combat Illicit Accumulation and Trafficking of Small Arms and Light Weapons* provides a platform for addressing yet another type of arms proliferation (Council 2006). This followed from the EU's experiences in the Western Balkans, where arms trafficking remained a major source of instability. Demand for such a policy also stemmed from the awareness of the consequences of such weapons falling into the hands of non-state actors and fuelling violent conflicts. Several of the instruments mentioned above have been used to implement this Strategy, including financial support from the IfS and CFSP budget. The EU has also worked to developed national, regional and global mechanisms to counter the spread of small arms and light weapons (SALW). Most notably, it has mounted an active campaign in favour of the 2013 Arms Trade Treaty (ATT), which is the first legally binding instrument establishing international standards for the transfer of conventional weapons (Council 2012g). While the EU has been a strong and visible proponent of the creation of the ATT, its advocacy was occasionally marred by internal differences, as exemplified by the failure to agree on a Council decision stipulating guidelines for negotiating the ATT on matters related to the CFSP (Depauw 2012). EU policy was criticized too. The often-limited financial resources for SALW projects made these efforts often more symbolic than substantive. More fundamentally, these policies only scratched the surface and ignored France, Germany, the UK and other member states' role as large worldwide weapons exporters (SIPRI 2012; Andersson 2013).

The EU has dealt with problem of weapon exports since its 1998 *Code of Conduct on Arms Exports*, which was replaced in 2008 by the *Common Position defining common rules governing control of exports of military technology and equipment* (Council 2008, 2011d). These initiatives had a positive effect on the gradual development of a common approach, increasing transparency and defining more stringent criteria for arms exports. However, they still leave application of criteria established in these agreements to the discretion of member states who, on a case-by-case basis, decide to transfer or deny the transfer of military technology and equipment to a third country. Both guiding documents mirror the delicate and difficult balance between security, human rights and non-proliferation concerns on the one hand, and the predominantly geostrategic, commercial and industrial interests on the other (see Bailes and Depauw 2011) (see also Chapter 8).

Remaining flaws in the Code of Conduct surfaced during the violent clashes of the Arab uprisings, where anti-riot guns and other weapons exported from the UK, Italy and Belgium were used by the authoritarian regimes in Libya and Bahrain to suppress protests (Bromley 2012). This was striking in light of the member states' commitment in the 2008 Common Position that they shall, 'deny an export licence if there is a clear risk that the military technology or equipment to be exported might be used for internal repression' (Council 2011d). Hence, the EU's policy did not fundamentally alter the fact that not only a significant proportion of illicitly trafficked weapons are 'Made in the EU', but a major part of weapons sold legally to authoritarian regimes are also EU manufactured (see Chapter 8).

The Fight against Terrorism

The close relationship between external and internal security both within the EU and within third countries (see also Chapter 10) has turned the fight against terrorism into another priority area for EU foreign policy (see Argomaniz and Rees 2013; Cottey 2013: 202–27; Ferreira-Pereira and Martins 2012; Inkster 2010). Although in the wake of the terrorist attacks against the US in September 2001 the EU treated terrorism more as an international problem, the Madrid (2004) and London (2005) bombings were an abrupt realization that 'home-grown' terrorism was equally on the agenda. The existence of 'sleeper cells' within the EU, composed of EU citizens or legal residents but trained abroad in 'failed' or 'fragile' states and belonging to loose international terrorist networks, threw up a new array of challenges relating to issues as diverse as the integration of immigrant communities and foreign policy choices. However, the majority of instruments for countering terrorism lied with the member states, not with the EU. Protecting its population is one of the core *raisons d'être* of the state, and tools to handle the terrorist threats, including intelligence, judicial and law enforcement systems, go to the very heart of national sovereignty. This also explains why the EU's counter-terrorism policy was always considered a complement to national efforts. Moreover, EU member states indicated different perceptions about the nature of terrorism, the urgency to deal with it and the need to tackle this issue at the EU level (Coolsaet 2010: 872–3).

The 9/11 attacks on the US and the bombings in Madrid and London precipitated a burst of activity at the EU level, with agreements reached on issues where divergence had previously proved insurmountable (see Argomaniz 2011; O'Neill 2012). At the institutional level, a Council Working Party on Terrorism was established, Europol and Eurojust were strengthened, and the position of Counter-Terrorism Coordinator was created, albeit with only limited powers and resources to act effectively. In terms of policy, following the 2001 *EU Action Plan on combating terrorism*, the EU adopted a *Counter-Terrorism Strategy* in 2005 composed of four strands: prevention (tackling the factors or root causes which can lead to radicalization and recruitment); protection (protecting citizens and infrastructure and reducing vulnerability, including through heightened border controls and security measures); pursue (pursuing, investigating and prosecuting terrorists transnationally and impeding terrorist attack by disrupting support networks, funding sources, travel, etc.); and response (managing and minimizing the consequences of terrorist attack) (Council 2005, 2011e). The Action Plan and Strategy were at the basis of a broad range of measures taken by the EU during the following decade. Furthermore, the EU adopted new legislative measures including a common definition of terrorism, a list of terrorist organizations, an EU-wide arrest warrant, rules for joint operations between national police forces, and legislation against money laundering and asset seizure.

As the list above indicates, the largest part of the EU's response to terrorism has been internal. However, many of these measures also require international cooperation. Counter-terrorism therefore became incorporated across the whole gamut of the EU's relations with third parties and also gradually became a strategic priority of EU foreign policy (Argomaniz 2011: 94–5; MacKenzie 2010). In line with its professed 'choice for multilateralism' (see Chapter 13), the EU has actively sought to develop cooperation in international fora. It has thrown its weight behind the adoption of the 2005 UN Convention for the Suppression of Acts of Nuclear Terrorism and the 2006 UN Global Counter-Terrorism Strategy; contributed to the sanctions regime against Al-Qaeda and other terrorist organizations; encouraged third countries to ratify and implement the existing anti-terrorism related UN Conventions; and supported international initiatives, including those constructed under other non-proliferation regimes (see previous section). One of the main motivations behind the increased cooperation in the field of non-proliferation was precisely to limit the chance that chemical, biological, nuclear and other dangerous materials would fall into the hands of terrorist or criminal groups.

The EU has equally attempted to streamline cooperation against terrorism in its foreign policy towards other countries. It included counter-terrorism clauses in agreements with third countries; initiated political dialogues on counter-terrorism; and provided support to third countries in the fight against terrorism, including through capacity-building initiatives financed through the IfS (see previous section). A major part of the aid was directed to Pakistan, the Sahel States, Yemen and the countries of the Horn of Africa (Coolsaet 2010: 871). Counter-terrorism assistance was often linked to support for the fight against international crime in general, as transnational terrorism and various forms of organized crime are often closely related (see Marsh and Rees 2012: 18–34; Commission 2012d) (see Chapter 10). Despite these initiatives, the EU has received criticism for the limited reach, funding and effectiveness of these various measures, and counter-terror clauses have also been criticized for having a purely rhetorical significance (Argomaniz 2011: 94–5). Such criticisms expose not only the often limited interest of and cooperation by the third country, but also the fact that the 'serious' counter-terror cooperation and information exchange occurred often not between the EU and the partner country, but rather between the most powerful EU member states (UK and France) and those countries. The limitation of the EU's own role also results from the reluctance of member states and the Commission to use too much development money to pursue security-related goals (Coolsaet 2010: 871).

In the bilateral relations, the EU has prioritized cooperation with the US in fighting terrorism, with US–EU counter-terrorism cooperation growing exponentially (including through the conclusion of agreements such as on extradition, mutual legal assistance and passenger-name records). In this regard, Argomaniz argues: 'No other international actor has influenced EU policies more comprehensively than the US, leading in some instances to an asymmetric process of internalization of US policies by the EU and concerns about the impact of this collaboration on European citizens' privacy rights' (2011: 95). Discussions on the exchange of data also resulted in arm wrestling between the Council and the EP as well as in cases before the European Court of Justice (respectively, e.g. the *SWIFT* case and the *Kadi* case – see Chapter 3).

Although successful in many respects, the close transatlantic cooperation in countering terrorist threats also brought drawbacks in other foreign policy domains. The American 'war on terror' sparked a debate about whether the West was undermining the values it wanted to promote, as a lack of respect for some basic freedoms was displayed by the US's detention of prisoners in Guantánamo and its use of torture in the interrogation of alleged terrorists, as well as certain EU member states' participation in or (at least) condoning of these practices. In combination with the West's aforementioned rejection of the democratic election of Hamas in the Palestinian Territories (see previous section), 'Guantánamo' and the condoning of torture further undermined American and European legitimacy in promoting 'Western' values.

One of the challenges for EU foreign policy has also been to understand the complexities behind so-called 'terrorist groups' and, in particular, Islamist terrorist organizations (see Coolsaet 2011). A group such as Al-Qaeda is 'as much an ideological movement as a terrorist organization, and is able to attach itself to a multiplicity of grievances' (Inkster 2010: 85). This also explains the attractiveness and legitimacy of Al-Qaeda and other Jihadi movements for part of the Muslim population in various parts of the world. Moreover, the lumping together of all varieties of armed struggle and the indiscriminate labelling of these struggles as 'Islamic terrorism' made it equally difficult to grasp the different dynamics and logics behind these movements (Roberts 2011: 31). This also hampered the development of a more sophisticated European foreign policy with a greater capacity to deal effectively with this complex, multifaceted phenomenon (see also Chapter 12).

Interestingly, CSDP did not initially emerge in the EU's counter-terror policy (Argomaniz 2011, 2012: 95; Merlingen 2012: 182). However, CSDP operations have recently attempted to deal more actively with so-called 'failed' or 'fragile' states and unstable regions, since these are often seen as 'ungoverned' 'safe havens' for Al-Qaeda-related groups and other Jihadi movements (Council 2012g: 15). An example is the EU's recently developed policy towards the Sahel and the Sahara region in Africa, where 'Al-Qaeda in the Islamic Maghreb' (AQIM), other Jihadist groups, Tuareg tribes and criminal networks expand their influence in areas increasingly outside government control. The 2012 takeover of northern Mali by AQIM and related movements is illustrative in this regard (Lacher 2012). The rising influence of these movements is worrying for the EU, as it contributes to further eroding stability in the neighbouring Mediterranean countries such as Libya, Algeria and Tunisia, which are still in turmoil after the Arab uprising of 2011. It is in this context that the EU launched its *EU Strategy for Security and Development in the Sahel*, the civilian missions EUCAP SAHEL Niger and EUBAM Libya, and the military training mission EUTM Mali, which strive to improve the capacities of these countries to fight terrorism and organized crime (see Simon *et al.* 2012) (see also Box 6.2 and Chapter 8).

In this way, CSDP may take up a task that it was endowed by the Treaty of Lisbon: contribute to 'the fight against terrorism, including by supporting third countries in combating terrorism in their territories' (Art. 43 TEU). However, as is indicated by the EU's Counter-Terrorism Coordinator, this can only have a chance at success if the EU contributes equally to strengthening governmental structures in the regions and to 'education, creation of economic and job opportunities for young people and prevention of violent radicalization, without which CT [counter terrorism] engagement cannot be successful' (Council 2012g: 22). This points to the need for a comprehensive approach referred to earlier in this chapter.

Conclusion

This chapter examined four key issues of EU foreign policy: human rights, democracy and the rule of law; conflict prevention, crisis management and peace-building; non-proliferation and control of arms exports; and the fight against terrorism. Through various documents, 'action plans', 'codes of conduct' or 'strategies', the EU has developed a broad conceptual basis on the importance of those issues for its foreign policy and the way it aims to implement them. In addition to this 'declaratory foreign policy', a range of toolboxes has been developed to go beyond mere declarations and to move into the direction of an 'operational foreign policy'. Two of the domains in which these key issues are operationalized are the CFSP and the CSDP. The four key issues discussed in this chapter indeed give substance to the CFSP and CSDP, which are analysed in the next two chapters.

Chapter 7

The Common Foreign and Security Policy (CFSP)

Chapter 2 argued that different and even conflicting motivations lay at the root of the Maastricht Treaty's creation of the CFSP. The decision to create CFSP stemmed as much from member states' interrelational, integration and identity objectives, as from their external objectives (see Chapter 1). For many member states, the main rationale was to allow the EU to manage interstate and inter-institutional dynamics within the Union and not, or not primarily, to deal with the outside world. It thus comes as no surprise that while member states could agree to create a CFSP at Maastricht, they initially had no intention of providing it with the necessary actors and instruments to turn it into a robust foreign policy tool. It was only from the late 1990s onwards that the majority of member states started to consider the CFSP framework useful to pursue external objectives. Since then, this has led to the development of both new actors with specific responsibilities for CFSP (see Chapter 3) and new instruments (see e.g. Chapter 8 on CSDP), making the initially hollow CFSP shell an increasingly useful operational facet of EU foreign policy.

This chapter provides a critical assessment of the formal set-up of the CFSP as outlined in the TEU and juxtaposes this treaty image against the empirical reality. It then evaluates the various modus operandi provided in the Treaty and turns to one of the most important, although often overlooked, elements of CFSP: systematic cooperation. Finally, the chapter briefly considers the scope and priorities of CFSP (which is further assessed in Chapters 6, 11 and 12), assessing both its declaratory and operational policies.

Formal Features and Nature of CFSP

CFSP: what's in a name?

Major expectations, but also misunderstandings, are created by the very name *common foreign and security policy* and by the first paragraph of the crucial Article 24(1) TEU:

The Union's competence in matters of common foreign and security policy shall cover all areas of foreign policy and all questions relating to the Union's security, including the progressive framing of a common defence policy that might lead to a common defence.

The name explicitly indicates that CFSP is a *'common'* policy. This gives the impression that it is on a par with long-standing common policies of the EU, such as the common agricultural policy and the common commercial policy. But, the Treaty does not provide for the same kind of common actors, common instruments or common budget that would be necessary to develop a *common* policy. Moreover, within these other policy fields, the term 'common' denotes policy domains in which the EU has exclusive or quasi-exclusive competence, denoting a transfer of sovereignty from the member states to the EU. Foreign and security policy is a special kind of EU competence, with the main powers remaining in member state hands. Two declarations cement this situation, which, particularly under British pressure, were added in annex to the TEU as an extra guarantee. First, Declaration 13 emphasizes that the CFSP provisions

do not affect the responsibilities of the Member States, as they currently exist, for the formulation and conduct of their foreign policy nor of their national representation in third countries and international organizations.

Second, to avoid any further misunderstanding, Declaration 14 specifies that the provisions covering the CFSP:

will not affect the existing legal basis, responsibilities, and powers of each Member State in relation to the formulation and conduct of its foreign policy, its national diplomatic service, relations with third countries and participation in international organizations, including a Member State's membership of the Security Council of the United Nations.

These declarations countered the expectation that the new provisions in the Lisbon Treaty would lead to a qualitative leap in the nature of EU foreign policy.

As far as the range of policy areas is concerned, the CFSP label and Article 24(1) TEU are misleading too. CFSP is not all encompassing, as it does not cover *'all* areas of foreign policy' and *'all* questions relating to the Union's security' (our emphasis). Member states' territorial defence, for example, is not covered by CFSP. For many member states, NATO remains the major forum for security policy. Chapter 8 also explains that the reference to 'the progressive framing of a common defence policy that might lead to a common defence' does not match reality. The word '*policy*' equally raises expectations, but hides the fact that cooperation between member states in at the heart of CFSP.

Equally interesting is the second paragraph of Article 24(2) TEU, which indicates that the EU shall conduct, define and implement a CFSP, 'based on the development of mutual political solidarity among Member States, the identification of questions of general interest and the achievement of an ever-increasing degree of convergence of Member' States action' (Art. 24(2)). This passage is remarkably sincere and revealing about the nature of CFSP. It indicates that political solidarity is not self-evident but must be developed. It concedes that questions of general interest must be identified and agreed upon – they are not inherently common among the member states. It admits that convergence cannot be assumed and that the aim is to increase the degree of convergence, not to reach full convergence. This also implies that member states still can undertake their own foreign policy actions. To sum up: the label 'common foreign and security policy' is misleading and has been one of the factors behind what Hill (1993, 1998) famously termed the EU's 'capability–expectations gap'.

The binding effect of CFSP

The Treaty also generates expectations about the level of commitment member states have entered into (Art. 24(3) TEU):

> The Member States shall support the Union's external and security policy actively and unreservedly in a spirit of loyalty and mutual solidarity and shall comply with the Union's action in this area.
>
> The Member States shall work together to enhance and develop their mutual political solidarity. They shall refrain from any action which is contrary to the interests of the Union or likely to impair its effectiveness as a cohesive force in international relations. The Council and the High Representative shall ensure compliance with these principles.

From a legal perspective, this provision, particularly the use of the word 'shall', is significant as it imposes respect for and participation in the CFSP upon the member states (Eeckhout 2011: 172). However, from a political perspective this is no more than a highly *conditional* binding power. The member states' active and unreserved support, loyalty and compliance, as demanded in this treaty article, in fact depend on the degree to which specific policies have actually been developed, to which EU interests have been specified, and to which the EU is indeed acting effectively as a cohesive force on a specific matter. When these conditions are not met, the Treaty provisions imply that the member states can go their own way – as they clearly are doing on many occasions.

In CFSP, the Council and the High Representative are responsible for ensuring that the above-mentioned commitments and principles are observed – and not the Commission and the Court of Justice, as is the case for external action and the external dimension of internal policies. As explained in Chapter 3, the Treaty provisions explicitly exclude CFSP from the jurisdiction of the Court of Justice (Art. 24(1) TEU and Art. 275 TFEU). Since the member states are not renowned for their ability to control each other, and as the High Representative has no political and legal authority over the member states, this arrangement clearly contributes to the limitations of CFSP's binding effect. The Council has not developed any enforcement mechanisms and the EEAS keeps no systematic record of whether member states have complied with CFSP engagements.

Member states with other 'responsibilities' and roles in international fora (notably UN Security Council, G8/20 or 'special relationships') sometimes divert from the EU line using these responsibilities as an excuse. However, where a well-elaborated and unambiguous policy has been developed towards a specific foreign policy issue, it becomes politically more problematic for member states to fall out of line. Peer pressure among member states and a degree of socialization do have their impact. Ultimately, the main problem for CFSP is not always member states deliberately embarking on policies that run counter to those developed within the EU. Major problems are the often too general nature of EU policies, which leave scope for member states' own interpretations and initiatives, and member states' apathy and lack of active support for specific policy initiatives (although this apathy can in some cases also facilitate policy-making – see Chapters 4 and 5).

Modus Operandi

Article 25 TEU further exposes the nature of CFSP and indicates that the EU shall conduct the common foreign and security policy by:

(a) defining the general guidelines;
(b) adopting decisions defining:
  (i) actions to be undertaken by the Union;
  (ii) positions to be taken by the Union;
  (iii) arrangements for the implementation of the decisions referred to in points (i) and (ii); and by

(c) strengthening systematic cooperation between Member States in the conduct of policy.

The content of this article and of the more detailed treaty provisions that follow seem logical (see also Eeckhout 2011: 469–77). General guidelines are defined by the highest political authority, the European Council. The Council of Ministers then adopts decisions to further develop and implement policy, utilizing operational actions and positions as well as arrangements to implement those actions and positions. And, to complement all this, member states strengthen their foreign policy cooperation. Accordingly, this final provision confirms the view about the nature of CFSP painted above, as it not only refers to the actions and position of the Union but also to systematic cooperation between the member states as a fully-fledged way to conduct the CFSP.

General guidelines

The Treaty does not define what 'general guidelines' are. To further complicate matters, the Treaty text also uses other similar terms, such as 'strategic lines' (Art. 26 TEU), 'strategic guidelines' (Art. 16(6) TEU), and 'decisions relating to the Union's strategic interests and objectives' (Arts. 22(1) and 31(2) TEU). The basic idea is clear: the European Council identifies the Union's strategic interests, determines the objectives of and defines general guidelines for the CFSP (Art. 26 TEU). This confusing terminology implies a certain sloppiness in drafting the CFSP provisions, but it also mirrors the European Council's dominant role in CFSP, where heads of state and government are less bound by treaty provisions (see also Chapter 3).

The European Council sets the course of CFSP through publicly available conclusions and declarations issued after each meeting and through informal conclusions, which remain confidential (and which may be agreed upon during the informal lunch meetings). In its conclusions, the European Council rarely uses the term 'general guidelines' or one of the other terms expressed in the treaty provisions.

Actions

The European Council's general guidelines can be translated into concrete policy through operational *actions* or through the definition of Union *positions*. A closer examination of the various relevant treaty provisions is useful as they exemplify the nature of CFSP and the prudence required when reading treaty texts.

Article 28 TEU is dedicated to decisions defining actions: 'Where the international situation requires operational action by the Union, the Council shall adopt the necessary decisions. They shall lay down their objectives, scope, the means to be made available to the Union, if necessary their duration, and the conditions for their implementation' (Art. 28(1) TEU). The subsequent subparagraphs articulate in detail what is expected from the member states. The decisions on operational action commit the member states in their positions and in the conduct of their activities. Whenever they plan to adopt a national position or take national action pursuant to an action, they shall provide information in time to allow, if necessary, for prior consultations within the Council. Should there be any major difficulties in implementing this decision, a member state has to refer them to the Council, which shall seek an appropriate solution. In short, Article 28 TEU is the Treaty basis to adopt decisions on operational action, and such decisions entail serious obligations for the member states and restrict their room to manoeuvre.

In practice, however, the story is rather different. Article 28 is mainly used for adopting decisions with regard to two categories of actions: for appointing EU Special Representatives (EUSR) and for launching crisis management operations within the CSDP framework (and for extending or modifying the mandate of the EUSR and CSDP missions). How should we interpret this?

First, it may indicate that the range of operational actions of the CFSP is indeed rather limited. This is somewhat misleading, however. Operational action can also follow from decisions adopted on the basis of ordinary decisions of the Council based on Art. 26(2) TEU (such as the activities promoting non-proliferation and fighting the spread of small arms) and of informal conclusions of the European Council or Foreign Affairs Council (leading to, for instance, diplomatic initiatives of the High Representative with regard to the Serbia–Kosovo dispute or the conflict with Iran) (see Box 7.1).

Second, the limited use of operational action on the basis of Article 28 TEU reveals member states' attitude towards CFSP. Member states may want to avoid decisions on the basis of that article precisely because it potentially restrains their freedom to act. The two categories of operational action that are undertaken on the basis of Article 28 TEU (related to CSDP operations and EUSR) do not automatically require additional commitment from the member states. This is even true for actions relating to crisis-management operations. CSDP missions require member states to make national personnel available for these missions, but this participation is in fact voluntary.

Positions

Similar conclusions apply to decisions defining 'positions', which are the subject of Article 29 TEU: 'The Council shall adopt decisions which shall define the approach of the Union to a particular matter of a geographical or thematic nature. Member States shall ensure that their national policies conform to the Union positions'.

In practice, instead of becoming the main tool to gradually define an EU approach towards a wide variety of foreign policy issues, decisions defining positions have been largely restricted to a very narrow field: the adoption of sanctions and restrictive measures against unsavoury regimes, against key individuals from the countries concerned, and against terrorist organizations (through arms embargos, travel bans, freezing of funds and economic resources, etc.). Moreover, many of these sanctions merely implement decisions adopted at the UN level and require further implementation through the EU's external action instruments (see Chapter 9). There are only a few exceptions where decisions have been adopted to define the EU's position towards other issues (such as the positions on the Review Conference of the Nuclear Non-Proliferation Treaty) (see Chapter 6).

Whereas Article 29 TEU requires the member states to ensure that their national policies conform to the Union positions, another provision requires them to 'coordinate their activities'. Article 32 TEU demands that member states 'consult' each other on any matter of general interest in order to determine a 'common approach'. The High Representative and ministers for foreign affairs have to coordinate their activities within the Council once a common approach has been defined by the European Council or Council. This underscores the importance of coordination and cooperation between the member states in the conduct of CFSP, which is the subject of the following section.

Systematic cooperation between Member States

'Strengthening systematic cooperation between Member States in the conduct of policy' (Art. 25(c) TEU) is one of the major modus operandi of CFSP, but also one of the most overlooked. Analysts of EU foreign policy often overlook this article because it is less visible and because it does not fit comfortably with the notion of a common policy. The fact that Article 25 TEU speaks about 'strengthening' systematic cooperation further testifies to this ambiguity, signifying as it does that systematic cooperation should not be taken for granted.

A number of other Treaty provisions provide additional information about the nature of systematic cooperation. Article 32 TEU not only points to the commitment of the member states to consult each other in order to determine a common approach. It also indicates that:

- '[b]efore undertaking any action on the international scene or entering into any commitment which could affect the Union's interests, each member state shall consult the others within the European Council or the Council';
- '[m]ember states shall ensure, through the convergence of their actions, that the Union is able to assert its interests and values on the international scene';
- 'diplomatic missions of the Member States and the Union delegations in third countries and at international organisations shall cooperate

and shall contribute to formulating and implementing the common approach'.

Systematic cooperation also carries treaty obligations regarding coordination, dialogue and information exchange in international organizations and conferences, including those fora in which not all member states are represented (Art. 34 TEU) (see Chapter 13).

Systematic cooperation between national diplomacies is a generic term incorporating different levels and forms of cooperation, including information exchange, consultation, coordination and convergent action. It is based on continuous interaction between national foreign ministries, their representatives in Brussels, their embassies in third countries, the EEAS and the EU Delegations. Exchanging information and consulting each other can contribute to member states basing their national policy positions on similar information and assessments of external developments and to developing common thinking regarding the issue at hand. This consultation also contributes to the interrelational objectives of EU foreign policy (see Chapter 1): it facilitates member states' understanding of the position of other member states; it helps to avoid external events leading to misunderstandings between them; and it can contribute to fostering mutual solidarity.

Shared information, consultation and common views can – but do not necessarily – lead to convergent action. Member states can agree on a course of action towards a specific policy issue, which they then pursue through national foreign policy instruments and actions. Hence, while the tone may differ, all member states convey the same basic message. Convergent action can be further strengthened through CFSP declarations or through public or confidential CFSP démarches by the High Representative or officials of the EEAS, including the Heads of Delegation in the capital of third countries or international organization concerned.

How can we evaluate the record of systematic cooperation? Overall, systematic cooperation has been strengthened over the last two decades, with member states accepting it as a familiar part of national foreign policy-making. By and large, exchanges of information and consultations occur more intensively and more automatically than in the past. However, this dynamic has not been felt in all policy issues or by all parts of national foreign policy bureaucracies. A consultation reflex clearly exists among Brussels-based national diplomats and those capital-based diplomats involved in the EU's main foreign policy issues. But, it is not as strong, and in some cases is absent, among the many capital-based diplomats responsible for their countries' bilateral relations with third countries or relations with other organizations. This means that the consultation reflex is much less widespread or intensive than is often suggested. Moreover, a consultation reflex not only takes place within

CFSP, but also in the context of other multilateral frameworks (such as NATO) or bilateral relations.

This critical remark on the limited scope of systematic cooperation in practice applies to both the small number of foreign policy issues at the top of the international agenda (the 'CNN issues') as well as the larger number of issues lower down the international agenda. On many 'CNN issues', there is no full exchange of information and no systematic consultation between member states. This can be because member states diverge in their position, because other international actors serve as primary interlocutors, or because these issues are considered too sensitive to share information with all EU member states.

At the same time, systematic cooperation does not always occur on foreign policy issues that are lower on the international agenda. This is because these matters only tend to be of interest to some member states, the EU is not seen as the most relevant setting for cooperation on that particular issue, or because a majority of the member states simply do not have the specialized desk officer or the embassy in a specific third country to allow them to be involved in intensive consultation. Thus, a consultation or coordination reflex might exist, but it might not be to consult all (or most) EU member states, and it is just as feasible that the consultation reflex will be played out in different fora and with other states.

Scope and Priorities

The CFSP's general nature having been analysed, this section now turns to CFSP's substance. It is important to recall that assessing CFSP in isolation from the EU's general foreign policy and particularly its external action is somewhat artificial. CFSP can also rely on crisis management and peace-building instruments of the CSDP, and can call on external action instruments that are politically steered through the CFSP framework or that are brought in through the external action mechanisms (such as financial support or association agreements). Accordingly, other chapters take a more comprehensive approach to the EU's policy with regard to the main thematic (see Chapters 6 and 8) and geographic priorities (Chapters 11 and 12).

The reach of CFSP becomes evident if we look at some quantitative indicators (Council 2011a, 2012i). Besides the thousands of messages touching on all parts of the world exchanged through the COREU network (see Bicchi 2011 and Chapter 4), there are annually many hundreds of CFSP statements and declarations directed towards nearly 100 countries, regions or international organizations; démarches towards almost all countries in the world (i.e. messages through diplomatic channels, including, for instance, protests against human rights violations); 'political dialogue' meetings on various (head of state/ government, ministerial or senior official) levels with a wide range of third countries and regional organizations. In addition, there were decisions covering dozens of countries, including sanctions (with regard to the Western Balkans, Iran, Iraq, North Korea, Myanmar and several African countries) and civilian and military crisis management operations in nearly a dozen countries (see Chapter 8).

The main focus of CFSP is the Eastern neighbours, the Western Balkans, the Mediterranean, the Middle East and Africa (see Chapter 11). Yet there are marked differences across these regions in terms of the intensity of the CFSP attention they receive. A low level of attention can indicate that the EU does not prioritize the issue at hand, that there are major disagreements between member states, or that dealing with these issues might undermine interests of the member states or the EU as a whole. For instance, notwithstanding the recent attention paid to the Mediterranean, it is remarkable how little attention is given to some individual countries and conflicts (such as Algeria and the conflict in Western Sahara), and how democracy promotion did not appear high on the EU's foreign policy agenda towards these countries until early 2011 (see Chapter 6). Human rights in the Gulf states and, for instance, the problematic situation of the millions of Asian immigrants working in those countries, are equally absent from the CFSP agenda. A last example is the lack of attention paid to the security situation in the Pacific: the growing tension and military rivalry between China, the US and various Asian countries is rarely the subject of EU deliberations and policies, denying the potential for this situation to affect Europe in long run (Song 2013). In this respect, for observers of CFSP, it is at least as interesting to examine which countries and issues are not the subject of CFSP declarations, démarches, etc., as it is to inquire into the countries and issues that do appear on the CFSP radar.

Nevertheless, the scope and reach of CFSP has widened greatly in the last two decades. Policy matters and regions of the world that in the past were beyond the reach of EPC and CFSP are now familiar points on the CFSP agenda and subject to systematic cooperation, common approaches, and concerted or common action. In the past, countries wanted to shield their '*domaines réservés*' from EU-level deliberations. Such attitudes proved a major constraint on EU foreign policy. Developments in member states' former colonies in Africa, for example, were for a long time deemed too sensitive or too important nationally to feature in the EU's political deliberations. Now, the opposite often occurs: member states want to 'Europeanize' national foreign policy priorities, but are faced with the difficult task of selling this to the other member states (see Chapter 5).

An example of the latter was the French attempt over several years to get EU attention for the deterioration of the situation in Mali and the

Sahel region in general (development of Al-Qaeda in the Islamic Maghreb, drug trafficking, kidnappings, etc.). These concerns were put forward during the French Presidency in 2008 and were followed by a call by eight member states upon the High Representative to increase the EU's involvement in the region (see Simón and Mattelaer 2011: 10). In 2011 the EU indeed adopted its 'Strategy for Security and Development in the Sahel', which testified that all member states by then understood the importance of the region, but also that it took nearly three years for the EU to get its acts together (see Box 6.2). Moreover, the EU Strategy neither prevented the crumbling of the Mali government, nor provided the basis for a robust common EU response. France therefore launched in early 2013 a military operation to avoid the complete takeover of Mali by Jihadist groups, which showed once again the EU's inability to react militarily to what was widely perceived as an imminent and serious threat. However, through the EU Training Mission (EUTM Mali), the EU agreed on a more modest contribution to supporting the Mali authorities (see also Chapter 8).

The example of Mali demonstrates too that the widening reach of CFSP has its limits: CFSP in general proves to be ineffective when positions need to be adopted on the potential use of military force. This again reflects the enduring relevance of the area of tension 'civilian power versus military power' in EU foreign policy (see Chapter 1). This was obvious in Mali, but equally in crises in the EU's more immediate neighbourhood, such as in Iraq, Syria or Libya (see Box 7.1). However, as is shown in Chapter 8, the EU in some cases is able to overcome its limitation of acting as a military power by entering into a new kind of business: engaging in capacity-building or training missions of the military and security forces of third countries (see Chapter 8 and Boxes 6.2 and 8.1). The long-standing violence in Syria since 2011 also demonstrated that the complexity of a conflict does not always allow external actors such as the EU to judge and to agree upon what the best course of action is: whether to intervene militarily; whether to recognize opposition movements (and, if so, which opposition movements); whether to provide support for armed groups (and, if so, which groups and through what kind of support); and so on.

Declaratory versus Operational Foreign Policy

The CFSP is vested with the standard diplomatic instruments to carry out foreign policy: informal talks and telephone calls, diplomatic demarches, high-level visits and meetings, participation in international conferences, mediation, sending observers, and so on. They are employed in order to consult, confirm, support, show solidarity, suggest solutions or options, meditate, reconcile, demand, protest, disapprove, accuse, reject, deter,

Box 7.1   CFSP and the use of force: the Libya crisis

In February 2011, shortly after the start of the Tunisian revolution, protests erupted in neighbouring Libya. Despite Gaddafi's violent repression, protesters managed to gain control over Benghazi, Libya's second biggest city and established a parallel government, the National Transitional Council, which was gradually recognized by the international community. Notwithstanding initial internal divisions, the EU agreed on an arms embargo against the Gaddafi regime in February 2011 (Balfour *et al.* 2012: 5–7).

Considering the increasing number of civilian casualties and the risks of heavy weapons being used by the Gaddafi regime against its own population, the UN Security Council adopted in March 2011 Resolution 1973 authorizing under Chapter VII of the UN Charter the use of 'all necessary measures' to protect civilians and the establishment of a no-fly zone. This strong but nevertheless ambiguous wording allowed France, the UK, the US (for the first time 'leading from behind') and some other countries to launch a military operation, which was subsequently taken over by NATO, in order to enforce the no-fly zone. This intervention took place among intense debates about the international community's 'responsibility to protect'. With Western help, the Libyan rebels finally succeeded in toppling Gaddafi, who was captured and killed in October 2011 (see Chapter 8).

While the operation was a military success, the EU's reaction to the crisis raised questions regarding its ability and willingness to act as a crisis-management actor in its neighbourhood. While France and the UK had taken the initiative on and had actively supported the adoption of the UNSC resolution and the start of the subsequent military operation, Germany and Italy were sceptical about the use of military means to solve the crisis. Germany's abstention on the vote of the UNSC resolution, thereby siding with Russia and China, represented the height of the European division. These internal disagreements can be explained by Germany's historical reluctance to send military troops in combat missions, but also by the business and political relations between Germany and Italy on the one hand and the Libyan regime on the other. Whatever the motivations behind the German behaviour were, the remaining chaos and violence in Libya in the years after the fall of Gaddafi may indicate that Germany had good reason to doubt the long-term effects of military intervention.

The Libya crisis was a blunt example of the failure of CFSP and CSDP to serve as a framework for effective EU foreign policy, despite European countries taking the lead and despite the presence of three (external) key conditions: a UN mandate, the support of the competent regional organization (the Arab League) and the unwillingness of the US to take the lead (see Cameron 2012: 99–101; Menon 2011a; Pinfari 2012).

sanction etc. When examining these diplomatic instruments, one can make a distinction between declaratory and operational foreign policy.

The broad scope of CFSP tells us little about its substance, added value and operationalization. When scrutinizing CFSP's output in more detail, it becomes clear that this is often limited to applying the EU's general principles and objectives to specific cases: a routine repetition of CFSP objectives such as peaceful resolution of conflicts, rejection of the use of violence or criticizing violations of human rights. Member states' views can be easily accommodated as long as CFSP output remains uncontroversial and limits itself to general goals. The EU's identity objectives (distinguishing itself vis-à-vis other countries on the basis of its specific values) dominate over the EU's external objectives (influencing the international environment) (see Chapter 1). This explains the dominance of *declaratory* foreign policy, wherein activities are rather routine and in which the policy position adopted is more about common sense than common policy.

It is important to nuance this argument. A basic function of diplomacy is to continuously indicate where you stand in the world and in relation to the constant stream of events. Declaratory foreign policy is therefore a standard part of CFSP (see Voncina 2011). It is important for the EU to project its identity and promote its values in international politics and even relatively anodyne declarations and demarches can have some impact. However, in most cases, a policy must go beyond routine declaratory foreign policy and have an operational aspect to make a difference on the international scene.

On many complex foreign policy issues, the EU has no or only limited *operational* foreign policy. When operational action is required, CFSP outputs are often of limited or no use because they are too vague and general. To have an operational foreign policy, the EU's representatives (the High Representative, diplomats from the EEAS and in EU Delegations in third countries) need to have the mandate, the flexibility and the instruments to intervene actively in a specific foreign policy issue. The EU must be able to react on a daily basis and in a flexible and detailed way to the demands, reactions, proposals, counter-proposals and often difficult dilemmas that characterize international politics.

Seen from this perspective, the CFSP's output is less substantial than it might seem at first glance. This is even the case when EU actors appear to be involved in an issue. A former Commissioner for External Relations (a function that today no longer exists as such) was cynical: 'We were consistent about one thing at least in Brussels. When we did not have a policy, we would go on a visit, or send [former High Representative] Javier Solana ... An active presence on the ground was too often an alternative to having anything very useful to say or do once we had got there' (Patten 2005: 164). This demonstrates that action can come down to *symbolic* rather than *substantial* foreign policy.

There are, however, a number of priority areas where CFSP has produced a significant operational foreign policy, albeit with varying levels of intensity, consistency and success. The yearly detailed evaluation or 'scorecard' compiled by one of the main European think-tanks, the European Council on Foreign Relations (ECFR), is in this respect revealing. It points to the diversity and wide range of CFSP operational policy, including mediation on Kosovo, democracy and human rights promotion in the Western Balkans, reacting to the Arab uprising, reacting to the crisis in Côte d'Ivoire, taking the lead in the negotiations on Iran's nuclear policy, contributing to the anti-piracy activities off the coast of Somalia, promoting human rights at the UN, and providing support for the International Criminal Court (Vaïsse and Kundnani 2012) (see Chapters 6 and 11).

But even though the EU's operational radius gradually widened and the number of successful operational foreign policy actions increased until the mid-2000s, thereafter, policy expansions became less common. The EU issued more declarations than ever, however, there were fewer diplomatic demarches, fewer 'political dialogue' meetings, and fewer new decisions on crisis management or peace-building missions, despite some major exceptions such as initiatives related to the Strategies towards the Sahel region and the Horn of Africa (see Boxes 6.2 and 8.1). There are two possible explanations: first, it potentially reflects transitional problems related to the set-up of the EEAS and the search for a clear role for the High Representative; second, it could be indicative of member states' and the EU institutions' more limited commitment to strengthening the EU's operational foreign policy.

The two 'successes' of European foreign policy detailed in Box 7.1, though, highlight the prudence required when analysing and judging foreign policy. Achieving success in foreign policy is indeed not evident, sometimes barely visible and often unavoidably modest. These examples, as well as the yearly evaluations provided by the ECFR, also demonstrate that the CFSP can only be seriously evaluated in conjunction with the foreign policy of (relevant) member states, with the CSDP, and with the EU's external action – which is the subject of the following chapters.

Conclusion

This chapter has shown that cooperation between member states is at least as important in CFSP as common actions or positions and that in some cases unilateral action continues to prevail. Moreover, CFSP's output is often less substantial than it might seem at first glance. Created

---

Box 7.2 'Successes' of EU diplomacy: Kosovo and Iran in February 2012

Early 2012 saw two successes of EU diplomacy that demonstrate the challenge of analysing foreign policy, as they exemplify that operational foreign policy can be hardly visible for those outside foreign policy circles. They also illustrate the subtlety of diplomatic successes within the given international contexts. Such successes, both announced within the span of (barely) one week, are particularly notable given the vivid criticism against the EU's foreign policy and the High Representative Catherine Ashton.

The first success story was the compromise reached in late February between Serbia and Kosovo on the participation of Kosovo in regional fora in the Western Balkans and on the cooperative management of the crossing points between both countries. The former touches upon how Kosovo would be allowed to present itself – a highly sensitive issue – in such fora (i.e. on the name plates), as it is not recognized as an independent state by Serbia. This compromise was a remarkable achievement given the bloody past of Serbia–Kosovo relations, the lack of formal relations between the two until one year before the compromise, the EU's internal division on the status of Kosovo (five EU member states not recognizing its independence), and the spurts of violence in north Kosovo in clashes with the Serbian minorities that occurred only a few months prior to the compromise.

The compromise was reached after months of very intensive confidential diplomatic negotiations conducted by a team of experienced EU diplomats and underpinned by frequent personal contacts between High Representative Ashton, Commissioner for Enlargement Füle, the political leaders of several EU member states, and the Serbian and Kosovar leaders. The US and NATO also lent their support and backed the talks.

→

---

by the Treaty of Maastricht as the successor of the EPC, the CFSP was for some member states as much about interrelational and identity goals as achieving external objectives (see Chapter 1). Nevertheless, the increasing institutionalization of CFSP has allowed CFSP to move from a declaratory to a more operational foreign policy. In this process, the new opportunities for civilian and military intervention provided by CSDP, and discussed in the next chapter, has been crucial.

Diplomatic efforts were only successful because of leverage provided by the use of other EU instruments that are part of the EU's external action and enlargement toolbox. These tools included the promise of candidate status for Serbia, a feasibility study for a Stabilisation and Association Agreement with Kosovo, a visa dialogue with Kosovo, etc. (Lehne 2012). This compromise and subsequent negotiations under the auspices of the EU led in April 2013 to a major breakthrough in the talks between Kosovo and Serbia, which led to an agreement paving the way for the opening of the membership negotiations with Serbia and for a Stabilisation and Association Agreement with Kosovo. The EU's success in the Western Balkans demonstrates that the potential leverage of this extensive toolbox could not be unleashed without the intensive and active diplomatic efforts of the EU.

This first success will likely have lasting effects, though such long-term impacts are not necessarily evident in our second success story: the offer to resume talks with Iran on nuclear issues. EU High Representative Ashton announced that Iran had finally answered an earlier proposal from the EU and the 5+1 powers (the US, Russia, China, France, the UK and Germany) and that, on behalf of these other powers, she had offered Iran to resume talks on the nuclear issue. The offer was extended against a background of 'carrots' (the promise of benefits in the nuclear, political and economic fields as part of a confidence-building process), 'sticks' (the EU increased economic sanctions merely six weeks earlier), and threats of potential violence (the fear of an Israeli military attack on Iran). Interestingly, non-European observers including the American Secretary of State Hillary Clinton and the international press emphasized the leading role played by the EU's High Representative. However, it is clear that 'success', although essential as a first step, remains limited and that the daunting threats of military escalation and violent regional conflict burden future peace-building efforts.

Chapter 8

The Common Security and Defence Policy (CSDP)

Security and defence have been taboo since the earliest days of the European integration project. The failure to ratify the European Defence Community Treaty in the 1950s and the Fouchet Plans of the early 1960s resulted in defence and security being taken off the 'menu'. From then onwards, West European cooperation in the field of defence was mainly organized within the framework of NATO, with France largely falling back on its own national defence policy (see Chapter 2).

It was not until exogenous pressure, and particularly that of the conflicts in the Western Balkans in the 1990s, that member states were forced to re-evaluate the status of European security policy. In the early 2000s, following an initiative of the UK and France and the resulting Saint-Malo Declaration (see Chapter 2), the 'European Security and Defence Policy' (ESDP) was launched. The ESDP was subsequently formalized and relabelled in the 2008 Lisbon Treaty as 'Common Security and Defence Policy' (or CSDP – the abbreviation used in the remainder of this chapter). Ten years after launching its first missions in 2003, the EU has conducted almost 30 military operations and civilian crisis management missions, ranging from small monitoring missions in Georgia and the Palestinian Territories to a comprehensive rule-of-law mission in Kosovo and a maritime anti-piracy operation near the Somali coast.

What explains the transformation of security and defence issues from taboo to a major component of CFSP? The end of the Kosovo crisis in the late 1990s created a context in which EU member states could for the first time at least partially overcome some of the major areas of tension outlined in the first chapter: European integration versus Atlantic solidarity, civilian power versus military power, and external versus internal objectives. CSDP emerged because a series of delicate balances could be found between France and the UK, between the EU and the US, between EU-oriented and NATO-oriented member states, between neutral member states and those who are NATO members, and between civilian and military crisis management traditions. Finding the right balances, though, remained a major challenge – these areas of tension were narrowed down but not eliminated. This explains both the remaining ambiguities and the boundaries that CSDP has to operate within (for a comprehensive analysis of CSDP, see Biscop and Whitman 2013; Biscop and Coelmont 2012, 2013; Ginsberg and Penksa 2012; Howorth 2007, 2014; Irondelle *et al.* 2011; Merlingen 2012; Norheim-Martinsen 2013; Vanhoonacker *et al.* 2010).

The Nature of CSDP

Ambiguity already appears in the very name 'Common Security and Defence Policy'. Like the name 'CFSP' (see Chapter 7), 'CSDP' is misrepresentative of both the intensions of the member states and the actual policy developed. The opening paragraph of the CSDP section in the Lisbon Treaty (Art. 42 TEU) summarizes what CSDP is really about:

> [The CSDP] shall provide the Union with an operational capacity drawing on civilian and military assets. The Union may use them on missions outside the Union for peace-keeping, conflict prevention and strengthening international security in accordance with the principles of the United Nations Charter. The performance of these tasks shall be undertaken using capabilities provided by the Member States.

This provision provides two clues to understanding the nature of CSDP. First, the possible military operations and civilian missions are limited to peacekeeping and conflict prevention outside the EU's territory (and are not related to the 'defence' of its territory). Second, the EU is to rely on member states' assets (and has no 'common' instruments, troops or headquarters of its own). These two caveats already nuance two of the pivotal terms used in the label 'CSDP'.

Not about defence

Member states did not consider CSDP as a locus for assuring their (territorial) defence, which most member states entrusted to NATO or to their domestic defence capacities. This stands in contrast to the Lisbon Treaty's call for CSDP to 'include the progressive framing of a common Union defence policy', which 'will lead to a common defence, when the European Council, acting unanimously, so decides' (Art. 42(2) TEU). It also puts into perspective the clause on mutual assistance: this clause obliges other member states to provide 'aid and assistance by all the means in their power' should another member state be the victim of an armed aggression on its territory (Art. 42(7)).

Member states wanted CSDP neither to compete with national foreign and security policy nor with NATO. This was reflected in the provision that specifies that the CSDP 'shall not prejudice the specific character of the security and defence policy of certain Member States and shall respect the obligations of certain Member States, which see their common defence realised in the North Atlantic Treaty Organization' (Art. 42(2) TEU). Indeed, the boundaries within which CSDP could develop are clear: it was allowed to build up if it was seen by member states (and the US) as not potentially harmful, as complementing or supporting NATO or national policies, and/or as a useful device to assume functions and missions which NATO or national member states were not (or were no more) willing or able to fulfil.

The types of missions and operations are stipulated in Article 43(1) TEU. They include, 'joint disarmament operations, humanitarian and rescue tasks, military advice and assistance tasks, conflict prevention and peace-keeping tasks, tasks of combat forces in crisis management, including peace-making and post-conflict stabilisation' (the so-called 'Petersberg Tasks'). The missions and operations can also contribute to 'the fight against terrorism, including by supporting third countries in combating terrorism in their territories'. However, CSDP was not devised to conduct large-scale offensive military operations like those in Afghanistan and Iraq in the early 2000s, or even short-term military offensives such as the Libyan campaign in 2011 (on Libya, see also Box 7.1).

Not that 'common'

CSDP is also less 'common' than its label may suggest, for three reasons. First, as will be explained below, the EU lacks 'common' capacities and has to rely on member states' assets, which are provided on a voluntary basis. Second, as Denmark expressed opposition to CSDP from the start, it was allowed to opt out of the CSDP arrangements, implying that it does not participate in the elaboration and implementation of decisions and actions within CSDP (see the 'Protocol (No. 22) on the position of Denmark' added to the TEU). Third, member states show a considerable variation in their commitment to participate in 'common' actions and capacity-building and they have vast differences in military capabilities (see Chapter 5). This explains why differentiation, specialization and division of labour are in fact major features of CSDP.

This differentiation is recognized in the Treaty on the European Union, which foresees several options (see also Biscop and Coelmont 2012: 74–98). First, when deciding on a CSDP mission or operation, the Council can 'entrust the implementation of a task to a group of member states which are willing and have the necessary capability for such a task'. Those member states, in association with the HR/VP, can agree among themselves on the management of this task (Art. 44 TEU). More far-reaching is the second option: to establish *permanent structured cooperation* between member states 'whose military capabilities fulfil higher criteria and which have made more binding commitments to one another in this area with a view to the most demanding missions' (Arts.

42(6) and 46 TEU – see also Chapter 4). A third option, which applies to all non-exclusive competences of the EU, is the possibility, under strict conditions, of 'enhanced cooperation' between at least nine member states (Art. 20 TEU). The fourth option, under the provisions on the European Defence Agency (EDA), implies that 'specific groups shall be set up within the Agency bringing together member states engaged in joint projects' (Art. 45(2) TEU).

The first three options have yet to be used in the CSDP domain. However, this does not mean that differentiation, specialization and cooperation between some member states have not developed in other forms. Examples include intensified cooperation between the UK and France following their 'Declaration on Defence and Security Cooperation' of 2010, the Weimar Triangle (France, Germany, Poland), Eurocorps (France, Germany, Spain, Belgium and Luxembourg), the 'Admiral Benelux' cooperation between the Belgian and Dutch navies, or the 'European Air Transport Command' (France, Germany, the Netherlands and Belgium) (Adebahr 2011; Biscop and Coelmont 2012: 65–8, 81–3). Even if these cooperation schemes occur outside the EU framework, they indirectly also have a positive effect on CSDP because they facilitate collaboration between member states.

The Military Dimension

Overcoming the EU–NATO divide

The Franco-British *Saint Malo Declaration* of December 1998 marked the first major step towards the CSDP. Itself a product of a particular geopolitical context (see Chapter 2), this Declaration was less a meeting of vision than a compromise between two opposing views on European security. France traditionally promoted the idea of a European military capability autonomous of the US and NATO. This position was juxtaposed against that of the UK, which focused first and foremost on the primacy of the US and NATO in European security. That the UK and France moved beyond these positions towards a common ground was the fundamental prerequisite for the start-up of CSDP.

In their 'Joint Declaration on European Defence' adopted at Saint Malo, Prime Minister Blair and President Chirac agreed that 'the Union must have the capacity for autonomous action, backed up by credible military forces, the means to decide to use them, and a readiness to do so, in order to respond to international crises'. In so doing, it was emphasized that Europe would be 'contributing to the vitality of a modernised Atlantic Alliance which is the foundation of the collective defence of its members' (Rutten 2001: 8–9). It is clear that the first quote met the French concerns, whereas the British position is reflected in the second one. This deal paved the way for the formal adoption of the goal to establish a CSDP by the European Council in Cologne in June 1999, which in its declaration practically repeated verbatim these crucial parts of the Saint Malo Declaration.

The US's calls for increased European military efforts meant that despite historic opposition to the Europeans developing autonomous military capabilities, the US had little option but to accept CSDP. However, this acceptance was on condition that the EU guaranteed to avoid the 'three Ds': no decoupling of CSDP from NATO; no duplication of capabilities; and no discrimination of non-EU NATO members (Rutten 2001: 10–12). The solution finally accepted in mid-December 2002 was termed the 'Berlin Plus' arrangements, which govern the relations between the EU and NATO in crisis management. Under these arrangements, the EU can either conduct an operation outside the NATO framework or make use of NATO assets and capabilities. In the second case, NATO guarantees that the EU has access to its planning facilities, can request NATO to make available a NATO European command option for an EU-led military operation, and can request the use of NATO assets and capabilities.

Berlin Plus was both pragmatic (Europeans alone lack core equipment and logistics necessary for high-intensity military operations) and symbolic (it institutionalizes what is for many member states and the US an essential interlinking of NATO and the EU institutions). At least partially overcoming the long-standing area of tension between European integration and Atlantic solidarity (see Chapter 1) was an essential step for CSDP to become operational and politically acceptable.

However, Berlin Plus did not solve all problems between the EU and NATO. The establishment of formal EU–NATO relations remained problematic due to France's specific position in NATO and due to the paralysing impact of the Turkey–Cyprus dispute. The first obstacle was largely solved in 2009 when France, following the pro-Atlantic course of then-President Sarkozy, rejoined the Allied military command of NATO. One of the French motivations for taking the lead in CSDP – to assert a 'European Europe' over an 'Atlantic Europe' – had indeed lost part of its strength (see Irondelle and Mérand 2010). Paradoxically, France's return to the military structure of NATO made CSDP less important for France, since this allowed France to work directly with and within NATO, without needing CSDP as a go-between. This is also considered one of the explanations for the French choice for NATO during the Libya crisis in 2011.

Relations between Cyprus and Turkey prompted a second obstacle for EU–NATO relations: Turkey blocked Cyprus's (and the EU's) engagement with NATO, and Cyprus blocked Turkey's (and NATO's) engagement with the EU. However, as Duke argues (2011b: 20), the Cyprus problem also provided a convenient pretext for avoiding some harder questions about NATO's relevance, American hegemony, and the political and military fundamentals of CSDP itself (on EU–NATO, see Biscop and Coelmont 2012; Ginsberg and Penksa 2012; Koops 2011, 2012; Michel 2013; Sperling 2011).

Soldiers and capabilities

The Treaty is unambiguous: the implementation of CSDP and the performance of CSDP operations depend on capabilities made available to the EU by the member states (Art. 42 TEU). The EU does not have 'common' troops or equipment. With in total around 1.7 million soldiers and a budget of nearly €200 billion for defence, finding the troops and military capabilities required for the rather modest CSDP tasks would appear to be a rather easy undertaking for the EU member states. In reality, this proved less evident than expected, as armies are only partially adapted from the Cold War modus to new security challenges. Merely one-tenth of the European armed forces are deemed to be really deployable. Inappropriate military equipment and political reluctance in member states to deploy troops under the EU flag explain why even these troops cannot always be brought into action (see Biscop and Coelmont 2012: 50–74; IISS 2011).

After an ambitious but failed attempt in the early 2000s to generate military forces of up to 50,000 to 60,000 persons (the *Helsinki Headline Goal 2003*) the EU in 2004 introduced the more modest *Battlegroup* concept to operationalize the military dimension of the CSDP at the European level (EEAS 2011b). Inspired by the experience with the small-scale Operation Artemis in DR Congo, the goal was to provide the EU with a capacity for rapid military response. For the EU, a Battlegroup is considered 1,500 troops (with appropriate support) at a high state of readiness (deployable within 15 days) and highly militarily effective (capable of high-intensity operations). The EU aims to be able to concurrently deploy two Battlegroups for a period up to 120 days if appropriately resupplied. Battlegroups can be formed by a single state or a group of states, including some non-EU member states such as Macedonia or Ukraine, and are capable of stand-alone operations or can execute the initial phase of larger operations (for instance, of the UN). On paper, two groups of countries are expected to take responsibility for a six-month standby period. As an example, two Battlegroups were on standby in the first half of 2013: one made up of Poland, Germany and France, and a second group including Belgium, France and Luxembourg. However, in the second half of 2013, only one Battlegroup made up of the UK and Sweden was on standby.

The Battlegroup concept has been at full operational capability since 2007, but as of early 2013, it has not been used in any concrete crisis. This mirrored doubts that had been raised from the start about operational challenges in real-life conflicts, difference in strategic cultures, problems of financing and, particularly, the dependence on the political authorization of the countries involved to use their Battlegroup. The operational future of Battlegroups in CSDP is therefore in doubt. On several occasions member states opposed the use of 'their' Battlegroup (and the risk of casualties among their soldiers) when they did not consider the proposed CSDP operation as essential for their own foreign policy interests. Occasions where deployment of Battlegroups could have been envisaged but were not agreed on include conflicts in DR Congo in 2008, South Sudan in 2010, Libya in 2011 and Mali early 2013 (House of Lords 2012: 29–32; Lindstrom 2007; Major and Mölling, 2011; Balossi-Restelli 2011).

The non-use of Battlegroups did not prevent the EU and its member states from engaging military forces. They did so in three ways: Europeanizing NATO troops, ad-hocism, and making troops available through other international organizations (NATO, UN). In each case, EU member states remained faithful to the basic principle of CSDP: European military capabilities are not achieved by creating permanent European forces, but are based on the voluntary and temporary contribution of member states.

First, a *Europeanization of NATO forces* occurred in the Western Balkans, with troops from European countries exchanging their NATO badge for an EU badge. In 2003, the NATO mission 'Allied Harmony' was taken over by the CSDP's Operation Concordia; one year later, the EUFOR Althea replaced NATO's SFOR in Bosnia and Herzegovina (Merlingen 2013).

Second, CSDP operations were launched on an ad hoc basis, depending on the entrepreneurship of one or more member states and/or the High Representative. Operation Artemis, EUFOR DR Congo, EUFOR Chad/RCA or EU NAVFOR Somalia are the product of such ad-hocism (see Brosig 2011). Its main advantage is flexibility and bottom-up cooperation, with the member states involved being committed as well as capable of providing a relevant contribution. Disadvantages, though, are the reoccurring problems of force generation, coordination, financing and, resultantly, burden sharing (as most costs are to be paid by the participating countries and not by the EU budget). Not surprisingly, the contribution of member states proved to be very uneven (Ginsberg and Penksa 2013: 145–9)

Third, EU member states can be engaged in *military operations outside the CSDP framework*, making troops available to the UN, NATO or coalitions of the willing. In some cases, these engagements are also discussed in the EU framework without producing a CSDP operation. For instance, in mid-2011, France and the UK took the lead in initiating and implementing the military campaign against the Gaddafi regime in Libya, with NATO further organizing the actual operation.

The choice for other settings can mirror capacity problems or political disagreement among EU member states, but can also follow from an understanding that UN or NATO operations can be preferable because of their operational expertise and military capabilities, the possibility to involve other countries or their greater legitimacy.

The French military action in Mali, launched in early 2013, demonstrated that other variations are possible too (see also Chapter 7). Facing the reluctance of other member states to launch a military CDSP mission, France, together with the armed forces from Mali and other African countries, initiated a military operation to stop and force back Jihadist groups. Behind the front line, logistic support was provided bilaterally to France by the US and about 10 EU member states. As part of the EU Strategy for Security and Development in the Sahel, the EU provided financial support to the African-led military operation to Mali through its African Peace Facility (see Chapter 6) and launched an EU Training Mission (EUTM Mali) to help improve the military capacity of the Malian Armed Forces (EEAS 2013c). However, the fact that most of the member states understood the need to intervene militarily in Mali but did not want to participate into an military operation raises questions about the value of CSDP. The risks about the situation in Mali were known since 2008 but there was no appetite to prepare the necessary military mission to address them (see Faleg 2013). However, the CSDP training missions that the EU member states managed to agree on in the Sahel Region (see Box 6.2), pointed to the 'niche' in the security sector which the EU became to focus on: capacity-building (see below).

Engaging in military crisis-management operations not only requires military personnel; it also requires hardware. When launching CSDP, the EU started a long process to identify shortfalls, define collective capability goals and reinforce military capabilities (see EEAS 2011c; Biscop and Coelmont 2012: 57–84). In 2008, the European Defence Agency (see Chapter 3) and the member states produced a comprehensive Capability Development Plan (CDP) with recommendations for member states. In early 2011, a list of top-10 priorities was approved, including intelligence surveillance and reconnaissance; increased availability of helicopters; cyber defence; strategic and tactical airlift management; fuel and energy; and mobility assurance. The nature of the exercise, though, was clearly emphasized: the CDP is 'not a supranational plan', but rather a tool for the member states to cooperate and coordinate actions in the field of military procurement (EEAS 2011c: 4; EDA 2008).

This intergovernmental approach is considered to be one of the reasons for the slow progress towards improved capabilities, as many of the CDP priorities were identified as early as 10 years before its launch. The overall method of capability development remains based on member states' voluntary contributions and measures, and on voluntary bottom-up cooperation. Importantly, this is not complemented with top-down guidance and coordination, which is crucial when coordination of national capability development on the strategic level is required (Biscop and Coelmont 2012: 70–1) (see also below).

The 2011 military intervention in Libya, more than the many detailed reports, uncovered the shortfalls of defence policies of many European countries (see Menon 2011a). Although it was a NATO operation, the gaps in capabilities became clear as the European countries led the operation. The Libya operation demonstrated that European countries were capable – within certain limits – of effectively undertaking serious military operations and taking lead roles, but that on their own they lacked military intelligence, surveillance and reconnaissance, air-to-air refuelling, smart munitions, and strategic and tactical transport capacities. On several crucial points, the US had to stand in, to 'lead from behind', and to fill the gaps in order to prevent the operation from failing. The operation also highlighted the different attitudes of member states: some were willing to take the lead (France and the UK) or to actively participate (Belgium, the Netherlands, Denmark and Sweden), while other large countries declined to take part (Germany) or did not make a meaningful contribution (Italy and Spain) (House of Lords 2012: 8–9, 49–50) (see also Box 7.1). Despite the economic and budgetary crisis and the resulting pressure on national defence budgets, the Libyan case was a wake-up call for the member states that when real military action is required, more investment and cooperation in the field of capability development is imperative.

Headquarters

Parallel to its military capabilities (military personnel and 'hardware'), institutions are needed to make CSDP policy operational. On a political level and institutionally located in the EEAS, the EU Military Committee (EUMC) and EU Military Staff (EUMS) provide the requisite expertise throughout the military–strategic planning process. They prepare detailed policy options and decisions on CSDP operations to be adopted by the PSC and Council (Merlingen 2012: 117–23) (see Chapter 3).

On the operational level, there are three possible options for undertaking a military CSDP operation, though none are particularly 'European' or 'integrated' in nature (see Biscop and Coelmont 2012: 103–7; Simón and Mattelaer 2011). The first option under the Berlin Plus arrangements is to utilize SHAPE (Supreme Headquarters Allied Powers Europe), NATO's Operational Headquarters located in Belgium, with NATO's Deputy SACEUR (Supreme Allied Commander Europe) serving as Operation Commander. This option has only been used for the two operations in the Western Balkans, where the EU took over from NATO: Operation Concordia in Macedonia and Operation Althea in Bosnia and Herzegovina.

A second option allows more 'autonomous' CSDP operations and involves the use of facilities provided by France, the UK, Germany, Italy or Greece's Operational Headquarters (OHQ) (EEAS 2013a). OHQs are then 'multinationalized' for the EU operation by including military staff from other member states and the EEAS. In this case, the Operational Commander is provided by the member state providing the headquarters. This option was chosen for e.g. Operation Artemis in the DRC and EUFOR Chad (using the French headquarters), EUFOR DRC (using the German headquarters), and EU NAVFOR Atalanta (using the British headquarters). The problem with this option is that these five EU member states are not always willing to put their OHQ at the EU's disposal, for instance because of the costs involved or because their national interests are not served by the CSDP operation in question (Balossi-Restelli 2011).

The third option is to command operations from Brussels utilizing the EU Operations Centre (OpsCen) which is located within the EU Military Staff under the command of a designated Operation Commander. OpsCen is not a standing or permanent headquarters, but can be activated by a Council decision for operations of up to 2000 troops and civilian experts. This option is designed particularly for situations where a joint civil–military response is envisaged and where no national headquarters is chosen. However, this option also faces disadvantages: it requires activation and installation before it can become operational; and its limited size does not make it suitable for larger and more complex operations. This third option has been available since January 2007, but the UK has blocked its usage for several years. The OpsCen was activated for the first time in early 2012 to provide support in the field of operational planning and conduct for the three CSDP operations in the Horn of Africa (see Box 8.1) (EEAS 2012d; Council 2012i).

An option not foreseen is to plan and conduct operations through an autonomous standing or permanent headquarters within the EU's institutional structures, as this is firmly opposed by the UK. The lack of a permanent structure limits the EU's possibilities to cope with more challenging operations, to react militarily rapidly, and achieve the goal to have boots on the ground no later than 10 days after the EU decision. This indeed would require substantial planning foresight that ad hoc operational planning and command structures cannot achieve (see Simón and Mattelaer 2011; Hynek 2011).

The Civilian Dimension

In addition to a military dimension, the CSDP also comprises a civilian dimension, which is focused on the deployment of non-military actors who contribute to security, such as police officers, judges or civil servants. The development of a civilian dimension to the CSDP originated from a Swedish–Finnish initiative. For the EU's traditionally neutral states, the development of civilian crisis management capabilities was a necessary complement to the development of military capabilities. They succeeded in convincing the other member states of the validity of their approach as experience in the Western Balkans made it clear that for longer-term stabilization, 'winning the war' was insufficient, and that special efforts were needed for 'winning the peace' (Ojanen 2000).

The Feira European Council of June 2000 defined four priority areas for the development of civilian capabilities: police, strengthening the rule of law, civil administration and civil protection. Two other priorities were added later: developing monitoring capabilities, and generic support capabilities to support EU Special Representatives or to be included in multifunctional missions (such as experts in mediation). The member states committed themselves to create a pool of police officers, judges, prosecutors and civilian administration experts, as well as assessment and intervention teams for deployment at short notice (see overview in Table 8.1). Progress was rapid: by January 2003 the EU had taken over from the UN the international police task force in Bosnia and Herzegovina and has since clocked up nearly 20 civilian missions. A major part of these missions relates to security sector reform (SSR), which refers to support for the creation, reform or strengthening of police, military, judicial or border management structures (Ekengren and Simons 2011; Gourlay 2013; Spence and Fluri 2008).

Like the military dimension, the civilian dimension of CSDP suffers from quantitative and qualitative shortfalls, which are only laboriously overcome in the process of civilian capability generation. Shortfalls are identified on the availability of specialized staff, mission and planning support capability, adequate financing, the ability to deploy at short notice, creating synergies between the various civilian capacities, coherence between civilian and military capabilities, and cooperation with other actors within and outside the EU (Council 2011f; Gourlay 2013; Hynek 2011).

The development and deployment of civilian capabilities comes with a particular set of challenges in terms of consistency and inter-actor coordination. Civilian crisis management implicates a wider set of national actors within foreign policy. Foreign or Defence Ministries, Ministries of Interior Affairs, Justice, Policing and others are involved, each with their own bureaucracy, procedures and cultures. Moreover, establishing and deploying civilian capabilities cannot be treated in the same way as military capabilities. First, difficulties exist in extracting civilian experts from their domestic duties. Whereas working abroad is normal for soldiers, extracting judges or policemen from domestic duties and asking them to leave on short notice is more complex and more expensive. Second, contributing governments can be rather reluctant to part with certain

Table 8.1   Civilian capabilities within CSDP

Priority sector	Task	Capacity goal
Police	Capable of carrying out any police operation from advisory, assistance and training tasks to substitution for local police forces.	A pool of more than 5,000 police officers, 1,400 are to be deployable in fewer than 30 days.
Rule of law	Capable of both strengthening and temporarily substituting for the local judiciary/legal system.	200 judges and prosecutors, part of whom are to be deployable within 30 days.
Civil administration	Capable of providing administrative services that the local administration is unable to offer (i.e. elections or taxation).	A pool of more than 500 experts.
Civil protection	To develop assessment and/or coordination teams.	Assessment or coordination teams of 10 experts to be dispatched within seven hours; intervention teams of up to 2,000 people and additional specialized services.
Monitoring missions	Monitoring missions including border monitoring, human rights monitoring or observing the general political situation.	More than 500 experts.
Generic support capabilities	Support the work of EU Special Representatives or form part of multifaceted CSDP missions.	A pool of 400 personnel including experts in political affairs, mediation, security sector reform, and disarmament, demobilization and reintegration (DDR).

Source: EU (2009).

resources, particularly where these are in relatively short supply at the national level.

To operationalize and lead civilian crisis management, the EU has developed structures at both the political and operational level (see Chapter 3). Situated within the EEAS, the Committee for Civilian Aspects of Crisis Management (CIVCOM) works at the political level, providing information, giving advice to the PSC and COREPER, and ensuring follow-up with regard to civilian crisis management capabilities and missions (see Chapter 3). On an operational level, the Civilian Planning and Conduct Capability (CPCC) is the locus for the planning, deployment, conduct and review of civilian CSDP missions. In institutional terms, the civilian side of CSDP is markedly smaller than its military counterpart. While there are over 200 people in the EUMS, only 60 people work in the CPCC (EEAS 2013a: 41). Furthermore, the military dimension has the luxury of recourse to NATO or national headquarters for planning and operational control, but the EU staff working on civilian missions do not have the potential back-up of external planning entities. The different approaches and different institutional set-up of the EU's civilian and military dimensions also explain the major challenges regarding civil–military coordination (Hynek 2011; Norheim-Martinsen 2010). This points to the role of the EEAS's Crisis Management and Planning Directorate (CMPD), which assumes responsibility for political–strategic planning of CSDP missions and operations and for ensuring coherence as part of the EU's comprehensive approach to crisis management.

Evaluating the CSDP's civilian crisis management capabilities in an isolated way is misleading. The CSDP missions are generally deployed – whether in a coordinated way or not – in addition to other civilian crisis management instruments from the EU's external action toolbox, such as the Instrument for Stability and the African Peace Facility (see Chapter 6). These are partially complementary and partially overlapping, strengthening the EU's crisis management policy, but sometimes also giving rise to turf battles and undermining consistency and effectiveness of EU policy. It is only when examining the various instruments and initiatives as a whole that the development and institutionalization of the EU's multifaceted crisis management policy can be fully understood (see also Gourlay 2013; Gross and Juncos 2011).

Military Operations and Civilian Missions

Considering that European security and defence cooperation has been a taboo for several decades, the EU's record with regard to civilian and military operations looks quite impressive. By early 2013, eight EU military operations, 18 civilian missions, and one combined civilian–military operation, have been launched; as of early 2013, 15 missions and operations were still deployed. They varied widely, with the length of missions ranging from merely a few months to nearly a decade, and the staff ranging from a scant dozen advisers to some thousands of soldiers (see Table 8.2) (for regularly updated overviews, see EEAS 2013c and CSDP MAP 2013).

The development and launch of CSDP operations and missions have been rather uneven, both in terms of time and geographically. The entrepreneurship of High Representative Solana and certain member states (particularly France), and the demand for EU action from third actors (NATO, UN and third countries) prompted a rapid succession of new missions and operations between 2003 and 2008. This was subsequently followed by a period of stagnation, a result of the transitional problems related to the setup of the EEAS, the more limited interest of both HR/VP Ashton and France (under President Sarkozy), and concerns about the financial costs of CSDP missions and operations. More recently, CSDP gained new momentum, with the Horn of Africa and the Sahel region replacing the Western Balkans as the main scene for CSDP action. The EU has or had CSDP missions and operations in several regions in the world: the Western Balkans, the Caucasus, the Middle East, sub-Saharan Africa and Asia. However, in terms of continuity, number and variety of missions and operations, the Western Balkans and Africa take centre stage, with a significant number directed at the DR Congo and, more recently, the Horn of Africa and the Sahel region (see Chapters 6 and 11).

As not every mission or operation can be analysed separately, the remainder of this section identifies some questions along which missions and operations, both past and future, can be understood. Detailed analyses and case studies have been made on the nature of the missions and operations, and of their objectives, relevance and impact (see Biscop and Whitman 2013; Blockmans *et al.* 2010; Dari *et al.* 2012; Ekengren and Simons 2011; Ginsberg and Penksa 2012; Grevi *et al.* 2009; Gross and Juncos 2011; Mattelaer 2013; Merlingen 2012).

A first set of questions pertains to the *military and civilian nature* of CSDP missions and operations and to their position on the *relational versus structural foreign policy axis*. How is a mission or operation to be situated in the range of tasks identified in the field of military and civilian crisis management (cf. Art. 43(1) TEU and the six priorities in the civilian domain)? The missions and operations have covered most of the tasks that have been enumerated. They are in most cases conducted in low-intensity crises and low-risk situations. Gun power and coercion by combat forces have thus been the exception, although a case like Operation Atalanta, which includes a mandate to undertake onshore military strikes against pirate bases, shows that it is possible. CSDP missions and operations recently moved into a new area with potentially a direct impact on military conflicts: the training of third countries'

Table 8.2   Overview of CSDP missions and operations

Mission/operation	Type of mission/operation	Scope
Western Balkans		
Operation Concordia (FYROM, 2003)	Military operation (Berlin Plus)	400 forces
EUPM (BiH, 2003–12)	Police mission	34 international and 47 local staff
Operation Proxima (FYROM, 2003–5)	Police mission	200 police experts
EUFOR Althea (BiH, 2004)	Military operation (Berlin Plus)	Around 1,400 forces
EUPAT (FYROM, 2005–6)	Police mission	30 police advisers
EULEX Kosovo (Kosovo, 2008–)	Police/rule-of-law mission	1,350 international and 1,150 local staff
Caucasus		
EUJUST THEMIS (Georgia, 2004–5)	Rule-of-law mission	10 international civilian experts
EUBAM to Moldova and Ukraine (Moldova/ Ukraine, 2005–)	Border assistance mission	Approx. 100 experts and 120 local support staff
EUMM Georgia (Georgia, 2008–)	Monitoring mission	Approx. 300 international and 100 local staff
Africa		
Operation Artemis (DRC, 2003)	Military autonomous operation (EU OHQ in France)	1,700 forces
EUPOL KINSHASA (DRC, 2005–7)	Police mission	Approx. 30 staff members
EUFOR DR Congo (DRC, 2006)	Military autonomous operation (EU OHQ in Germany)	Over 1,000 forces; rapid force available
EUSEC DR Congo (DRC, 2005–)	Security sector reform	51 staff
EU support to Amis II (Darfur)(Sudan, 2005–6)	Civilian–military mission	31 police, 27 military experts and observers
EUPOL DR Congo (Congo, 2007–)	Police mission	50 international police officers
EUFOR Chad/RCA (Chad, 2008–9)	Military autonomous operation (EU OHQ in France)	3,700 forces

→

Mission/operation	Type of mission/operation	Scope
EU SSR Guinea-Bissau (Guinea-Bissau, 2008–10)	Security sector reform	8 international and 16 local staff
EU NAVFOR Somalia (Operation Atalanta) (Somalia, 2008–)	Military autonomous maritime operation (EU OHQ in the UK)	1,400 troops
EUTM Somalia (Uganda, 2010–)	Military Training mission of Somali soldiers (EU Mission HQ in Uganda)	106 troops
EUFOR Libya (Libya, 2011, not launched in absence of a request from the UN)	Military autonomous operation (EU OHQ, Italy)	
EUCAP Nestor (Horn of Africa, 2012–)	Civilian training mission / Regional maritime capacity building	29 staff
EUCAP Sahel (Niger, 2012–)	Civilian training and capacity building mission	26 staff
EUAVSEC South Sudan (2012–)	Aviation security mission	13 staff
EUTM Mali (Mali, 2013–)	Military training mission	450 total staff
EUBAM Libya (Libya, 2013, to be deployed)	Border assistance mission	110 staff
Middle East		
EUJUST LEX (Iraq, 2005–)	Rule of law	800 judges and police officers
EUBAM Rafah (Palestinian Territories 2005–)	Border assistance mission	9 EU and 8 local staff
EUPOL COPPS (Palestinian Territories 2006–)	Police	70 international and 41 local staff
Asia		
Aceh Monitoring Mission (AMM) (Aceh, Indonesia, 2005–6)	Monitoring mission	80 unarmed personnel
EUPOL Afghanistan (Afghanistan, 2007–)	Police	350 international staff and 200 local staff

Note: Situation as of May 2013.

Source: EEAS (2013c).

armed forces, which are subsequently sent to the battlefield, as was the case with the EUTM Somalia mission (see Box 8.1) (see Oksamytna 2011). The EU military Training Mission in Mali (EUTM Mali), launched in early 2013, has equally the objective to strengthen the capabilities of the Malian army to operate more effectively in its territory (see Box 6.2).

Whereas the Treaty focuses to a large extent on tasks involving military capabilities, the EU has mainly deployed civilian missions. The boundary between military operations and civilian missions is, nevertheless, not always clear. For instance, the EUCAP Nestor mission, which has the mandate to support regional maritime capacity-building in the Horn of Africa, is described by the EU as a civilian mission augmented by military expertise. Likewise, EUSEC DR Congo is a civilian mission paid from the CFSP budget, but conducted by military staff in support of reforms of the Congolese army (EEAS 2013c).

Looking at CSDP missions and operations through the relational versus structural foreign policy lens provides further insights into the nature of the mission or operation (see Chapter 1). Some missions and operations are clearly focused on managing conflictual relations between third actors in the framework of conflict prevention or peacekeeping. Hence, they rather serve a relational foreign policy objective. Examples include the military operations in the Western Balkans (Merlingen 2013), in Chad/RCA and the DR Congo (Brosig 2011; Wittebrood and Gadry 2010; Mattelaer 2013), or the monitoring missions in Aceh and Georgia (Davies J. 2010; Bosse 2011). Other missions demonstrate a structural foreign policy approach, aimed at shaping or supporting new institutions and rules. Illustrations are the regional maritime capacity-building mission in the Horn of Africa as well as the EULEX Kosovo mission (Keukeleire and Metais 2014) and the various smaller rule-of-law and security sector reform missions (Ekengren and Simons 2011; Justaert 2014). The purpose is increasingly not to provide security in the short run through direct action, but rather to contribute in the longer run to the strengthening or establishment of effective security structures.

A second set of questions touches upon the positioning of CSDP missions and operations within the broader *multifaceted, multilevel and multilateral nature* of the EU's foreign policy (see Chapters 1 and 13), also raising questions regarding consistency (see Chapter 4). Is a CSDP mission or operation a relatively isolated endeavour, or is it part of a policy that is meant to be comprehensive and in which other parts of the EU's toolbox are also used coherently (see also Chapter 6 and 11)? An example of the latter is the EULEX Kosovo mission, which from the start was complemented by long-term assistance programmes and intense diplomatic involvement (Keukeleire *et al.* 2011) (see also Chapter 7). Other examples are the CSDP missions and operations that are framed within the EU Strategies towards the Sahel Region (see Box 6.2) and towards the Horn of Africa (see Box 8.1).

On the contrary, whereas the EUJUST LEX Iraq and the EUPOL Afghanistan missions initially suggested that the EU has a clear policy towards those countries, this is not really the case (Gross 2010, 2011; Sedra 2011). The latter also points to a particular phenomenon: a 'CSDP without CFSP' or, more exactly, a CSDP operation without the EU having a clear foreign policy towards the related crisis or conflict. CSDP missions or operations can give the misleading impression that the EU has an agreed foreign policy for the issue at hand. A common foreign policy on a specific issue may indeed exist in terms of general objectives, but a substantive or deep agreement on how to deal with an issue is often absent (see Chapter 7). Agreeing to a limited and 'harmless' CSDP mission or operation can then become a surrogate for a comprehensive and detailed common foreign policy towards specific issues.

It is also useful to gauge the role of CSDP in the context of the overall international response to crises. CSDP missions and operations are nearly always part of a broader multilateral effort and are often launched after an explicit external demand to support, complement or replace other organizations such as the UN, NATO and the AU (see Biscop and Whitman 2013: 253–301; Ginsberg and Penksa 2013: 161–229; Gourlay 2010; Hofmann 2011; Kirchner 2011; Koops 2011; Lucarelli *et al.* 2013). As mentioned, the EU took over from NATO in the Western Balkans and, more generally, 'emerges as a not inconsequential actor in the Atlantic security system' (Sperling 2011: 53). EUFOR Chad/RCA and Operation Artemis bridged operations for UN missions, whereas EUFOR DR Congo reinforced the UN during the sensitive period of the first democratic elections. Complementing other multilateral naval forces (including of NATO), Operation Atalanta also supports vessels of the AU and the World Food Programme. And through its support for security sector reform and capacity-building (including military training) the EU found a 'niche' in which the EU usefully contributed to wider multilateral efforts in post-conflict situations (Spence 2011). In their evaluation of the impact of CSDP on other international security providers, Ginsberg and Penksa (2012: 228) therefore conclude that the EU is increasingly considered as a relevant security actor.

A third set of questions relates to *the objectives and rationales behind a mission or an operation*. Do CSDP missions and operations correspond to strategic and other external policy objectives of the EU, or do they reflect other types of objectives? The strategic rationale behind decisions to launch the various CSDP missions and operations is often far from clear (Biscop and Coelmont 2012: 36–7). In fact, the three sets of missions and operations that most seem to stem from the EU's strategic objectives are the operations in the Western Balkans (to stop the destabilizing impact of conflicts in that area), in the Horn of Africa (to safeguard crucial trade routes to Asia) and, more recently, in the Sahel region (to avoid increasing instability and growing Jihadist influence spilling over

---

Box 8.1   CSDP and the EU Strategy for the Horn of Africa

The three CSDP actions in the Horn of Africa – Operation Atalanta, EUCAP Nestor and EUTM Somalia – are part of the 'EU Strategy for the Horn of Africa' (Council 2011g; EEAS 2013e), which, for once, seems to deserve the label 'strategy'. Like other initiatives of the EU in the region, these CSDP actions are all aimed at the same goal: securing the strategic naval trade routes to the Asia-Pacific region. This requires order and development in the 'failed state' Somalia, which was controlled by the Islamist armed group al-Shabaab and other groups. The Strategy encompasses both relational and structural foreign policy dimensions; reflects the 'comprehensive approach' discussed in Chapter 6, including diplomatic, civilian, military, judicial, humanitarian and development components; is supported through the EUSR for the Horn of Africa; and is part of broader multilateral efforts (see also Ehrhardt and Petretto 2012a, 2012b; Kaunert and Zwolski 2012).

Relational foreign policy is mainly pursued through the naval *Operation EUNAVFOR Atalanta*. With its 1,800 troops it is the largest military CSDP operation outside Europe. Since 2008 it has been combating piracy and protecting vessels from the UN World Food Programme in the Indian Ocean, including through the use of force. This is complemented by the structural foreign policy of the capacity-building mission *EUCAP Nestor*, which aims to strengthen the capacities of five countries in the region to combat piracy and strengthen related rule-of-law systems. These actions are complemented by other EU actions, including capacity-building programmes by the IfS, an anti-piracy programme of EUROPOL, as well as by the EU's support for programmes of INTERPOL and UN agencies.

→

on the Mediterranean). Other CSDP missions and operations correspond to general foreign policy objectives, such as strengthening the rule of law or supporting UN missions, without always being clear why these objectives lead to CSDP action in some countries and not in others. This again reflects an ad hocism which, as Gross and Juncos (2011: 148) emphasize, often negatively affects the EU's performance.

Recalling the internal objectives of the EU's foreign policy – integration, identity and interrelational objectives – can equally help to explain the launch of CSDP missions and operations (see Chapter 1). At least initially, civilian missions like those in Iraq and Afghanistan aimed to alleviate internal tensions within the EU and to appease external pressures from the US regarding the EU's minimal involvement in these two hotbeds. Several smaller and short-term missions and operations sought to expand the reach of CSDP or to demonstrate that the

In the longer term, the anti-piracy actions can only be tackled if order is re-established in Somalia itself. Despite initial doubts, the EU and other international actors supported the Somali Transitional Federal Government (TFG). Since 2010, the CSDP EU Training Mission *EUTM Somalia* complements the EU's active diplomatic policy in favour of the TFG by providing operational support for its efforts to regain control over Somali territory. Despite its small staff of 100 people and its modest budget, the EUTM Somalia was considered as effective in training troops that were subsequently used in successfully combating al-Shabaab and regaining control over part of the Somali territory in cooperation with the African Union Mission in Somalia (AMISOM). The African Peace Facility – managed by the Commission (see Chapter 6) – has provided considerable budgetary support for AMISOM (which comprised 1,7000 troops of the African Union), including for troop allowances and salaries for police officers.

Other Commission managed instruments have also been used as part of the EU's Strategy for the Horn of Africa: humanitarian aid as a response to the famine; substantial EDF support for the development of Somalia and the wider region; funding for a wide range of programmes through the EIDHR and the IfS (such as support for civil society or for counteracting trafficking of firearms); and support for various initiatives to combat illegal fishing (such as the 'ACP FISH II' programme). However, the limited priority given to the fight against illegal fishing raises doubts about the EU's seriousness in tackling another root source of the piracy problem: the presence of large illegal fleets of European and Asian industrial fishing ships that contributed to stock depletion (Anderson 2010).

Sources: EEAS (2013c).

EU is an international actor, irrespective of whether these missions and operations had the potential to make a difference in the field.

Member states' (and particularly France's) policy entrepreneurship offer another explanation for the launch of missions and operations, prompted by their success in uploading or Europeanizing national preferences and foreign policy objectives (Biscop and Coelmont 2012: 36) (see Chapter 5). However, this often results in CSDP missions or operations that are supported by all member states on paper, but in fact struggle to obtain sufficient funding and staff from member states other than those who initiated the mission or operation. In practice, other member states may pursue parallel foreign policy activities or provide operational support to actions initiated by other international organizations, thereby bypassing EU action (as was the case with the EUPOL DR Congo mission) (Justaert and Keukeleire 2010; Justaert 2012). This also raises doubts about the 'common' character of these CSDP missions and operations and it may undermine their credibility, as well as the credibility of CSDP at large.

This leads to a fourth set of questions, pertaining to the *effectiveness and added value of CSDP missions and operations* (see also Gross and Juncos 2011: 148). Determining the success of CSDP missions and operations is not straightforward, as it depends on both the explicit and hidden objectives of these missions. That missions and operations are generally part of broader European and international efforts makes it harder to determine the impact of a CSDP action as such. For a considerable number of missions and operations, the impact and added value is rather limited, reflecting their often-limited size, short duration or lack of alignment (Justaert 2014). CSDP can be seen, though, as relatively successful in the Western Balkans (Merlingen 2013). Other successes – within the framework of their more limited mandates – include the Aceh Monitoring Mission (Davies J. 2010), EUTM Somalia and EUSEC DR Congo (Martinelli 2010). However, this last example illustrates how a mission may be successful in realizing the objectives within a specific aspect of a security problem (such as contributing to the implementation of some aspects of the reform plan of the defence forces of the DR Congo), but how the remaining general security problems in a target country can overshadow a mission's success in terms of reaching long-term and strategic foreign policy objectives (see also Chapter 7).

The Industrial and Technological Aspect

The EU's capacity to undertake operations is considerably limited as a result of serious shortfalls in military and technological capabilities. These shortfalls are linked to both the fragmented and inefficiently used defence budgets and the fragmented defence and technology market.

A first shortfall that hinders the EU's operational capacities is related to the fragmentation and inefficiency of the European defence budgets. Indeed, the US has long lambasted its European partners for the size of their defence budgets – in 2010 the annual defence budget of the EDA member states (i.e. all EU member states except Denmark) was €194 billion, or 1.6 per cent of their common GDP, while that of the US was around €520 billion or 4.8 per cent of the American GDP. Whereas the US's defence budget was steadily rising (with an increase of nearly 25 per cent in five years), the defence budget of the Europeans was below that of five years earlier (EDA 2012: 2). On paper, €194 billion should be ample to meet European defence ambitions. Nonetheless, both the fragmentation of expenditure and the total amounts being spent prove to be stumbling blocks. For example, in 2010 only 22 per cent of defence equipment procurement occurred in European collaborative schemes and only 11.8

per cent of defence R&T (research and technology) expenditure was spent collectively (EDA 2011: 13–16). Member states do not have the budget to individually bankroll large-scale procurement or research projects, and by failing to coordinate defence expenditure, major short-falls at the EU level are not addressed.

The EU's attempt to meet this challenge consists of more research and development of weapons systems at the European level. This is considered a tool to ensure interoperability of member states' armed forces and to meet high costs. One of the functions of the EDA is to push forward the *European Defence Research and Technology* (EDRT) strategy. This involves pursuing collaborative use of national defence R&T budgets to meet priorities set at the EU level. The voluntary nature of the strategy and the general constraints to which EDA is subject (see Chapter 4), limit the EDA's potential to enforce significant progress. Cooperating and coordinating research efforts has also been targeted by the Commission as an area in which common action can add value, even if in formal terms the Commission can only support civilian rather than defence research. However, under the multiannual Research Framework Programmes, the Commission has major leverage, allocating considerable budget resources to aeronautics and space, supporting dual-use research, and establishing the *European Security Research Programme*, which amounted to €1.4 billion for a period of seven years (Jeandesboz and Ragazzi 2010). The Commission also established a forum of representatives of defence and security industries, research institutes and national Ministries of Defence and Interior. A comprehensive roadmap designed to inform policy-making for a period of 20 years resulted from this forum, providing for example the development of information and communication technologies and unmanned aerial vehicles (UAVs or 'drones') (ESRIF 2009; Commission 2009).

A second reason for the EU's limited operational capacities is that defence-related industries have largely been left outside the regulatory framework governing the EU internal market, resulting in a fragmented defence and technology market instead of a common EU-wide market. Article 346 TFEU serves as the legal basis for a security-based exemption to the general internal market rules, as it states that any member state, 'may take such measures as it considers necessary for the protection of the essential interests of its security which are connected with the production of or trade in arms, munitions and war material'. This security exemption in part accounts for the fragmented nature of the defence markets. This leads to a lack of competition and in turn drives up prices and negatively impacts innovation. The fragmentation and lack of coordination in equipment procurement also explains why a considerable number of the member states' weapon systems and armaments are not compatible, further undermining the interoperability and deployment ability of European forces (Chang 2011).

This challenge has been acknowledged by the EU. For instance, by launching a *European Defence Equipment Market* (EDEM), managed by the EDA, the EU hoped to increase competition and transparency in defence procurement. But because the intergovernmental regime is voluntary, its impact is limited: national governments remain reluctant to hand juicy defence procurement contracts to companies from other member states if this risks to having a negative effect on the national defence industry. Accordingly, expectations of various Commission-steered initiatives and the 'Defence Package' legislation of 2009 are higher, as these are binding rules and as they limit the scope of the above-mentioned security exemption (Bailes and Depauw 2011; Commission 2012g; Edwards 2011).

Member states also cooperated in the field of joint procurement initiatives outside the EU framework. Specific joint ventures include the production of fighter jets such as Eurofighter (Germany, Italy, Spain and the UK) and the military transport aircraft Airbus A400M (the same four countries plus France, Belgium, Luxembourg and Turkey). However, such cooperative ventures have suffered from major financial, organizational and technical problems, leading to significant delays and overspending (Mölling and Brune 2011: 56).

The responses of the EU member states, the EDA and the European Commission were affected by the financial crisis. This crisis had a twofold effect. On the one hand, it resulted in more cuts in the defence budgets of several member states. On the other hand, it also gave a new impetus for more 'pooling and sharing' of military capabilities (EDA 2011; Council 2012j), although it is not yet clear whether this will have substantial long-term effects on the EU's attempts to counter fragmentation (Faleg and Giovannini 2012).

The necessity to overcome fragmentation of budgets and markets was recognized and dealt with much earlier for space technology, a strategically important domain. In this respect, the *European Space Agency* (ESA) oversees the development of *Ariane* satellite launchers, which may become fundamental to various kinds of security operations (Darnis and Veclani 2011; FRS *et al.* 2011). Two other flagship strategic projects of the ESA and the Commission are the EU's earth observation system GMES (Global Monitoring for Environment and Security) and the *Galileo* satellite radio navigation system, which is to launch 24 satellites by late 2015. While initially designed for civilian use, both have ramifications for the EU's security and defence capabilities (ESA 2009; Commission 2011a; Veclani *et al.* 2011).

It is clear that the industrial and technological aspects of the EU's security and defence policy are growing and that this development brings the EU closer to a 'martial potency' (Manners 2006: 182). As Manners emphasizes, the gradual but pervasive securitization and militarization of EU policies is not only an answer to the challenges that are raised by the international environment. It is also the result of what he labels the European 'military–industrial simplex': 'the way in which both the military–armaments lobby and the technology–industrial lobby have worked at the EU level to create a simple but compelling relationship between the need for forces capable of robust intervention [and] the technological and industrial benefits of defence and aerospace research' (Manners 2006: 193). The predominance of major defence and security companies also emerges in the analysis of the Commission's security research policy and the 'EU security–industrial complex', leading to questions about democratic oversight and potential threats to citizen's fundamental freedoms and rights (Jeandesboz and Ragazzi 2010; Statewatch 2009). The political power of the European defence and space industry also stems from its economic importance. It employs some 700,000 people, contributes to 2 per cent of EU GDP, and includes industrial giants, such as the European Aeronautic Defence and Space Company (EADS), BAE Systems (formerly British Aerospace), Finmeccanica of Italy and Thales of France – all belonging to the top 10 of the world's largest defence industry companies (Andersson 2013; see also Meijer 2010).

The involvement of powerful private actors and networks generally remains under the radar of both public attention and academic research. Nevertheless, technology and defence industry giants may be a crucial factor in explaining the growth and development of both the CSDP and the EU's internal security policies (see Chapter 10) (see also Bechtel and Schneider 2010; Cross 2011). Turning to the EU actors, it also implies that, in addition to those actors that are usually in the spotlight (the Foreign Affairs Council, HR/VP and EEAS), the 'Competitiveness Council of Ministers' (responsible for internal market, industry, research and space) and the DGs for Research and Innovation and for Enterprise and Industry in the Commission may gain importance for the future of the CSDP capabilities and operations.

Conclusion

The speed of change in CSDP is rather remarkable when considering both the sensitive nature of the policy field and the various impediments discussed. However, the label 'CSDP' is misleading as this policy is not related to territorial defence and as it is less common than the word suggests. Indeed, CSDP is fully dependent on the voluntary contributions of the member states. In the last decade, more than 25 military operations and civilian missions have been deployed, leading to an active involvement of the EU in several crisis areas, mainly in the Western Balkans and Africa. CSDP has been able to move forward when the member states considered the relation between CSDP, their national foreign policies and the actions of other international organizations as a positive-sum game. The added value of CSDP is indeed that it can complement unilateral actions and/or civilian and military crisis management operations of the UN, NATO, the African Union and other international organizations.

Chapter 9

Trade, Development and Other External Action

This chapter analyses policy fields that are developed under what the Treaty calls the Union's 'external action' (Part five of the TFEU) (see Chapter 1). This includes trade, association and cooperation agreements; enlargement; development cooperation; sanctions; and humanitarian aid. In many cases, the EU's external action represents the cornerstone of the EU's foreign policy. These external action policies have shaped EU foreign policy and, in some cases, are foreign policies in and of themselves. They constitute the major instruments of EU foreign policy yet can also hinder the achievement of EU foreign policy objectives.

We look here at the manner in which the EU uses these external action fields and instruments to pursue a foreign policy, what this foreign policy actually looks like and how effective it is. In this context, it is useful to question the dominant perspectives of foreign policy and to use the concept of structural foreign policy (see Chapters 1 and 14). Structural foreign policy provides an analytical perspective and allows us to broaden and update our view of foreign policy without falling into the pitfall of portraying all the relations the EU has with external partners in various fields as foreign policy. This concept makes it easier to recognize the foreign policy dimension – actual or potential – of the EU's external action.

Trade

The common commercial policy

The EU is the world's largest trading bloc. It accounts for approximately one-sixth of world trade in goods and more than one-fifth of world trade in services (see Table 9.1) (see also Verdun 2011: 257–61). The EU's market and resulting bargaining power has grown through the various enlargement rounds over the last decades. The EU's only direct trading competitor is – and certainly has been – the US. The EU has a larger market than the US (a population of 500 million compared to the America's 300 million), but this pales in comparison to the growing economies of China and India with their populations of more than 1.3

Table 9.1   Share of world trade (2010)

| | Goods | | Services | |
	import	export	import	export
EU27	16.54%	15.06%	21.88%	24.39%
US	12.78%	8.39%	10.20%	14.04%
China	9.06%	10.36%	5.47%	4.61%
Japan	4.51%	5.05%	4.44%	3.76%
India	2.12%	1.44%	3.31%	3.34%
Canada	2.61%	2.55%	1.83%	2.56%
Russia	1.61%	2.63%	2.00%	1.19%
Brazil	1.24%	1.33%	1.70%	0.82%
South Africa	0.61%	0.54%	0.51%	0.37%

Source: WTO (2012).

billion and 1.1 billion respectively. With growth rates far outstripping the EU and the US, China and India are key economic competitors, and increasing market access to fast growing markets is essential for the EU to maintain its trade dominance.

The EU has exclusive competences on the common commercial policy (CCP) (Art. 207 TFEU) not only covering trade in goods, but also trade in services, trade-related intellectual property rights and foreign direct investment. Although the CCP was already included in the Treaty of Rome, the issue of distribution of competences has been a controversial process, certainly as 'new trade issues' such as services and intellectual property rights entered the international trading system (Meunier and Nicolaïdis 2011; Young and Peterson 2006).

The main consequence of the exclusive nature of the EU's trade competences is that the European Commission enjoys the sole responsibility of conducting trade negotiations for the EU (see Chapter 4). However, the Commission negotiates in an interdependent relationship with the Council, since it needs an authorization (and 'negotiating directives' or a 'mandate') from the Council to negotiate and since trade agreements only become legally binding for the EU once they are ratified by the Council and the EP. In many cases, trade agreements also need to be ratified by the member states individually due to the inclusion of elements 'beyond trade', such as provisions on good governance or labour standards, which are not exclusive EU competences. In many cases, interim agreements are concluded that can enter into force before all member states have ratified the full agreement (for an overview of EU trade policy and trade policy-making, see Poletti and De Bièvre 2013).

The delegation of trade negotiation authority to the Commission may be a bit misleading: the Commission is not a completely autonomous actor in trade negotiations. The Commission needs to ensure that the member states follow so that they will ultimately accept the deal – and the concessions – made by the Commission. The Commission is thus constantly negotiating at two levels, aiming to find a deal at the international level that is still covered by the member states at the EU level (see da Conceicão-Heldt 2010; Delreux and Kerremans 2010; Kerremans 2004a; Meunier 2005). In trade politics, the Commission and the member states operate under intense pressure of interest groups – and particularly lobbyists defending the interests of European exporting companies – making that also the negotiation position of the EU is largely influenced by interest group pressure (Dür 2008, 2011; Dür and De Bièvre 2007).

Although the EU is largely a 'single' actor in international trade, this does not make it a monolith. Member states not only differ in their economic interests in third countries or regions, but also in their preference for the extent to which trade-related interests should dominate foreign policy interests or development objectives (Sicurelli 2010: 103–7). Clearly, third countries can and do make use of such points of divergence within the EU and use their contacts with 'friendly' EU member states to promote their cause (see Bretherton and Vogler 2006: 78–80; Kerremans 2004b, 2006).

The EU uses a combination of three venues to conduct its CCP: its own unilateral trade policies, multilateral agreements and bilateral (or interregional) agreements. The EU can apply trade defence instruments against trade-distorting practices of other countries, such as anti-dumping or anti-subsidy measures. The application of this type of unilateral trade measures must always comply with WTO rules. The application of unilateral trade policy instruments has consequences for the general relations of the EU with the third country in question and, as a consequence, also for its foreign policy with that country.

Besides the unilateral application of trade measures, the most important trade instruments are international trade agreements. Until the second half of the 2000s, the EU clearly expressed favour for the multilateral venue, in which international trade is governed within the WTO with common trade rules for the more than 150 WTO members. However, since the second half of the 2000s, the EU has shifted its focus from the multilateral to the bilateral venue (Elsig 2007). It has negotiated or is negotiating preferential trade agreements bilaterally with key partners such as the US (on the so-called Transatlantic Trade and Investment Partnership, see Chapter 12), South Korea, Canada and Japan, as well as interregionally with Mercosur and the ACP regions. The result is a web of preferential trade agreements. The shift towards the bilateral venue – the EU's 'plan B' or second best option – is closely linked to the impasse in the WTO Doha Development Round, the latest multilateral trade round (see Poletti 2012). Indeed, when realizing the multilateral venue does not seem possible because of international negotiation dynamics, the EU opts for the bilateral and interregional venues.

Trade power with foreign policy fallout

The origins of the EU's role as an international actor lie in the CCP. Trade policy forced the EU to define its relations with the rest of the world and also created expectations in third countries that the EU was a major power (see Redmond 1992). This gradually demanded foreign policy-related choices. The EU quietly became an international actor and, later, also a foreign policy actor even though such a role had not initially been foreseen or supported by all member states. Today, the EU can exercise power and influence international affairs through its large single market and the externalization of market-related policies and regulatory measures (Damro 2012).

The EU's trade and foreign policies are inextricably linked for three reasons. First, since the CCP is fully part of the EU's external action, it should follow its principles and objectives – democracy, the rule of law, human rights, fundamental, equality and solidarity – which have broader foreign policy implications (Arts. 205 TFEU and 21 TEU). However, in practice, trade objectives in many cases prevail over these foreign policy objectives (see Chapter 6).

Second, trade policy provides essential instruments for foreign policy, including through sanctions and embargoes and support measures (see further). That trade policy is used as a foreign policy tool and that pure foreign policy considerations play a role in the common commercial policy can be illustrated by the fact that the EU granted increased market access to Pakistan after the summer 2010 floods that ravaged the country, a decision that was mainly driven by humanitarian objectives. Another example includes the EU's sanctions against the regime of Laurent Gbagbo in Côte d'Ivoire, who did not accept his electoral defeat in early 2010 (Hoffmeister 2011: 87–90). As illustrated in Chapter 11, support measures also serve to assist third countries in pursuing structural reforms.

Third, the EU's trade and agricultural policies can undermine foreign and development policy objectives, including poverty reduction. Trade is not 'just' an external policy. The type of trade policy conducted by the EU, both in multilateral fora and with regard to specific third countries, can affect their economies and, indirectly, their political systems, societies and the welfare of individuals. This impact – positive or negative in terms of human security, societal security and political stability – also determines the international security context in which the EU is embedded and in which it operates as a foreign policy actor.

Trade has never been apolitical, but the furore surrounding WTO meetings, including the vehement protests led by anti-globalization protestors since the meeting in Seattle in 1999, is testimony to its increasing level of politicization. The Doha Development Round has been deadlocked since July 2006. It collapsed amid highly vocal mutual recriminations between the EU, the US, India and developing countries. These tensions revolved around agriculture (developing countries sought increased developed-world market access for their agricultural products and reductions in agricultural production and export subsidies) and non-agricultural market access (the US and EU sought increased market access to emerging economies like China, Brazil and India for their industrial goods through a reduction in industrial tariffs). The EU had also been pushing two additional interests: services liberalization, reflecting the fact that services represent over 70 per cent of its economy; and other behind-the-border measures like investment, competition policy, government procurement and trade facilitation (the so-called 'Singapore issues') (see Meunier and Nicolaïdis 2011). By putting these issues on the agenda, the EU also aimed to broaden the agenda in order to be able to make European concessions on agricultural trade in exchange for concessions by external partners on these 'new issues'. Since the 2000s, the EU's more ambitious trade agenda is apparent, but the EU has not been effective in realizing these ambitions. Three of the four Singapore issues were removed from the agenda in 2004, for example, when aiming to rescue the Doha Development Round (Young 2011).

While the EU's rhetoric vocally touts international trade liberalization, the EU in practice does not bring this to fruition across the board. As Meunier and Nicolaïdis put it: 'the issue is not only how much liberalisation, but also what kind of liberalisation and for whose benefit' (2005: 260). Agriculture related debates best illustrate this issue. The EU's determination to defend its common agricultural policy (CAP), which also soaks up 40 per cent of its budget, has a serious negative impact on its capacity to achieve goals in international trade negotiations, as well as foreign policy goals such as poverty eradication. Agriculture makes up a small proportion of the EU economy, but it is the mainstay of many developing countries' economies, especially the poorest. Agricultural concessions are traditionally difficult for the Commission since a group of member states, usually led by France, is particularly reluctant to further liberalize the agricultural market.

The EU has taken initiatives to reform the CAP since the beginning of the 1990s, namely the MacSharry Reform (1992), the Mid Term Review (2003) and the Health Check reform (2008) (see Grant 2011). On the one hand, a system which linked financial support to farmers with the volume of production is gradually replaced by direct incomes for farmers (i.e. 'decoupling'). This reduces pressure to overproduce and to dump overproduction (financially supported by export subsidies) on the world market, which would lead to distortions of local markets. In the course of the Doha Development Round negotiations, the EU also conceded to phase out export subsidies. However, market price support reforms, reliant on high import tariffs to maintain artificially high prices, have not been sufficiently far-reaching to have a substantial positive impact on external competitors. This is combined with tariffs and non-tariff barriers (administrative procedures or health and safety standards, for example) on agricultural goods entering the EU market, effectively limiting imports and protecting domestic producers. On the other hand, agricultural policy reforms have brought the 'multifunctionality of the CAP' to the forefront, emphasizing the protection of the countryside and related issues like ecotourism as equally important as the production of food as an economic sector.

In its decision-making, the EU often disregards the political dimension and the broader external impact of its trade policy. Core EU foreign policy objectives, including the integration of developing countries into the world economy, are fragile when pitched against the realpolitik of protecting Europe's farmers. Where trade objectives are weighed against development or foreign policy objectives, the trade perspective indeed tends to dominate.

Through its 'Everything but Arms' (EBA) initiative adopted in February 2001 (and the current cycle lasting to 2015), the EU tried to mitigate the negative side effects of its trade and agricultural policies on developing countries (see Faber and Orbie 2007). The initiative provides the 48 countries belonging to the least developed countries (LDC) group duty-free access for all exports to the EU market (except arms and munitions) without any quantitative restrictions. But, imports of bananas, rice and sugar (key markets for many LDCs) were not fully liberalized immediately given their sensitivity to EU producers. Proponents argue EBA is an important development tool. A counterargument is that these countries are so removed from competing in the international economy that they have virtually nothing to trade anyway, which makes the initiative quite 'cheap' for the EU.

The fact that the EU's economic dominance led the EU to develop an international role and subsequently a foreign policy highlights trade's influence in shaping the nature and form of EU foreign policy. It is unlikely that EU foreign policy would rely so heavily on contractual agreements, through which the EU provides preferential access to the internal market as well as financial and technical aid, if it were not such a strong actor in trade. As illustrated in the following section, the decision to conclude a trade or association and cooperation agreement with a third country/regional organization, as well as the depth and scope of this agreement, is to a large extent foreign policy. The EU also attempts to use trade agreements to pursue specific foreign policy objectives, for example seeking to incorporate environmental and labour standards. The EU's attempts to expand its regulatory practice and values have been resisted by developing countries, which perceive such moves as yet another form of protectionism (Bretherton and Vogler 2006: 86).

Association and Cooperation Agreements

The nature of agreements

Association and cooperation agreements are based on economic instruments such as access to the internal market and the provision of aid. However, these agreements have become increasingly political over the last decades. There are three types of agreements (see Lenaerts and Van Nuffel 2011: 977–90):

- pure trade agreements (Art. 207 TFEU);
- trade and economic cooperation agreements (Arts. 207 and 218 TFEU) (they can also incorporate Art. 211 TFEU if there is a development component or Art. 212 TFEU for non-development focused economic, financial and technical cooperation, as well as other Treaty articles on e.g. the approximation of laws or Trans-European networks);
- association agreements (Art. 217 TFEU);
- agreements with the EU's (southern and eastern) neighbouring countries (Art. 8 TEU) (see Chapter 11).

Normally they will not actually be called 'trade and economic cooperation agreement' or 'association agreement' – they are given a name such as a Stabilisation and Association Agreement (with the Western Balkan countries), a Partnership and Cooperation Agreement (with for instance Russia, Ukraine, countries from the South Caucasus and Central Asia – a lot of them covered by the European Neighbourhood Policy, see Chapter 11), or a Partnership Agreement (such as the Cotonou Agreement with ACP countries). In practice, most of these agreements are 'mixed agreements'. This is because, in addition to issues that fall under the EU's exclusive competence, agreements generally incorporate other areas where competence is shared with the member states (see Chapter 4).

Scope, contents and motivation

The EU has some form of trade, association or cooperation agreement with nearly every country in the world. In terms of geographical scope, this network of formalized relations is more extensive than the bilateral network of any member state alone. This means that each member state, via the EU, can maintain some form of foreign policy with regard to third countries/regions at minimal cost.

It is mainly the EU's economic power that first and foremost makes it an attractive partner for third countries. However, the EU uses this economic allure to build leverage on political issues. The issues covered in agreements vary substantially. In terms of market access, the level of trade preference accorded is highly variable. The EU's agreement with Turkey, for example, extends its customs union, and the Stabilization and Association Agreements with Western Balkan states create a free trade area. The relationship with Malaysia, on the other hand, does not provide for bilateral preferential trade arrangements at all. The objective of the trade partnership with the Mediterranean countries is to create a 'Euro-Mediterranean Free Trade Area'. Agreements also create the structure through which the EU channels financial and technical aid. They provide for cooperation in various socio-economic fields and in a host of other areas of interest including migration, justice and home affairs issues, CFSP, drugs, science, culture or the environment. They can also provide for support to the political structures of a country or region (for example capacity-building of state institutions, good governance and rule of law). The scope and depth of issues subject to cooperation varies depending on several factors: geographic location relative to the EU, prospect of EU membership, level and nature of political relations, and (a)symmetry of the relationship between the EU and the third country. Timing also factors into the level of cooperation and is indicative of the scope and breadth of an agreement: the scope of policy issues deliberated in the EU framework has increased over time, as has the breadth of issues incorporated into agreements.

This last point relates to one of the pitfalls of the EU's continuously expanding relations with third countries and regions. With each new round of negotiations, there is a tendency to broaden the range of issues in the agreements, to upgrade the text, and to adjust the relationship's label to demonstrate the importance attached to the process (e.g. from 'Partnership' to 'Strategic Partnership'). However, enhancing the terminology and broadening the issues covered by the agreement is often not matched by concrete improvements or increased budgets. Moreover, broadening the scope of agreements often mirrors the continuously expanding competences of the EU rather than reflecting new opportunities for substantive cooperation or real new commitments from the EU or the partners involved. Combined, these factors contribute to the EU's famous 'capability–expectations gap' (Hill 1993).

Concluding – or refusing to conclude – agreements with third states has been a trump card for the EU. The EU can decide to conclude an agreement as a reward for 'good behaviour'. The prospect of an agreement is also used as an incentive to affect desired changes within a country. And conversely, by rejecting an agreement with a third country or rejecting the inclusion of issues that are advantageous for that country, the EU can pressure or sanction it.

The examples given above indicate that the agreements concluded by the EU can be an instrument of both conventional and structural foreign policy. Agreements are used as part of the EU toolbox to react to specific conflicts or crises, allowing the EU to reward, sanction or pressure third states. And, in view of their longer time-frame and the broad scope of policy fields involved, cooperation and association agreements can (at least on paper) provide a firm basis for a structural foreign policy. They can be instrumental in supporting or inducing structural reforms or in strengthening existing political, legal and socio-economic structures in third countries and regions (see Holden 2009). Conditionality and political dialogue instruments, both discussed below, provide further support to this dynamic.

Conditionality

Conditionality refers to the practice of making the conclusion and implementation of agreements, cooperation, and assistance by the EU dependent on certain conditions being met by third countries. It is often applied in enlargement policy, as well as in trade and development agreements, where access to the European market or financial aid is exchanged for changes in domestic practices. It takes several forms: positive and negative, political and economic, *ex ante* and *ex post*. It 'promis[es] benefit(s) to a state if it fulfils the political and/or economic conditions' (positive conditionality), or 'reduc[es], suspend[s] or terminat[es] those benefits if the state in question violates the conditions' (negative conditionality) (Smith K. 2008: 58).

Ex ante conditionality refers to conditions that must be met *before* an agreement is concluded. As Fierro argues in relation to EU candidate countries, '*ex ante* conditionality represents the most sophisticated form of conditionality because when it applies to European countries, conditions are spelled out with great detail. They are also periodically examined and regularly monitored' (2003: 377–8). However, where *ex ante* conditionality is applied to non-European countries, it becomes a less sophisticated instrument as monitoring is much more superficial (Fierro 2003: 378).

Ex post conditionality, which is more common, refers to conditions or 'essential elements' which must be met *after* an agreement has been concluded. Since 1995, almost all EU agreements contain at least a human rights clause and often provisions to make the respect for democratic principles and the rule-of-law essential elements of the agreement (see Hafner-Burton 2009). Since 2004, the EU has also pressured its partners into accepting the inclusion of a non-proliferation clause which makes the fight against the proliferation of WMD an essential element of the agreement. If either party to the agreement does not respect one of its essential elements then the agreement, and thus the cooperation and aid arrangements for which it provides, can be suspended in whole or in part. This would normally follow a period of consultations in which parties attempt to find a mutually acceptable solution.

Because of the difficulty of applying these measures, Fierro argues that *ex post* conditionality 'tends to be static rather than dynamic and symbolic rather than substantial' (2003: 377–8). The EU has made much greater use of conditionality provisions in the EU–ACP Cotonou Agreement (see further) than in its relations with Asia, Latin America, the Middle East or the Mediterranean (see Chapter 11). However, as Mbangu (2005) argues, even in EU–ACP relations, conditionality tends to be a reactive instrument only invoked where the violation of an essential element was so blatant that it was quasi-impossible to ignore. The prevailing negative image of 'essential elements' clauses in some ACP countries has deterred the EU from opening early-stage consultations in states where respect for democracy and human rights is deteriorating. For countries subject to it, conditionality is an unwelcome practice. The EU's extensive use of terms like 'essential elements' or 'political dialogue' allows for the circumvention of the word 'conditionality', which is by many third states considered as an unacceptable word. Large, emerging powers like India particularly disapprove of the EU's tendency to link the conclusion of trade agreements with political considerations. Paradoxically, whereas within the EU the intensified use of conditionality is seen as a positive instrument of a strong foreign policy, invoking such conditionality can sour the EU's trade and foreign policy relations with third parties.

It is difficult to draw conclusions about the effectiveness of the EU's use of conditionality. The Commission rhetoric suggests that it is indeed effective, but evidence is more mixed (Meunier and Nicolaïdis 2006). However, it is interesting to note that the landscape is changing. The West does not have a monopoly on donorship or on buying African exports, particularly oil and commodities. Donors such as China and India are willing to trade and to provide aid without the constraints of Western-style conditionality. Moreover, their aid is potentially more effective and more visible to the local population than that from the EU (see Cheru and Obi 2010; Men and Barton 2011) (see Chapter 12).

Political dialogue

The provisions for political dialogue in agreements are particularly important from a foreign policy perspective (see Devuyst and Men 2012). The EU now incorporates political dialogue into its agreements as a matter of course. Generally, agreements establish political dialogue on ministerial, senior official and expert levels. Although the precise aims of political dialogue vary, generally they incorporate some of the following aspects: increasing convergence of positions on international issues of mutual concern; cooperation on matters pertaining to the strengthening of stability and security in Europe and the region in question; and reinforcing democracy and the respect and promotion of human rights, including minority rights and the rule of law.

Each cooperation and association agreement creates foreign policy machinery through provisions for 'institutions of the agreement' as well as the regular meetings foreseen for political dialogue. For example, the Euro-Med Association Agreement with Morocco provides for an Association Council (ministerial level) and an Association Committee (official level), supplemented by several subcommittees (including one on human rights, democratization and governance) (see Van Hüllen 2012). The creation of this bilateral apparatus deepens the level of cooperation between the EU and the third country or region. Meetings touch on all sectors of the economy and government.

By forming joint institutions, a potentially powerful instrument for foreign policy is created. However, this can also be counterproductive. The high frequency of meetings at ministerial level adds to an already overburdened agenda and the modus operandi of meetings often precludes a true dialogue. Furthermore, the EU is eager to formulate positive joint statements and nice declarations following meetings to give the appearance of a positive result of 'foreign policy'. Sensitive foreign policy issues – such as the abuse of human rights or the involvement of a third country in a violent conflict – are therefore often just mentioned as a passing formality, or are not mentioned at all if the 'partner' is too powerful (as in the case with Russia or China). Moreover, EU representatives (but also member states' representatives) often prioritize trade and cooperation issues and do not want to disturb negotiations on these issues by tough talks on problematic foreign policy issues. The result is that political dialogue is not exercised to its full foreign policy potential, and cases are limited where it is used as leverage to promote and obtain concrete EU foreign policy goals.

Enlargement

Enlargement policy is the EU's most powerful tool of structural foreign policy in its immediate neighbourhood (see Smith K. 2011). The rationale is twofold. First, enlargement has allowed the EU to pursue its basic interests in its neighbourhood, which is primarily stability and peace on the continent. Both the southern enlargement wave of the 1980s and the Eastern wave of the 2000s exemplify successful attempts of the EU to stabilize its 'backyard' and to avoid new instances of conflict emerging from unstable regimes or disputing countries. Second, by its enlargement policy, the EU is able to transform various types of structures in its neighbouring countries that are eager to join the EU. By offering those countries the carrot of membership, the EU can disseminate its policies and approaches not only in the economic and political structures of the future member states, but also in their societal structures, as 'every aspect of state action is captured in the accession sweep' (Meunier and Nicolaïdis 2006: 913).

The logic behind enlargement as a foreign policy tool is thus also conditionality (see Grabbe 2006; Schimmelfennig 2008). The conditions mandatory to be eligible for accession, the so-called 'Copenhagen criteria', are threefold: countries must have a stable political system that guarantees democracy, rule of law, human rights and protection of minorities; a functioning market economy; and they must adopt the *acquis communautaire* (although phase-in stages are usually foreseen for a new member states' first few years).

In addition to the conditions required of applicant countries, additional criteria have more recently been formulated in the EU's enlargement policy. A first new criterion is the EU's integration capacity. The Turkish bid for EU membership best exemplifies the augmented importance of this criterion as it has allowed national governments to publicize rationales and discourses rooted in geopolitical, financial or cultural issues that argue the EU is not ready to accept Turkey as a full member (see Noutcheva and Aydin-Dzigit 2012; Schimmelfennig 2011). Furthermore, in the enlargement discussions regarding the Western Balkans (see Chapter 11), region-specific conditions surfaced mandating the Western Balkans to cooperate with the International Criminal Tribunal for the former Yugoslavia and to resolve disputes with neighbouring countries (such as between Croatia and Slovenia, and between Serbia and Kosovo) (Freyburg and Richter 2010; Noutcheva 2012).

In order to apply the conditionality strategy in the field, the Commission monitors progress in successive reports, publishes benchmarks, provides best practices and offers financial and technical assistance. However, it is the Council that takes the final decision on the different steps in an enlargement process. Enlargement negotiations are conducted on the basis of so-called 'chapters', in which progress in the different policy domains is discussed. The decisions to open and to close these chapters are taken by the Council, where other political concerns and national interests also play a role. Diffusing policies and institutional structures to adjust existing structures in neighbouring future member states is generally a successful EU foreign policy strategy. The question remains whether the changes realized in the structures remain permanent and sustainable once enlargement has taken place and the carrot of membership has disappeared (see Epstein and Sedelmeier 2009; Schimmelfennig 2008; Sedelmeier 2012). Moreover, the question is whether conditionality can also always work well for states like those in the Western Balkans, where the EU is faced with a more complex situation (see Chapter 11) (Stahl 2011).

The generally successful transformation, democratization, stabilization and incorporation of the Central and Eastern European countries (CEECs) in the EU in 2004 and 2007 concluded one of the most geostrategically significant foreign policy achievements of the EU, and indeed of the 'West' more globally (see Chapter 2). The EU was exporting its structures and values beyond its territory and embedding the CEECs within its own structures, policies and beliefs. This reflected deep 'governance by conditionality' on the part of the EU and led to the gradual socialization and Europeanization of the CEECs (see Schimmelfennig and Sedelmeier 2005; Grabbe 2006). Not surprisingly, the approach adopted towards the Central and Eastern European neighbours was and is often taken as a model for developing the EU's policy towards other regions of the world. However, using this as a point of reference is misleading, for several reasons.

First, despite obvious ambiguities and hesitations, the EU developed a long-term and comprehensive policy that tackled the political, legal, socio-economic and other structures on all relevant levels. The member states also agreed to provide the necessary sustained budgetary support for this policy. The only structure that the EU could not tackle alone – the military security structure – was taken care of by NATO and the US. It is clear that this long-term, comprehensive effort and such budgetary dedication cannot be generated for all regions of the world.

Second, the EU structural foreign policy towards the CEECs was largely successful because the EU could promise an ultimate reward for the often painful structural changes: EU membership. This prospect cannot be offered to non-European countries, explaining why the EU faces considerably more obstacles to diffuse norms beyond Europe and to develop effective tools of 'external governance beyond membership' (see Box 9.1) This external governance can be successful with regard to some specific policy domains, but cannot have the same all-encompassing structural impact as was the case with the EU's enlargement policy. Moreover, it is difficult to distinguish the impact of the EU from the impact of other actors or dynamics when one observes change in third countries' policies or governance systems. Not all changes in countries that are targeted by EU foreign policy are indeed caused by the EU.

Third, in most CEECs the EU's policy was facilitated by existing endogenous dynamics and preferences. Although the EU has been criticized for not sufficiently taking into consideration domestic actors and sensitivities, in general terms, the elites and the population of most CEECs shared the values and wanted the transformations and structures the EU was promoting. This also explains why the new values and rules of the game were in most countries quite easily internalized and gradually became part of the mindset of the population and elites. The EU strengthened and

Box 9.1   'External governance' and 'diffusion'

The analysis of the EU's structural foreign policy can profit from the research on external governance and norm diffusion. At its most concise, the term *external governance* can be defined as 'the expansion of EU rules beyond EU borders' (Lavenex and Schimmelfennig 2009a: 807). Some of the early work on external governance analysed rule transfer in the context of the EU's Eastern enlargement, and was hence closely linked to the literature on Europeanization and conditionality (Lavenex 2004; Schimmelfennig and Sedelmeier 2004, 2005; Schimmelfennig and Wagner 2004). However, in view of the limits to further enlargement and the interdependence between the EU and its new neighbours, the concept has since then been developed by Lavenex and Schimmelfennig to better understand 'forms of integration into the European system of rules that remain below the threshold of membership' (2009a: 792). They differentiate between three modes of external governance: hierarchy, networks and markets. These three forms of external governance relate to variations in the types of relations between the EU and the third country, the levels of institutionalization and the mechanisms of rule expansion, leading to different degrees of effectiveness. External governance has been studied in a wide variety of specific sectors, ranging from environmental and energy policy to democracy promotion and internal security. The majority of studies on external governance has analysed EU relations with the countries in the European neighbourhood, with the application on other countries being scarce (Lavenex 2011; Lavenex and Schimmelfennig 2009b, 2010, 2012; Lavenex and Wichmann 2009; Schimmelfennig and Scholtz 2008).

Closely related to external governance is the concept of *diffusion*. Börzel and Risse (2012a) have argued that the 'Europeanization' framework focuses too exclusively on top-down and hierarchical patterns of spreading norms, hence neglecting more indirect ways in which the EU influences changes in institutions, norms and policies abroad. Such indirect mechanisms are particularly important when looking beyond candidate countries and immediate neighbours to EU relations with more distant parts of the world. Drawing on the literature on transnational diffusion, Börzel and Risse propose to fill this gap through the concept of 'diffusion', which is defined as 'a process through which ideas, normative standards, or ... policies and institutions spread across time and space' (2012a: 5). They distinguish different types of diffusion mechanisms as well as different scope conditions for the institutional change. The diffusion mechanisms are analysed with regard to a variety of thematic areas (including judicial reform and anti-corruption policies, democracy promotion, European-style international courts and regional integration models) and with regard to regions and organizations beyond the EU's immediate neighbourhood (see case studies in Börzel and Risse 2012b).

channelled the existing reformist dynamic, alleviated some of the pain of reforms, and helped bring countries back on the right track when they diverted from the reformist course or slackened in their efforts. Evidently, such positive endogenous forces do not always exist in other countries and regions where the EU promotes similar structural changes. Recent political developments in several CEECs – including Romania, Bulgaria and even former model-state Hungary – also revealed that the internalization of values occurred unevenly and should not be taken for granted (see also Morlino and Sadurski 2010).

Fourth, the EU was able to successfully pursue its long-term structural foreign policy objectives because these goals were not overshadowed by manifest military security threats or other conventional foreign policy concerns. This is also a major difference with, for instance, the EU's policy towards the Mediterranean area and the Middle East conflict where security threats and violent conflicts undermine a more structural foreign policy approach (see Chapter 11).

Finally, in its policy towards its Central and Eastern European neighbours, the EU was seen by both the member states and other international actors (such as the US and initially also the Soviet Union/Russia) as a useful actor that provided clear added value, was complementary in its approach, and in general posed no threat to their own interests. Again, this is not the case for other parts of the world, where other actors or movements exert structural power too – Russia in the former Soviet republics, China in Africa, or 'political Islam' in the Arab world (see Chapters 11 and 12).

Development Cooperation

The EU as a development world power

If we total the development budgets at the European level and those at the member state levels, the EU is the world's largest donor of Official Development Assistance (ODA), providing over 50 per cent of global ODA. The numbers, like those in trade policy, suggest that the EU is a real power in development policy (see Carbone 2011a, 2011b, 2013; Gänzle *et al.* 2012; Holden 2009; Holland and Doidge 2012; Schrijver 2009). By virtue of its position as the largest international donor, the EU should theoretically be able to use development cooperation to effect changes within third countries that parallel its world-view and foreign policy objectives, like conflict prevention, dialogue and cooperation between countries in conflict, good governance and democracy, the rule of law and respect for human rights.

Article 208(1) TFEU gives development policy the following objective: 'the reduction and, in the long term, the eradication of poverty', continuing that 'the Union shall take account of the objectives of development cooperation in the policies that it implements which are likely to affect developing countries'. The EU's goal of poverty reduction can be understood from a foreign policy angle. Poverty reduction improves welfare and stability and assists in the integration of developing countries into the international system. Indirectly, this contributes to core foreign policy objectives. As the 2003 European Security Strategy emphasized: '[t]rade and development policies can be powerful tools for promoting reform ... A world seen as offering justice and opportunity for everyone will be more secure for the European Union and its citizens' (European Council 2003a: 10). Improving individuals' human security is also an important element of avoiding a situation in which alternative actors or structures gain power and legitimacy because, in the absence of a well functioning state, it is these alternative actors and structures that step in to provide financial and food support, education, health care or a minimum of 'order' at a grass-roots level. Examples of such shifts include Hamas in the Palestinian Territories, Hezbollah in Lebanon and Islamic courts in Somalia.

EU development policy operates within a large international framework, including the UN system, IMF and World Bank (see Chapter 13). In development policy, 'the Union and the member states shall comply with the commitments and take account of the objectives they have approved in the context of the United Nations and other competent international organisations' (Art. 208(2) TFEU). Because multilateral governance structures above the EU also deal with development issues, the appropriateness of also organising development cooperation at the EU level, in addition to the multilateral level, is sometimes questioned, e.g. by the Scandinavian member states. Other member states, such as the UK, prefer bilateral development aid and are not in favour of strong EU involvement. The most important of the current multilateral initiatives are the UN Millennium Development Goals (MDGs). The eight MDGs, which were agreed to by all countries and prominent development institutions in 2000, range from halving extreme poverty to halting the spread of HIV/AIDS and providing universal primary education, all by 2015. However, as the yearly UN reports indicate, it is not likely that all MDGs will be achieved (UN 2012a).

The Union's development policy is a shared competence, although the exercise by the EU of that competence 'may not result in member states being prevented from exercising theirs' (Art 4(4) TFEU). This means that the EU's development policies are characterized by 'the parallel existence of 28+1 development policies' (adapted from Carbone 2011a: 342). A consequence of the coexistence of European and national development policies is that the Commission's role, besides its traditional role as donor, is increasingly that of 'coordinator' of national development policies at the European level through 'soft' mechanisms such as benchmarking, peer pressure or name-and-shame strategies (Orbie 2012).

EU development policy is based on the following three principles: coherence of EU policies (i.e. 'horizontal consistency', see Chapter 4); coordination between EU and member state action (i.e. 'vertical consistency'); and complementarity between policies and programmes of the Union and member states (related to the shared nature of the development competences). However, translating this '3 Cs principle' into practice is quite a challenge. Even if we only focus on the objectives of development policy as outlined in Article 208 TFEU, it is clear that there is a risk of incoherent or competing objectives, a basis for horizontal inconsistency. Foreign policy goals (developing democracy, for example) on the one hand and pure development objectives and the fight against poverty on the other hand risk being incoherent or at least competing, leading to horizontal inconsistency. For instance, to what extent should the EU fight poverty in countries where there is no possibility that it will be able to promote democracy and where the human rights situation is appalling? The international fisheries agreements the EU has concluded with many African countries, which allow EU fleets to (over)fish African fishing grounds, provide a second example. This not only has negative consequences for the marine environment, but also for the economic and social development in these countries.

Since development policy is a shared competence and the '28+1 development policies' situation prevails, ensuring vertical consistency is as important as ensuring horizontal consistency. The Treaty provisions on development cooperation therefore pay considerable attention to mutual consultation, coordination and cooperation between the EU and the member states. However, in practice, levels of coordination between member states and the Union tend to be low, with progress proving rather difficult. Whereas some member states aim to act via the EU, others prefer international action (see above), and some others are not really interested in development cooperation or prefer to keep their hands free in their national development policies, which are also considered a useful tool to raise the national flag around the world.

In the second half of the 2000s, growing awareness of policy inconsistencies prompted several initiatives to tackle this issue. The 'Policy Coherence on Development' was adopted in 2005 (Commission 2005a) and the Commission adopted a work programme in 2010 on the basis of this initiative (Commission 2010c). Moreover, the 'Code of conduct on complementarity and division of labour' was adopted in 2007 (Commission 2007). Whereas the former aims to increase synergies between the external action, the external dimensions of internal policies and various other components of the EU's foreign policy, the latter intends to come to a division of labour between member states. This arrangement allows each member state to focus on priority areas in priority countries so that a better balance between 'aid darlings' and 'aid orphans' can be established (Carbone 2011a: 338). However, the implementation of these Commission-steered initiatives is far from evident (Delputte and Söderbaum 2012).

The shifting sands of development policy priorities

EU development policy can be conceptualized as a two-dimensional patchwork in terms of its geographical coverage and its policy priorities.

Geographical priorities

Historically speaking, the EU's development cooperation has focused on the ACP (African, Caribbean and Pacific) countries. Development aid for these countries is financed through the European Development Fund (EDF). The EDF does not fall under the general budget. As a result, the EP has no powers over the EDF, which raises legitimacy concerns about the EDF. It is funded by the member states and the budget, which has its own financial rules and is managed by its own committee (the EDF Committee), is set in the Council. The EDF allocation for the five-year period 2014–20 is €29.1 billion.

EU–ACP relations started with the conclusion of the Yaoundé Agreement in 1963, followed by a succession of Lomé Agreements and today managed through the Cotonou Agreement. With each agreement, the scope of cooperation has broadened and, since Lomé III and IV, has become increasingly political and conditional (i.e. 'beyond trade'). The Cotonou Agreement between the EU, the member states and 77 ACP countries is the current legal framework of EU–ACP relations. Signed in March 2000 and entered into force in April 2003, it has a duration of 20 years, with five-year reviews (see Holland and Doidge 2012: 70–82).

Cotonou brought about three main developments: in trade provisions, broadened participation and political dialogue. However, these evolutions were more reflective of the changing global context and the EU's own agenda, interests and values, than a response to the demands and concerns of the African partners. Indeed, whereas the EU aims to present itself as a 'distinct development partner', the ACP countries still consider the EU as a player acting on the basis of its own economic interests (Weinhardt 2011).

First, it was Cotonou's trade provisions that marked the most significant break with the preceding four decades of cooperation. Under the Lomé Agreements, the ACP countries benefited from non-reciprocal preferential market access arrangements. This trade arrangement ran counter to the WTO's rules in the 1990s, which was one of the reasons for a new, free trade-based approach under the Cotonou regime. The Lomé Agreements were also widely criticized for reinforcing developing countries' reliance on primary commodities and for contributing little to promoting an increase in higher value manufactured goods (Sourd 2005: 15). Despite reluctance by many ACP countries, trade liberalization prevailed in the Cotonou Agreement, which provided for new *Economic Partnership Agreements* (EPAs) to be negotiated between the EU and seven regional groups of ACP countries (five in Africa, one in the Pacific, and one in the Caribbean region) by the end 2008. The EPAs are meant to create free trade areas between the EU and various groups of ACP countries, and to encourage subregional economic integration (see Bartelt 2012; Elgström 2009; Elgström and Frennhoff Larsén 2010; Holland and Doidge 2012: 82–7). By designing EPAs as free trade agreements, implying trade reciprocity between the EU and the ACP countries, the incompatibility with WTO rules of the previous EU–ACP regime is meant to be solved. However, EPAs are supposed to be more than merely trade agreements, as they intended to cover also issues related to aid, agriculture, fishing or labour rights (Elgström and Pilegaard 2008).

The parties did not meet the deadline of concluding EPAs by December 2008 and most EPA negotiations are deadlocked, which reflects the critical assessment on the side of many ACP countries as well as European NGOs. A full EPA has been concluded only with the Caribbean countries (in 2007). As for the other regions, significant doubts still prevail concerning the feasibility and potential impact of EPAs. These doubts are grounded in the threat of (subsidized) European agricultural products crowding out local products, a lack of additional financial support to cover the anticipated adjustment costs, and capacity problems on the African side (see Develtere 2012; Sicurelli 2010: 86–91). Moreover, the main bone of contention between the EU and the ACP countries relates to their diverging interpretations of the relationship between development objectives and trade liberalization (see Stocchetti 2010).

A second major development with the Cotonou Agreement was its provision for broadening the participation of civil society, local actors and the private sector in EU–ACP relations and political dialogue. The aim in encouraging a broader participation was to increase the feeling of 'ownership', to encourage the development of civil society and to broaden the EU's interlocutors on the ground. However, in practice, this approach is difficult to implement. In countries with a vibrant civil society accustomed to participating in political processes, the level of engagement within the Cotonou process is high. Where chaos and insecurity rule, conversely, or where the enabling environment provided by the state is restrictive, civil society struggles to fulfil its role (Saferworld 2005).

A third innovation relates to a more vigorous promotion of the political elements of the agreement's agenda and mirrors the official name of the Cotonou Agreement, the *ACP–EU Partnership Agreement*. These political elements have developed in line with evolving concerns on the EU's side, and are a stark demonstration that the EU–ACP relationship is only a 'partnership' on paper. Nevertheless, the intention was that political dialogue would become deeper, wider and more dynamic than in the past, covering a broad range of political issues that fall outside traditional development cooperation (such as peace and security or migration). The objective of political dialogue is to exchange information, to foster mutual understanding, and to facilitate the establishment of agreed priorities and shared agendas (see above).

Development cooperation with non-ACP developing countries, particularly in Asia and Latin America, is rather different and much less tangible. EU development policy with regard to ACP countries differs from development policy with regard to non-ACP countries in two ways. First, historically speaking, non-ACP developing countries have received considerably less attention (and money) from EU development policy than the ACP countries (Carbone 2011a). Funding does not occur through the EDF, but through the separate Development Cooperation Instrument (DCI), an instrument linked to the annual EU budget, which covers among others cooperation with developing countries in Latin America, Asia, the Gulf region and South Africa (see Chapter 4). Yet, the DCI also finances thematic programmes benefitting all developing countries, including the ACP ones.

Second, the EU's approach to development is different for the ACP region and the non-ACP region. On the one hand, development policy towards the ACP states was initially focused on aid. But since the Cotonou era, trade liberalization has come more to the forefront of EU–ACP relations. Indeed, the Cotonou Agreement dislodged the ACP from the apex of the EU's pyramid of trade preferences with non-reciprocal preferential market access only retained through the EBA initiative (see above), which is open to all LDCs, not just ACP states (see Holland and Doidge 2012: 87–92). This to some extent normalizes EU relations with the poorest developing countries and moves these relations beyond previous historical preferences. On the other hand, the EU's development policy with non-ACP countries is historically by and large defined by a trade liberalization approach and reciprocity in market access, although political discourse may suggest something else. Indeed, the approach with regard to the ACP region that started with the Cotonou Agreement was already deployed with regard to non-ACP countries much earlier. On EU relations with Asian development countries, Holland and Doidge conclude that they 'essentially constitute an economic dialogue to which development rhetoric has been attached' (2012: 181–2).

Mirroring the reasoning in the European Commission's 'Agenda for Change' (Commission 2011b), the Commission proposed to stop bilateral development aid to around 20 countries, which have recently advanced to the middle-income category in the Multiannual Financial Framework 2014–20. The bulk comes from Latin America (including Argentina, Brazil, Chile, Mexico but also countries such as Costa Rica and Peru) and Asia (including countries such as China, India, Indonesia and Thailand), thus including several of the emerging powers (see Chapter 12). Nonetheless, these countries will continue to receive funding through the thematic and regional programs of the DCI and the new Partnership Instrument (Commission 2011c; EU 2011).

Policy priorities

In addition to increasing the emphasis on political dialogue, Cotonou built on a trend that had already begun under the Lomé Agreements of building political conditionality into the agreement (see above). Respect for human rights, democracy and the rule of law became 'essential elements' of the agreement. Against the wishes of the ACP states, the agreement also includes a non-execution clause under which the violation of an 'essential element' forms the basis of consultation procedures and the eventual application of 'appropriate measures', a process which potentially leads to the whole or partial suspension of cooperation and aid. During negotiations, the EU also pushed for 'good governance' to be an 'essential element' of the agreement. This frustrated the ACP partners who argued that it was unnecessary given the democracy and rule-of-law provisions already present. Ultimately, a different procedure was agreed for good governance: it would be a 'fundamental element', meaning that its violation would not constitute grounds for suspension. Reflecting both the EU's own strategic concerns and the extent to which it de facto determines the agenda of this partnership agreement, the revised Cotonou Agreement of 2005 also included new provisions on WMD (through a 'non-proliferation clause' as a new 'essential element') and on the fight against terrorism and support for the ICC (see Hadfield 2007).

Another evolution of EU development policy from the early 1960s to today is that the EU increasingly links development with security, as was confirmed in the 2003 European Security Strategy: 'security is a precondition of development' (European Council 2003a: 2). The so-called 'security–development nexus' reflects the EU's growing attention to conflict prevention and peace-building in development policy (see Gänzle 2012; Gänzle *et al.* 2012; Keukeleire and Raube 2013; Merket 2012; Smith M. E. 2013b; Stern and Öjendal 2010). In this context, although the above analysis tends to suggest that ACP countries are becoming less prioritized in strict development terms, Africa is becoming increasingly important in foreign policy terms. This is illustrated by the deployment of CSDP operations on the African continent, support provided by the African Peace Facility (which is part of the EDF) and the Instrument for Stability, and the prominent place for security issues in both the Cotonou Agreement and the EU's strategies towards Africa (see Chapters 6 and 11) (see Mangala 2013).

The link between development and security needs to be qualified. On the one hand, both are interlinked and can be mutually reinforcing.

Insecure situations can impede economic development just as a lack of development can cause conflicts. On the other hand, the danger exists that security issues will dominate the development agenda and that development actions to reduce poverty will be overshadowed by security concerns. Certainly after the 9/11 terrorist attacks, security motivations and tackling the root causes of conflict increasingly play a role in the EU's development policy. The tension between two sets of possibly competing and diverging concerns and interests poses a dilemma summarized by Orbie (2012: 33): 'while it opens new opportunities to broaden the scope of [the EU's] activities and increase their relevance, there is also a risk that development policy will be absorbed by the foreign policy and security policy machinery'.

Sanctions

Sanctions, or 'restrictive measures' in EU jargon, are a frequently used foreign policy instrument. The Treaties endow the EU with a concrete power to use its economic and financial leverage to achieve foreign policy goals, as they explicitly foresee the possibility to take decisions on 'the interruption or reduction, in part or completely, of economic and financial relations with one or more third countries' and on 'restrictive measures ... against natural and legal persons and groups or non-State entities' (Art. 215 TFEU).

Sanctions aim to bring about change in the activities or policies of third states, individuals (often political leaders or elites of a state) and non-state entities such as terrorist groups. Sanctions imposed on individuals or non-state entities are often referred to as 'smart' or 'targeted' sanctions (see Portela 2010). Smart sanctions receive this title because they seek to only focus on the individuals responsible for the behaviour that the EU wants to adjust, and are not directed at a whole population or country. The shift from 'comprehensive' sanctions, which are directed at countries as a whole, to 'smart' sanctions is a trend mirroring the UN's sanctions regime (Giumelli 2011). Comprehensive sanctions undertaken by the EU mostly include the interruption of trade relations (including arms embargoes), whereas smart sanctions usually take the form of financial sanctions (such as the freezing of funds) and visa bans. Yet, suspending cooperation with a third country, interrupting or reducing diplomatic relations, boycotting sports or cultural events and imposing flight bans also form part of the EU's sanctions repertoire.

Sanctions can be either autonomous EU sanctions or (more often) sanctions implementing UN Security Council Resolutions (see Eeckhout 2011: 501–48). Autonomous EU sanctions usually complement or intensify UN sanctions. Sometimes they are taken when the Security Council fails to adopt sanctions (Brummer 2009). The basic framework for the use of such sanctions is the 'Basic Principles on the Use of Restrictive Measures' (Council 2004). These Principles state that sanctions will be adopted 'in support of efforts to fight terrorism and the proliferation of weapons of mass destruction and as a restrictive measure to uphold respect for human rights, democracy, the rule of law and good governance', and that they should be 'part of an integrated, comprehensive policy approach' that also includes other foreign policy instruments such as political dialogue and conditionality.

As an external action policy, sanctions are closely linked to CFSP, since an explicit and binding CFSP decision is needed to take a restrictive measure, be it against states, individuals or non-state actors. Indeed, the political decision to use sanctions is taken through a CFSP decision defining a position to be taken by the EU (Arts. 25 and 29 TEU). This is a necessary step before the High Representative and the Commission can jointly propose a measure to the Council, which decides on the target, type and duration of the sanction on the basis of QMV (Art. 215 TFEU) (see Chapter 4). The Commission then implements the measure(s) decided upon in relation to the third country concerned.

In 2012, EU sanctions were in force against more than 25 countries, as well as against Al-Qaeda and other foreign terrorist organizations (Commission 2012h). Usual targets include Belarus, the DR Congo, Côte d'Ivoire, Iran, Iraq, North Korea, Libya, Sudan and Syria. In quantitative terms, most current EU sanctions are targeted at terrorist groups. The gradual removal in 2012–13 of the trade, economic and individual sanctions in response to political reforms in Myanmar demonstrated that the sanctions instrument can also be used the other way around: ending sanctions is equally a tool to provide support to positive changes (and to allow European companies to equally profit from new business opportunities).

Although sanctions are usually considered an important foreign policy tool (Eckes 2012: 114), their effectiveness is often questioned. They are 'generally ineffective tools for accomplishing the objectives they aim for, which are predominantly related to the protection of human rights and democracies' (Portela 2010: 101). The jury is still out, however, on the identifications of the conditions determining the effectiveness of EU sanctions (see Druláková *et al.* 2010, Giumelli 2010). Another problem with the EU's sanctions policy is that it lacks consistency on three fronts: the EU seems to be very selective and thus inconsistent in choosing the countries against which it adopts sanctions; there is no consistent pattern in the underlying reasons for sanctions; and exemptions are used in a relatively arbitrary way (Brummer 2009). Finally, as discussed in Chapter 3, Council decisions on sanctions are also challenged before the Court of Justice (best exemplified by the *Kadi* case) as in some cases they do not respect basic principles of human rights and rule of law, and counter the ideas the EU attempts to promote in its external action.

Humanitarian Aid

With its humanitarian aid policy, the EU provides 'ad hoc assistance and relief and protection for people in third countries who are victims of natural or man-made disasters, in order to meet the humanitarian needs resulting from these different situations' (Art 214 TFEU). Since humanitarian aid competences are shared with the member states, action by the EU does not exclude such action by the member states. The EU is the world's second largest humanitarian aid donor, but the EU and the member states together are by far the most important donor of humanitarian aid in the world. Since humanitarian aid policy allows the EU to distinguish itself as a benevolent actor on the international scene, concerned about human suffering, the EU's humanitarian policy is also driven by identity objectives (see Chapter 1).

Humanitarian aid policy is coordinated and managed by the Humanitarian Aid & Civil Protection Directorate-General of the Commission, commonly referred to as ECHO (the old acronym for European Community Humanitarian Office). ECHO spends an annual budget of approximately €1.1 billion, and more than 40 per cent is dedicated to humanitarian aid in Africa. Another apex of the EU's humanitarian aid policy is its focus on 'forgotten crises' – such as the Bhutanese refugees in Nepal or the populations affected by the internal armed conflict in Colombia – which receive little visibility and attention from other partners in the world.

ECHO acts relatively autonomously from the College of Commissioners and the Council since it is able to take decisions through a fast-track procedure. For instance, it can immediately spend a maximum of €3 million without the political approval of the College in order to react rapidly to international crisis. Although its strong bureaucratization is often criticized, ECHO is usually able to deploy humanitarian aid relatively swiftly, certainly in the cases of natural disasters, which are less politically sensitive than humanitarian aid in crisis situations. Even though the Treaty of Lisbon foresees the establishment of a European Voluntary Humanitarian Aid Corps (Art. 214(5) TFEU), through which young volunteers will be able to help in humanitarian aid operations of the EU, the EU's operational capacity on the ground is relatively limited. This is why the EU cooperates with more than 200 partners worldwide, such as NGOs, UN agencies and the International Committee of the Red Cross.

Four principles drive the EU's humanitarian aid policy: humanity, neutrality, impartiality and independence. Contrary to development cooperation (where conditionality largely determines the EU's policy), humanitarian aid is guided by the 'humanitarian imperative' (Versluys 2008). The elaboration of military and civilian crisis management tools under CFSP/CSDP (see Chapters 7 and 8) allows ECHO to take a neutral role and to focus on the humanitarian needs of the people most in need. However, the further development of CFSP/CSDP has also a downside for the neutrality and the humanitarian imperative of the EU's humanitarian aid policy: when the EU is both conducting civilian and/or military missions (which are not politically neutral at all) and delivering humanitarian aid (which is meant to be apolitical), it comes as no surprise that the people in third countries cannot clearly distinguish between these two and that the recipients' perception of EU neutrality and impartiality of the humanitarian aid is put in danger (Versluys 2008).

Conclusion

In addition to the foreign policy goals that the EU determined for itself – such as consolidating respect for human rights and fundamental freedoms, the rule of law and democracy, and promoting these values externally – the EU also has narrower strategic and trade interests to protect, which in many cases prevail over and undermine these stated foreign policy goals. The external action policies discussed in this chapter constitute the backbone of the EU's structural foreign policy, including its ability to enter into long-term contractual agreements, to offer trade concessions or the prospect of membership, or to support development. Nonetheless, as is discussed in Chapter 11, with the exception of the CEECs and the Western Balkans, these policies have often not been sufficiently steered or backed up with enough resources to actually shape the political, legal, socio-economic, security and ideational structures of third countries or regions.

Chapter 10

The External Dimension of Internal Policies

In Chapter 1 we argued that the European Union functions as a shield and an agent of globalization, seeking to contain, manage and order this process. Acting alone, member state governments are unable to adequately protect themselves from the negative consequences of globalization, or to steer its direction. Through the Treaties and the case law of the Court of Justice of the EU (see Chapters 3 and 4), the EU has been vested with external competences in a range of 'Union policies and internal actions' (Part Three of the TFEU) to try to shape external developments. As we argued in Chapter 1, this means that the foreign policy of the EU is not limited to CFSP/CSDP (Chapters 7 and 8) and external action such as trade, development or enlargement policy (Chapter 9), but also includes internal policies that have an external dimension. This chapter focuses particularly on the external dimension and the foreign policy relevance of three internal policy domains: energy; environment and climate change; and freedom, security and justice. Finally, it briefly discusses two challenges without a real external policy: health and demography. This is not an exhaustive list of internal policies with an external dimension, however. Almost all internal policies have in one way or another an external dimension and the EU is also active internationally e.g. the areas of fisheries, transport or competition policies. The external dimension of other internal policy fields with an external dimension are discussed elsewhere in this book, such as research and technological development policy (see Chapter 8) or agricultural policy (see Chapter 9).

Energy

Energy security is a hotly debated topic in the EU, but it is not a new issue. It has been widely discussed at least since the 1973–4 Arab oil embargo, which triggered one of the first major foreign policy actions of the fledgling EPC (see Chapter 2). However, as was the case then, the looming threat to energy security has not automatically led to member states developing a genuine 'common' energy policy. On the contrary, the oil crises of the 1970s have led to a strengthened nationalization of energy policy and to a growing reaction of the member states to see energy policy as part of their national sovereignty (Belyi 2008).

It was not until the entry into force of the Lisbon Treaty in 2009 that energy policy was given a specific legal basis in the Treaties. An objective of the EU's energy policy is to 'ensure security of energy supply in the Union' (Art. 194(1) TFEU). However, that article immediately tempers the expectations of those hoping for a entirely common energy policy, since it also states that European energy measures 'shall not affect a Member State's right to determine the conditions for exploiting its energy resources, its choice between different energy sources and the general structure of its energy supply' (Art. 194(2)), thus still emphasizing a large role for the member states.

Challenges

The EU faces a number of pressing challenges in the energy field. The first challenge is the EU's growing import dependence. In 2010, the EU's energy dependence rate was 53.7 per cent, although this picture varied considerably across the member states. Denmark has been a net energy exporter since 1999, and the UK only became a net importer for the first time in 2004. All other member states are sizeable importers, with energy dependence rates of around 60 per cent in Germany, 50 per cent in France, 80 per cent in Italy, 75 per cent in Spain and 30 per cent in Poland (Eurostat 2012b). The origins of the imports also differ from member state to member state, which may have broader foreign policy consequences. For instance, the high level of Italian dependency on Libyan oil (22 per cent, IEA/OECD 2011) partially explains its initial resistance to EU sanctions against that country in 2011. These varying dependence rates also have an impact on the way member states position themselves in the internal policy-making process on external energy policy and on the EU's foreign policy towards Russia or the Middle East. Consequently, energy should not only be understood as an internal policy with an external dimension. It also provides an explanation for member states' positions on other foreign policy issues and for the EU's (in)ability to define and implement a common foreign and security policy.

The second challenge is that, with the exception of Norway, most of the main energy producers are in unstable regions (such as the Middle East), are countries with which the EU has a difficult relationship (such as Russia), or are countries with a fundamentally different political system and value system (see Chapters 11 and 12). As far as oil is concerned, the EU has maintained political relationships with Saudi Arabia to guarantee oil access despite this country's poor human rights record and lack of democracy. Even Saudi Arabia's violent oppression of the unfolding revolt in Bahrain in 2011 did not lead to any serious reaction from the EU and its member states (International Crisis Group 2011) (see Chapter 11).

Revealing in this regard is the overview of the main origin of primary energy imports in the EU in 2010, the year before the Arab uprising resulted in turmoil on the energy market. Four countries provided for more than 80 per cent of the natural gas supply: Russia (31.8 per cent), Norway (28.2 per cent), Algeria (14.4 per cent) and Qatar (8.6 per cent). Russia also leads the ranking of crude oil suppliers with 34.5 per cent, followed by Norway (13.8 per cent), Libya (10.2 per cent) and Saudi Arabia, Iran, Kazakhstan, Nigeria and Azerbaijan, each of which provided between 4 and 6 per cent of the crude oil from outside the EU (Eurostat 2012c). The top position of Russia in both the natural gas and crude oil rankings explain the strength of Russia (and its state-owned Gazprom company) vis-à-vis the EU. Russia has made it clear that it is prepared to exploit its energy dominance for foreign policy purposes, which can have serious consequences for the EU. For example, in 2006 and 2009, Russia flexed its energy muscles, temporarily cutting off supplies to Ukraine. When Russia turned off the tap it also led to shortages of gas and oil within the EU, with some member states experiencing a fall of Russian energy supply of between one-third and one-quarter (see De Jong *et al.* 2010; Pirani 2012; Smith Stegen 2011).

The growing international demand for energy, combined with the scarcity of sources of fossil fuels is a third challenge for the EU. A consequence of this development is that competition for energy sources will continue to grow, bringing the EU in an ever-increasing dependent situation with regard to energy exporting countries. China, India and other rapidly industrializing states are increasingly competing for global energy resources, while energy consumption in developed countries, including the US and the EU's member states, continues to rise, albeit at a slower rate. World energy demand is expected to rise by 40 per cent by 2030 (Commission 2011d: 2). China in particular is developing a very proactive foreign policy in which guaranteeing future energy supplies plays a central role. Hence, the EU may be forced to increasingly take up responsibility for ensuring its own energy supply. The US already gives less consideration to the energy factor in its foreign policy, as the recent rise of shale gas found in the US itself allows it to diminish its dependence on energy imports (see Riley *et al.* 2012).

The EU's energy dependence increasingly thwarts EU foreign policy with regard to human rights and democracy, particularly in Africa (see Chapters 6 and 11). A quick glance at a map of global oil and gas reserves indicates that the future of energy supply is unlikely to be any easier for the EU. Countries with significant reserves include Venezuela, Kazakhstan, Turkmenistan, Russia, Iran, Iraq, Kuwait, Saudi Arabia, the United Arab Emirates, Qatar and Nigeria (BP 2012: 6, 20). This simple list of countries clearly demonstrates the potential competition between energy supply objectives and other foreign policy goals.

The fourth challenge relates to the necessary transition from fossil fuel-based production and consumption patterns to a low-carbon economy, driven by environmental and climate change concerns. Indeed, the EU's external energy policy should not only take into account energy security, but also the promotion of renewable energy and an efficient use of existing energy sources. The scientific evidence and the increasing awareness that greenhouse gas emissions must be reduced have put the issue of sustainable energy at the forefront. This has not only forced the EU to adopt internal energy objectives (the 20–20–20 objectives, see below), but also has important foreign policy implications, not the least in the area of development cooperation (see Chapter 9). Using more renewable energy sources and increasing energy efficiency in developing countries and emerging powers are considered to contribute to a higher level of sustainability of the economies of these countries and to the achievement of the Millennium Development Goals (Commission 2010a, 2011d).

Finally, the EU faces an internal challenge, as it is confronted with obstacles preventing it from adopting a common (external) energy policy. On the one hand, member states still apply a national sovereignty reflex regarding their energy mix and their energy security. Their preferences for a European energy policy still diverge, mainly because the energy structures and energy mixes of the different member states remain highly heterogeneous (Andoura 2011). Some member states, such as France or Finland, prefer nuclear energy, whereas others such as Germany opted to close nuclear power plants. The foreign policy consequence of such a sovereignty reflex is that member states prefer bilateral agreements with external energy suppliers, such as Germany, France and Italy having committed themselves to long-term gas imports from Russia (see Belyi 2008). On the other hand, and also resulting from the sovereignty reflex among the member states, the EU is still lacking a single energy market and insufficient interconnectedness between the national markets. As long as this continues to be the case, energy issues are likely to remain national security concerns and not become collective ones (Kirchner and Berk 2010: 868).

Foreign policy response

In its 2011 Communication *The EU Energy Policy: Engaging with Partners beyond Our Borders* (Commission 2011d), the Commission again proposed a comprehensive strategy for the EU's external relations in the energy domain. This Communication was preceded by similar Commission documents the decade before, all focusing on the development of a strategic external energy policy of the EU. Yet, reaching agreement on how and what to do to achieve this is rather more complex, with the sovereignty reflex still existing and with member states proving extremely reluctant to hand responsibility over to the EU level. From a foreign policy perspective, there are a number of interesting issues, of which the following are discussed here: the development of critical infrastructure, securing and diversifying energy supplies, and developing relationships with the main energy suppliers (see Andoura 2013; Kuzemko *et al.* 2012).

First, the development of critical infrastructure revolves around identifying priorities for upgrading and constructing new infrastructure to ensure supply security. Several initiatives supported by the Commission are, however, undermined by member states' bilateral actions. The best-known example is the *Nabucco* gas pipeline project, aimed at constructing a 3,400 km pipeline across South-East Europe to the end of Anatolia in eastern Turkey, to facilitate the transit of oil supplies from countries such as Azerbaijan and Turkmenistan to the EU and to reduce European dependency on Russia. This project was supported both politically and (to a limited extent) financially by the Commission. However, the notion of developing a common approach has been overtaken by member states' realpolitik and attempts to develop privileged bilateral contacts and contracts with energy suppliers. Hence, the momentum for the construction of Nabucco – once seen as the 'the flagship project of the EU's emerging energy policy' (Barysch 2010) – seems to be lost and the likelihood that the pipeline will actually be built is relatively low (Socor 2012).

One of the competing and more successful projects is the German–Russian construction of a pipeline through the Baltic Sea (the *North Stream* project), but strongly opposed by Poland and the Baltic member states who were not involved in this project. The pipeline has been technically operational since 2011 and since then has been carrying large volumes of Russian gas directly to Germany. This not only undermines the common external policy approach towards energy supply but also the objective of developing energy transit routes which bypass Russia. Another example of such bilateral projects that put a common EU approach at risk is the *South Stream* project, based on bilateral deals between Russia on the one hand and EU member states Bulgaria, Hungary and Austria on the other and aims at transporting Russian gas into Europe via the Black Sea (see de Jong and Schunz 2012: 172–3; Youngs 2009). This brings de Jong and Schunz to the conclusion that '[w]hereas the Commission and Parliament firmly advocated diversifying natural gas supplies and transit routes away from Russia, member states in many instances seem to have in fact strengthened their energy ties to Gazprom' (2012: 174).

The second issue at stake is diversifying energy sources, the main objective being to reduce dependence on Russia and the Middle East. The Nabucco gas pipeline project was one example. The Commission received a negotiation mandate in 2011 to negotiate a treaty with Azerbaijan and Turkmenistan to build a *Trans Caspian Pipeline System,* but the chances of success of this initiative seem to be very low. Therefore, the need to secure and diversify energy sources might in the future imply looking to different regions, including Africa's oil-producing states.

Third, furthering energy dialogues with the main energy suppliers and strategic partners (see Chapter 12) appears as an objective in most recent EU texts on energy security. Energy dialogues have been inserted as part of agreements with a large number of third countries, such as Brazil and China but also Norway and Ukraine. However, the effectiveness of this dialogue is doubtful, particularly with regard to Russia. As early as 2000, the EU and Russia launched an Energy Dialogue that covered security of supply and infrastructure. Although this has resulted in regular meetings of experts and high-level political discussions at annual EU–Russia summits, the result has been of a more symbolic than substantive nature. In this respect, it is illustrative that the main concrete outcome of that dialogue has been the conclusion of a memorandum in 2009 (and an updated version in 2011) on an early-warning mechanism that aims to signal problems with energy supply from Russia to the EU so that measures can be taken in time to solve the issues.

The EU's failure to develop a common external energy policy limits its potential to effect change in the high geopolitics of energy. This is not to argue, however, that the EU is impotent in this regard. Economically powerful, the EU is a large consumer and a large trading partner, particularly for Russia, with more than 70 per cent of Russian gas and oil exports going to the EU. Moreover, Russia depends on EU investment to improve its energy infrastructure. Whether the EU's advancing foreign policy will equip it to merely react to crises, or to proactively influence the structures and rules of the game that will determine the following decades, will be pivotal to its future energy security.

Environment and Climate Change

In terms of the legal basis for external action in the field of environmental policy, the Treaty explicitly defines 'promoting measures at international level to deal with regional or worldwide environmental problems, and in particular combating climate change' (Art. 191(1) TFEU) as one of the four objectives to which EU environmental policy should contribute. To this end, it foresees that 'within their respective spheres of competence, the Union and the Member States shall cooperate with third countries and with the competent international organisations' as long as this does not prejudice the competence of the member states to negotiate in international bodies and to conclude international agreements (Art. 191(4) TFEU).

This treaty provision reveals two important points regarding the EU's legal competences in this field (see Delreux 2011a: 15–18). First, it

provides an explicit and direct authorization for the EU to act externally. However, most external environmental competences of the EU
are so-called 'implied powers'. These powers are the result of the parallelism doctrine established by the *ERTA* case, which in practice means
that the EU can act internationally on all those issues on which it has
adopted internal legislation (see Chapter 3). Second, the aforementioned treaty article also confirms that environmental competences are
shared competences, which has an effect on the way the EU is externally represented in international environmental negotiations (see
Chapter 13 and Box 13.1).

The vexed question of leadership in global environmental governance

Being an advocate of strong environmentally friendly measures at the
international level, the EU is usually considered to be a leader in global
environmental governance (see Kelemen 2010; Vogler 2011; Vogler and
Stephan 2007; Zito 2005). Although the EU's leadership in the field of
climate change governance is increasingly questioned, it should be
remembered that global environmental governance is of course broader
than just climate change. As far as other environmental issues are
concerned, the EU's leadership is under less pressure. Indeed, the EU has
assumed a leadership role in many environmental regimes as it was at the
forefront of negotiations aimed at protecting biodiversity, regulating
GMOs or the transboundary movements of waste. European environmental leadership started somewhere in the 1980s, when it replaced the
US as the global environmental leader (Kelemen and Vogel 2010). This
leadership has manifested itself on three main fronts.

First, bilateral agreements with third countries generally incorporate
environmental clauses whereby these countries have to meet certain environmental standards to trade with the EU. Both with its eastern neighbours and with Mediterranean countries, the EU is engaging in dialogue
and providing technical assistance and funding (for instance through the
ENP – see Chapter 11). This type of bilateral relations also serves to a
large extent the EU's self-interest, since the EU wants to decrease the
chances of suffering from transboundary environmental pollution
emanating from these countries. Second, through its enlargement process
and accession policies (see Chapter 9), the EU has contributed to the
dissemination of environmental practices and standards. By virtue of the
transposition of the *acquis* into the national law of new member states,
an extensive corpus of environmental legislation has gradually spread to
other European countries. Third, the EU has strongly contributed to the
development of environmental governance at the multilateral level. The
EU is now a party to more than 60 multilateral environmental agreements (MEAs) which cover a broad range of environmental domains

including air, biotechnology, chemicals, climate change, biodiversity, soil, waste or water policies (Delreux 2012b).

Although the EU's leadership on *climate change* has declined substantially over the last decade (see further), the EU retains global leadership ambitions in the broader field of *environment*. The origins of this environmental leadership at the multilateral level can be explained in three ways. The first reason is that the EU is generally committed to multilateralism (see Chapter 13). In the environmental domain, this commitment takes the form of favouring legally binding agreements (MEAs) stipulating rights and duties with which parties have to comply. In this regard, the EU prefers, for instance, international environmental conventions negotiated in the UN framework. However, many emerging powers tend to be less favourable to such an approach as they feel that this impacts on their national sovereignty, not only in the environmental domain *sensu strictu*, but also with regard to the economic consequences environmental regimes may have.

The second way to understand the EU's global environmental leadership is that this has demonstrated the EU's potential to act as a structural power on the international scene and has played an important role in asserting and shaping its international identity (see Chapter 1). For instance, the EU strongly distinguishes itself from the US and the emerging powers as a forerunner in global environmental politics.

Third, it may also serve the EU's (economic) self-interest since European leadership at the international level can also be prompted by the desire of (producers in) the member states to maintain a competitive position at global markets. The EU indeed aims to create a level playing field by exporting its own relatively stringent environmental legislation to the international level so that not only European producers, but also their global competitors, need to meet similar standards (Kelemen 2010). The fact that the EU strives for strong regulations on the use and trade of chemicals, based on its own internal directives and regulations on chemicals policy, is illustrative in this regard.

Climate change as a foreign policy issue: EU leadership under pressure

Climate change is not only an important foreign policy issue because of environmental concerns (global warming threatening our daily environments, including biodiversity) or because of the economic consequences it may have (making it a transition towards a sustainable economic system necessary), but also because it has two main security components (see van Schaik and Schunz 2012). First, stronger climate change policies can contribute to a higher level of energy security in the EU. The more the EU is successful in reducing greenhouse gas emissions, the less fossil fuels will be needed and the less import dependent the EU is likely to become vis-à-vis big gas and oil exporters such as Russia and the Middle East (see above). Second, the impact of climate change, such as desertification, may generate conflicts over scarce natural resources such as water. Such conflicts may destabilize various regions, which may in turn have security consequences as, for instance, the need for military and humanitarian interventions or a growing wave of climate refugees (see Scheffran *et al.* 2012). Although many scientific reports deal with the long term and structural consequences of climate change, the EU does not seem to sufficiently take into account these scenarios in its external climate policies.

Since the EU's internal and external climate policies are closely interwoven, the existence of a strong regulatory climate framework explains the EU's activism at the international level (see Jordan *et al.* 2010; Oberthür and Pallemaerts 2010). Therefore, it is primarily in the area of climate change that the EU has been characterized as a leader (see Oberthür and Roche Kelly 2008; Parker and Karlsson 2010; Wurzel and Connelly 2010). The EU's leadership is, nevertheless, also qualified in the literature. It has been stated that the EU has not (yet) fulfilled its leadership potential, that it is only able to attempt leadership and that its actions do not correspond to its rhetoric (see Schunz 2011; Bourblanc 2011).

The EU's leadership in climate change governance was shown in the past through its support for the Kyoto Protocol. This was despite the fact the EU was initially not in favour of the Kyoto market mechanisms such as emissions trading, which ironically later became the cornerstone of the EU's climate policies. The EU's diplomatic efforts to achieve the necessary threshold to get the Protocol ratified and thus entering into force demonstrated its leadership role. In this respect, the deal the EU reached with Russia on Russian ratification of the Kyoto Protocol in exchange for EU support for Russia's WTO membership bid is one of the EU's biggest foreign policy successes in this area (Bretherton and Vogler 2006: 109).

The EU also tried to take on a leadership role in the post-2012 climate regime (i.e. the negotiations on a global climate change regime to succeed the Kyoto Protocol regime, of which the first commitment period ended in 2012). The EU was the first major actor to propose strong internal targets with the so-called 'climate and energy package' (or the '20–20–20 objectives'), thereby aiming to lead by example. In this package, the EU committed itself to reduce greenhouse gas emissions by 20 per cent, to have 20 per cent of its energy mix coming from renewables, and to increase energy efficiency by 20 per cent, all by 2020 (see Kulovesi *et al.* 2011). In another attempt of leadership, the EU pushed for the inclusion of the 2 degree target (i.e. limiting global warming to a maximum of 2 degrees Celsius above pre-industrial levels) as the basis of the post-2012 regime. This can be seen as one of the few modest achievements of the EU in recent climate talks.

The outcome of the 2009 Copenhagen conference was a clear indication that the EU's climate leadership in the current international power constellation has declined. All three pillars of its external climate policies are under pressure: multilateralism (informal gatherings such as the G20 or the Major Economies Forum are increasingly preferred to discuss climate change by other countries), a preference for legally binding instruments (others tend to be in favour of soft law outcomes, such as a pledge and review system) and environmental integrity (scientific reports by the Intergovernmental Panel on Climate Change show that the current measures are not sufficient to effectively tackle global warming) (Delreux 2012b). In terms of external climate policy effectiveness, the EU suffers from a mismatch between its ambitions, like the 20–20–20 objectives, and its ability to deliver. The EU has failed to export its own solutions to the multilateral level, proving that its 'leading by example' strategy simply did not work. The EU is still more able to influence the agenda of the climate change regime (e.g. the 2 degree target) than the outcome.

Whereas the climate change conference of Copenhagen was a clear failure for EU leadership, the climate change conferences of those taking place in the years after Copenhagen – i.e. those in Cancún (2010), Durban (2011) and Doha (2012) – indicate that the EU may have turned the corner and that it may have found a new role for itself in multilateral climate change negotiations. That new role now consists of a combination of defending ambitious preferences and attempting to play the role of bridge builder, coalition maker or mediator at the international level (see Groen *et al.* 2012; Pavese and Torney 2012). Particularly in Durban in 2011, the EU played a crucial role in gathering developed and developing countries together to commit themselves to reach by 2015 an encompassing global deal to cut greenhouse gas emissions (the so-called 'Durban Platform').

How does one explain the problematic leadership (ambitions) of the EU in global climate change politics? First, although the EU has very detailed position papers on all technical issues that are discussed internationally at the technical level, it pays insufficient attention to outreach and it lacks an overall strategy and a sufficient level of pragmatism in the (political) endgame of the negotiations. Indeed, when the level of politicization increases and when the real political knots need to be cut, the negotiation strength of the EU seems to weaken.

Second, the EU focuses too much on climate negotiations under the umbrella of the UN Framework Convention on Climate Change (UNFCCC), whereas the issue has largely passed beyond the UN framework. The formal UNFCCC process is increasingly paralleled by informal talks in new multilateral fora, where the EU is absent, where the EU is not as outspoken as it is in the technical working groups of the UNFCCC negotiation process, or where the EU uses different external representation and internal coordination arrangements than in the UNFCCC context (see Chapter 13).

Third, the EU's performance not only depends on intra-EU factors, but also on the external context in which in the EU acts. Indeed, international climate change negotiations work on the basis of consensus and they thus often result in a lowest common denominator outcome. Hence, it is not only the EU, with its usually reformist positions, that should be blamed for underperforming. It is also the positions of other major countries, including the US and the various 'strategic partners' of the EU (see Chapter 12), that have meant that the global climate change regime remains far from the EU's preferences in this regard.

Freedom, Security and Justice

Member states have been involved in a loose form of cooperation on internal security since the early 1970s. However, it was the implementation of the Schengen zone which provided the major catalyst to heighten cooperation, as dismantling national borders necessitated 'compensatory measures' in border-related issues such as migration, asylum and organized crime. Cooperation has been gradually formalized and institutionalized. Simultaneously, it is now recognized that merely internal measures and procedures will not lead to an effective approach to the challenges at stake. This means that the external dimensions of these policies (that initially were to address internal security concerns) are now considerably developed. As a result, the EU is quite active in the external dimension of the various domains that are covered by the Area of Freedom, Security and Justice (AFSJ) (see Wessel *et al.* 2011).

The fall of the Iron Curtain gave rise to popular concerns about a wave of immigration and organized crime in Europe. It was in this context that competences on *justice and home affairs* (JHA) were attributed to the EU in the Maastricht Treaty, although they were still organized in an intergovernmental manner. In the context of the EU's enlargement to the east, conflict in the Western Balkans and an increasing frustration with difficult intergovernmental decision-making processes, the Amsterdam Treaty called for the development of *an area of freedom, security and justice*. While retaining internal security measures involving *police and judicial cooperation in criminal matters* in the intergovernmental so-called 'third pillar', the Amsterdam Treaty 'communitarized' measures aimed at facilitating the free movement of persons (asylum, immigration, etc.) (see Lavenex 2006). Although the Amsterdam Treaty already foresaw the possibility of cooperation with third countries in this field, the political green light was given at the 1999 Tampere European Council, where the heads of state and government acknowledged the importance of creating stronger external relations in the field of JHA (Marsh and

Rees 2012; Trauner and Carrapiço 2012). Moreover, the Amsterdam Treaty also incorporated the Schengen agreement, initially an intergovernmental agreement between some member states outside the EU framework, into the EU's legal order.

Under the Lisbon Treaty, the AFSJ was fully integrated in the TFEU, applying the Community method to policies on border controls, asylum, immigration, judicial cooperation in civil and criminal matters and police cooperation (Arts. 78, 81, 82 and 87 TFEU). Yet its external dimension also developed quickly. The overall AFSJ objective of the EU is to 'offer its citizens an area of freedom, security and justice without internal frontiers, in which the free movement of persons is ensured in conjunction with appropriate measures with respect to external border controls, asylum, immigration and the prevention and combating of crime' (Art. 3(2) TEU). This objective has been challenged by societal events and dynamics such as immigration, organized crime or terrorism (see Chapter 6)

Schengen and border controls

Prior to the 2004 and 2007 enlargement wave, the Central and Eastern European countries acted as a buffer zone between the EU and the rest of the world. Before the mid-2000s, the EU prioritized issues related to the AFSJ in its relations with these countries. The 2004 and 2007 enlargements meant that the EU's external frontiers moved to the east and that countries such as Ukraine, Belarus and Moldova became direct neighbours of the enlarged EU. This led to new internal security challenges emanating from these new borders.

The Schengen area – created through both the dismantling of internal borders and the strengthening of control and security measures at the external borders – consists of most EU member states (Bulgaria, Cyprus, Ireland, Romania and the UK do not participate) as well as non-EU member states (Iceland, Norway, Switzerland and Liechtenstein). The existence of Schengen has heightened the need to control migration and to fight organized crime at the external borders of the Schengen area. Indeed, once organized criminal groups have entered the area, there are no longer border obstacles that could prevent them from taking up their activities, such as drug trafficking, in all Schengen countries (Rees 2011).

The enlargements also provided the impetus behind the launching of a range of new measures, legislation and mechanisms. For example, the accession of new member states to the Schengen *acquis* led to the upgrading of the Schengen Information System. This database allows participating member states to alert each other to, *inter alia*, people who have been refused admission, those wanted for arrest, extradition or to testify in court, or people who are fugitives.

Aiming to coordinate the cooperation between the member states on the management of their common external borders, the European

Agency for the Management of Operational Cooperation at the External Borders (Frontex) supports national authorities with training, technical support and risk assessment in border control (see Pollak and Slominski 2009; Rijpma 2012). Based in Warsaw (Poland being one of the EU member states with a large external border), Frontex faces a daunting task. Frontex has undertaken many operations, patrolling the EU's borders at sea, land and in the air. Most sea patrolling operations take place within the Mediterranean coastal area to stem the influx of illegal immigrants crossing from North Africa to Europe. In recent years, the EU has faced a highly visible and growing immigration crisis on its Mediterranean border. It was estimated that in 2011 more than 58,000 people arrived in Europe via the Mediterranean, while more than 1,500 lives were lost at sea that year (UNHCR 2012). Frontex operations have also included patrolling the shores of Mauritania, Senegal, Cape Verde and the Canary Islands to try to stop immigration at its source.

Frontex's operations risk contributing to an ever-growing securitization of the EU's borders. There is indeed a difficult balance to be found between internal security threats and larger foreign policy goals. As such, developing rigorous external border controls is deemed essential for internal 'security' (to prevent widespread immigration or organized crime), yet enhancing the stability of the circle of states surrounding the EU is essential to structural foreign policy goals. EU border controls can negatively affect this latter goal.

Immigration and asylum

The EU's response to the perceived need to tackle immigration and asylum has included the adoption of a range of 'remote-control' (beyond its borders) policies. The aim of such policies is to prevent migrants reaching the EU in the first place. The 2011 'Global Approach to Migration and Mobility' (Commission 2011e), very much in line with the first 'Global Approach' of 2005, puts forward a comprehensive approach to migration, and aims to combine two aspects of remote-control policies. First, it aims at better controlling illegal migration, using primarily restrictive tools such as border controls, visa policy and facilitating return through readmission agreements. Second, a 'preventive' aspect complements the more 'repressive' one, addressing the root causes of migration, namely factors outside the territory of the member states that make people decide to move, such as poverty or the lack of job opportunities (Trauner and Carrapiço 2012). This comprehensive approach has also been the rationale behind the five-year priority programmes on AFSJ issues (the 1999 Tampere Programme, the 2004 The Hague Programme and the Stockholm Programme, presenting the priorities for 2010–14).

Critics point out that the EU does not succeed in fully realizing this comprehensive approach (Sterckx 2008). Priority is given to the repressive aspect, such as the conclusion of readmission agreements or the fight against illegal immigration. Moreover, budget allocation also seems to suggest that the comprehensive approach between repression and prevention is unbalanced, leading Sterckx to conclude that 'the comprehensive approach is no more than empty rhetoric' (2008: 135).

There are two factors preventing the EU from successfully developing a fully-fledged external asylum and migration policy and translating its (rhetorical) ambitions into reality (2008: 123–8). First, the EU is not able to create sufficient leverage in its negotiations with third countries, for instance on readmission agreements. Indeed, those countries have little to gain from such agreements and the EU thus needs leverage for them to be effective. Leverage is usually found in the areas of trade or development, since they can provide the necessary carrots for third countries. However, the Commission DGs that are responsible for trade and development – and in particular for the trade and development budgets – do not seem to be very keen to use their resources for migration and asylum purposes, although the Commission's 'Policy Coherence for Development' document (see Chapter 9) acknowledged that migration and development are mutually dependent (De Bruycker and Weyembergh 2009). The second factor refers to the low degree of vertical consistency in the EU's external AFSJ policies (see Chapter 4). Because the AFSJ is explicitly an area of shared competence (Art 4 TFEU), member states retain the right to maintain their bilateral relations with third countries in this field, but they do not necessarily always follow the EU line. Although the Commission has a mandate to negotiate EU-wide readmission agreements, member states also negotiate such agreements bilaterally, focusing on those countries from where they have the largest influx.

The challenge for the EU is to find a balance between meeting growing popular concerns that immigration will destabilize national labour markets and even affect the European identity (Marsh and Rees 2012), while not building the regulatory equivalent of the Berlin Wall. In any case, three points on the foreign policy dimension of immigration and asylum policies are quite clear.

First, the area of freedom, security and justice has been developed first and foremost for EU citizens and, although achieving internal AFSJ goals requires an external dimension, there is little evidence that the freedom, security and justice of third-country citizens has been of major concern. Indeed, the external dimension of the AFSJ emerged mainly as a tool for achieving internal AFSJ objectives (Wessel *et al.* 2011). Obviously, this calls into question claims of the EU as a 'normative power' (see Box 6.1).

Second, the EU's external asylum and immigration policy is characterized by an 'externalization trend' (Sterckx 2008: 134–5). This means that the EU increasingly implements its own migration and asylum measures at and beyond its borders with origin and transit countries. For example, in order to export its policies and responsibilities outside its territories, the EU invests in capacity-building in third countries or in transferring migration control to these countries, aiming to prevent illegal immigration from transiting third countries on their way to the EU (Marsh and Rees 2012) (see Box 6.2).

Third, the EU's approach has been criticized for a one-sided emphasis on 'security' at the expense of the elements of 'justice' and 'freedom'. This 'securitization' process occurred in a broad spectrum of issues, some of which (particularly immigration or asylum) were clearly not a security threat per se but were nonetheless framed like that (see Huysmans 2006; Cross 2011). One consequence of this has been that AFSJ issues increasingly dominate over foreign and security issues. A second consequence is that the EU has been portrayed as 'Fortress Europe', unwelcoming towards those people who seek prosperity and security within the EU (see Bretherton and Vogler 2006: 238).

Agreements

The EU can incorporate AFSJ issues into its cooperation and association agreements with third countries, and can also conclude specific AFSJ agreements with third countries/organizations. Together with providing technical assistance (like know-how, training officials or legislative advice), such agreements are the main operational instruments of foreign policy-making in AFSJ. Indeed, the EU has deemed working with third countries essential to responding to terrorism, organized crime, corruption and drugs and managing migration (see Chapter 6).

The EU can also negotiate readmission agreements with third countries which provide for the return of illegal residents to their country of origin or transit (Art. 79(3) TFEU), as well as visa facilitation agreements, which makes it easier and cheaper for third country citizens to acquire short-stay visas to the EU (Art. 77(2) TFEU) (see Peers 2011: 290–3). The EU has concluded readmission and/or visa facilitation agreements with most Western Balkan countries, Georgia, Ukraine, Moldova and Russia.

The EU can also conclude agreements with third states and international organizations on police and judicial cooperation in criminal matters (Art. 82(1) TFEU). Examples include agreements on mutual legal assistance with countries such as the US and Japan, as well as agreements between European agencies in this field such as the European Police Office (Europol) and Judicial Cooperation Unit (Eurojust) on the one hand and third countries and international organizations on the other.

The inclusion of AFSJ issues in agreements with third countries has become a priority in the EU's relations with its neighbourhood. In concrete terms, EU policy takes several forms ranging from incorporation of AFSJ issues in political dialogue (see Chapter 9) to the development and implementation of specific projects financed by the EU. By incorporating

AFSJ issues in the European Neighbourhood Policy (see Chapter 11), the EU wants to achieve the cooperation of its neighbours in realizing its internal security concerns (see Lavenex and Wichmann 2009).

AFSJ issues are certainly a priority in the EU's relations with the Mediterranean. This is particularly the case since the Arab uprisings, which have led to increased concerns in Europe regarding uncontrolled migration. In this respect, it was illustrative that the first reactions of the Council of Ministers to the 2011 Arab uprisings was to secure borders and avoid a high flow of migration rather than to provide structural support to the peoples and the countries concerned. The internal security aspects of issues like migration or police and judicial cooperation now dominate the EU's agenda towards the southern Mediterranean countries (see Wolff 2012). Demonstrative of this is the fact that agreements with Northern African countries mostly include clauses on counter-terrorism and the management of migration (Rees 2011: 240).

From a foreign policy perspective, this strong emphasis on AFSJ issues in the EU's relationship with its neighbourhood has had major implications. A comprehensive approach towards the 'human dimension' in relations with neighbouring countries, aimed at promoting fundamental structural changes, has been abandoned in favour of a much narrower focus on internal security and migration issues. Thus, to some extent the AFSJ approach hijacked and undermined the structural foreign policy approach. Furthermore, since the EU relies on these countries' cooperation to achieve its AFSJ priorities, the EU has also weakened its leverage with regard to human rights and democratization issues. Arguing that particularly Northern African countries perceive the EU as aiming to resolve European problems at their expense, Marsh and Rees conclude that 'countries with their own demographic and economic problems have been reluctant to accede to EU demands which they regard as motivated by European self-interest' (Marsh and Rees 2012: 25). For political leaders and public opinion, tackling AFSJ concerns has become more urgent than foreign policy objectives which, particularly in the case of the Mediterranean, in any case had minimal prospect of success (see also Chapter 11).

Challenges without a Real External Policy: Health and Demography

This chapter has discussed issues that have both external and internal factors, such as energy supply, internal security issues or environmental degradation. In addition to this, the EU also faces threats on which no real policy has been developed but which may nonetheless be major foreign policy and security issues in the future. This chapter concludes by briefly looking at challenges related to health and to the impact of demographic change on the EU.

Health

Over the last decade, health has grown in importance on the international agenda, and is increasingly framed as a security risk. Disease figures as a 'global challenge' in the European Security Strategy: 'In much of the developing world, poverty and disease cause untold suffering and give rise to pressing security concerns ... AIDS is now one of the most devastating pandemics in human history and contributes to the breakdown of societies. New diseases can spread rapidly and become global threats' (European Council 2003a: 2). There are two dimensions to the intersection between health and foreign/security policy: first, the use of foreign policy to protect against health threats to the domestic population; and, second, the use of foreign policy to promote global public health.

The first dimension relates to the fact that foreign policy can be used to protect the domestic population from health threats. This particularly refers to vulnerability to transnational health risks. One of the many side effects of globalization is that population movements and wide-scale access to international travel mean infectious disease can now spread quickly across the globe. The H5N1 (avian influenza, 2005) or H1N1 (swine flu, 2009) pandemics were among some of the cases of transnational diseases that threatened Europe in the last decade. In the EU, such health issues have been treated first and foremost as an internal issue, mainly focusing on vaccine development and vaccination strategies, with minimal foreign policy relevance.

The spread of infectious disease can also be the result of bio-terrorist attack. The EU is vulnerable to the deliberate release of biological/chemical agents with the potential to cause widespread harm. As the European Security Strategy acknowledges, '[a]dvances in the biological sciences may increase the potency of biological weapons in the coming years; attacks with chemical and radiological materials are also a serious possibility' (European Council 2003a: 3). The EU supports initiatives to strengthen and promote international regimes such as the Biological and Toxin Weapons Convention and has taken other initiatives to prevent unauthorized access to, and risks of diversion of, lethal biological products (see Chapter 6).

The second dimension to the health–foreign/security policy intersection is focused on the promotion of global public health. This is both a question of solidarity and compassion as well as of far-reaching self-interest. As McInnes and Lee argue (2006: 16), we can understand the promotion of global health as being in an actor's own interests if we agree that poor health is destabilizing because it undermines state economic and social structures, and because tools to maintain state order (security forces) are particularly prone to sexually transmitted diseases, including HIV/AIDS. In this context, it is clear that the chance of foreign policy initiatives succeeding in stabilizing the countries of Southern Africa – where, for example, HIV infection rates stand at a staggering 25 per cent in Botswana and 26 per cent in Swaziland – is critically hampered by the devastating impact of this pandemic (UNAIDS/WHO 2009).

The EU promotes global public health both through its development policy and through particular trade initiatives. For example, it played a role in negotiating amendments to the WTO's Agreement on Intellectual Property (TRIPS) to improve access to medicines by allowing poor countries without manufacturing capacities in the pharmaceutical sector to import generic medicines for humanitarian purposes. However, as van Schaik (2011: 699) demonstrates, in the World Health Organization (WHO), member states have diverging views on issues such as reproductive rights, which undermines the EU's performance on these issues.

Furthermore, global public health scarcely features on foreign ministers' agendas. In their analysis of the relationship between health, security and foreign policy, McInnes and Lee (2006: 22) argue that:

[t]he relationship between the two policy communities [global public health and foreign/security] tends to be unidirectional, namely how selected health issues may create risks for (inter)national security or economic growth, and how therefore they might be issues of concern to foreign and security policy. The agenda is not one of how foreign and security policy can promote global public health.

This point is highly pertinent, as it relates to questions regarding which issues are considered to lie within the foreign policy remit and which goals should structure foreign policy. For example, why is it that democratic elections or free speech are firmly on the foreign policy agenda and are clear objectives of EU foreign policy when this is not the case with public health issues, even though on an individual basis, health is clearly of more vital and pressing concern than the ballot box? This is also linked to the West's conceptual fixation with human rights, and its neglect of wider human security issues and socio-economic rights (see Zhang C. 2012) (see Chapter 6).

Taking a non-Western-centric view of health also puts the EU's focus on bio-terrorism and terrorism into perspective. Globally speaking, in quantitative terms, the threat to life from biological weapons is probably rather small. However, terrorism is, and is seen to be, a threat to the West. The level of response thus depends on perspective rather than on the level of objective global threat. In its 2011 Human Development Report, the United Nations Development Programme states that some 2 million children under the age of 5 die annually as a result of diarrhoea (UNDP 2011: 63). Yet the issue of diarrhoea is yet to figure on the EU foreign policy agenda. Bio-terrorism is not the only way that disease can be used as an instrument of aggression. An example is the use of rape as a weapon of war (Carter 2010). Above and beyond the psychological, social and physical harm to victims, this plays a role in the spread of HIV/AIDS, has a long-term disruptive effect on societies and undermines efforts to pursue post-conflict stabilization. Rape has been systematically used as a weapon of war in, for example, Sudan and the DRC. Yet, this dimension of 'bio-terrorism' is not a priority in EU foreign policy.

Demography

The change in Europe's demographics ranks alongside climate change and energy security as a major issue for Europe in the decades to come. Faithful to its responsibility to act in the general interests of the EU, the European Commission is increasingly drawing attention to the dramatic demographic challenges facing the EU. For instance, every two years since 2006 it has organized the European Demography Forum, where policy-makers, stakeholders and experts discuss demographic change. The combination of two demographic changes seems to challenge the EU, including its foreign policy (see Langton 2010).

The first challenge is falling birth rates. The fertility rate required to renew Europe's population is around 2.1 children per woman. However, in many member states, the birth rate has fallen below 1.5 children per woman and immigration has become essential for population growth. Demography is not a foreign policy issue per se. However, shrinking populations do constitute a threat to a nation's vital interests and to its societal security. Combined with the relative increasing demographic size of other regions in the world, the consequence of demographic patterns in Europe is that the share of the EU of world population between 2000–30 is likely to fall from 12 per cent to 6 per cent (Commission 2005b: 16). This development, together with its budgetary implications, is likely to have a significant impact on the EU's weight in international affairs.

The second major issue is Europe's ageing population. The decrease in size of the EU's population is much more pronounced when we consider only the working age population (see Commission 2006a). The Commission estimates that the working age population is projected to fall by 16 per cent by 2050. In contrast, the elderly population will rise sharply by 77 per cent in that period, leading to a situation where by 2050 'the EU will change from having four to only two persons of working age for each citizen aged 65 and above' (Commission 2006a: 4). The increasing dependency ratios of the number of people working to the number of elderly citizens not only challenge competitiveness (decrease in number of persons employed, decline in GDP growth) but also the continued existence of the European socially corrected market economy model (increases in public spending for pensions, health care and long-term care). In addition, this change implies foreign policy related choices. For example, should the EU expedite Turkey's accession because its younger population could help redress Europe's demographic imbalance? In a similar vein, the EU will have to decide whether, despite popular concerns regarding immigration, EU countries should in fact be increasing immigration both over the short term (to bolster the workforce) and the long term (to have an impact on dependency ratios).

Conclusion

In steering change in the policy fields considered here – energy; environment and climate change; freedom, security and justice; health and demographics – there are a number of recurring themes. In the majority of policy fields discussed, the Commission has presented itself as an actor able to design comprehensive long-term programmes to tackle the challenges it had recognized and to further common interests.

In most of these fields, with the notable exception of environmental policy, member states within the Council have only reluctantly accepted the formulation of common policies, the transfer of new competences to the EU level and the operational involvement of central EU actors. Although this is understandable from the member states' perspective, it remains paradoxical since the ability of individual states to tackle the inherently transnational risks and challenges invoked in this chapter is often limited. Perhaps unsurprisingly, advances have often only been possible in the aftermath of sudden crises which demonstrated the EU's vulnerability (such as gas shortages when Russia cut off supplies to Ukraine and Belarus).

Finally, characteristic of each policy field mentioned here is that other institutional actors on both the EU and national levels play a role in developing new policies, with ministers, ministries, DGs and civil servants responsible for justice, the environment, energy and health being central. The blurring of the inside–outside divide in policy is thus paralleled by a blurring of the traditional picture of foreign policy actors being responsible for managing relations with the outside world.

Chapter 11

EU Foreign Policy towards the Neighbourhood

This chapter analyses the EU's foreign policy towards its neighbourhood and more particularly the Western Balkans, the eastern neighbourhood, the Mediterranean and the Middle East. For each region discussed, we assess the extent to which the EU has gone beyond trade and contractual relations towards developing a relational and structural foreign policy (see Chapter 1). This chapter mainly focuses on developments during the last decade in two categories of regions (for the developments in the 1990s and early 2000s, see Keukeleire and MacNaughtan 2008: 255–97). First, the EU's foreign policy towards the Western Balkans and Turkey is or was developed within the framework of their (potential) membership. This provides the EU with a unique leverage and set of carrots and sticks that it cannot use with regard to the other regions (see also Chapter 9). Second, since 2004, the EU's relations with most former Soviet republics, the countries of the Mediterranean and the Middle East are structured through the *European Neighbourhood Policy* (ENP). We discuss the ENP separately before analysing more in detail the EU's foreign policy towards the Eastern neighbourhood and the Mediterranean.

The Western Balkans and Turkey

Interaction with the Western Balkans has had a major defining impact on the image, nature and development of the EU's foreign policy. Throughout the 1990s, the Western Balkans was the site of European foreign policy's most resounding failure, with neither EPC nor CFSP able to stop the wars in the EU's immediate backyard that resulted in more than 100,000 casualties and around 2 million people displaced. Since the early 2000s and particularly after the Eastern enlargement wave (see Chapters 2 and 9), the Western Balkans has become the site of the EU's most comprehensive structural foreign policy and has emerged as the main testing ground of EU leadership and of an increasingly robust CFSP/CSDP (see also Rupnik 2011). The case of the Western Balkans also demonstrates clearly that EU foreign policy is embedded within a wider multi-location foreign policy, including NATO, the UN and the

OSCE. The EU wields the full spectrum of its policy toolbox in the region, reflecting its current position as the de facto leader of the international community's stabilization efforts. By 'Western Balkans' we refer to the countries of the former Yugoslavia and Albania – Albania, Bosnia and Herzegovina (BiH), Macedonia (formally called the 'Former Yugoslav Republic of Macedonia' or FYROM), Montenegro, Serbia and Kosovo (as defined by UNSCR 1244). At the end of this section, we also briefly discuss Turkey – not a Balkan country *per se*, but a candidate country with a long and difficult accession history which is in a process of redefining its relationship to the EU.

Structural foreign policy

The foreign policy efforts of the international community in the Western Balkans intertwine relational and structural foreign policy. After the peace agreements at the end of the Bosnian and Kosovo wars it was clear that the continued presence of extensive military forces would not alone achieve sustainable peace and that a fundamental transformation of the region was needed. It is in this transformation process that the EU's role has been key. From a position of impotence in the 1990s, the EU has evolved into a key actor in the region, employing the full range of instruments at its disposal. The EU is undertaking its most comprehensive and challenging structural foreign policy, which works on the majority of structures (political, legal, socio-economic, security) and levels (individual, societal, intrastate, interstate, intersociety, regional) (see Chapter 1). The EU's structural foreign policy towards the Western Balkans could, however, only be successful because its actions have initially been complemented by NATO's strong conventional foreign policy in the region and because EU membership was seen by the Balkan countries as the ultimate goal.

One of the cornerstones of the EU's policy is the Stabilization and Association Process (SAP), complemented by its enlargement policy. Launched in 1999, the SAP is based on a progressive partnership with each Western Balkan country, in which the EU offers a mixture of trade concessions, economic and financial assistance (through the Instrument for Pre-Accession) and contractual relationships (through Stabilization and Association Agreements (SAAs)) which govern the political, trade and economic relations of the EU with the Western Balkan countries. SAAs cover the creation of a free trade area; the approximation of legislation to the EU *acquis*; political dialogue; and cooperation in all areas of EU policies, including in the area of freedom, security and justice. Similar to the Europe Agreements with the CEECs that were concluded in the 1990s after the end of the Cold War, they provide the contractual framework for relations between the EU and the individual countries until their foreseen accession to the EU. Large sums of financial assistance aside, it is indeed the prospect of accession that again gives the EU its greatest leverage.

The EU has gone beyond the common elements of conditionality that governed its relations with the CEECs pre-accession (democracy, rule of law, human rights and market economy reforms) and, in Partnership Agreements with the countries concerned, has added further conditions related to the Western Balkans' specific post-war situation and the need to overcome regional tension (see Bieber 2012; Noutcheva 2012). These conditions include a commitment to good neighbourly relations and a readiness to engage in cross-border cooperation with neighbouring countries; compliance with obligations under the various peace agreements and with the International Criminal Tribunal for the former Yugoslavia (ICTY) in The Hague; and commitments on protecting minorities and on facilitating the return of displaced people. These conditions may sound self-evident, but they pose serious challenges in view of the high level of inter-state and intra-state animosity in the region. This explains why 'whereas the "end goal" (i.e. EU membership) is societally approved (some of) the criteria for membership are disapproved' (Freyburg and Richter, 2010: 276).

Widening the list of conditions also has resulted in 'conditionality dilemmas' for the EU as a country's compliance pattern often differs according to the issue. This required the EU to reward states in some fields, whereas non-compliance in other fields led to the need for sanctions (Richter 2012). This reflects multiple contradictions and ambiguities which hinder the EU's structural foreign policy towards Macedonia, Bosnia and Herzegovina and Kosovo in particular. As Juncos (2012: 58) argues, the EU's enlargement policy and state-building agenda are undermined by a series of internal contradictions:

> between the EU's technocratic approach and the politics of state-building; between state-strengthening and state-weakening dynamics associated with the EU's intervention; between the external promotion of EU demands and local ownership; and more generally, between member state-building and peacebuilding.

Other dilemmas and contradictions can be added: between the EU's multi-ethnic paradigm and actual state-building and societal preference which often underpin ethnic separation; between the EU's reform paradigm and its stability paradigm; between the EU's focus on structural changes and local leaders' reluctance to accept such reforms and respect the rule of law; and between the EU's focus on institution-building and the local demand for economy-building and job creation (Keukeleire *et al.* 2011: see also Fagan 2010).

An additional complicating factor is the disagreement among EU member states about the formal status of two countries that emerged from the break-up of Yugoslavia: Macedonia and Kosovo (which in 2008 declared itself independent from Serbia). The very use of the term 'Macedonia' is at the heart of a dispute between Greece and Macedonia. Macedonia, or formally FYROM, had been granted candidate-country status in 2005, as a reward for the peaceful resolution of the inter-ethnic conflict within the country. Because of domestic concerns (the fear that the Kosovar example would fuel separatist movements in their countries) Spain, Romania, Slovakia, Greece and Cyprus refused to recognize Kosovo as an independent state. Remarkably, disagreement on these fundamental issues of statehood did not prevent the EU from developing a comprehensive policy towards both countries and towards Kosovo in particular, even though Kosovo's contested statehood hampered the effectiveness of the EU's policy (see Papadimitriou and Petrov 2012).

The EU's internal divisions on Macedonia and Kosovo and the very different pace of compliance with the EU's conditions explain the quite different status of the various countries in their relationship to the EU. After accession negotiations were launched in 1995, Croatia became in July 2013 the 28th member state of the EU. Montenegro, Macedonia and Serbia were granted the status of EU candidate. In early 2013, negotiations had started with Montenegro, whereas negotiations with Macedonia were blocked by Greece. Albania, Bosnia and Herzegovina and Kosovo have not yet received the status of candidate country.

Both Serbia and Kosovo were awarded in 2012 with an upgrade of their relations with the EU, following Serbia's fulfilment of the ICTY conditions (with the arrest and extradition of former leaders that were charged with war crimes) and the conclusion of the first agreement between Serbia and Kosovo (Lehne 2012). This proved that the combination of the prospect of closer relations with the EU, conditionality and intensive diplomatic meditation could allow the EU to slowly resolve deadlock, even if structural reforms within the various countries remains more problematic than is hoped for (see Chapter 7). Negotiations under the auspices of the EU led in April 2013 to a breakthrough in the relations between Kosovo and Serbia which in principle should pave the way for the opening of the membership negotiations with Serbia and for an SAA with Kosovo.

Relational foreign policy

Before focusing on current relational foreign policies, it is useful to reflect on the EU's abject failures at the start of the Yugoslav war and to point to some paradoxes therein. As the Yugoslav War was starting in mid-1991, European Political Cooperation (EPC) (see Chapter 2) was still in place; member states were embroiled in negotiations over the Maastricht Treaty which, along with its new provisions for a CFSP, would only come into force two years later. Although EPC/EC demonstrably failed to prevent escalation in the Western Balkans, in the first stages of the crisis in 1991 it did assume responsibility and mediated actively between the warring parties (see Ginsberg 2001: 57–104). However, EPC/EC efforts did not bear fruit in the conflicts in Croatia and Bosnia and Herzegovina, not only because of their complexity but also because of the inability of the EC/EPC to back up its intensive diplomatic efforts with the necessary military instruments to monitor ceasefires or take up positions in buffer zones. Paradoxically, countries such as the UK that were most critical of the EPC/EC failure to tackle conflict in the Western Balkans were also the most fiercely opposed to endowing the EPC (and CFSP) with military crisis management instruments. The Maastricht Treaty did not lead to a strengthening of the EU's crisis management capabilities (see Chapter 2). Unsurprisingly, during the subsequent Bosnian and Kosovo wars, CFSP was not able to perform any better than had EPC. Ultimately, after refusing for several years to be involved in the conflict, NATO's military intervention countered the Serbian forces and ended the conflicts in Bosnia and Herzegovina (in 1995) and Kosovo (in 1999).

From 1999 on, the demands of conflict in the Western Balkans became a lever to breathe life into CFSP and create CSDP (see Chapters 2 and 8). The Kosovo debacle in 1999 influenced the EU's choice for the first High Representative of the CFSP – then NATO Secretary General Javier Solana – who had extensive experience in the Western Balkans and had led NATO through the Kosovo War. As the member states were determined that the EU should now succeed in the Western Balkans, they gave the High Representative the necessary room for manoeuvre to develop a highly intensive diplomacy in the region. This was evident during the successful conflict prevention campaign in 2002–3 in Macedonia, which then was at the brink of a new civil war, and during the equally successful mediation between Serbia and Montenegro in view of a peaceful separation of both entities (Piana 2002; Friis 2007). From 2011 onwards, HR/VP Catherine Ashton and senior EEAS staff actively mediated between Serbia and Kosovo and succeeded in gradually defusing the tense relationship between both countries (see Chapter 7).

The EU's diplomacy in the Western Balkans is underpinned by a whole array of instruments, including in the framework of CSDP. The Western Balkans proved to be a testing ground for the CSDP and provided its *raison d'être*. Since its inception in 2003 up to early 2013 the EU has undertaken several CSDP operations and missions in the Western Balkans (see also Collantes-Celador and Juncos 2011; Ioannides and Collantes-Celador 2011; Merlingen 2013). The *EU Police Mission in Bosnia-Herzegovina* (EUPM) was the EU's first ever civilian CSDP operation. It took over from the UN in January 2003 and acted as the leading force for supporting police reform in the country (until 2012). *Operation Concordia* was the EU's first military operation and the first operation to make use of the Berlin Plus arrangements with NATO (see Chapter 8), involving 400 troops and took over from NATO in March 2003 until the end of that year. Its mandate was to ensure a stable, secure environment in Macedonia to facilitate the implementation of the Ohrid Framework Agreement. *Operation Proxima*, the EU police mission (of 200 police advisers), took over from Concordia in Macedonia in December 2003. Its aim was to support the reform process within the Macedonian police service – a role which in 2005–6 was taken over by the much smaller EU Police Advisory Team (EUPAT).

In early 2013, the EU was conducting one military operation and one civilian mission in the Western Balkans. *Operation EUFOR Althea*, the EU's largest military operation, took over from the NATO-led multilateral Stabilization Force in Bosnia and Herzegovina (SFOR) in 2004. With initially 7000 troops (and in early 2013 still 600 troops), in a context of continued interethnic tensions and weak state institutions, its objective is to provide a safe environment for the population, to ensure compliance with the peace agreements and to support the international and local authorities. *EULEX Kosovo*, the EU's rule-of-law mission towards Kosovo, is the largest civilian mission ever launched under the CSDP (initially 3,200, later on 2,200 staff). Launched in 2008 under the general framework of UN Security Council Resolution 1244, it assists the Kosovar authorities in shaping police, justice and border management structures (see also below). Until 2012, the mission also had limited executive powers, implying that it could take decisions instead of the Kosovar authorities (see also below).

The EULEX Kosovo mission and the EU's general support for security sector reform demonstrate that CSDP missions not only serve as relational foreign policy tools (mediating between conflicting parties) but also as structural foreign policy tools (Keukeleire and Thiers 2010; Keukeleire and Metais 2014). However, these missions suffer from the same dilemmas and ambiguities which also hamper the EU's broader structural foreign policy towards the region (see above).

In the Western Balkans, we see a CSDP coming of age as the scope and size of missions and operations increase. The use of CSDP demonstrated the EU's potential as a post-crisis stabilization force able to conduct mutually reinforcing military and civilian operations. However, this occurred in a context where, despite their decreasing involvement, NATO and the US were still considered as the ultimate security guarantors in case things went wrong.

Turkey: between EU membership and emerging power

Discussions on the prospective membership of states in the Western Balkans have been closely linked to that of Turkey. In both cases EU enlargement has been seen in the first place through a foreign policy prism. Holding out the carrot of accession has been viewed as essential to trigger structural changes in these countries, to smooth tensions and conflicts, and to gradually embark on a process of Europeanization. However, Turkey has a longer experience of the trials and tribulations of seeking EU membership. The possibility of Turkey's accession to the EC/EU was first established by the 1963 Ankara Agreement, and it formally applied for membership in 1987, prior to any of the countries that have joined the EU in its successive enlargement waves since 1995. In December 2004, the EU finally decided to begin the Turkish accession process, opening membership negotiations in October 2005. Since then, however, the support in EU member states for Turkish membership has waned, the pace of reform within Turkey has slowed, and Turkey has gradually redefined its position and identity as a regional power in the wider Middle East and Mediterranean than as future EU member state.

Meanwhile, the EU has failed to use accession to solve one of the major problems in EU–Turkey relations: the conflict over Cyprus, an island divided into Greek and Turkish parts. In April 2004, on the eve of their accession to the EU, the population of Cyprus rejected the UN plan on Cyprus's unification, but were allowed to join the EU nonetheless. It was at this point that the EU lost its significant leverage to tackle the conflict. The Cyprus conflict has thus been allowed to continue to paralyse various EU policies, not least relations with Turkey and NATO (see Chapter 8). Disagreement on Cyprus led to the virtual suspension of the negotiation on some 'chapters' (see Chapter 9) in the EU–Turkey accession negotiations in 2006.

Turkey, like all prospective members, has to meet the Copenhagen Criteria to join. As is the case with the Western Balkans, further areas of conditionality have also been specifically designed for Turkey. The carrot of EU membership has brought about wide-ranging reforms on all levels within Turkey. However, in failing to offer resolute support to its membership, the EU has undermined the willingness of Turkey to achieve painful and often politically costly reforms *ad infinitum*. The processes of Europeanization and socialization proved to have their limits in a context of an open-ended membership prospect, particularly as the EU's politics of accession have been increasingly perceived as a politics of exclusion. Not surprisingly, levels of popular support for EU membership within Turkey have also waned, a development which deepened as the EU fell prey to the financial crisis (Engert 2010; Hughes 2011; Noutcheva and Aydin-Dzigit 2012; Ugur 2010).

The EU's main concerns about Turkish membership, in addition to the dispute over Cyprus, can be summarized in three points (see Bogdani 2010; Hughes 2011). The first is the political situation, and more concretely the state of democracy, the role of the military and respect for human rights, the rule of law, minority rights (particularly the Kurds) and fundamental freedoms, including freedom of speech, the press and assembly (see Usul 2010). After initial progress in the first years of the reign of the Prime Minister Erdogan and his Islamist-rooted AKP (Justice and Development Party), recent years have shown a worsening of the situation, including for example a sharp rise of the number of journalists that are imprisoned.

The second concern is more complex and related to matters of identity on both the Turkey and the EU side: that Turkey is a Muslim, though secular, state, and that its credentials as a 'European' country have been questioned. Objections to Turkish entry are indeed increasingly defined in these religious and cultural terms, particularly in two of the largest EU member states, Germany and France (Macmillan 2010).

This is linked to the third issue, demography. With its (still steadily growing) population of 73 million people (in 2010) Turkey would overtake Germany as the largest EU member state in less than a decade. This would change the balance of power in the EU's institutional framework, thereby weakening the position of the current largest EU states. Not surprisingly from this perspective, leading politicians particularly in Germany have pleaded for a 'privileged partnership' with Turkey rather than for Turkish accession.

However, the EU potentially has also much to gain from Turkish membership, in addition to contributing to the economic recovery in Europe. Turkish accession could be a counterweight to the 'clash of civilizations' thesis, ending the image of the EU as a Christian club, and helping to redefine its relationship with the Muslim world. Its accession could also make a concrete contribution to the difficult relations between EU member states and their Muslim populations (see Chapter 11). As a Muslim country generally embracing Western structures of democracy, respect for human rights and fundamental freedoms, Turkey is perceived as a positive model for other Muslim states worldwide, even if recent developments with regard to freedom of press and rights of minorities give reasons for concern.

Instead of seeing Turkey's assertive foreign policy as an obstacle to EU membership, the EU could take advantage of Turkey's valuable geostrategic position, especially in terms of its potential to improve energy-supply security as a transit route for oil and gas (see Chapter 9), to act as a mediator in various conflicts in the region, to support structural reforms in the Mediterranean, and to augment the EU's potential to make its voice heard and increase its influence on developments in the Southern Caucasus, the Middle East and the Mediterranean. This also implies that, parallel to Turkish membership, the EU would have to seriously upgrade its foreign policy towards and increase its engagement with these new neighbouring countries. Furthermore, since Turkey is a member of NATO, the relations between CSDP and NATO could benefit from a Turkish accession to the EU (see Gürsel 2013; Kirisci 2012; Murinson 2012) (see Chapter 8).

In view of the waning appeal of EU membership in Turkey and Turkey's rising status as an independent political and economic regional power, the EU may, from a foreign policy perspective, have missed an invaluable geostrategic opportunity. Turkey increasingly presents itself and is perceived in the Mediterranean region and Muslim world as a competing and more attractive and effective structural power than the EU. This is particularly the case the more Turkey develops its foreign policy as based on a neo-Ottoman vision and on the importance of Muslim solidarity and the transnational concept of *ummah*, the Muslim community (Murinson 2012: 12–13) (see also below and Chapter 12).

The European Neighbourhood Policy (ENP)

Launched in 2004 and revamped in 2011–12, the ENP serves as the overarching framework for the EU's policy towards its eastern and southern neighbours: in Eastern Europe (Ukraine, Moldova, Belarus), South Caucasus (Georgia, Armenia, Azerbaijan), the Middle East (Israel, Palestinian Territory, Jordan, Lebanon, Syria), and Northern Africa (Morocco, Algeria, Tunisia, Libya, Egypt). The ENP is a crystallization of the goal formulated in Article 8 TEU, which is also labelled the 'Neighbourhood Clause' (Hanf 2012):

> The Union shall develop a special relationship with neighbouring countries, aiming to establish an area of prosperity and good neighbourliness, founded on the values of the Union and characterised by close and peaceful relations based on cooperation.

The ENP is complemented by other EU policies towards these countries and regions, including bilateral relations and agreements (such as Association Agreements), additional regional frameworks (such as the Eastern Partnership and the Union for the Mediterranean), and initiatives in the framework of the CFSP and CSDP. Following an evaluation of the ENP in this section, these policies as well as the region-specific evaluation of the ENP are analysed in the sections on the eastern neighbourhood and on the Mediterranean and the Middle East (see below) (for a detailed analysis of the ENP, see Lannon 2012; Whitman and Wolff 2012b).

Parallel to its first enlargement with Central and Eastern European countries, the EU launched the ENP in order to strengthen prosperity, stability and security in its neighbourhood and avoid new dividing lines emerging between the enlarged EU and its neighbours (Commission 2003, 2004). Being unable or – with regard to the eastern neighbours – unwilling to offer the incentive of accession, the ENP offered the neighbours a deepening of the political, economic, social, cultural and security relations. The ENP was and still is designed to support the ENP countries in their political, economic and institutional reforms; to strengthen democracy, good governance, the rule of law and human rights; and to promote economic modernization and liberalization, including a gradual integration in the internal market and a participation in EU sectoral programmes and policies. The ENP's approach is founded on the principles of partnership, common interests, joint ownership and differentiation, with the latter depending on the partner countries' ambition to pursue reforms and willingness to accept the 'common values'.

The ENP's general framework has been translated into specific *ENP Action Plans* negotiated with 12 of the 16 ENP countries, which allowed for a more tailor-made approach for each country. Belarus, Algeria, Libya and Syria do not (yet) figure on this list in view of their refusal to enter into the ENP logic or due to a refusal of the EU to start negotiations, although negotiations were foreseen with Libya after the 2011 regime change in that country (Commission 2012i). The ENP Action Plans include a jointly defined agenda of reforms, an extensive list of short and medium-term priorities in a wide range of policy sectors, and incentives in the form of EU assistance, market access and integration in EU programmes and networks. The implementation process is managed and closely monitored by the European Commission (DG DEVCO) and the EU Delegations in the partner countries, with financial support provided through the EU's various financial instruments and, particularly, the European Neighbourhood Instrument (ENI) (see Chapter 4).

At first glance, the ENP provides a perfect example of a comprehensive structural foreign policy. Not only does it support structural changes on a declaratory level, it also made this policy operational through a comprehensive set of implementation mechanisms, underpinned by significant budgetary means and managed by an extensive bureaucratic apparatus. The emphasis on partnership, common interests and joint ownership are to guarantee a sufficient degree of legitimacy and endogenous support needed for an effective structural foreign policy (see Chapter 1).

The actual effect of the ENP was and is very uneven – across countries, sectors and over time. The Commission's yearly progress reports indicate that the ENP Action Plans are made a major point of reference in the domestic reform strategies of a limited number of ENP countries, including Morocco, Moldova and initially also Ukraine (Bicchi 2010; Commission 2012i; Sasse 2012; Solonenko 2012). However, the general impact and relevance are more limited or even negligible in a range of other countries, including an important country such as Egypt (see Bicchi 2012; Ghazaryan 2012; Echeverria Jesús 2012). In combination with Association Agreements concluded with the partner countries, the ENP has contributed to a norms transfer and expansion of EU rules beyond EU borders in various policy sectors, such as environmental policy and migration policy. This norms diffusion has taken various forms, however, depending on a variety of factors, with rule adoption by the ENP partners not necessarily meaning that the rules have also been applied and respected in practice (see Börzel and Risse 2012b; Casier 2011; Lavenex and Schimmelfennig 2009a, 2012).

On the whole, the ENP has not induced the expected structural reforms. It has also failed in achieving some other major objectives: promoting prosperity, security and stability in the EU's neighbourhood and limiting the feelings of exclusion in partner countries. As Whitman and Wolff emphasize (2012a: 13), despite some cooperation 'the EU is still surrounded by unstable neighbours affected by low living standards, high levels of corruption and organized crime, volatile political systems and violent domestic conflicts', in addition to both ongoing and 'frozen' conflicts.

It is useful to look for some explanations for the mixed results of the ENP, as these can also be useful to evaluate the adaptation of the ENP pursued since the 2011 revolts in the Arab world. In its very first evaluation of the ENP, the Commission (2006b, 2006c) already provided some explanations, pointing to three areas in which partner countries have been disappointed by the ENP process. One decade later, these three sore points remains largely valid: too little effort by the EU to resolve conflicts in the region; a failure to improve access to the EU market for the products most important to them; and the lack of progress in terms of people-to-people contacts and improving the movement of citizens from partner countries to the EU. These disappointments are symptomatic of a major flaw in the EU's structural foreign policy towards the region: while the EU wants far-reaching structural change within these states, it refuses to make the internal changes necessary to achieve this. By refusing to consider the ENP as a preparation for EU membership, and by rejecting the free movement of their products and their population, the EU has made clear that it will not structurally reform the political, economic and human patterns that define its relations with its ENP partners.

The disappointing impact of the ENP is related to its ambiguity, in terms of both objective and methodology, which results from what can be labelled as the shadow of enlargement. In terms of objectives and underlying motivations, the ENP was conceived by the majority of EU member states as a way to avoid further enlargement. However, for several of the ENP partners, constructive cooperation within the ENP had as its main objective to ultimately 'escape' the ENP and to receive what the ENP was designed to exclude: a membership perspective or, for the Mediterranean partners, greater integration in EU programmes and networks (Whitman and Wolff 2010a: 13). When this membership perspective proved to be elusive, so too did the cooperative behaviour and EU inclination of several ENP partners. The ENP thus did not overcome but rather exacerbated the border and boundary problems, in terms of territory, policy and identity (see Dimitrovova 2010; Tonra 2012).

In terms of methodology, the ENP largely relies on the accession approach: conditionality, action plans covering a broad range of policy sectors, and a Commission-led bureaucratic implementation and monitoring process. However, as Sasse rightly emphasizes: 'The ENP is built on "conditionality-lite" – the incentives and the commitment on the side of the ENP countries as well as the EU are vague and limited' (2012: 200). As the advantages offered by the EU are generally seen as too little or too ambiguous – belonging more to the realm of 'possibilities' than of real commitments – the conditionality tool could not function as it did (and does) in the enlargement process. It did not motivate the partner countries to make the necessary fundamental steps and to accept the costs and risks related to structural reforms (Ghazaryan 2012: 236, 240; Whitman and Wolff 201a: 12). Moreover, disillusionment rose as it became clear that the ENP Action Plans mainly reflected the EU agenda, with a strong emphasis on the approximation of the legal and institutional framework of the ENP countries to that of the EU, whereas the EU itself made little extra effort and played down the demands put forward by the neighbouring countries themselves (Casier 2012: 108; 2011).

Providing tangible financial and other incentives is essential, however, as structural reforms inevitably take time, with political, economic and human costs of ambitious reform programmes often being paid up front, while reforms often only come to fruition later. The latter is true for the elites as well as for the population. Elites often risk losing political power and economic control as a result of the political liberalization processes sought by the EU, while the population in the short-term risks feeling the disadvantages of the economic liberalization processes sought by the EU.

This issue relates to another explanation for the limited impact of the ENP, reflecting two of the conditions for a successful structural foreign policy (see Chapter 1). The first condition is the existence of endogenous support within the ENP countries for the various structural reforms (and for accepting the costs in pursuing these reforms). Whereas in some of the eastern neighbourhood countries the local context initially seemed to be conducive to structural changes, this context became gradually less favourable for structural reforms. Endogenous support for structural reforms seemed to be largely absent in the southern neighbourhood, although the 2011–12 upheavals would prove this perception to be wrong.

The second condition is comprehensiveness, implying that the individual and societal level are also to be taken into account. However, the ENP was clearly out of touch with some societal dynamics that were taking place, particularly in the Mediterranean countries, including both the quest for freedom or the increasing importance of the religious dimension within society. Whereas the EU and its member states accepted to cooperate with undemocratic regimes which questioned the basic values the EU was said to promote – thereby also undermining the EU's own credibility – the population in several Mediterranean countries from 2011 on protested against and, in some cases, also ousted their authoritarian leaders.

The 2011 Arab revolutions and uprisings in Tunisia, Libya, Egypt and other Mediterranean countries also affected the ENP. The EU had to deal with the perception that structural changes took place despite, rather than thanks to, the ENP. This concurred with the negative experience in the eastern neighbourhood where the ENP had not been able to avoid the fact that – and was even seen as one of the reasons why – reforms faltered or were turned back in countries that initially seemed to be on the right track (such as Ukraine and Georgia) (see below).

Based on the Joint Communication by the HR/VP and the European Commission (2011), the EU introduced in May 2011 a 'new approach' for its ENP, including an upgrade of objectives and principles. The goal was no longer merely to support democracy but rather to support 'deep democracy'; not merely economic development but 'sustainable economic and social development'; not merely to create free trade areas but 'Deep and Comprehensive Free Trade Areas' (DCFTAs). The DCFTAs not only provide for the gradual dismantling of trade barriers but also aim for regulatory convergence in areas that have an impact on trade, such as sanitary rules, animal welfare or public procurement. This implies the need for a complex and broad-ranging reform process and approximation of EU rules and practices by the partner countries. Sustainable economic and social development implies support for policies conducive to inclusive growth, to the development of micro, small and medium-sized companies and to job creation. 'Deep democracy' mirrored the recognition that the organization of free elections is not sufficient, but that other factors are needed to make democracy sustainable, including free press and freedom of expression, an impartial judicial system with independent judges, a non-corrupt civil service, democratic control over armed forces and justice, and a vibrant civil society.

The latter was also translated in the EU's commitment to develop partnerships not only with governments but also with civil society. This was an answer to the criticism voiced about the EU during the Arab revolts, namely that it engaged mainly with the authoritarian regimes and not with the population in the surrounding countries. In order to engage more with societies in the partner countries, the EU created two new financial instruments: the 'European Endowment for Democracy' and the 'Civil Society Facility' (see Chapter 6).

'More for more', 'markets, mobility and money', and greater differentiation are the principles that were put forward in the EU's new approach for the ENP (HR/VP and Commission 2011, Commission and HR/VP 2012a). First, 'more for more' implies a further strengthening of the conditionality principle. Continuing internal reforms were expected with regard to economic liberalization and political liberalization (with respect for democracy, rule of law and human rights). Second, the more and the faster a partner country progresses in its internal reforms, the more can be expected from the EU with regard to the three Ms: markets (a further opening of the EU market for products from the partner countries), mobility (including 'mobility partnerships' and progress in terms of visa facilitation or visa liberalization) and money (enhanced financial support by the EU). Third, and unavoidably, in combination with the specificities of the neighbourhood countries, this intensified conditionality has to lead to more differentiation in the EU's policy towards the various ENP partners (see Van Elsuwege 2012).

The EU's upgraded ENP was met with serious criticism. First of all, the Southern Mediterranean countries discovered that now that they had embarked on the difficult road of political reforms, paradoxically, the EU was stricter on conditionality in its relations with the fledgling democracies, than it was with the former dictatorships.

Second, instead of 'more for more', the EU's policy seemed in many respects to be rather 'more of the same'. The EU did not provide the population in its neighbourhood with fundamentally new prospects or advantages that would convince them to consider the EU as a major beacon for their reforms. Particularly in a context of financial and economic crisis in Europe, EU member states were no less reluctant than before to open up markets and borders or to provide such considerable financial support that would allow the EU to make a difference in the region.

Third, the DCFTAs place the burden of reforms on the partner countries, without the EU offering sufficient incentives or proposing concrete measures to increase the standard of living of the population and to mitigate in the short term the problematic economic situation. As Martin (2012: 247) emphasized: the EU's 'norm-promoting capacities are weak precisely where they are most needed: in relation to the "human face" of its economic model'.

Finally, the EU's attempt to engage more with societies also proved to be problematic. This is due in part to the EU's interpretation of 'civil society', which does not match the various forms of civil society in the neighbouring countries, which could be much more nationalist, traditional and/or religious (see further).

The two last aspects – the neglect of the human face of the economic model and of the deeper identity issues – partially explain the waning influence and credibility of the EU in the ENP countries. It also explains the gradually strengthened position of other development models and competing structural powers: Russia in the Eastern neighbourhood, and Islamic movements and states in the southern neighbourhood (see below and Chapter 12). This underlines the fact that the ENP does not exist in a vacuum but is to be seen more within the broader geostrategic context, with surrounding regions as Central Asia, the Gulf, the Middle East and the Sahel region. In order to stabilize or transform its neighbourhood, the EU also has to deal more with crucial problems in these regions such as the uncertain spillover effects of the 'Arab Spring', regional conflicts, state failures, strengthened Jihadist movements, food crises, terrorism, trafficking and organized crime. In other words, in order to stabilize or transform its neighbourhood in a sustainable way, the EU has to also deal more intensively with the 'neighbours of the EU's neighbours' (Gstöhl and Lannon 2014) (see also the following sections).

The Eastern Neighbourhood

The ENP does not tell the whole story of the EU's foreign policy towards its Eastern neighbourhood. The EU's enlargement to incorporate the CEECs had a profound impact on its eastern flank and affected the EU's relations with countries in the post-Soviet space which had for a long time remained a blind spot in EU foreign policy: in Eastern Europe (Ukraine, Belarus, Moldova), in the South Caucasus (Armenia, Azerbaijan, Georgia) and in Central Asia (Kazakhstan, Kyrgyzstan, Uzbekistan, Tajikistan and Turkmenistan). Enlargement turned Belarus, Ukraine and Moldova into immediate neighbours, and brought distant conflicts and authoritarian regimes closer to home. It fuelled new hopes and aspirations, increased pressure on neighbouring countries, but also prompted new dividing lines and areas of tension. By drastically redrawing the European map, the EU and Russia became potential direct competitors, leading to a 'clash of integration processes' (Casier 2007) (see Chapter 12). In this region, the EU's main emphasis is on developing contractual relations, which only to some extent constitutes a basis for a structural foreign policy. Only recently has the EU also undertaken some elements of a relational foreign policy, a development which has been limited by Russia's influence over the former Soviet republics and its global strategic importance.

Structural foreign policy

As the enlargement came closer, the EU was compelled to define its relations with what would become its new neighbourhood and, more in general, with the post-Soviet space. Currently, the main tools of EU cooperation with the post-Soviet states are: bilateral Partnership and Cooperation Agreements (PCAs) concluded with all former Soviet republics; the European Neighbourhood Policy (ENP) with the countries in Eastern Europe and the Southern Caucasus (but not Central Asia); the Eastern Partnership; and the European Neighbourhood Instrument

(ENI) as the main financial instrument to support these policies (on the ENI, see Chapter 4).

Partnership and Cooperation Agreements constitute the legal framework for the political, economic and trade relations between the EU and its Eastern partner countries. PCAs were concluded in the late 1990s with all countries in the region, although some of these have not been ratified or have been suspended because of problems with human rights and democracy. There is no PCA with one of the EU's closest neighbours, Belarus, as the EU did not ratify the agreement in view of the authoritarian rule of President Lukashenko. The contents of the PCAs vary considerably – those with the Eastern European countries are more elaborate and extensive than those with the countries of Central Asia and the Caucasus, for example. However, they all contain the classical ingredients of the EU's contractual relations with third countries including: supporting efforts to consolidate democracy and economic development; promoting trade and investment; cooperating in various policy fields; and providing a framework for political dialogue.

Launched in 2004, the *European Neighbourhood Policy* (ENP) included the countries in Eastern Europe and the South Caucasus, but not Central Asia (see above). The ENP and ENP Action Plans complement rather than supersede the PCAs. For the Eastern neighbourhood, Action Plans have been adopted for Ukraine, Moldova, Georgia, Armenia and Azerbaijan, whereas Belarus was excluded from the ENP process. The ENP Action Plans rest on a shared commitment to 'common values' and aim to support structural changes or consolidation in the direction of democracy, rule of law, good governance, respect for human rights and market economy principles. In this sense, the ENP had the potential to provide an alternative or complementary institutional context to the predominant context of Russian influence and of inward-looking authoritarian regimes.

However, disappointment and failure of the ENP was unavoidable considering the widely diverging views on the ultimate goal of this policy. The ENP had sought to assuage the aspirations of Georgia and Ukraine towards EU accession following democratic revolutions in those countries in 2003–4 but without the major incentive of accession. Whereas Georgia and Ukraine saw EU membership as a strategic priority and the ENP as a tool to achieve this goal, the majority of EU member states considered granting a membership perspective as politically and economically out of the question – despite the insistent support of the Baltic countries and Poland (Whitman and Wolff 2012; Sasse 2012). Hence, whereas particularly Ukraine and Moldova had initially made the ENP Action Plans a major point of reference in their domestic reform strategies, disillusionment grew in these countries about the ability to profit more from the ENP and to redefine the ENP as a step towards EU membership. This also partially explains why political reforms faltered or were turned back in countries that initially seemed to be on the right track (such as Ukraine and Georgia) (see below).

The apparent need to upgrade relations with the Eastern neighbours and to counterbalance the newly established 'Union for the Mediterranean' with the countries in the southern neighbourhood (see next section) resulted in 2009 in the launch of the *Eastern Partnership* (EaP), which had to lead to strengthened cooperation and deepened economic integration (Council 2009b; Korosteleva 2011, 2013; Lannon and Van Elsuwege 2012). The inauguration of the EaP was also accelerated by the 2008 Russian–Georgian war and Russian–Ukrainian gas crisis in 2009 (see Chapter 10), when the EU realized that the stability and prosperity in the Eastern neighbourhood is also essential for its own interests and that strengthening relations with these countries was important to counter the growing assertiveness and influence of Russia in this region (see below). The purpose was to deepen political cooperation and economic integration with six Eastern neighbouring countries: Moldova, Ukraine, Belarus, Georgia, Armenia, and Azerbaijan. The inclusion of Belarus was seen as an opening to the regime in Minsk, as a reward for some prudent first steps towards reforms. However, compared with the ENP, the EaP did not fundamentally alter the terms of the relationship. Doubts arise about the added value for the Eastern neighbours, particularly because the key elements of the partnership have been forged mainly by the EU rather than by the Eastern 'partners' and because the EU had difficulties taking into account the partners' needs and internal dilemmas (Korosteleva 2012, 2013). Hence, similar to the ENP, whereas the EU presents the EaP as a 'politics of inclusion', it is perceived rather as a 'politics of exclusion' in the countries concerned, with 'the EU reinforc[ing] the boundaries rather than accommodating them, and much less transforming them' (Radchuk 2011: 22).

It is against this background that scepticism was voiced when the EU, in the context of upgrading the ENP, proposed a new EaP Roadmap which again included the traditional objectives: political association and economic integration, enhanced mobility of citizens 'in a secure and well managed environment', and strengthened sector cooperation (European Commission and High Representative 2012b). As a translation of the 'more for more' principle, the question was whether the goals and implementation of this Roadmap was not in the first place 'more of the same', particularly as the political and financial constraints surrounding the implementation of the EaP did not disappear (see Lannon and Van Elsuwege: 2012: 321).

By early 2013, the very mixed results of the EU's policy towards its Eastern neighbours were quite obvious, with Ukraine being a case in point (see Balfour 2012; Stewart 2011; Solonenko 2012). In late 2011, Ukraine was the first country to conclude negotiations with the EU on a new Association Agreement (AA), including a DCFTA, reflecting a further approximation of Ukraine to the EU's legislation and standards, particularly in the economic field. However, despite its fulfilment of the economic conditions, the signing of the agreement with Ukraine was put on hold in view of the curtailing of the political liberalization process and, particularly, the imprisonment of former Prime Minister Tymoshenko in what was considered as a politically motivated trial. This demonstrated the EU's failure to export rule of law, human rights and 'deep democracy' and, in general, to shape the political and societal structures of Ukraine – notwithstanding Ukraine initially be seen as one of the successes of the EU's neighbourhood policy. The victory of Russia-oriented politicians in the 2010 elections and the defeat of the EU-minded president and parties also demonstrated the doubts of a majority of the population about the pertinence and practical advantages of the previously followed pro-EU course. It reflected a general failure of the EU's ENP and EaP, that is to positively contribute to a 'process of redefinition of regional identities in the wider-European space' (Simao 2011) in a direction of the EU's view, with Russia proving to be a more successful structural power than expected (see Chapter 12).

Beyond its relations with the countries of Eastern Europe and the South Caucasus, the EU's capacity to influence is even more limited in the Central Asian countries which are not part of the ENP and EaP. Reflecting the EU's struggle with the question of how to deal with the oppressive regimes in Central Asia, the EU has negotiated Partnership and Cooperation Agreements with the Central Asian countries (Kazakhstan, Kyrgyzstan, Uzbekistan, Tajikistan and Turkmenistan), although the one with Turkmenistan has not yet entered into force. The EU is indeed staggering between upholding its own values and yielding to the enticements of realpolitik given the strategic importance of this region (in the supply of energy, the 'war on terrorism' and as a transit area for European troops to Afghanistan) and the competition with other structural powers (not only Russia, but also China). The formal welcoming of authoritarian presidents in the EU's headquarters in Brussels and the signing of bilateral 'strategic partnerships' between, for instance, Germany and Kazakhstan (including guaranteed access to raw materials) indicated that realpolitik reigned on both the EU side and member states side (see Bossuyt and Kubicek 2011; Kavalski 2012).

Relational foreign policy

The EU and Russia have managed to defuse a range of potentially highly conflictual foreign policy issues in the post-Soviet space, such as the difficult problem of the Russian enclave Kaliningrad, the situation of the Russian minorities in the Baltic states and, more generally the accession of the Baltic states to the EU. With enlargement bringing the post-Soviet arena closer to the EU, the EU began to use its diplomatic and crisis management toolbox to develop policy towards the post-Soviet states' various conflicts and crises. The results are varied, ranging from some initial successes (Ukraine, Georgia and Moldova) to non-involvement (Nagorno-Karabakh) (Huff 2011; Popescu 2011).

The EU's main diplomatic success seems to be the way it handled the political revolutions in Georgia and particularly Ukraine during the Orange Revolution in late 2004. In the midst of the crisis, High Representative Javier Solana and the Polish and Lithuanian presidents worked in Kiev to negotiate the contours of a democratic solution between the rival interests. The EU's diplomatic pressure on the Yanukovych government in the run-up to and aftermath of presidential elections in Ukraine in 2004 has been seen as contributing to the peaceful revolution (Karatnycky 2005). One year later, the EU became actively engaged in another regional crisis, launching its first Border Assistance Mission (EUBAM Moldova and Ukraine) along the 800 km Ukraine–Moldova border. In so doing, the EU supports Ukraine and Moldova in countering the secessionist leaders of Transnistria, which are in turn supported by Russia. Together with the EU Special Representative for Moldova and complementary Commission initiatives, this CSDP operation effectively contributed to the easing of tensions – though without being able to find a fundamental solution (see Popescu 2011: 38–65).

However, a backlash followed these successful EU interventions. The emergence of an increasingly assertive Russian foreign policy, with Russian leaders and a Russian public opinion that wanted to stop increasing Western influence and regain control over its 'Near Abroad' put the EU's diplomatic achievements in another perspective. Moreover, as seen in the previous section, the EU did not manage to translate its success in terms of relational foreign policy into a successful structural foreign policy, as the EU could not engage Ukrainian elites to enter into enduring political liberalization processes.

Russia's increasing firmness culminated in 2008 in the Russian invasion of Georgia in order to support the secessionist regions of South Ossetia and Abkhazia. In contrast to the US, the OSCE and UN, the EU could take 'the key role as the primary conflict manager' in the Georgian–Russian confrontation (Sinkkonen 2011: 265). A ceasefire was mediated by the French President Sarkozy, who at that time held the rotating Presidency of the European Council. The 'Sarkozy–Medvedev Plan' (referring to the then presidents of France and Russia) foresaw the withdrawal of Russian troops from Georgia and the deployment of 200 civilian EU monitors in the conflict zones. The EU managed to decide swiftly on launching a civilian CSDP mission (the EU Monitoring Mission (EUMM) Georgia). EU monitors were in fact deployed some weeks later, and a financial assistance package was granted to Georgia, including for the breakaway regions (see Bosse 2011; Popescu 2011:

66–94). The EUMM is still present in Georgia, with an 'EU Special Representative for the South Caucasus and the crisis in Georgia' underpinning the EU's policy, without having much political clout, however.

The EU thus proved to be able to react swiftly and successfully to crises, although two caveats need to be mentioned in this context. First, the EUMM never had access to the territory of South Ossetia and Abkhazia, the two regions that had declared independence, and whose independence was recognized by Russia and securitized by Russian troops. The EU could not force Russia to withdraw its troops and comply with all aspects of the peace agreement. The EU's conflict management initiatives indeed contributed to ending the war and to avoiding a resumption of hostilities in the following years, but the EU was unable to forge a fundamental solution for the territorial disputes – thus in fact ensuring Russia's preferred outcome.

Second, the EU's diplomatic success was perhaps less an EU success than a success of a strong and assertive member state. France at that time was holding the rotating Presidency and in this context also skilfully used the available EU foreign policy tools. Larsen (2012) in this context suggests that the Georgia crisis can be better explained by referring to a 'European great power concert', with the large EU member states and Russia being the main players, particularly when deals have to be struck on the most sensitive issues. This is also valid in other cases where EU foreign policy is quite invisible, such as the crisis in Nagorno-Karabakh between Armenia and Azerbaijan where again France plays a leading role (Popescu 2011: 95–121). It also applies in the relations with the former Soviet republics in Central Asia where the above-mentioned enticements of realpolitik dominate and where the appointment of an EUSR for Central Asia mainly serves to hide the absence of a firm EU foreign policy towards that area (Kavalski 2012: 77–99).

To conclude, whereas the EU had proven to be an active, pertinent and in some cases also successful diplomatic player and conflict manager in the second half of the 2000s, its role was drastically sized down when Russia started to pull rank and assert itself as the main regional power. As Popescu (2009: 458) notes, despite the growing CSDP and the high-level declaratory commitment of a strong EU engagement in the neighbourhood, the level of EU engagement in conflict resolution in the eastern neighbourhood does not stand out and even pales in comparison to EU commitment in other regions such as the Western Balkans or sub-Sahara Africa. Several factors help to explain this: the perception that most of the conflicts did not have a direct negative impact on the majority of the EU member states, the willingness of the large member states to remain the main players in the most sensitive conflicts, and the desire to avoid the EU's other strategic objectives and more important relationship with Russia being further undermined by a more assertive EU policy in Russia's 'near abroad' (see Chapter 12). In this sense, the EU's current prudent policy towards its Eastern neighbourhood may not be the reflection of a toothless foreign policy, but rather of what can be labelled as rationally chosen 'strategic non-engagement' (Klinke 2007).

The Mediterranean Region and the Middle East

The Arab uprising that started in early 2011 confronted the EU with the limitations of its long-standing structural foreign policy towards the Mediterranean region and the Middle East, as well as with its limitations when sudden crises and violent conflicts arise (see Peters 2012a). At the heart of the EU's strongly developed but barely effective structural foreign policy is the *European Neighbourhood Policy* (ENP) which was launched in 2004 and renewed in 2011–12 in response to the Arab revolts (see above). For the Mediterranean region and the Middle East, the ENP complemented and succeeded the promising but equally unsuccessful *Euro-Mediterranean Partnership* (EMP) that was established in 1995 in Barcelona, together with a comprehensive structural foreign policy towards the then newly created Palestinian Territories. The *Union for the Mediterranean*, launched in 2008, and the bilateral Association Agreements with most countries complements this picture of complementary and partially overlapping frameworks in the Euro-Mediterranean region (see Barbé and Herranz-Surrallés 2012). The Arab upheaval also put renewed pressure on EU member states to take a position on various crises in the region, on the use of mediation and diplomacy versus coercive instruments (including military force), and on whether to deal with these crises through the EU or other multilateral settings. Important factors influencing the EU's policy are the historical links of EU member states with particular countries in this region, the continued predominance of the largest member states, the geopolitical importance of this energy rich region, the major impact of the US, and competing agendas of key international players (see Möckli and Maurer 2011; Müller 2012).

Structural foreign policy

It is useful to look back at the EU's long-standing structural foreign policy towards the region in order to assess the EU's current attempts to support structural transformations in the southern neighbourhood. The EMP was the first major initiative to promote structural changes in the region and to link the EU and the Mediterranean countries (at that time 14 countries from the Maghreb and the Middle East, including Israel and Palestine) (see Gomez 2003). The EMP, also labelled the 'Barcelona Process', was designed to build a comprehensive multilateral framework for dialogue and cooperation in three dimensions of the partnership: the political and security partnership; the economic and financial partnership; and the partnership in social, cultural and human affairs. The EMP established a detailed Working Programme, created an institutional mechanism with regular meetings of a wide range of actors, and provided for considerable budgetary resources. It was complemented by a new set of bilateral agreements which allowed the EU to differentiate its policy in relation to its different partners, gradually replacing cooperation agreements with more ambitious Association Agreements, which also included stronger conditionality.

At the same time as launching a structural foreign policy on a regional scale, the EU also conducted a comprehensive structural foreign policy towards one of the new entities in the Mediterranean area: the Palestinian Territories and Palestinian Authority, which had been created following the 1993 Oslo Accords. Through its support for the idea of a sovereign Palestinian State – translated subsequently in the goal of a 'two-state solution' – the Europeans had already contributed to framing the terms of the international debate, paving the way for the peace negotiations (Allen and Hauri 2011). Following the peace agreement, EU funding allowed for the establishment of a Palestinian administration, the organization of the first democratic elections, the creation of Palestinian police forces, the development of basic economic structures, etc. At first sight, the EU's policy was successful: the various structures were established in a remarkably short period and the newly created Palestinian Authority and democratically elected President Arafat could function thanks to the EU's political and financial support (see Müller and Spencer 2011; Bouris 2010).

Both the EMP and the EU's policy towards the Palestinian Territories looked promising. They focused on genuine structural reforms, were comprehensive in nature and could rely on a wide set of policy instruments. However, disappointment quickly became predominant. Although the structural foreign policy dimension was strong in both intent and set-up, it was weak in terms of output and effects.

In Palestine, the EU was involved in what in fact proved to be 'stillborn state-building', in view of the gradual resumption of violence and ultimate collapse of the Israeli–Palestinian peace process. The EU too played a role in the failure of state-building as it has never really used its strongest tool: conditionality (Bouris 2010: 387). The EU only very reluctantly used its leverage over the Palestinian leaders and turned a blind eye to increasing authoritarianism and corruption. It failed to ensure that its massive financial aid had positive effects on the standard of living and well-being of the Palestinian people. The EU also shied away from using its extensive trade and contractual relations with Israel to compel that country to restrict its military operations against civilian targets, halt its settlement policy, and stop its sanctions against the Palestinians in Gaza and the West Bank. The death blow to the EU's approach was given by the Palestinian population, electing in 2006 the radical Islamic movement Hamas, which was also a response to the deteriorating societal security situation in the Palestinian Territories. The victory of the Islamic movement demonstrated the painful gap between the perception of the majority of the Palestinian population and the EU, which had included Hamas on its list of terrorist organizations. The EU's refusal to deal with Hamas after the latter's victory in the EU-sponsored fair and free elections undermined the credibility of one of the main rules of the game that the EU was trying to promote in the Middle East and the Mediterranean, namely democracy (see Al-Fattal Eeckelaert 2013; Schulz 2012) (see also Chapter 6).

The faltering of the peace process in the Middle East is one of the explanations for the failure of the EMP (see Maresceau and Lannon 2001). As explained in Chapter 1, developing a successful structural foreign policy is problematic if related conflicts and crises are not resolved. Moreover, the EU had wanted to apply to its relations with the Mediterranean the objectives and methodology that had proved so successful with the Central and Eastern European countries, though without being able to play its trump card, the prospect of accession. The envisaged structural changes could not count on the same level of endogenous support in the countries concerned, particularly as the stated objectives were not realized. The EMP aimed to promote the EU's values, but in fact buttressed the authoritarian regimes in the region. The economic liberalization process was to improve the economic situation, but the socio-economic situation of the weaker strata of society deteriorated. Whereas the EMP aimed to promote dialogue and exchange between societies, it could not counter the growing distrust between the West and the Muslim world. Most importantly, the attractiveness of the EU and of the structures the EU was promoting increasingly paled in comparison to those promoted by Islamist movements and parties, which paid more attention to the basic material needs as well as to the immaterial identity related desires of the population (see Chapter 12).

It is against this background of a failed EMP that the EU's *European Neighbourhood Policy* has to be evaluated. The ENP was to 'rescue' the Euro-Mediterranean Partnership and upgrade the EU's relations with the Southern neighbours, in addition to smoothening out the potential negative consequences of the EU's enlargement process for the Eastern neighbours. The preceding section on the ENP already explained the main features as well as the weaknesses of the ENP. Generally speaking, the ENP did not fundamentally change the basic parameters of the EU's structural foreign policy towards its Southern Neighbours, particularly in providing no answer to the problematic socio-economic situation, neglecting the societal changes in favour of Islamic movements, and in continuing to deal with authoritarian regimes. The *Union for the*

Mediterranean (UfM) was also unable to provide satisfactory answers (Bicchi and Gillespie 2011). Launched at the initiative of the French President Sarkozy, it aimed to promote economic cooperation through specific projects (for example, related to energy and infrastructure), irrespective of political reforms in Mediterranean countries. That the French and Egyptian Presidents, Sarkozy and Mubarak, acted as the co-Presidents of the UfM did not help, as the Egyptian president was one of the leaders who was ousted during the Arab uprising of 2011.

The Arab uprising painfully pointed to the ENP's failure in terms of objectives, methodology and underlying paradigm. Whereas the main frustration of the *Eastern* partners was that the ENP did not offer them a ticket to EU membership, the frustration for the *Mediterranean* populations was that the ENP and the EU in general did not offer them a ticket to freedom, democracy, welfare and strengthened identity. The ENP, just as the preceding UfM and EMP, had not contributed to prosperity, security and stability in the EU's neighbourhood and had not diminished the feelings of exclusion in the partner countries. With a few exceptions, poverty and unemployment, poor economic performance, corruption, bleak prospects for the population, weak or undemocratic government, and in some cases also violent domestic conflicts remain major challenges (see Lannon 2012; Whitman and Wolff 2012b). Also, in the handful of countries with a (moderately) reformist leadership, endogenous public support for modernization, liberalization and 'Western' reforms were fading among sections of society, with support for the competing Islamic structures increasing (see Chapter 12).

The methodology cherished by the EU – based on positive and negative conditionality, financial and technical assistance, and institutionalized dialogue – has proved to be ineffective. The EU mistakenly believed in a top-down approach and had readily embraced the delusion that interaction with the EU would induce authoritarian leaders to engage into structural reforms that could endanger their very survival. The Arab revolts disclosed that the EU – and the West in general – in fact had no real problem (or better: saw it as unavoidable) dealing with authoritarian but nevertheless stable regimes in the region (with the exception of those that caused concerns for other reasons, such as Iraq). In this sense, the refusal of many of the Mediterranean governments to respect the engagements made in the EMP and ENP was paralleled by the EU's reluctance to use the ENP conditionality and, earlier, the Barcelona provisions to exert pressure on the states in the Mediterranean and the Middle East that failed to observe their commitments.

That the EU and its member states accepted the dictatorial regimes also became clear in the years before the Arab revolts. In 2010, Tunisia and the EU had started negotiations on upgrading the former's status to 'advanced status' in the ENP. The Europeans also renewed relations with the Libyan leader, Gaddafi, who was overthrown in 2011 after a military campaign led by France and the UK. In late 2009, the EU had started negotiations to conclude an Association Agreement with Syria based on the commitment to economic (but not political) reforms of President Bashar al-Assad, the leader who violently suppressed the revolts in his country. More positively, in the same period the EU had also granted 'advanced status' to the two countries within the ENP that had started a prudent liberalization process: Morocco and Jordan (Whitman and Juncos: 2012: 153).

In his analysis of the EU and the 'Arab Spring', Peters emphasizes that '[h]uman rights and democracy promotion ultimately lost out to a more urgent and competing set of European priorities in the region' (2012b: xiii), including the need for stability and security in the region, control of the flow of illegal migration, and the protection of European economic interests. Especially since 9/11, European countries also saw the ruling Arab regimes as crucial allies against the rise of Islamic radicalism, implying too that violent repression of political dissent was often met with silent acquiescence (2012b: xiii–ix). This reflected the EU's difficult relationship with democracy promotion in a region where authoritarian regimes prevailed, but where the EU insufficiently saw the underlying dynamics within the various societies, including the rising popularity of Islamic movements that were often seen by the population as the only countervailing force against the dictators (Cavatorta and Pace 2010b; Pace and Seeberg 2009) (see also Chapter 6).

The EU's strategy failed completely. The revolts sweeping across North Africa and the Middle East have contradicted the prognosis of sustainability of these regimes. The authoritarian regimes proved not to be a guarantee for stability and security. The population in various countries exhorted democratic elections, and indeed in most countries elected a variety of Islamic parties which proved to be much more popular than the generally quite small Western-oriented and secular political parties.

The EU and its member states at first hesitated and sent contradictory signals on how to react to the Arab upheaval and political changes within Mediterranean societies (see Peters 2012a; Schumacher 2014). However, in March 2011 the European Commission and the High Representative (2011) proposed a '*Partnership for Democracy and Shared Prosperity with the Southern Mediterranean*' aimed at building a stronger partnership with people and civil society actors, at democratic transformation, tackling the inequalities and creating job opportunities. This proposal was the precursor of the revision of the ENP, based on the 'more for more' principle, the three 'M's ('markets, mobility and money'), and greater differentiation. However, as was discussed earlier in this chapter (see section on the ENP), a first evaluation of this revamped ENP was that it was again rather more of the same (as has already been the case with the creation of the ENP following the failed EMP). Moreover, there was no indication that the new ENP would lead to a more genuine 'partnership', more 'prosperity' and jobs for the people concerned, or an understanding by the EU of the specific features of 'civil society' in the Mediterranean countries and for the way in which the population would exercise their democratic rights.

In addition to the general weaknesses of the 'new' ENP, some problems were pronounced even more sharply in the context of the Mediterranean countries (see also Schumacher 2014). First, quite remarkably, 'despite rhetorical statements, and even after the evidence and experience of the 2011 social revolts in the Mediterranean neighbourhood, the EU does not consider social policy (and by extension also social justice) as a key dimension of stability and security in its neighbourhood' (Martin, 2012: 247). Second, the EU's emphasis on 'civil society' does not closely match the many traditional forms of 'civil society' which do not necessarily fit Western criteria (Pace 2010: 621–2), particularly as the Southern Mediterranean society is in essence a very 'religious society' based on the Islamic faith with a strong emphasis on 'social justice'. This unveils a third set of dilemmas, which cannot be solved by the EU's focus on 'deep democracy': what if more democracy leads to a weakened respect for or a different view on human rights, or if it leads to the supremacy of Islamic political parties that have a different view on human and civilian rights and on the role of religion in society and politics?

This is linked to the last, major challenge for the EU: the rise of competing structural powers, in the form of increasingly influential Islamic states (including mainly Saudi Arabia and Qatar) and of what can be labelled with the generic term 'political Islam'. Much more substantial and attractive than the EU's 'three M's' are the 'five M's' from the Gulf: Mohammed, Mecca, money, migration and media (Thépaut and Keukeleire 2012). Paradoxically, the regional power that seems to be able to provide some counterweight to the growing impact of the Gulf states is Turkey, with whom the EU is not able to define its relationship (see above and Chapter 12).

Relational foreign policy

With the uprisings in various Arab countries and the wars in Libya and Syria, new challenges were emerging in addition to some long-lasting crises such as the Iranian nuclear ambitions and the Israeli–Palestinian conflict.

The Israeli–Palestinian conflict has been on the EU's foreign policy agenda for several decades (see Möckli and Maurer 2011). The EU's lack of success in this crisis reflects the failure of the international community in general. After the collapse of the Oslo Accords between Israelis and Palestinians, the EU attempted to assume a more proactive role through its diplomatic activities in the framework of the 'Middle East Quartet', made up of the EU, the US, Russia and the UN (see Musu 2011; Tocci 2013). The Quartet not only ensures a more visible involvement for the EU in Middle East diplomacy, but also is 'an important vehicle for refining EU policy, cementing EU cohesion, and enhancing the EU's ability to speak effectively and with one voice in the Israeli–Palestinian conflict' (Musu, 2011: 136). The EU was largely responsible for drawing up the 'Roadmap' which was accepted in 2003 as the basis of the Quartet's intervention. The Roadmap lays out reciprocal steps for both Israel and the Palestinian Authority in political, security, economic, humanitarian and institution-building fields, with a negotiated two-state solution to the conflict at its core. However, although the EU still considers the Roadmap as a major point of reference, the Roadmap no longer fits a conflict that has significantly escalated. Moreover, while the EU has been the principal driver behind the Quartet, the Quartet 'has failed to engage in effective multilateral mediation, while providing a multilateral fig leaf for dynamics that have remained quintessentially unilateral (and at most bilateral) in character, and which have rarely served the goal of promoting peace in the Middle East' (Tocci 2013: 44).

For the EU, the Quartet's activities mainly revolved around engaging the US, which also implied that the EU also often chose to follow American positions. This included the boycott of Hamas after its electoral victory in 2006 and its takeover of Gaza in 2007, which also implied that the EU de facto put itself aside and left the field to other actors to mediate (Saudi Arabia, Egypt and Turkey). The EU and the Quartet no longer undertook major new policy initiatives to relaunch peace negotiations (Tocci 2013: 38–40). The EU's refusal to deal with Hamas also undermined the two small civilian CSDP missions in the Palestinian Territories that were launched in 2005–6: the police mission 'EU COPPS' and the border assistance mission 'EU BAM Rafah' between the Gaza Strip and Egypt (Musu 2013: 176–7).

The EU's potential effectiveness is also undermined by the fact that both the US and the Israelis harbour distrust of an EU perceived as maintaining a pro-Arab bias, whereas on the other hand the Palestinians and Arab countries denounce the EU's highly accommodating attitude towards Israel. Using conditionality or sanctions in EU–Israel relations is one of the strongest taboos in EU foreign policy, even though Israel's settlement policy, blockade of Gaza, use of violence against civilians, violation of human rights of the Palestinians, destruction of EU-funded Palestinian infrastructure, or simply withholding Palestinian revenues have given ample reason for sanctions or at least countermeasures. The EU merely condemned the Israeli policy in its many declarations, but this did not hamper the continuous intensification of economic relations with Israel, with Israel enjoying free access to the EU's internal market and participating in an increasing number of EU policies. In short, Israel and the EU member states have managed neatly to shield economic and contractual relations from foreign policy issues. This reluctance to adopt a more assertive position towards Israel is not only affected by the influence of the US and the historical links of EU member states with Israel, but also by the shadow of the past (particularly for Germany, in view of the Holocaust) (see Peters 2012b). The divisions which these factors cause were also reflected in the position of the EU member states on the Palestinian's quest for statehood at the UN, which was strongly opposed by Israel and the US. This appeared in 2012 when the Palestinians gained recognition as an observer non-member state at the UN General Assembly, with half of EU member states voting in favour (including France), 13 abstaining (including the UK and Germany) and one country voting against (the Czech Republic) (UN 2012b).

The position of Israel also relates to a second conflict in the Middle East that is a recurrent theme on the EU's agenda: the long-lasting conflict between the West and the Islamic Republic of Iran, particularly on Iran's nuclear ambitions (see Pant 2011; Posch 2013; see also Chapters 6 and 7). The Europeans had initially hoped that positive engagement and a mix of sanctions and offers would 'push relations with Iran towards the pattern of pragmatic accommodation' (Nonneman 2011: 209–10). The three largest EU member states took the lead in negotiations with Iran to find a solution to the dispute over its nuclear programme. In addition to their diplomatic clout (France and the UK as permanent members of the UNSC, Germany as major trading partner), the 'E-3' or 'EU-3' could also fall back on the possibility of economic incentives provided by the EU.

As the reformist leaders in Iran were replaced by more nationalist leaders, the EU-3's diplomatic efforts faltered. The European efforts were therefore embedded in a broader framework, including now also the US, China and Russia, leading to negotiations through the 'EU-3+3'. The EU's High Representative was designated as the spokesperson of the six countries in negotiations with Iran, representing recognition of the EU as a primary actor. However, the EU's chances of successful meditation remained limited in view of the internal dynamics in Iran (where its nuclear ambition is largely shared by the population) and the diverging positions of the US and the EU on the one hand (with the latter increasingly sharing the American view on imposing tougher sanctions) and China and Russia (reluctant to use sanctions) on the other hand (Pant 2011). Nevertheless, the efforts towards Iran resulted in some modest successes, even though successes were rarely durable and comprehensive, as is also illustrated in Box 7.1. The American factor in this case also heavily influenced the EU's foreign policy, similar to what has occurred regarding the Israel–Palestinian conflict. As Posch indicates, 'the EU's engagement policy with Iran centred on bringing the Iranians and the Americans to the negotiations table, directly or indirectly', with success or failure ultimately being a bilateral Iran–American affair (2013: 185, 187).

The EU's response to the Arab revolts and to the resulting violent clashes and conflicts has been touched upon in several other chapters in this book (such as Chapter 6 and 8) (see also Peters 2012a). The EU initially struggled to formulate a 'foreign policy' response to the Arab upheaval, with other concerns initially dominating the debate. The question of how to avoid and manage a large influx of refugees was most prominent on the agenda of the EU, not how to support the democratic transition in the Arab countries or how to formulate long-term solutions. The revolts in the various countries also met varied responses, with member states holding different positions and the EU in general defining different policies (or avoiding to define policies) depending on the Arab country concerned.

The first real test was how to manage the crisis in Libya. The EU supported a Libya no-fly zone imposed by the UN Security Council in March 2011 and adopted an arms embargo and sanctions against the Gaddafi regime, including oil and gas revenues. Yet the EU was divided over the military interventions, particularly with Germany actively opposing any military action and deciding not to vote in favour of the UN Security Council Resolution imposing a no-fly zone. Ultimately, a French–British-led coalition with American support and within the framework of NATO launched a military intervention against the Libyan regime, which also ousted the Libyan leader (see Box 7.1) (see Pinfari 2012). However, following this military success, the EU was unable to provide security, stability and order in post-war Libya – just as the Western countries had also not been able to contribute to security and order in Iraq, being another country that one decade earlier had been 'liberated' by Western forces (see Burke 2010).

With regard to Syria, where the situation is more complex and where external opposition to military intervention is more prominent, the divergences between member states were initially not whether to launch a military intervention, but whether and how the rebellions against the Assad regime should be supported (Berg 2012). Various dilemmas appeared in this context: accepting the growing number of casualties as a result of non-intervention versus the risk that intervention would lead to a protracted war and instability and even more casualties, as in Iraq or Afghanistan; supporting opponents of Assad versus the 'risk' of another Arab country dominated by Islamist parties; the position of member states that force had to be considered versus those that wanted to exclude that option; and the position of countries (such as France and the UK) that weapons had to be provided versus the EU's own common position that forbids the export of weapons to conflict areas (see Chapter 6).

Whereas the EU mainly focused on the Mediterranean states, it largely neglected the revolts in other Arab countries, such as Yemen and particularly Bahrain (see Schumacher 2012). In response to the use of violence against the anti-regime protests, the EU mainly responded with prudent declarations. The EU and its member states also closed their eyes to the military intervention in Bahrain in 2011 by the other Gulf states, led by Saudi Arabia, aimed at knocking out pro-democracy demonstrations (see also Chapter 10). The intervention by Saudi Arabia and other states of the Gulf Cooperation Council did not lead to any sanctions against these Gulf states, if only because of their importance in terms of energy supply, providing stability, helping the West to fight Al-Qaeda and countering the rising power of Iran.

Some final observations on the EU's relational foreign policy in the Mediterranean region and the Middle East are linked to the analysis provided in other chapters of this book. The first finding is the remarkable irrelevance of CSDP in the various crises and conflicts in this region. In addition to the small but nearly abandoned missions in the Palestinian Territories, the EU only launched the barely effective rule-of-law mission EUJUST LEX in Iraq. In 2011 it decided on the EUFOR Libya operation to provide humanitarian aid. However this was not launched in practice, but a small border assistance mission was decided upon in early 2013. This reflects the analysis in Chapter 8 that CSDP operations and missions only fit a quite limited and specific set of purposes.

The second observation is that the EU's inability to provide stability, security and order in its southern neighbourhood opened the way for other regional powers (such as Turkey, Iran and the Gulf states) to determine the structures that would rule the countries concerned (see Chapter 12).

Third, the remaining insecurity and chaos in several Mediterranean countries also had a negative spillover effect on other adjacent regions, including in the Sahel and Sahara regions (see Gstöhl and Lannon 2014). This explains why the EU felt compelled to enhance its involvement in this region through its Strategy for the Sahel region and why France in 2013 initiated a military campaign in Mali to counter the rise of Jihadist forces (see Chapters 7 and 8).

Conclusion

This chapter assessed to what extent and how the EU moved beyond trade and contractual relations to developing a relational and structural foreign policy towards the regions in its eastern and southern neighbourhood: the Western Balkans, Eastern Europe and the South Caucasus, the Mediterranean and the Middle East. The EU has gradually adopted policies to resolve conflicts and military threats in these regions. In contrast to the ambitions raised in the late 1990s and early 2000s, the EU increasingly faces problems in further developing an effective structural foreign policy in its neighbourhood. This can to some extent be explained by the relative decline of the EU's structural power. Not only the lack of a membership carrot and the prospect of accession with the neighbouring countries, but also the rise and the increasing presence of other structural powers in the EU's eastern and southern neighbourhood, explain this. The latter is analysed in the next chapter.

Chapter 12

Competition with Major Powers: The US, Russia, China, Emerging Powers and Islamism

This chapter evaluates the EU's foreign policy towards and relationship with other major powers. In each case, we not only assess the relationship in terms of relational foreign policy, that is, policies towards crises and conflicts. We also evaluate it in terms of structural foreign policy and we assess the capacity of the other powers to behave as a 'structural power', that is, a power that has the capacity to set or influence the organizing principles and rules of the game (see Chapter 1). In addition, this chapter seeks to answer other questions: to what extent are the structures shaped or promoted by these other powers similar to or compatible with those promoted by the EU? And to what extent is the EU able to influence, gain support from or, if necessary, counter those other powers? In so doing, we explore how the EU copes with the strategic opportunities and challenges emanating from the (manifest or potential) structural power of the other major players on the world scene.

This chapter first turns to the three most important 'strategic partners' of the EU: the US, Russia and China. Table 12.1 compares the basic demographic, economic and military ingredients of power of these three countries with those of the EU. Showing the significant differences between these four powers, it allows for a better understanding of the context in which these powers compete and in which the EU conducts its foreign policy. Both the US and Russia have already been dealt with in other parts of the book. The EU's relationship with the US and the American position towards EU foreign policy emerges in nearly all chapters of the book; the relationship with Russia is discussed in particular in the section on energy in Chapter 10 and in the section on the eastern neighbourhood in Chapter 11. However, less attention has been devoted to the relationship with China and to China's structural power, although the EU and China are increasingly intertwined and although the continued rise of China will unavoidably have a major impact on the EU in the next few decades. The EU's relationship with China and its different views on how to structure politics, economics and societies are therefore elaborated somewhat more extensively in this chapter. After having

Table 12.1   The EU, US, Russia and China: ingredients of power

Country	Population (millions, 2010)[1]	GDP (in $ billion, 2011)[2]	EU27 Import (€ million, 2011)[3]	EU27 Export (€ million, 2011)[3]	Defence expenditure ($ million, 2012)[4]	Total active armed forces (2013)[4]
EU	504.9	17,646.9	–	–	250,108	1,586,000
US	310.4	14,991.3	190,911.0	263,638.5	645,700	1,520,000
Russia	143.0	1,857.8	198,178.2	108,448.9	59,851	845,000
China	1,341.4	7,318.5	292,070.9	136,216.9	102,346	2,285,000

Sources: [1]UN Department of Economic and Social Affairs (2011); [2]United Nations (2013); [3]Commission (2013b); [4]International Institute for Strategic Studies (2013)

discussed China, the following section broadens this perspective by focusing on the EU's relationship with other emerging powers, thereby evaluating the EU's 'strategic partnerships' with countries such as India, Brazil and South Africa. Finally, the last section broadens the analysis even further, looking beyond the traditional state actors and assessing the increasingly influential structures under the umbrella term 'Islamism'.

The United States

The United States is the actor with the most extensive structural power in today's international system. Following the Second World War, the US defined the main international (though originally 'Western') structures which are still largely predominant: democracy, the rule of law, free market economy and international organizations such as the IMF and the WTO that organize this economy on a global scale. While the US is the EU's most important partner on the international stage, this is also a relationship which the EU manages with difficulty, and with mixed results. The transatlantic relationship spans an incredibly diverse range of issues and policy fields and, irrespective of events such as the high-profile clash over Iraq in 2003, the vast majority of this business continues without incident. The EU and US economies are highly interdependent and together account for approximately 30 per cent of world trade and half of world GDP (see also Chapter 9). The US and the EU share many common domestic features and international goals. However, these similarities can be deceptive, in the same way that the occasional highly publicized disagreements over foreign policy issues mask a more complex reality.

It is worth recalling that the European integration process is to a large extent a construct of a US structural foreign policy made operational through its post-Second World War Marshall Plan (see Chapter 2). The continued expansion of the European integration project has remained an objective of US foreign policy until the present day – support for Turkey's accession to the EU being a case in point. Since the 1990s, transatlantic relations became increasingly institutionalized by a number of EU–US agreements, such as the 1990 Transatlantic Declaration, the 1995 New Transatlantic Agenda, the 1998 Transatlantic Economic Partnership or the establishment of the Transatlantic Economic Council in 2007. This process of institutionalization has created a dense network of ministerial meetings, working groups, task forces, steering groups, dialogues and fora between policy-makers from both sides of the Atlantic focusing on a broad range of issues, including climate change, financial market regulation, biotechnology, terrorist financing and higher education (Smith and Steffenson 2011: 415–16).

The most visible transatlantic institution is the annual EU–US Summit, consisting of the President of the US, President of the European Council, and President of the European Commission, often assisted by the HR/VP and/or the Trade Commissioner. However, particularly on the side of the US, questions are increasingly raised about the continued usefulness of these summits, which have been described as 'grand but largely empty diplomatic occasions' (Zaborowski 2011: 109). President Obama's decision not to attend the Summit that was to take place in February 2010 in Madrid was illustrative in this regard.

In 2013 the parties launched talks on the Transatlantic Trade and Investment Partnership (TTIP), which is supposed to become, in the words of the then Trade Commissioner De Gucht 'the biggest bilateral trade negotiations ever undertaken' by the EU (Commission 2013c). These bilateral trade negotiations are another example of the increasing importance of bilateral agreements in the EU's overall trade policy, with the negotiations under the multilateral venue of the WTO being completely deadlocked (see Chapter 9). The TTIP intends to create a free trade area between the EU and the US, to promote greater transatlantic cooperation and to further stimulate investment, growth and jobs. It aims to be a response both to the economic crisis and to the rise of China and other emerging economies.

In fields where there is clear EU competence, such as in trade, the US deals directly with the EU. However, in many other cases, the US prefers to structure its relations bilaterally with individual member states. This can be explained by the American preference to apply pressure or rely on like-minded countries (as during the George W. Bush era) or to work directly with the most powerful EU member states: the UK, France and Germany (as during the Obama era) (Zaborowski 2011). Particularly with regard to crises and military interventions in the Middle East, the US's preference to cooperate intensively with only a part of the EU member states equally reflects the widely diverging policies as well as capabilities of the European countries (Möckli and Mauer 2011). The US has frequently attempted to play the divide-and-rule game with the EU member states in areas that were not that deeply integrated in the EU. This occurred during negotiations on issues related to the area of freedom, security and justice, such as talks on passenger name records or visa waivers (Smith and Steffenson 2011) but also at the end of the 1990s in the area of aviation policy, when the US concluded bilateral Open Sky agreements with the member states separately (Meunier 2005: 144–65). However, in both cases, this situation prompted the Commission to take initiatives for more integration and a common European approach, ultimately leading to, for instance, the SWIFT and the EU–US Open Skies Agreement (Delreux 2011b; Dobson 2009; Servent and MacKenzie 2012).

This preference of the US to deal with member states bilaterally adds to the field of tension between European integration and Atlantic solidarity in EU foreign policy-making (see Chapter 1). Member states are divided along a spectrum on the importance they attribute to the 'what would the Americans think?' test. The division between the group of 'Europeanist' member states led by France and the group of 'Atlanticist' member states led by the UK is the most commonly discussed. While France in general views the development of the EU as an effective actor on the international stage as a prospective counterweight to US *hyper-puissance* (see Howorth 2010), for the UK building EU foreign policy capability is basically about making the EU a more effective partner for the US. A distinction also exists between the 'old' member states for whom military threat from a third country is a relatively distant memory and the 'new' Central and Eastern European member states for whom memories of the Soviet military threat and the fear of a Russian display of strength are vivid. This explains why the CEECs are more sensitive to the continued relevance of the US security umbrella and hence keener to keep the US happy (see Hynek and Eichler 2012).

On one level, the EU and US share many features and common goals. Domestically, they share the same values of democracy, rule of law, human rights and individual freedoms, free market economies, and so on. On the trade front, both parties support a global free market economy, prioritizing stability and trade growth to ensure their continued economic prosperity. Together, the EU and US largely regulate the global economy. They also face similar challenges, such as recovering from the financial crisis, energy import dependency and competition from the emerging economies of the BRICS. Common concerns and goals are shared on both sides of the Atlantic in terms of declining natural resources, fighting international terrorism and international crime, resolving conflicts, and promoting functioning democratic government.

However, beyond these broad brushstrokes which form the basic foundations of the European and the American political systems and of their intensive cooperation, there lies a remarkable array of divergences which go to the very core of the EU and the US relationship (see Fröhlich 2012; Zielonka 2011). Their diverging views on tackling climate change, on energy security, on genetically modified foods or hormone beef, or on the relationship between the state and the market have significant consequences for transatlantic cooperation. This also explains why negotiations on a TTIP are to overcome substantial hurdles. The divergences are also played out both in the different global structures that the two powers promote and in their approach to multilateralism. Whereas the EU is in general committed to multilateralism, negotiation and non-military power (see Chapter 13), the US is generally less reluctant towards unilateral action, coercion and military power (Smith M. E. 2011). This distinction was particularly apparent during the era of the George W. Bush Administration. The stark contrast between the EU and the US in terms of support for the major international treaties is striking in this regard. While EU member states have, with very few exceptions, signed up to nearly all major international treaties, the US has either not ratified or not signed up to over half of these, including treaties on the abolition of the death penalty, the ICC, the Kyoto Protocol, the Comprehensive Nuclear Test Ban, the prohibition of anti-personnel mines, biological diversity, economic social and cultural rights, civil and political rights, elimination of discrimination against women, the rights of the child and the status of refugees. While the EU and US are systematically lumped together as 'the West', the differences in their voting patterns on these treaties are greater than the differences between the EU and either China or Russia (although this in and of itself is no guarantee of either China or Russia adopting EU-style behaviour) (Keukeleire and MacNaughtan 2008: 300–1).

On both sides of the Atlantic, different values are attributed to the multilateral system and the international rule of law. In general terms, the EU promotes a rules-based international order while the US tends to be highly suspicious of multilateralism, international rules and frameworks where these restrain its ability to act autonomously. However, this does vary depending on the issue at hand and the administration in power. Democratic Administrations under Obama or Clinton adopted a less hostile approach to international institutions, using them as a legitimizing device and a tool for substantive consensus-building, than did the Republican George W. Bush Administration (Stepak and Whitlark 2012: 55). Most importantly, the existing multilateral architecture is to a large extent the result of American initiatives. Moreover, where the US has deemed it to be in its own interest, it has been significantly more effective than the EU in using multilateral structures such as the IMF and the World Bank to promote its objectives. In terms of choosing multilateralism, the US is thus highly effective, if highly selective (see Lake 2010; Patrick 2010; Skidmore 2011).

After the election of President Obama in November 2008, governments and public opinion in Europe hoped for a renewal of the transatlantic relationship after the eight years of the George W. Bush Administration in which transatlantic relations reached rock bottom. However, after Obama's first term, it is clear that these expectations have not been fully fulfilled and that both sides of the Atlantic are somewhat disappointed in each other (Zaborowski 2011). The US criticized the refusal by many European countries to augment their troop contributions to the NATO mission in Afghanistan, as well as the too slow and insufficiently profound way in which the EU was handling the financial crisis in the eurozone. European countries were primarily concerned about falling in the priority list of the US, which increasingly focuses its foreign policy on the Asia-Pacific region (Obama's so-called 'pivot' to Asia) (see Chapter 13). The fact that the US disregarded the EU at the climate change conference in Copenhagen and drafted the Copenhagen Accord with the emerging powers shows that this changed world order has implications for the transatlantic relationship and for EU foreign policy in concrete negotiations (see Chapter 10). However, the Arab revolts required more cooperation between both sides, for instance through the NATO operation in Libya in 2011, when the US supported the military campaign initiated by the UK and France (see Chapters 6 and 8). The launch of the negotiations of the TTIP in 2013 also demonstrates that the transatlantic relationship remains important for both the US and the EU.

Russia

The EU's relationship with Russia is quite a peculiar one, with the shadow of the past still looming over the current relationship. First of all, since 10 of the current 28 EU member states were until the late 1980s part of the Moscow-dominated Soviet bloc or (in the case of the Baltic states) Soviet territory, there remains a strong suspicion towards Russia and Russia–EU rapprochement. Second, Russia is the successor of the Soviet Union, which for half a century was the main antagonist of the West. The end of the Cold War, the fading away of the communist structures exported internationally by Russia, and internal upheaval across the former Soviet bloc forced Moscow's global influence – and potential to shape the rules of the game – into rapid decline. Russia's position changed from being the main competing structural power in the four decades following the Second World War, to one of an initially economically and politically weak junior partner. EU–Russia relations were initially highly asymmetrical, with the EU putting itself in the position of 'helper' and 'guide' of Russia. The EU aimed to reshape Russia in its own image by promoting its principles and rules to trigger change in its economic, political and legal structures (Casier 2014). However, from the late 1990s Russia increasingly claimed to be treated as an equal partner and was no more willing to be merely the subject of a structural foreign policy by the EU in the same way as the Central and Eastern European countries. Since the mid-2000s, there has been a resurgence in Russian assertiveness on the international stage, even if Russia is not (yet) competing as a global structural power beyond its near abroad.

The EU's relations with Russia are structured through the now rather old 'Partnership and Cooperation Agreement' (PCA) (since 1997), which has been extended through 'Common Spaces' since 2003. Negotiations on a new EU–Russia treaty (launched in 2008) and on the elaboration of a 'Partnership for Modernization' (2010) proceed very slowly. The EU–Russia PCA sets out the principal common objectives, establishes the institutional framework for bilateral contacts (including two summit meetings a year), and provides for cooperation in a broad range of policy fields. When the EU in 2003 launched the European Neighbourhood Policy (ENP, see Chapter 11), Russia declined the EU's invitation to participate, refusing to be treated as just another third country and considering the positive and negative conditionalities therein unacceptable.

As an alternative to the ENP the EU and Russia agreed to focus cooperation on the long-term creation of four jointly agreed Common Spaces in the framework of the PCA: a Common economic Space; a Common Space of freedom, security and justice; a Common Space of external security; and a Common Space of research, education and cultural aspects. However, these Common Spaces in fact concealed quite separate visions (Adomeit 2012: 382). This appeared clearly in the difficulties in elaborating so-called 'Road Maps' which include short- and medium-term instruments for the implementation of the 'Common Spaces' and which can be considered as the equivalent of Actions Plans under the ENP. Moscow refused to accept that the EU should be involved in determining its internal rules of the game. This implies that – in contrast to its relationship with other countries in its neighbourhood – the EU was not able to assert its values and norms in the development of the four Common Spaces, also leading to a virtual absence of political conditionality. While the President of the European Council or the HR/VP occasionally still voice the EU's concerns over the state of democracy or human rights in Russia, these normative concerns play only a marginal role in the various significant documents related to EU–Russia relations (Casier 2014). The once asymmetrical EU–Russia relationship has thus evolved into a much more symmetric relationship, with relations in one major geopolitical policy area – energy – even tilting in the other direction due to the EU's dependency on Russian oil and gas (see Chapter 10).

The difficulty to find a convergence of views can also be observed in the lack of substantial follow-up on the idea launched in 2007 by the EU to create an EU–Russia Strategic Partnership and in the very slow pace of negotiations that started in 2008 on a new EU–Russia treaty (to replace the PCA) (Haukkala 2010; Giusti and Penkova 2012). One of the main obstacles for the latter was overcome with the EU's support for Russian accession to the WTO (in exchange for Russia's previous support for and ratification of the Kyoto Protocol) (see Chapter 10). However, the negotiation process was slow, with negotiations blocked twice due to a veto by EU member states (Poland and Lithuania), frozen for 18 months as a result of the Georgia–Russia war, and complicated by disagreement on a whole list of policy issues and by mistrust about each other's regional ambitions. The launch in 2010 of the EU–Russia 'Partnership for Modernization', as an attempt to revamp relations, did not fundamentally improve their mutual relations, despite the continued regular dialogues and interaction and despite strong economic links (with Russia being the third trade partner of the EU, behind the US and China) (Giusti and Penkova 2012: 123–7).

As was emphasized in Chapter 11, the EU and Russia increasingly saw each other as direct competitors in what Russia called its 'Near Abroad' and the EU its 'European neighbourhood'. This competition between both structural powers was also leading to a 'clash of integration processes' (Casier 2007) and to a battle about this 'shared neighbourhood' which was more and more characterized by 'zero-sum calculations and geopolitical competition' (Gower and Timmins 2010: 2). In this battle, Russia proved to be increasingly effective. It is important to recall that with its 2004 and 2007 enlargements and its European Neighbourhood Policy and Eastern Partnership with former Soviet republics, the EU has cut swathes through Russia's sphere of political and economic domination, a fact which is too often overlooked in assessments of EU–Russia relations. From this perspective, Russia's growing assertiveness can be considered a kind of counter-offensive to recover lost ground and avoid further chipping away at Russian influence in its immediate neighbourhood. The fact that Russia could indeed gradually recover its old assertiveness and economic strength was largely attributable to rising gas and oil prices. Nevertheless, 'Russia envisages itself as a completely independent world player that tolerates no interference with its foreign or domestic affairs from the Union (Haukkala 2010: 103). Russia has recently adopted a more confrontational international posture, leading to more clashes with the EU as well as with countries that once belonged to its zone of influence. They have adopted a pro-Western course, while at the same time also strengthening relations with the other countries of the post-Soviet region (see Adomeit 2012; Freire and Kanet 2012).

Russia's increasing emphasis on its vital national interests, particularly in its near abroad, was not only closely linked to the objective to regain Russia's great power status but also to reaffirm its identity (Laenen 2012). Interestingly, Russia's increasing strength has occurred almost in tandem with the gradual deterioration domestically of 'Western' structures of democracy, free speech, separation of the state and the economy, and respect for human rights and rule of law. Russia has seen in this period the promotion of the idea of 'sovereign democracy' (with one party dominating the political system), the increased control of society and politics, and the return of Vladimir Putin to the president's office in 2012. This has been described as a 'retreat from the EU's vision of Russia's "transformation" to a liberal, pluralist democracy, a market-based economy with fair competition, and a law-based state with a civil society' (Adomeit 2012: 383).

The increasingly active structural foreign policy of Russia also included attempts to strengthen and to institutionalize its relations with neighbouring countries. Russia could thereby make use of its position as a natural centre of gravity – politically, economically but also in terms of identity – for various countries that had been part of the Soviet Union. Russian leaders could in this context point to the growing attractiveness of their model, which was also evident in the victory of pro-Russia parties and leaders in the elections in various countries, such as Ukraine which one decade earlier was heading in a clear pro-Western direction (see Chapter 11). Whereas Russia had failed to bring all parts of the former Soviet Union together in the Commonwealth of Independent States (CIS) (see Malfliet *et al.* 2007), it now adopted a more pragmatic approach, including the launch of a common market between Russia, Belarus and Kazakhstan in 2012 as a first step towards an ambitious but not very evident project of regional integration which is intended to lead to a Eurasian Economic Union (Keukeleire and Petrova 2014; Saivetz 2012).

In order to (re)gain influence in its Near Abroad, Russia has also employed a confrontational approach, which peaked at various moments. A first example was in 2009 when Russia temporarily cut off energy supplies to Ukraine, also leading to a disruption of natural gas supply to several EU countries (see Chapter 10). A second one was the use of military forces by Russia against Georgia in 2008, followed by recognition of the independence of the secessionist regions. Indeed, the Russian–Georgian war demonstrated Russia's ability and willingness to exercise power in the regions of strategic importance. Although it accepted the EU and particularly the then French President Sarkozy as a mediator, Russia's intervention was a warning to the EU to downgrade its 'stealth interventions' in Russia's zone of influence (Popescu 2011) (see Chapter 11).

Whereas Russia was often criticized by the EU for its use of force, it is often overlooked that Russia too had some reasons to distrust the EU and the West in general. In dealing with international crises, Russia was mostly more sceptical or even outright negative about the use of military force, sanctions and coercion in general against third countries (Kaczmarski 2011). In 2011 Russia (together with Germany and China) criticized the broad interpretation by France, the UK and some other EU member states of the UNSC resolution authorizing military action in Libya to protect civilians (see Box 7.1). Russia's recognition in 2008 of the secessionist Georgian regions, Abkhazia and South Ossetia, can in this respect also be considered as a retaliation against the recognition earlier that year of Kosovo's independence by a majority of EU member states, despite the lack of consensus on that issue in the UN (Giusti and Penkova 2012; Ker-Lindsay 2011).

The question of how to handle a newly resurgent Russia has received contradictory answers within the EU, with member states defending very diverse positions and interests (David *et al.* 2011, 2013). Particularly the Central and Eastern European member states, along with the EP, are generally in favour of the EU adopting a more assertive attitude towards Russia and stress the importance of democracy and human rights in foreign policy deliberations. Other member states prioritize their national economic interests or the need to gain Russia's strategic partnership in crucial foreign policy issues, including the fight against terrorism, negotiations with Iran over its development of nuclear capabilities, and gaining support for or at least avoiding Russian obstruction in international crises such as Afghanistan, Syria or Libya. In conjunction with growing concerns about the EU's energy dependence, these factors have restrained part of the member states – particularly Germany and France – to openly criticize developments within Russia. The determination of Germany and France as well as Italy and Spain to foster a special or strategic partnership with Russia and to underpin this with separate bilateral agreements (Timmins 2011) contrasts strongly with the UK that – inspired by its more transatlantic orientation – traditionally has a more problematic relationship with Russia, including frequent bilateral disputes (David 2011).

The different interests of the EU's member states is one of the explanations for the EU's failure to develop an effective policy. As 'Europe loses its glitter', Russia may also become less interested in the EU. However, the picture becomes different when looked at from a wider perspective: 'Europe may become less important globally but Russia is becoming less important globally too' (Baranovsky and Utkin 2012: 64, 78). This observation is linked to the rising power of China and other Southern countries, which is the topic of the following two sections of this chapter.

China

The term used by the EU to qualify its relationship with China is that of a 'Strategic Partnership' (EEAS 2013e). This section examines what this strategic partnership entails, points to the rising disputes within a context of a shifting balance of power, and presents explanations for the rather disappointing partnership by illuminating 'conceptual gaps' between the EU and China. It also demonstrates how the EU initially saw China as a subject of its structural foreign policy, but is increasingly confronted by China as a competing structural power.

During the sixth China–EU Summit in 2003, both partners put forward the 'development of an overall strategic partnership' (EU 2003). In 2006, the EU and China agreed to upgrade their contractual relations and to start negotiations on a single overarching Partnership and Cooperation Agreement (PCA) which should replace the Trade and Cooperation Agreement (TCA) of 1985 (Men and Balducci 2010). However, in 2013, the negotiations on the PCA had not yet been finalized, although China and the EU are strongly tied, both economically and institutionally. The EU is China's biggest trading partner and most favoured destination of overseas direct investment, whereas China is the EU's largest source of imports and the EU's second largest trading partner (behind the US). In addition to the commitment to organize annual summits, frequent economic, political and trade dialogue meetings are also held. Over 50 sectoral dialogues and agreements are in place, covering sectors from environment and energy to human rights and international security. Interaction has been further upgraded through the establishment of a High Level Economic and Trade Dialogue (since 2008), a High Level Strategic Dialogue (since 2010) and a High Level People-to-People Dialogue (since 2012).

In its approach towards China, the EU basically used the same structural foreign policy approach as it employs in its dealing with other regions of the world. The main rationale was indeed that the development of a comprehensive partnership and of intensive interactions would gradually lead China to adopt the structures which the EU promotes. In other words, the EU demonstrated a 'stubborn belief that it can socialize China', assuming 'that by entangling the Asian power into a web of international institutions and rules, Beijing will adopt the norms that Europe has enshrined in its own political charters' (Holslag, 2011a: 309). However, such a 'unilateral socialization' – in contrast to a 'bilateral socialization' – has little chance of success with a country as powerful as China (Lirong 2011: 33–5).

This is particularly true as, over the last decade, the balance of power between both partners has changed dramatically, particularly in the economic field (see Dai 2012; Defraigne 2012; Wang 2012). China's massive and rapidly growing economy has been the driving force behind its gradual emergence – or 're-emergence' – as a global power, with its military capabilities also being strengthened considerably (see Table 12.1). China has succeeded in developing this power by partially adapting itself to, and embedding itself within, the predominant 'global' – but originally Western – economic structures, including through its membership of the WTO in 2001. China now enjoys the highest economic growth rates of all major and emerging world economies, with rates of on average 6.8 per cent to be expected until 2020 (compared to less than 2 per cent in the Euro area). China is also the world's largest foreign currency reserve country with more than $3 trillion at hand in 2012 (OECD 2013).

Taken together, these indicators point to the impressive leverage China possesses – economically but potentially also politically – which also explains China's increasing assertiveness in world politics. However, the Chinese leadership has considerable challenges before it. These include guaranteeing its population of 1.3 billion people a steadily growing economy and welfare, as a requirement for continued internal stability. Furthermore, there is the challenge of ensuring supplies of food, energy and other resources from third countries. This also has external implications, including for the EU's position in the Middle East, Africa and other parts of the world where China and the EU compete for the same resources, markets and political influence.

The EU, on the other hand, saw its position fundamentally weakened: 'If China believed that Europe was still a rising power before 2008, with the arrival of the global financial crisis in 2008 and the Euro crisis in 2009, such a view became less persuasive in China' (Chen 2012: 19). These crises also undermined the belief in the effectiveness and sustainability both of Europe's socio-economic model and of the financial and economic structures it promotes internationally. Symbolizing the reversal in their relative weight, China in 2010–11 agreed to contribute to international efforts to tackle the eurozone crisis.

This shift in the relative balance of power did not make it easier for the EU and China to live up to the high hopes and rhetoric of the strategic partnership: both partners proved to be reluctant to make concessions and no breakthroughs of crucial importance were achieved. The 'honeymoon' between China and the EU was clearly over and what emerged was in fact 'deepening cooperation amid rising disputes' (Chen 2012: 18–9). The EU–China Strategic Partnership had proved to be an 'elusive axis' (Holslag 2011a).

In the economic field, negotiations on the PCA became blocked on issues such as market access, intellectual property rights and state aid, with conflicts within the WTO also growing (Men and Balducci 2010; Wouters and Burnay 2012). Hence, despite the spectacularly increased ties between the European and Chinese economies, the three decades old TCA continues to serve as the main legal framework for EU–China relations. Whereas the EU was mainly disappointed about the lack of Chinese concessions on the above-mentioned issues, China saw the EU's reluctance to grant China 'market economy status' under WTO rules as proof of the EU's inability to act strategically and treat China as a genuine partner. Such market economy status would remove restrictions for Chinese companies that want to export to the EU. China is now confronted with the EU not willing to grant that market economy status automatically, as was in principle foreseen when China acceded to the WTO in 2001. Other areas of contention also emerged, despite the 'strategic partnership' and the so-called joint priorities. One example is climate change policy (Wouters *et al.* 2012b: 202–65). Open confrontation surfaced in the 2009 Copenhagen conference (see Chapter 10), but also later on over other issues, such as the EU's unilateral decision to also subject non-European airlines using European airports to the EU's Emissions Trading Scheme. From a Chinese perspective, the European Commission's DG Trade and DG Climate Action dominate the EU–China agenda through their assertive sectoral policies and in fact undermine the possibility of developing a genuine strategic partnership (Chen 2013: 188).

Hence, what emerged was not a 'partnership' but rather growing distrust and mutual misunderstanding, which was also related both to the internal situation in China and to foreign policy issues. In order to allow for the development of an EU–China strategic partnership, European leaders in the early 2000s had pushed politically sensitive issues to the background, including human rights, political and religious freedoms, and the situation in Tibet and Xinjiang. However, these themes gradually regained importance in the political debate in Europe and increasingly overshadowed the EU–China partnership. Particularly the meetings of various European heads of state or government with the Tibetan Dalai Lama – seen in the West as a spiritual leader, but in China as the leader of a separatist movement – resulted in China's temporarily freezing its relations with the EU member states concerned. This too, in turn, had a negative impact on EU–China relations (Freeman and Geeraerts 2012; Zhang C. 2012). The arms embargo against China which the EU had imposed after the 1989 Tiananmen massacre when military forces crushed the protest movements was also symbolically important. Following strong pressure from the US and shifting positions in some member states, the EU reconsidered in 2005 its earlier decision to lift its arms embargo against China. This turned the issue into a remaining sore point in EU–China relations (Cuyckens 2012; de Wilde d'Estmael 2012).

In the field of foreign policy, the results of the envisaged strategic partnership were equally sobering. In official declarations, the EU and China emphasize their strengthened collaboration on important international security issues, such as in the E3+3 talks on Iran (see Chapters 7 and 11) and in fighting piracy off the coasts of Somalia (see Chapter 8) (Larik and Weiler 2011; Song 2013). However, the strategic partnership did not materialize in practice, as appears in an evaluation of the policy outputs with regard to what both China and the EU endorsed as joint priorities, including Africa, North Korea, Afghanistan but also Iran (Holslag 2011a). The EU and China in general disagree on how to tackle authoritarian regimes. Whereas China pursues closer diplomatic relations with countries such as North Korea, Iran, Sudan or Zimbabwe (often in order to secure energy supplies), the EU denounces China's disregard for the human rights situation and the nature of the political regimes in these countries. European distrust is particularly focused on China's Africa policy, as China is not only considered as a competitor for resources, but also as undermining the EU's human rights, democratization and development policies (Holslag 2011b; Lirong 2011; Men and Barton 2011).

Outspoken conflicts arose over the EU's proactive diplomacy to foster regime change in the Arab world and on the handling of the crises in Libya and Syria. Although it had supported international sanctions against the Gaddafi regime in early 2011, China (together with Russia and Germany) was critical of the military operation against the Libyan dictator, arguing that this operation went beyond the UNSC resolution authorizing the protection of Libyan civilians (see also Box 7.1). The military campaign in Libya, led by the UK and France, had a direct negative effect on Chinese interests in that country. Many thousands of Chinese workers were forced to leave the country and strategic Chinese investments in and energy supplies from Libya were nullified. This negative experience prompted China, together with Russia, to veto draft resolutions in the UN proposed by European countries calling for a more assertive policy against the Assad regime in Syria (Chen 2013: 181).

When moving from a relational foreign policy to a structural foreign policy perspective, it appears that the gradual rise of China as a competing structural power is a major concern for the EU. This not only reveals itself in multilateral organizations (see Chapter 13), but also in third regions in the world. China successfully embodies a development model for other (developing or emerging) countries that seems more attractive than the model promoted by the EU. The Chinese model consists of economic liberalization and development that do not necessarily go hand in hand with political liberalization and development towards Western norms. The remarkably swift modernization of the Chinese economy, combined with internal political stability and sustained control of domestic political and societal dynamics, are attractive for many political and economic elites in other countries who want progress without risking losing political control.

This resulted in the notion of a 'Beijing Consensus' – a term coined in the West as a twist on the discredited 'Washington Consensus' (see Chapter 13) – meaning that 'China is marking a path for other nations around the world who are trying to figure out not simply how to develop their countries, but also how to fit into the international order' (Ramo 2004: 3). In other words, 'emerging markets [are] learning to combine market economics with traditional autocratic or semi-autocratic politics' (Halper 2010: 2–3). China itself rejects the notion of a 'Beijing Consensus' and claims that, in contrast to the EU, it is not promoting its structures and rules of the game in other parts of the world. However, through its expanding presence in Africa and other parts of the world it challenges the structures promoted and conceived by the West, particularly when its model is considered more effective and legitimate in these countries (Liu 2012; Wagner Givens 2011). Moreover, China's cultural and public diplomacy aims to strengthen its position in the long run, including through the active promotion of the study of the Chinese language, the promotion of Chinese students studying abroad and foreign student enrolment domestically, all mirroring an eagerness to strengthen China's soft power (Chen and Song 2012). However, rising nationalism, growing military capabilities, increasing domestic social inequity in the country, and fear for its economic dominance can undermine the attractiveness of the Chinese model.

It is evident that the often conflicting interests between the EU and China explain in large part the generally disappointing development of the EU–China relationship. Yet, there are other explanations, one of them being the existence of 'conceptual gaps' (Pan 2012a). Indeed, the EU and China often use different conceptualizations of the same notions and values, with the Europeans often ignoring or even not knowing about concepts that are important for China (see Shambaugh and Xiao 2012; Liqun 2010). These conceptual gaps also illuminate why China and the EU often position themselves differently at the international stage as they propose different rules of the game for world politics. Examples of such conceptual gaps include the notions of sovereignty; human rights; democracy; global governance and multilateralism; and 'strategic partnership', which we will discuss in the rest of this section.

First, the conceptual gap on *sovereignty* is related to the EU and China being different types of players in international politics. The gap starts with the EU's being labelled as a post-Westphalian or post-sovereign polity, which follows from the specific historical trajectory of Europe (Pan 2012b: 4). This contrasts with the Chinese view of sovereignty as absolute, inseparable and infrangible and as the core principle of international relations (Carlson 2011; Ding 2012; Gottwald and Duggan 2012; Pan 2012c). The concept of sovereignty is also at the heart of the 'Principles of Peaceful Co-Existence' which have formed since the mid-1950s the cornerstone of Chinese relations with other states. These include respect for territorial integrity, non-aggression, non-interference in each other's internal affairs, equality and mutual benefit (Zhang Q. 2010). China's adherence to these core principles explains the frequent disagreements between the EU and China. As post-sovereign actors, the Europeans consider interference mostly as acceptable and sometimes even as morally imperative, including through the use of coercive measures and political conditionality (see Chapter 9). This implies that, under certain circumstances, military force can be used and territorial integrity of third countries can be infringed, as was applied in the European involvement in military interventions in the Balkans, Afghanistan, Iraq, Libya, Côte d'Ivoire and other places. China considered these interventions as contrary to the above-mentioned principles. In the same vein, from a Chinese perspective, the European concerns over Tibet are considered as undermining the important principles of respect for China's territorial integrity and non-interference in its internal affairs.

With its systematic emphasis on respect for sovereignty, China has made its imprint on the structure of international relations. Its nearly systematic opposition in the UN Security Council to intervention in third countries is illustrative in this regard. So too is its reluctance to global commitments and its preference for a unilateral 'pledge and review' approach in the fight against climate change (see Chapter 10). The

Chinese adherence to sovereignty also resonates positively in a major part of the Southern Hemisphere. Experience with European colonialism and Western multinationals explain why territorial integrity, non-aggression, non-interference, equality and mutual benefit are seen as principles to be cherished. Interestingly, whereas the Europeans often depict China's principled choice for non-intervention and against political conditionality as an unwillingness to take up responsibility and uphold universal values, this choice is precisely considered in China as a 'value' and as a sign that China respects its partner countries and treats them as equals (see Li and Liu 2013; Wu 2012).

Second, different views exist on *human rights*, which not only reflects a political choice by the dominant elites, but also different societal orientations (Freeman and Geeraerts 2012; Men 2011; Taylor 2011). Whereas the EU blames China for not respecting individual human rights and liberties and for neglecting human rights in its dealing with third countries, China points to the EU's 'double standards' (see Chapter 6), particularly the EU's lack of attention for collective human rights, such as the 'right to subsistence' (i.e. having the minimum necessary to support life) and the 'right to development'. This also reflects the fact that Chinese society traditionally focuses more on the group than on the individual (Zhang C. 2012), which also often resonates in countries in the South.

Third, a similar discussion arises with regard to *democracy*. Whereas the EU urges China to pursue democratic reforms, China argues that it has a 'multifaceted democracy with Chinese characteristics'. When making this argument, it emphasizes that its current circumstances do not allow for Western-style democracy, referring to the chaos and decline of the Soviet Union after introducing such democracy (see Weil and Jing 2012). China also points to the need of 'international democracy', which requires European countries to relinquish their privileges in the main international organizations, such as their overrepresentation in the UNSC and in the executive boards of the international financial institutions (IFIs) such as the IMF and the World Bank (see Chapter 13).

Fourth, there are conceptual gaps on *global governance* and *multilateralism*. Both the EU and China declare being committed to these principles, but their understandings of these concepts vary considerably (Gross and Jian 2012; Qin 2011; Scott 2013; Zhang X. 2012). Whereas the EU urges China to take up more responsibility in the various global governance structures, concomitant to its rising economic power, China urges the Europeans to engage in reforms of the existing Western-dominated international structures, again referring to the European overrepresentation in many multilateral organizations. Moreover, multipolarity rather than multilateralism is what China is interested in. These different perspectives affect the positions of the EU and China in various international institutions and regimes (see case studies in Wouters *et al.* 2012b).

Fifth, a conceptual gap exists on the very concept of *strategic partnership* (Stumbaum and Xiong 2012). Whereas the EU mainly focuses on current challenges and regrets that China is not more cooperative in tackling these challenges, this notion of immediacy contrasts with the long-term perspective taken by China. For the Chinese leadership, a strategic partnership means that the cooperation should be comprehensive, long-term and stable, and based on the principles of equality, mutual respect, mutual trust and mutual benefit ('win-win'). This explains why China often sees the EU as being unwilling to treat China as an equal partner. This is shown, for example, in the EU's continued emphasis on Tibet and human rights and in its reluctance to grant China market economy status, to lift the 25-year-old arms embargo, or to accept further Chinese participation in the strategic European Galileo satellite navigation system (see Chapter 8). For China, this demonstrates the EU's inability to act strategically and explains why the EU is decreasingly seen as a key strategic partner, in contrast to the more central place it had in China's foreign policy in 1995–2005 (Chen 2012).

Emerging Powers and Strategic Partners

The EU considers the US, Russia and China as the most important powers. However, several other countries are also increasingly establishing themselves on the world scene, compelling the EU to find ways to deal with them strategically (see Smith M. 2013). Therefore, the EU has launched 'strategic partnerships' with the newly emerging powers Brazil, India, Mexico, South Africa and South Korea, in addition to the partnerships it already had with Russia, China, and with the three long-standing partners Japan, Canada and the US (Grevi 2013; Grevi and Khandekar 2011; Renard and Biscop 2012) (see overview in Box 12.1 and Figure 13.1). In the Report on the Implementation of the European Security Strategy, the EU explained that it considers these strategic partnerships as building blocks of an effective multilateral order with the UN at its apex (European Council 2008).

In general, the formal relations with the 'strategic partners' follow largely the same pattern. The legal bases for these strategic partnerships are long-term partnership and cooperation agreements or trade and cooperation agreements. Joint action plans or common declarations outline a medium-term vision for the partnership, including an overview of fields of cooperation and dialogue. Furthermore, the annual summits, ministerial meetings as well as the sectoral dialogues between EU officials and representatives of third countries take place on a regular basis, leading to a dense web of institutional frameworks.

Notwithstanding that recurring pattern, the nature of the EU's relations with its strategic partners is very diverse as well as ambiguous (see

Renard 2011; Sautenet 2012). In most cases, the 'strategic partnership' with the emerging or re-emerging powers is rather a goal to be pursued through a gradual process of interaction than a reflection of reality. An analysis of the strategic partnerships demonstrates that, despite some common features, they are neither identical nor equal. Moreover, they are not truly strategic, leading Renard (2011: 23–4) to conclude that 'cooperation of the EU with its partners on international strategic issues is limited at best', as becomes clear in areas such as WMD proliferation, conflict management or climate change policy. Although cooperation and dialogue have intensified in general terms, the launch of the strategic partnerships has in most cases not contributed to an increased shared understanding of international affairs, to a more common vision for global governance, or at least to a greater appreciation of the EU. An analysis of perceptions in the emerging countries on the contrary points to the generally negative image of the EU (Fioramonti 2012; Pew Research Center 2011: 63).

The use of the label 'strategic partnership' functions to a large extent as a rhetorical façade which masks the fact that the EU has to a large extent failed to transform its relations with the various powers into strategic partnerships. The partnerships generally did not help the EU in its relational foreign policy (tackling specific crises and conflicts), nor did they contribute to a structural foreign policy (influencing the rules of the game in third countries and on the global level). The proliferation of strategic partnerships also reflects the EU's inability to agree and decide upon which third actors are genuine strategic partners and consequently to behave strategically in relation to these partners. The agreements and action plans with the EU's various 'strategic partners' indeed read more as a catalogue of policy domains that are on the agenda of their meetings, rather than as well-formulated strategies to pursue well-defined objectives through intensive and purposeful common actions. Whereas the EU has not been able to turn its relationships with Russia and China into genuine strategic partnerships (see previous sections), the other countries with which the EU has a strategic partnership were even lower on the EU's priority list to build a genuine strategic partnership. In reality, for most EU member states the only genuine strategic partnership seems to be the one with the US (Keukeleire and Bruyninckx 2011: 389–91).

A closer look at the position adopted by the emerging powers on major issues of international relations reveal the limits of the strategic partnerships, even if the EU were to start to consider them as real strategic partners (Keukeleire *et al.* 2011). First, emerging powers share the common goal to counter Western dominance in the main international organizations as well as the common resentment against the Europeans who are reluctant to scale down their privileged position in the various international fora. They share the goal to counter Western-dominated rules of the game and gain a greater voice in global governance, as was

---

Box 12.1   The EU's 'strategic partnerships'

The EU has launched 'strategic partnerships' with 10 countries. In addition to the US, Russia and China – discussed earlier in this chapter – these are:

Canada

The 1976 Framework Agreement for Commercial and Economic Cooperation governs EU–Canada relations. The 2004 Partnership Agenda followed this Framework Agreement, and negotiations are currently ongoing for an EU–Canada Comprehensive Economic and Trade Agreement (CETA) aiming to create a free trade area. The EU considers its relationship with Canada to be intrinsically 'strategic' and uses the term 'strategic partner', but there is no official document entitled 'EU–Canada strategic partnership'.

Japan

EU–Japan relations are based on the 2001 Action Plan. Negotiations on a free trade agreement were launched in the beginning of 2013. Despite the use of the term 'strategic partner' there is no official document entitled 'strategic partnership' with Japan. Similar to the EU–Canada relationship, the EU considers the relationship with Japan to be intrinsically 'strategic' (see Keck 2013; Nakamura 2013; Söderberg 2012; Tanaka 2013).

India

The Cooperation Agreement of 1994 provides the framework for current EU–India cooperation. In 2004 the EU and India launched the 'EU–India Strategic Partnership' and Joint Action Plan, which were both further strengthened and expanded in 2008. The EU and India in 2007 started negotiations on a free trade agreement, but negotiations have been deadlocked for a long time (see Allen 2013; Bava 2013; Jain 2012).

→

---

already visible in international negotiations on the international financial system, climate change or the OECD/DAC rules on development aid. Multilateral frameworks such as the IBSA Dialogue Forum (India, Brazil, South Africa) and BASIC (the same three countries plus China) allow them to coordinate their positions and to influence the debates in other forums (Bava 2011; Stephen 2012; Wade 2011) (see also Chapter 13).

Second, with their common experience as former colonies of European countries, they cherish national sovereignty and non-intervention in

South Africa

Relations between the EU and South Africa are based on the Trade, Development and Cooperation Agreement, which created a free trade area in 2000 and which was upgraded in 2009 with new arrangements to strengthen political and economic cooperation between both partners. In 2007, both partners signed the South Africa–EU Strategic Partnership as well as a Joint Action Plan (Helly 2012).

Brazil

The 1992 bilateral Framework Cooperation Agreement governs the current relations between Brazil and the EU. In 2007, during their first summit, the EU and Brazil decided to launch a Strategic Partnership in order to upgrade mutual ties. In 2011, a Joint Action Plan was approved, which upgrades the relations towards a comprehensive strategic partnership. Free trade negotiations with Mercosur, of which Brazil is the largest member, are currently deadlocked (see Saraiva 2012; Whitman and Rodt 2012).

Mexico

EU–Mexico relations are governed by the Economic Partnership, Political Coordination and Cooperation Agreement of 1997 and a Free Trade Agreement of 2000. Mexico has been a strategic partner of the EU since 2008. Two years later, this partnership was upgraded through a Joint Executive Plan (Gratius 2012).

South Korea

The EU and Korea signed a new Framework Agreement in 2010 and a Free Trade Agreement in 2011, which replaces the 2001 Framework Agreement for Trade and Cooperation. On the basis of these two agreements, both parties decided in 2010 to upgrade their relationship to a strategic partnership (see Kelly 2012; Wissenbach 2013).

Sources: EEAS (2013f); Renard (2011); Sautenet 2012.

internal affairs. This explains why even democratic countries such as India, Brazil and South Africa are not natural allies for the EU in tackling authoritarian regimes or in promoting democracy and human rights 'EU style'. This also appears in their voting behaviour in the UN, where the EU cannot count on their systematic support on these issues (Keukeleire *et al.* 2011: 10–16; Vieira and Alden 2011).

Third, India, Brazil and other emerging powers manifest themselves as increasingly important players in South–South cooperation. They usually emphasize values as mutual benefit, equality and non-interference in internal affairs – and thus generally oppose the EU's approaches such as political conditionality. Together, they become daunting competitors for the EU and its member states in the search for markets, resources and political influence, which combined with their different approach towards South–South cooperation implies that a partnership with the EU – let alone a strategic one – is not evident (Chaturvedi *et al.* 2012; Grimm and Hackenesch 2012; Hengari 2012).

Islamism: Challenging the Dominant Structures

Lacking statehood and being neither an international organization, institution nor a regime, Islamism is a 'power' which does not fit within conventional categories and conceptions of foreign policy. Islamism is multifaceted, with no clearly defined centre or leadership. Despite its ambiguous character, Islamism can be understood as a formidable structural power in the same league as the US, Russia, China, the EU or major international organizations. It has a growing influence in large parts of the world: from Indonesia and Pakistan to the Middle East and half of Africa, many European cities and beyond. It is a competing power which is developing partially inside, but also partially outside and against the dominant structures established and sustained by the West. Several inter-related mechanisms, processes and actors contributed to the growing influence of Islamism over the last decades. These include the generally increasing religiosity of Muslims; state-controlled (re-)Islamization; financial support for Islamic groups, mosques, Islamic schools and centres worldwide; and the provision of essential public goods to an often impoverished population and the construction of parallel social and economic structures in the absence of a properly functioning state. For us to assess the EU's approach towards this structural power, we must first explain what we understand by 'Islamism'. We first describe what the various manifestations of Islamism have in common, followed by a discussion of the differences between those manifestations.

Common to all manifestations of Islamism is the belief that Islam provides an answer to the political, economic, social, moral and identity questions of Muslim societies and states. It is based on the claim that Islam is able to structure all aspects of life, with the Quran and the Sharia playing a central role. The Sharia offers what is believed to be a divinely inspired legal framework which regulates politics, economics, business, banking and finance, family relations, social relations, education and the day-to-day personal behaviour of Muslims. As Azzam argues, for most Muslims, the Sharia is a fundamentally positive force which, when upheld, will offer security for Muslim citizens against the tyranny of political leaders, will counter corruption and other abuses committed by the state, and will counter secular and Western values, which are viewed as mistaken, immoral and corrupting. Hence, 'the issue here is not only secular versus religious; it is also a search for justice versus repression' (Azzam 2006: 1130). This also explains why the Sharia is probably at the heart of one of the major misunderstandings or conceptual gaps between the West and the Muslim world, with the former seeing the Sharia predominantly as a threat and a negative force and the latter seeing it as a solution, relief and a positive force.

Islamism is as such also a reaction against the secular state and against 'Western' models and ideologies (such as modernization, nationalism, socialism, liberalism, capitalism and, particularly, secularism). Most of these models have been applied in Islamic countries, but they have largely failed to provide welfare, security and identity to Muslim people. The rise of Islamism is also a reaction against globalization which is perceived as an extension of colonialism and part of the general Western and secular assault (Halliday 2005; Rahman 2009). Historically, the development of Islamism is thus closely linked to post-colonial identity building. In societies that experienced the cultural influence of colonial powers, Islam has often served as a basis to develop a reactive identity to Western models and to counter growing feelings of societal insecurity (see Box 1.1) (see Burgat 2009).

Generally speaking, structures upheld and promoted by Islamism are on one point of a fundamentally different order than those promoted by the West: they not only question or reject the Western conception of separating religion and politics, but also assert the relevance of religion, and in some cases also the dominance of religion over politics. More specifically, they not only provide for different norms or sources of inspiration, but also translate into different ways of organizing politics, economics and social relations than in the West. One example is Islamic banking and finance, which allows for transnational economic transactions and capital flows to occur largely outside 'Western' international economic and financial structures (see Kettell 2011).

Coming to the variation within Islamism, it is clear that Islamism is not a monolithic movement, but a complex multifaceted phenomenon that expresses itself through a variety of groups, movements and currents on various levels (see Rubin 2013). Differences relate to questions such as the extent to which a literal reading of the founding religious texts is required, and whether Islamic solutions and structures can be combined with non-Islamic (secular and 'Western') solutions and structures. Divergences also relate to the approaches to be employed: the focus can be on the faith of the individual Muslim; on grass-root action aimed at the gradual Islamization of society from below; on direct political action and the seizure of political power; on bringing about drastic socio-political changes, including through violent action within specific national contexts; or on the holy war or 'jihad' against the unfaithful in both the Muslim world and the West (such as the Al-Qaeda network) (Denoeux 2002; Thépaut 2012). These last two variants – combined with other dynamics and grievances – also pose direct challenges to the EU's foreign policy (Coolsaet 2011). This is the case in the Mediterranean and the Middle East, but also in sub-Saharan Africa, as appeared in the policies towards Somalia, Mali and the broader Sahel region (see Chapters 6, 7, 8 and 11).

The EU for a long time seemed to ignore the structural power emanating from the rise of Islamism. It is difficult for the EU – and the West in general – to counter or contain Islamism as a structural power, as the traditional instruments of foreign policy are largely irrelevant to its unconventional actors, instruments, networks and immaterial dimensions. As the Islamist assertion in the Muslim world is basically religious and cultural, this makes it all the more difficult to contend with its growth in traditional foreign policy terms (Azzam 2006: 1130). The EU's answer has been to attempt to export Western structures, norms and values to Muslim countries in its southern neighbourhood mainly through the Euro-Mediterranean Partnership, the ENP and the Union for the Mediterranean (see Chapter 11). However, the EU's policies towards the Mediterranean did not help to tackle the problematic socio-economic situation or the deteriorating societal security in the region. They consisted mainly of interactions with and support for the elites in the various authoritarian regimes (instead of the population) and basically ignored the identity and religious dimension (Burgat 2009; Cavatorta and Pace 2010a). As Bicchi (2006: 10) noted, in the implementation of its policies the EU in fact preferred 'not to engage with Islamic organizations, regardless of how moderate or how central they are to the social and political scene of Mediterranean Arab countries'. Moreover, the EU's rejection of the democratic election of Islam-rooted parties, such as Hamas in the Palestinian Territories, further alienated the Muslim world from the West (Tocci 2007) (see Chapters 6 and 11). The EU's historic neglect of the Islamic dimension in its policies towards Muslim countries is indicative of the struggle of secular Europeans to understand religious non-Western societies, to take into account non-Western beliefs and cultures, and to respond positively to their desire for recognition.

The 2011 Arab uprisings functioned as a wake-up call for the EU, which was no longer able to neglect the Islamic dimension in its foreign policy towards that region. The toppling of authoritarian regimes in Tunisia and Egypt paved the way for free elections dominated by Islamic parties, while conservative Islamic parties also gained political influence in other Mediterranean countries. The EU applauded the revolutions made in the name of EU-supported values such as democracy, but the rise of Islamist political parties posed new dilemmas, since the elections had resulted in different outcomes than the EU had envisaged in its democracy promotion discourse (see Behr 2013; de Vasconcelos 2012; Peters

2012a). Although each country and party has its own specificities, a certain number of factors explains the Islamic parties' success. First, their years of resistance against regimes widely perceived as violent and corrupt gave those parties and movements a strong local legitimacy. Second, they developed networks of social aid and educational support to a large part of the poor populations, which increased their appeal as dedicated actors that responded to what the people needed. Third, they were seen as genuine promoters of values that had been heavily flouted by previous regimes such as sincerity and justice – explaining too why the term 'justice' appears in the name of several Islamic parties. Finally, Islamic political parties have also stressed the importance of economic development in their programmes, often following policies inspired by the free market. The EU policies, particularly in its revised ENP and its Partnership for Democracy and Shared Prosperity with the Southern Mediterranean (see Chapter 11), did not provide a substantial and credible answer to these factors.

In contrast, Islam as a vector of influence in international relations can be observed in the role played by some key countries in the Gulf, as well as Turkey. Together, their influence takes both an ideational and a material form (see Tocci *et al.*: 2012). The influence of Gulf states as Saudi Arabia and Qatar can be summarized in the five 'M's: Mohammed, Mecca, media, money, and migration (Thépaut and Keukeleire 2012). In addition to the central position of the Prophet *Mohammed* in all Muslim countries, Saudi Arabia and Qatar exert ideational influence through their direct financial support to Islamist groups and parties, and Saudi Arabia attracts additional attention through the pilgrimage to *Mecca*. *Media*, such as the TV channels Al-Jazeera (Qatar) and Al-Arabiya (Saudi Arabia), are very influential in the region. The abundant availability of *money* is central in the support for material activities in the form of investments in the major economic sectors. *Migration* is the final source of influence, as the booming Gulf economies have attracted many Mediterranean workers who have adapted to local customs before returning to their home countries. Taken together, these five 'M's from the Gulf prove to be much more appealing and substantial than the 'three 'M's' (markets, mobility and money), proposed by the EU (see Chapter 11).

Turkey is also increasingly emerging as a structural power in the region (Tocci *et al.* 2012; Sadik 2012). Turkey's political and economic presence in the Arab world grew dramatically, while its ideational influence is also important in the context of the post-Arab revolutions. As a Muslim but secular country, with a functioning democracy and efficient market economy, and with social policies grounded in Islamic norms, Turkey under the Islamic AKP party serves as one of the models for new Islamist parties (on Turkey, see also Chapter 11).

Moreover, the impact of the countries from the region is also demonstrated in the role played by the Gulf Cooperation Council and the Arab

League. The Arab League, for instance, played a key role in the 2011 military intervention in Libya, where its call to impose a no-fly zone over Libya was crucial in bringing France and the UK to the decision to actually start the military operation (with Qatar also participating in the operation) (see Box 7.1).

Confronted with the structural power emanating from Islamism in general and leading Islamic countries and organizations specifically, the EU is challenged to reconsider its policies towards the Mediterranean and the broader Muslim world (Behr 2013; Cassarino 2012). This is also important for the EU for another reason. The challenge posed by Islamism is one of the best examples of the blurring inside–outside divide in foreign policy: the boundaries of the '*umma*', or community of the faithful, have stretched beyond Muslim states to European cities, with a shared sense of belonging to a common faith (Azzam 2006: 1119). From this perspective, it is of vital interest for the EU to develop a sophisticated answer to the multifarious challenges and demands of a growing Muslim community and an increasingly globalized Islam. This is not only important because of the potential threat posed by jihadism, but it is of particular importance to counter a growing feeling of alienation and of societal insecurity among both Muslim and non-Muslim sections of Europe's population.

Conclusion

This chapter has analysed the EU's relationship with competing powers: global powers (such as the United States, Russia and China) and the group of emerging powers (such as India and Brazil), and the increasingly influential structures under the umbrella term of 'Islamism'. It has shown that the US remains the most important structural power and, despite remaining divergences on various policy issues, the EU's most preferred partner. However, the EU is increasingly facing competition from Russia and China at the global level, particularly in regions like the Eastern neighbourhood or Africa. The EU has also experienced the fact that that the emerging powers do not always share its foreign policy priorities and methods, undermining the EU's influence in shaping structures both in other parts of the world and at the multilateral level, which will be further explored in the following chapter.

Chapter 13

The EU and Multilateral Organizations

This chapter focuses on the EU's position in global governance and particularly on the EU's relations with multilateral organizations. It first discusses the EU's choice of multilateralism and its status, coordination and representation practices in international fora. Next, the chapter examines the participation of the EU in the UN, international financial institutions such as the IMF and the World Bank, and in more informal systems of 'club governance' such as the Gx system (i.e. G7, G8 and G20). Finally, it discusses the EU's position in so-called 'competing multilateralisms' in the Asia-Pacific region. The EU's relations towards some other major international organizations are described elsewhere in this book (see Chapter 8 for NATO and Chapter 9 for WTO).

Major political, economic and financial international organizations, such as the UN; the IMF and the World Bank, and the Gx system, define, shape and influence the structures to which countries and other actors in the international system must adapt. Although many EU and national policies find their origins in international organizations, there are different ways in which international regimes, organizations and institutions influence the EU (see Costa and Jørgensen 2012). Structural power emanating from international organizations has an impact on European welfare and security, provides opportunities and challenges for EU foreign policy, and also influences the parameters within which EU foreign policy operates.

Therefore, the EU aims to have an impact on these multilateral organizations and their output. Although the EU's participation in international organizations is often hindered by both external and internal legal constraints and by the divergences in member states' preferences on the desirability of European unity in international organizations, the EU has established close relationships and practical working methods to engage in the global governance architecture. Mirroring our conceptualization of EU foreign policy as 'multilevel' and 'multi-locational', EU foreign policy actions are in most cases explicitly adopted alongside or in support of the initiatives of other international organizations (see Chapter 1).

The EU's Choice of Effective Multilateralism

The EU is seen as a frontrunner and advocate of multilateral cooperation and of a global order based on international organizations and rules. Its support for cooperation through international organizations and international agreements is stronger than is the case in many countries, especially in the EU's 'strategic partners' and some 'major powers' (see Chapter 12) .

The EU's adherence to multilateralism is clearly reflected in the European treaties. The EU 'seeks to develop relations and build partnerships with ... international, regional or global organisations' and it shall 'promote multilateral solutions to common problems' (Art. 21(1) TEU). Moreover, one of the objectives of its external action is to 'promote an international system based on stronger multilateral cooperation and good global governance' (Art. 21(2) TEU). In order to operationalize this, the EU considers the UN as the cornerstone of global governance, yet the EU's relations with other regional entities and its promotion of interregionalism are also important in this regard (see De Lombaerde and Schulz 2010; Murray and Rees 2010; Telò 2014; Warleigh-Lack *et al.* 2011).

In its 2003 European Security Strategy, the EU defined 'effective multilateralism' as a core principle and objective of its foreign policy (see Chapter 2). One of the three strategic objectives defined in this Strategy is an 'international order based on effective multilateralism'. The EU's approach is to develop 'a stronger international society, well functioning international institutions and a rule-based international order' (European Council 2003a: 9). The Strategy equally emphasizes the importance of 'key institutions in the international system', of regional organizations and of the development of international law in response to new challenges. In the 2008 Report on the Implementation of the European Security Strategy, the EU committed itself to 'lead a renewal of the multilateral order' (European Council 2008). However, the notion of 'effective multilateralism' has not been put into practice and the concept has been used in policy documents and academic analyses in various ways and with different emphases (see Blavoukos and Bourantonis 2011; Bouchard *et al.* 2013; Drieskens and van Schaik 2014). As a result, the meaning of 'effective multilateralism' seems to have been eroded and its practical usefulness can be questioned.

The EU's preference for international agreements and its adherence to international law are an external reflection of the EU's internal efforts to base interstate relations on common rules and institutions. This reflects Europe's negative experience with the consequences of unrestrained sovereignty. The EU has a strong record in ratifying international treaties, with the EU being a party to many of the major international and UN-wide treaties. It also plays a pivotal role in the development, adoption and implementation of important multilateral legal instruments such as multilateral environmental agreements or various disarmament regimes (see Chapters 10 and 6). The EU itself is also a political system based on (far-reaching and in-depth) multilateral cooperation and it can be seen as a 'multilateral microcosm of the international system itself' (Oberthür and Roche Kelly 2008: 43) and multilateralism can even be considered as a 'way of life in Europe' (Groom 2006: 460). In short, the EU's commitment to a multilateral approach can be seen as part of its DNA.

How would one evaluate the EU's track record on pursuing multilateralism? First, the EU has in particular cases certainly succeeded in playing an activist or mediating role (see Van Vooren *et al.* 2013). The EU's role in environmental governance (see Chapter 10) is often considered as to be one of leadership, the EU has played a strong role in the promotion of the 'responsibility to protect' (R2P) principle at the multilateral level and it has succeeded in advocating social aspects in trade and aid agreements (Kerremans and Orbie 2009) (see Chapter 9). The EU has also contributed to multilateralism by attempting to play a 'bridge-builder' or mediator role rather than an activist one. This is the case, for instance, with development issues, where the EU has positioned itself between the US and the developing countries (Kissack 2010). However, in other cases, the EU and its member states do not manage to agree on either an activist or mediating EU approach and remain too divided to 'promote multilateral solutions to common problems' (Degrand-Guillaud 2009: 414). Hence, the EU's adherence to multilateralism needs to be qualified since there often seems to be a gap between the EU's rhetoric and the positions it is actually taking.

Second, the extent to which the EU is able to influence multilateralism not only depends on the institutional and interstate consistency within the EU (see Chapter 4), but also on other factors, such as the legal rules determining the EU's status, its ability to agree on common positions (see further) and the international context. The rise of emerging powers in the multilateral system has in particular diminished the relative (bargaining) power of the EU and with it the EU's performance in international organizations (Jørgensen *et al.* 2011).

The EU in International Fora: Legal Status, Coordination and Representation

Legal status

At first sight, the EU's legal status in international organizations seems to indicate that it would be difficult for the EU to be an influential multilateral actor. With some notable exceptions, both the EU's member states and third states have proved extremely reluctant to accept the EU as a member of international organizations – a privilege they have sought to retain for themselves. The EU's legal status in international organizations varies considerably between different international fora, ranging from full membership to observer.

The EU is a full member of a small number of international organizations (see Hoffmeister 2007; Jørgensen and Wessel 2011). The best-known examples are the World Trade Organization (WTO) and the Food and Agricultural Organization (FAO), but the EU also enjoys membership of the European Bank for Reconstruction and Development (EBRD, see Chapter 3), the Codex Alimentarius Commission (CAC, under the joint auspices of the FAO and the World Health Organization), Eurocontrol, the Energy Commission, the Hague Conference on Private International Law, the Intergovernmental Organization for International Carriage by Rail (OTIF), as well as several regional fisheries organizations. Moreover, the EU is a 'de facto member' of the World Customs Organization (Wessel 2011b: 627–8) and its participation in the Organization for Economic Cooperation and Development (OECD) 'comes close to full membership' (Jørgensen and Wessel 2011: 269).

The case for EU membership in an international organization is strongest in those areas where the EU enjoys exclusive competence, such as trade policy. The main factor determining the EU's legal status in international organizations, however, is the statutes of the international organizations themselves. Indeed, many constituent treaties of international organizations, such as the United Nations Charter (see further), only allow membership for states and not for regional organizations such as the EU. The international rules of the game are often the main impediment preventing the EU from becoming a member of an international organization, including international fora which deal with issues covered by strong, even exclusive EU competences. International law and the statutes of international organizations are not the only obstacles to EU membership. Even in cases where full EU membership is allowed, divergences between member states and between EU institutions could still impede the EU obtaining membership status (Wessel 2011b).

Since external and internal constraints – both political and legal – often prevent the EU from becoming a full member of many international organizations, the EU has achieved the status of observer in many international organizations. Generally speaking, this means that the EU can participate in meetings, but that it does not have the right to vote. The extent to which the EU, being an observer, can exercise other rights such as the right to make amendments, to take part in discussions on procedural issues or to chair committees, varies considerably from organization to organization. The EU is often labelled 'full participant' when it enjoys all rights of membership short of voting rights.

Not being a state, the EU is usually recognized as a 'Regional Economic Integration Organization' (REIO) in those international organizations where the EU is a member or an observer. There is a recent development whereby the concept of 'RIO' (Regional Integration Organization) is used, emphasizing and acknowledging the political – and not merely economic – nature of regional integration projects. The R(E)IO status is used far more often to allow the EU to become a party to international agreements than to grant the EU membership of an international organization, since the latter is much more problematic.

Coordination

Irrespective of whether the EU is a member or an observer of an international organization, the EU member states are usually also members of that international organization in their own right. This implies that coordination between EU member states (and the Commission) is necessary to make the EU's voice heard in multilateral fora, with different mechanisms being used for CFSP and for non-CFSP (external action and external dimension of internal policy) issues.

With regard to CFSP issues, Article 34 TEU includes a set of co-ordination and consultation obligations for member states, which can be summarized as follows:

- member states are to coordinate their action and uphold the Union's positions in international organizations;
- this coordination is to be organized by the High Representative;
- where not all the member states participate in an international organization, those which do participate are to uphold common positions and keep the other member states, as well as the High Representative informed of any matters of common interest; and
- member states which are members of the UN Security Council (UNSC) are to 'concert' and keep the other member states fully informed and defend the EU's positions and interests, which is 'without prejudice to their responsibilities under the provisions of the United Nations Charter'.

Furthermore, the Treaty foresees that the 'diplomatic missions of the Member States and the Union delegations ... at international organisations shall cooperate and shall contribute to formulating and implementing the common approach' (Art. 32 TEU) and that the 'diplomatic and consular missions of the Member States and the Union delegations ... and their representations to international organisations shall cooperate in ensuring that decisions defining Union positions and actions adopted pursuant to [the CFSP] are complied with and implemented' (Art. 35 TEU). Nevertheless, the member states have also emphasized in the

Treaty that these articles do not affect their responsibilities and powers with regard to their participation in international organizations, particularly their membership of the UN Security Council (Declaration 14, see Chapter 6).

Coordination practices in international organizations on non-CFSP issues vary considerably in two main ways. First, the extent of coordination differs from strong in organizations like the WTO, to medium in arenas like the UN General Assembly or the OECD, to rather weak in international fora like the UNSC or the G8 (Gstöhl 2009). In a situation where certain EU member states have a privileged position (like the permanent UNSC members France and the UK or the EU countries that are member of the G8/G20), the legal obligation and the political practice of coordination among EU actors is likely to be much lower than in cases where all member states have the same participation rights.

Second, the focal point of EU coordination varies from forum to forum (Jørgensen *et al.* 2011). Member states coordinate their positions in the framework of the Council, for example, in the WTO (in particular in the Trade Policy Committee) (see Kerremans 2011; Meunier and Nicolaïdis 2011: 282–6) or in international environmental negotiations (in the Working Party on International Environmental Issues) (see Delreux 2012b: 295–8). Coordination also sometimes takes place at the seat of the international organization in question like at the International Labour Organization (ILO) (see Kissack 2011; Riddervold and Sjursen 2012) or the World Health Organization (WHO) (see van Schaik 2011).

Two additional elements need to be considered when evaluating the EU's coordination practices in international organizations. First, more coordination and a more strictly coordinated EU position do not necessarily lead to a better performance or a higher impact of the EU at the international level (Jørgensen and Wessel 2011). In case the decision-making process in the international organization is based on majority rule, like in the UN Human Rights Council, a strongly coordinated and highly ambitious EU position risks being outvoted (Kissack 2010). Second, the EU often invests too much time in internal coordination processes and neglects engaging in outreach with third states necessary to convince other actors. Political deals during international negotiations are often made in the corridors, where the EU is not always sufficiently active. This phenomenon has been witnessed on many issues, including trade, human rights and environment, as well as in the UN in general (Brantner and Gowan 2008; Degrand-Guillaud 2009; Delreux 2011a; Elgström 2007; Smith K. 2006, 2010a).

Representation

The EU's external representation arrangements differ to a large extent between CFSP and non-CFSP issues (i.e. external action and the external dimension of internal policies). For CFSP issues, the Treaty is straight-forward: 'The High Representative shall represent the Union for matters relating to the common foreign and security policy. He shall ... express the Union's position in international organisations and at international conferences' (Art. 27(2) TEU) (see also Chapter 3). On a day-to-day basis, this task can also be executed by EU Delegations (Art. 221(1) TFEU). However, Declaration 13 to the Lisbon Treaty demonstrates that the member states have legally anchored their reluctance to delegate a high level of representation power to the HR/VP or EU Delegations (see Chapter 7). This Declaration states that the aforementioned articles 'do not affect the responsibilities of the Member States, as they currently exist, for the formulation and conduct of their foreign policy nor of their national representation in third countries *and international organisations*' (our emphasis). Indeed, in addition to the High Representative or the EU Delegations, the member states also take the floor on these issues.

Article 34 TEU stipulates that the EU member states which sit on the UN Security Council 'shall request that the High Representative be invited to present the Union's position' when the EU has defined a position that is on the UNSC's agenda. Following this provision, in May 2010 HR/VP Catherine Ashton for the first time made an EU statement at the UNSC, speaking on the issue of EU–UN cooperation in the field of peace and security.

The representation of the EU in international organizations and international treaty regimes dealing with non-CFSP issues takes various forms with different roles for the Commission, the rotating Presidency, the member states, EU Delegations, etc. To determine who speaks for the EU, competences matter (Wessel 2011a). The general rule of thumb is that the Commission represents the EU for exclusive competences, that the rotating Presidency and the Commission play a representation role when shared competences are negotiated, and that member states negotiate separately or through a single spokesperson whom they choose themselves when national competences are concerned. In international financial institutions (see further), the European Central Bank may also play a role.

The entry into force of the Lisbon Treaty in December 2009 generated divergences between member states and tensions between the Commission and the Council with regard to the external representation of the EU in international organizations. These divergences and inter-institutional turf wars emerged from different readings of the Lisbon Treaty provisions and some member states interpreting them as a threat to their national sovereignty in international organizations. It was particularly the questions on who is responsible for drafting EU statements, on behalf of whom these statements are to be issued and who was to present them in policy fields of shared competences – and not in CFSP-related or exclusive competence areas – that raised major controversies in the EU.

Particularly the UK raised concerns about external representation in that area, fearing that member states would be excluded from international activities and exercising these shared competences in international organizations at the expense of a growing role for the Commission. The UK is said to have blocked more than 70 EU statements on issues of shared competences in the UN framework in that period (PIIA 2012: 14). Hence, these tensions paralysed the EU in a couple of cases, leading to embarrassing situations at the international level, such as in the first negotiation session on a new treaty on the chemical substance mercury in January 2010, where the disunity in the EU on the external representation became clearly visible for the negotiation partners (Corthaut and Van Eeckhoutte 2012; Delreux 2012a). These tensions were mainly calmed down by the adoption by COREPER of general arrangements with regard to the delivery of EU statements in international organizations in October 2011. Although these arrangements did not provide a solution for all the issues, they broke the deadlock, weakened the turf wars and steered the EU external representation into calmer waters after a turbulent period following the entry into force of the Lisbon Treaty.

Practice shows in many international settings that formal rules are only seldom strictly applied and that the choice for a particular EU negotiation arrangement is the result of pragmatic considerations. Indeed, 'a reference to legal competence is useful yet often insufficient for understanding practices that may diverge significantly from what formal rules would lead us to expect' (Jørgensen *et al.* 2011: 601). This leads to the existence of many different negotiation arrangements, which means that the EU's representation in international organizations and treaty regimes can be best characterized as a 'fragmented representation' or even a 'patchwork pattern' (Gstöhl 2009: 386; 2012). The EU's representation in environmental negotiations provides a good example of such a pragmatic approach (Delreux 2009, 2011a) and the illustration presented in Box 13.1 exemplifies this practice of informal division of labour (see also Chapter 4).

The question of the EU's representation in external fora has often been narrowed down to the question of the EU's 'single voice'. This is, however, a rather vague debate that risks equating the EU's ability 'to speak with a single voice' with a high level of influence or performance at the international scene. Both aspects deserve some qualification.

First, a 'single voice' can refer to the unity or coherence of the position conveyed by the EU on the one hand or to the question whether there is a single negotiator speaking for the EU on the other hand. Therefore, former Trade Commissioner Pascal Lamy suggested in 2002 to make a distinction between the EU's 'single voice' (referring to its message) and the EU's 'single mouth' (referring to the messenger) (Lamy 2002).

Second, there is no automatic causal link between a more unified EU representation and a better EU performance – or a higher level of effectiveness – on the international stage (Thomas 2012; van Schaik 2013).

**Box 13.1   Informal division of labour in the EU's representation
in international environmental negotiations**

Environmental competences are shared competences, which suggests that EU representation in international environmental negotiations should be 'dual', consisting of the Commission (for the EU part of the shared competences) and the Presidency (for the member state part). Whereas granting negotiation authority to the Commission for EU competences is a legal obligation for the member states (Arts. 218 TFEU and 17 TEU), appointing the rotating Presidency as their spokesperson is a political option (Delreux 2012b).

What we see, however, is that the EU has developed informal practices that do not correspond to this 'dual representation' model. This way, the EU aims to overcome the problems related to the shared nature of environmental competences. An illustrative example is the employment of the so-called 'lead country system' in the UN Commission on Sustainable Development (CSD), or the use of 'lead negotiators' and 'issue leaders' in negotiations on climate change (Delreux and Van den Brande 2013). The work of preparing and/or representing EU positions is informally divided among member states which have an interest in the issues at stake, which are interested or which just have the necessary skills to deal with these issues. In practice, this means that an EU position can be expressed by, for example, a Dutch official, speaking from behind a Swedish nameplate, on behalf of the EU.

Such an informal system has advantages for the EU: it guarantees continuity, it allows the burden of representing the EU to be shared, it allows for pooling the available expertise, and for involving interested member states in the international negotiation process (Delreux and Van den Brande 2013). Once such an informal representation system is established, it is quickly taken up by the actors in the EU and becomes standard practice (Cœuré and Pisani-Ferry 2007).

The rationale behind these informal systems is to increase the EU's effectiveness. This aim, however, is not always achieved. Whereas such an informal system works quite smoothly and cooperatively in negotiations that take place at the level of officials in so-called preparatory 'contact groups' or 'working groups' (which is the lion's share of international environmental negotiations), this is not the case once negotiations reach their end game and their salience increases. Indeed, informality in the EU's external representation arrangements is only effective up to a certain level of politicization. When ministers enter the scene – or even heads of state and government, as the 2009 Copenhagen conference on climate change witnessed – the informal and relatively well functioning system that is used when negotiations are conducted at the level of officials is set aside. It is then often replaced by an internal struggle regarding who should represent the EU, leading to European navel-gazing, which impedes outreach activities.

Indeed, the 'WTO formula', with the Commission speaking for the EU, is not necessarily the magic formula for all international fora. In some contexts, like the WTO, the EU performs rather well thanks to this arrangement, but in other fora, it is sometimes neither feasible nor functional – or it may even turn out to be counterproductive. Hence, the 'single voice' should not be considered an absolute mantra for EU foreign policy.

One of the strategies that seems to function better than the 'WTO formula' in many international negotiations is attempting to convey a single message through many negotiators and even diplomatic channels. For instance, this became clear under the UN framework in the UN General Assembly debate on the moratorium of the death penalty (Kissack 2012), in the UN Human Rights Council where the EU's operation 'as a bloc' undermines its ambitions to advance human rights objectives (Smith K. 2010a; Macaj 2011; see also Chapter 6) or in environmental negotiations where the EU may benefit from having multiple 'mouths' rephrasing and supporting the same 'voice' (Delreux 2011a: 172–4). One of the lessons drawn from the 2009 Copenhagen climate conference by European Climate Action Commissioner Connie Hedegaard is revealing in that regard: 'A lot of Europeans in the room is not a problem, but there is only an advantage if we sing from the same hymn sheet. We need to think about this and reflect on this very seriously, or we will lose our leadership role in the world' (in her hearing as candidate commissioner before the European Parliament in January 2010).

This is not only the case for 'low politics'. The same conclusion about the ineffectiveness of the single voice can be drawn from analyses of the EU's performance in 'high politics' areas, such as its participation in the Review conference of the Parties to the Treaty on the Non-Proliferation of Nuclear Weapons, where the EU performs well with regard to some agenda items by not employing the single voice strategy, but by opting for many European spokespersons and mobilizing diplomatic structures of the member states to convey the EU message (Dee 2012).

The EU and the UN

One of the main manifestations of the EU's commitment to effective multilateralism (see above) is the fact that the UN and its Charter are considered as a central point of reference in the foreign policy of the EU. Much more than any other international organization or institution, the UN and its principles are given 'overwhelming' attention in the EU Treaties (Wessel 2011b: 632). The EU has put forward an objective to contribute to the 'respect for the principles of the United Nations Charter' (Art. 3(5) TEU). Its action on the international scene 'shall be guided by ... respect for the principles of the United Nations Charter' (Art. 21(1) TEU) and it aims to 'preserve peace, prevent conflicts and strengthen international security, in accordance with the purposes and principles of the United Nations Charter' (Art. 21(2) TEU). In addition to these general objectives, the Treaty also refers to the UN, e.g. by making CSDP missions possible under a UN framework (see Chapter 8), or by emphasizing the strong correlation between the EU's own development cooperation and humanitarian aid policy on the one hand and the UN framework on the other hand (see Chapter 9).

The EU plays an important role in sustaining the UN, not only politically but also financially (for an overview of recent studies, see Bouchard and Drieskens 2013). Combined, the member states provide approximately 40 per cent of its regular budget, 50 per cent of contributions to UN funds and programmes and more than 40 per cent of UN peacekeeping operations. Moreover, the Commission contributes more than €1 billion in support of UN external assistance programmes and projects (EU Delegation to the UN 2012).

Since 2011, the EU enjoys a so-called 'enhanced observer status' at the UN General Assembly (UNGA), which implies that the EU enjoys the same rights to speak, make proposals and amendments, or circulate documents like full UN member states and that the only thing that distinguishes the EU from 'full' members is its inability to vote. It is, however, unclear what the impact of this enhanced observer status in the UNGA will be on the EU's status in other programmes, funds and organs of the UN. A first attempt to upgrade its status in the UN, dating from September 2010, failed rather painfully for the EU since its draft resolution was objected by other countries which were concerned about the effect of an enhanced status for the EU on other regional groups or organizations in the UN. These countries included, on the one hand, Caribbean and Latin American countries that benefit largely from EU development cooperation (see Chapter 9) and, on the other hand, countries with whom the EU established strategic partnerships (see Chapter 12). This indicates that these types of foreign policy initiatives do not necessarily increase the leverage of the EU over these countries. The EU's reattempt in 2011 has resulted in a 'watered down' resolution that fails to meet its original purpose because it only secures speaking rights for the permanent President of the European Council and the High Representative, but it does not give the EU sufficient legal leverage in the everyday work of the UNGA (Wouters *et al.* 2011).

Whereas all member states participate in the UNGA, only a few of them participate in the UNSC. Nor is the EU as such represented there, although it is possible for the HR/VP to make statements on behalf of the EU (see above). The UNSC is still dominated by intergovernmental dynamics with a major role for those member states that are serving in the UNSC and a minor one for the EU and its CFSP. The institutional set-up of the EU and its working practices do not seem to fit well with the EU's aspirations as global actor. They allow EU member states to 'act freely in a national capacity and may feel less bound by expectations that they should act collectively as the EU' (Smith K. 2010a: 224). Furthermore, information sharing between those EU member states that are UNSC members and those who are not, let alone EU coordination for the UNSC, is rather problematic (Blavoukos and Bourantonis 2011).

How would one evaluate the EU's relations with the UN? On the one hand, it is clear that the EU is an advocate of the UN through its financial commitment and rhetorical support. On the other hand, detailed scrutiny paints a less impressive picture of the EU's record in the UN. On the basis of a broad scale of case studies, Laatikainen and Smith concluded that the EU does not contribute to more effective UN multilateralism and that, in general, 'the intersection of EU and UN multilateralisms is dysfunctional' (2006a: 21–2). Moreover, the EU's influence falls well short of its economic and political weight. Two reasons explain this.

First, the EU struggles in relation to the UN reform process. Broadly speaking, it has supported the reforms proposed by the former UN Secretary General Kofi Annan to strengthen the UN. However, the member states have no common view on what is probably the most important aspect of UN reform: that of the Security Council. With the UK and France opposing any reform that challenges their privileged position as permanent members and with the Germans and Italians competing for their own permanent seats, a common position was clearly impossible (Blavoukos and Bourantonis 2011, 2013). Moreover, any talk of a common EU seat is merely theoretical (see Drieskens *et al.* 2014). At first sight, the EU has an interest in maintaining the status quo, since it currently is overrepresented in the UNSC with 2 of the 5 permanent members (France and the UK), as well as up to 3 of the 10 elected UNSC members being EU member states (2 from the Western European and Others Group and 1 from the Group of Eastern European States) (Emerson *et al.* 2011: 68). However, the EU's reluctance in the UN reform debate may undermine its legitimacy in its relationship with emerging powers, which are underrepresented in the UNSC.

Second, EU member states have proved reluctant to respond positively to the UN Secretary General's repeated request for them to provide more troops for UN peacekeeping operations in order to have more well-trained and well-equipped troops. The number of European soldiers deployed in UN peace operations has decreased considerably over the last few years (Laatikainen 2010). Although member states' reluctance is understandable in view of previous negative experiences with UN operations, this position makes the declaratory support for a stronger UN role in international security somewhat ambiguous. On the other hand, the EU supports and complements UN operations through various CSDP operations and through the assistance provided by the Instrument for

Stability and the African Peace Facility (see Hynek 2011; Knudsen 2013) (see Chapters 6 and 8). However, this type of EU support does not compensate for the poor performance of the UN blue helmets in various conflicts, as was demonstrated in the violent conflict at the border between the DR Congo and Rwanda in late 2012.

The EU and International Financial Institutions

Until recently, the EU demonstrated a systematic neglect of multilateralism in its attitude towards international financial institutions (IFIs) such as the IMF and the World Bank despite the major foreign policy implications of decisions adopted by these organizations. Whereas in the WTO the EU speaks with one voice and through one mouth, and in the UN it at least tries to get its act together, in the IFIs, the EU plays a less prominent role than one would expect, given its economic importance. Unified European representation is certainly out of the question today. This is not only true in the main IFIs, but also in more specific regimes on global financial governance, like those dealing with banking regulation, accounting standards or capital market regulation (Mügge 2011). The global financial crisis has not changed this observation, nor has it changed the member states' willingness to rely on the EU in these fora.

Part of the explanation for the EU's problems in dealing with the IFIs is the complicated institutional set-up at both the EU/EMU and the IMF/World Bank side. The external representation of the EMU is complex (see Glöckler and Truchlewski 2011), leading to a cacophony of voices on the part of European states, with the Commission, the rotating Presidency of the ECOFIN Council (Ministers of Economics and Finance of all EU member states), the presidency of the Eurogroup (including only the ministers from the eurozone countries), the European Central Bank (ECB) and the member states all playing a role. This reflects the internal ambiguities and divisions regarding the EMU and related issues within the EU. Not all member states have adopted the euro, and the responsibility for the monetary policy of eurozone members is assumed by the ECB but for exchange rate competences it is shared between the ECB and the Eurogroup, and broader economic competences are shared between all member states and the EU (Gstöhl 2009). Moreover, the adoption in 2012 of the Treaty on Stability, Coordination and Governance in the EMU (the 'Fiscal Compact'), to which only 25 member states participate, shows that financial issues are increasingly the subject of differentiated integration in the EU (see Holzinger and Schimmelfennig 2012).

The EU is not directly represented in the Executive Board of the IMF, which is responsible for the day-to-day operations of the Fund. The ECB has only an observer status for those agenda items with relevance to it, but there is no formal representation role for the presidencies of ECOFIN or the Eurogroup, nor for the Commission (Emerson *et al.* 2011; Wouters and Van Kerckhoven 2013). In the absence of a single representation of the EU or the eurozone in the Executive Board, member states play a major role and are even overrepresented. They have a relatively high combined voting share of approximately 30 per cent, which exceeds the voting power of the US and, if used together, would allow the EU to form a blocking minority on a lot of issues. The 24 Executive Directors who make up the Executive Board each represent a so-called 'constituency' in the IMF. Three EU member states – the UK, Germany and France – have a single state constituency, meaning that they are always represented. Other member states are grouped in constituencies with colleague member states. A third group of member states share a constituency with non-European countries, like Spain being grouped with Latin American countries and also Ireland and Poland being part of a constituency that includes no other EU member states. Whereas this system allows for European overrepresentation on the Board, it is simultaneously an impediment for a more unified EU or EMU representation.

Internal coordination with regard to the IMF is rather weak and there is generally no coordinated stance on issues such as IMF country programmes, rescue packages for third countries or the far-reaching conditionality that the IMF imposes. The existing coordination efforts that take place are always in an EU setting and not in a eurozone format. Member states coordinate their views on IMF issues in two ways (Wouters and Van Kerckhoven 2013). First, quasi-monthly coordination meetings are organized in Brussels in the 'Subcommittee on the IMF and Related Issues' (SCIMF) within the Council, which prepares the Economic and Financial Committee (in which the ECB also participates). Second, the Executive Directors of the member states meet on a weekly basis on-the-spot in Washington, DC in so-called EURIMF meetings. Although 'they rarely agree on common positions' (Giovannini *et al.* 2012: 8), the on-the-spot EURIMF coordination meetings are considered to be more important than the Brussels-based SCIMF ones.

Given the limited performance of the EU, both in terms of representation and coordination, in an increasingly important international organization like the IMF, the question of a single EU or EMU seat has been on the table for a couple of years. The Commission and the European Parliament have repeatedly called for such a unified representation (see Commission 2008: 142–5; European Parliament 2011). Little progress has been made on this issue, although the Lisbon Treaty explicitly allows for this. Article 138(2) TFEU reads as follows: 'The Council, on a proposal from the Commission, may adopt appropriate measures to ensure unified representation within the international financial institutions and conferences. The Council shall act after consulting the European Central Bank'. The next paragraph clarifies that only eurozone members can vote on this in the Council. However, political obstacles remain: member states fear that a unified representation would bring an end to the European overrepresentation and that they would lose national prestige. Furthermore, the IMF's rules of the game remain state based. Finally, the question remains whether the EU – or the eurozone – should have one seat, or whether they should represent one constituency in the Executive Board (Glöckler and Truchlewski 2011: 130–2).

In the context of the financial crisis and the shift of power in the direction of the emerging powers, the European countries have come under pressure to accept a reduction of voting weight and seats in the IMF. The G20 Pittsburgh Summit of 2009 agreed upon a transfer of at least 5 per cent of the quota share in favour of the emerging powers and developing countries, which was confirmed one year later at the G20 of late 2010. The changes in quota share implied that China would become the third largest shareholder after the US and Japan, now leaving behind Germany, France and the UK. The top 10 shareholders included Italy, Russia and – for the first time – India and Brazil, meaning that it now includes four of the five BRICS. The European countries were also forced to commit themselves to cede two of their eight seats in the 24-seat Executive Board. The Europeans and the US were able to prevent any change in the political agreement that the respective heads of the IMF and the World Bank are automatically a European and an American, but it was clear that this tradition might very well come to an end in the future under the pressure of non-Western countries (Cherry and Dobson 2012; Wade 2011: 363–5).

These developments clearly demonstrate the gradually changing financial and political balance of power at the expense of the Europeans. This trend was also evident in mid-2012 when, in contrast to the US, the BRICS countries agreed to make a substantial contribution to the $460 billion IMF bailout fund, which was to serve as firewall to prevent contagion from the eurozone crisis (Emerson 2012). During their informal meeting ahead of the G20 summit in Mexico, the leaders of the BRICS countries emphasized that their new contributions to the IMF were being made 'in anticipation that all the reforms agreed upon in 2010 will be fully implemented in a timely manner, including a comprehensive reform of voting power and reform of quota' (Ministry of External Affairs India 2012).

The EU's participation in the World Bank resembles to a large extent the situation in the IMF. The World Bank plays a major role in development cooperation policies. The EU member states combined are the largest donor to the World Bank and they can jointly put more than 30 per cent of the voting weight on the table, but the EU is nevertheless not represented in the Board of Directors (Baroncelli 2013; Emerson *et al.* 2011). Whereas the ECB enjoys observer status at the IMF, it does not enjoy such status at the World Bank. Mirroring the IMF situation, France, Germany and the UK have the privilege of a single-state constituency in the Board whereas the other member states are scattered across a range of other constituencies. However, the internal coordination practices in the framework of the World Bank differ from those deployed in the IMF since coordination only takes place on the spot in Washington, DC and not in Brussels. Mirroring the gradual reforms in the IMF, in the World Bank the Europeans also had to accept a (still limited) reduction of its share in favour of an increase in the representation and influence of emerging powers (Wade 2011: 359–63).

The fact that the EU is not able to punch at its weight in the IFIs has quite serious implications for the effectiveness of EU foreign policy. The impact of the IFIs' prescriptions extends beyond the economic policy of third countries. Even if, economically, the IFI policies do have a positive effect over the longer term, they can have a highly negative impact on the societal and human security situation in third countries, on internal political developments and stability, and in some cases also on regional stability and security.

The EU tries to develop its own structural foreign policy towards third countries and regions, but it insufficiently acknowledges the far-reaching structural impact of the IFIs' policies. It seems that the EU has too readily adopted the IMF and World Bank recipes and integrated them within the EU's own policy. This reflects a broader pattern that we have already seen in previous chapters regarding the EU's trade policy – it promotes neo-liberal policies and pursues free trade agreements with third countries and regions often without due regard to their wider foreign policy implications.

In practice, particularly during the period of the 'Washington Consensus' (see Serra and Stiglitz 2008), the IFIs have systematically based their policies on the neo-liberal model of capitalism, with its focus on the market, the withdrawal of the state and the subordination of societal objectives and values to free market principles. This approach can be appropriate in some contexts, but it clearly does not work across the board. It is in this respect that the Europeans might have played a constructive role, because the European social–economic model has traditionally combined a free market economy with a larger role for the state and civil society actors, as well as with greater provision of safety nets and public services. This is not to advocate that the models used by European countries could be simply transplanted to other countries. However, they could have provided a source of inspiration for developing strategies of global governance.

Since the end of 2010, this mismatch between the approach by the IFIs and the European model has slightly diminished due to a shift in the policy focus of the IFIs, leading to a so-called 'post-Washington Consensus' (see Arrébola Rodríguez 2011; Murphy 2008). Under this new approach, a larger role is attributed to the state, as state intervention in, for example, the regulation of the financial system, the education system or the fight against poverty is no longer seen as something that should be avoided. However, referring to the 'European rescue of the Washington Consensus', Lütz and Kanke argue that '[t]he IMF may have carried much of the Washington Consensus to the grave, but the EU has revived a good deal of these policies' (Lütz and Kranke 2011: 7). They mainly refer to the joint EU–IMF loan programmes to EU member states as Hungary, Latvia, Romania, Greece and Ireland, which only partly reflect the Keynesian approach now promoted by the IMF.

The financial and sovereign debt crisis in Europe has also led to a fundamental shift in the EU's position in relation to the IFIs. Instead of being a potential policy-shaper in those fora, some European countries have now become recipients and the eurozone crisis has been raised on the agenda of the IMF (see also Della Posta and Talani 2011; Nousios *et al.* 2012). Indeed, the IMF started to play an increasingly important role in Europe in the context of the management of the financial and budgetary crisis in the eurozone. Three members of the eurozone – Greece, Ireland and Portugal – accessed IMF resources. In these countries, the IMF works closely together with the Commission and the ECB under the so-called 'troika' format. Poland and non-EU European countries – Kosovo, Serbia, Ukraine, Moldova and Macedonia – have also concluded arrangements with the IMF to arm themselves against the crisis. Furthermore, the IMF plays a monitoring role in the context of Spain's banking recapitalization programme that is conducted with European financial assistance (see IMF 2012).

Another consequence of financial and sovereign debt crisis in Europe was a growing pressure on the Europeans as well as the increasing resentment in non-Western countries against Europeans who, while pretending to be the champion of multilateralism, in fact mainly defended the old multilateral order in which they enjoyed privileged positions. The resentment and degradation of reputation of the EU in the Global South could be more harmful for the EU than the potential loss of some of its privileges (see Emerson 2012).

The EU and the G7/8 and G20

One of the main characteristics of recent developments in global governance is the growing importance of informal fora and non-binding decisions. The most visible manifestation of this trend is probably the so-called 'Gx system', consisting of a complex arrangement of gatherings at different levels – heads of state and government, ministers, central bank governors, diplomats, officials – in the G7, G8 and G20. Whereas the G7 still reflects the Western dominance characteristic of the twentieth century (enlarged to G8 when Russia joined the club in the 1990s), the G20 includes the emerging economic and political powers. This mirrored the changing balance of power in the early twenty-first century and the ambition of the emerging powers to reform the multilateral system of global financial and economic governance (Jokela 2011b; Wade 2011).

As the Gx is not mentioned in the European Treaties, there are no formal rules on the EU's participation or representation in these fora. The absence of formal institutional rules on the Gx system also means that the question whether the EU enjoys formal membership of the G7 and G8 is disputed. It is generally acknowledged that the EU is a 'fully accepted participant' that is 'generally treated on par with the real G8 members' (Niemann and Huigens 2011: 426). In contrast to its situation in the G7 and the G8, the EU is a full member of the G20. Irrespective of its formal status, the EU is the only non-state actor participating in the Gx system. In addition to the EU, the so-called 'EU4' – the UK, France, Germany and Italy – are all members of the G7, G8 and G20. Moreover, Spain is a permanent guest at the G20 and the Netherlands has been invited to attend G20 meetings. Along with these member states with a privileged position, the EU is represented as follows in the Gx (see Emerson *et al.* 2011: 105–8; Debaere and Orbie 2013: 313):

- in the G7, which principally discusses financial and monetary issues, the President of the ECB and sometimes the president of the Eurogroup participate (representing the eurozone, not the whole EU) when issues related to their competences are on the table;
- when the G8 meets at the level of heads of state and government ('G8 summits'), the EU is represented jointly by the President of the European Council and the President of the Commission. Whereas the former takes the lead in preparing the G8 on behalf of the EU, the latter does so for the G20. The exact division of labour between the two presidents is usually determined on a case-by-case basis. At the ministerial level, the EU representation is led by the responsible commissioner (or by the HR/VP when CFSP issues are debated), occasionally accompanied by the responsible minister from the rotating Council Presidency. Generally speaking, the role of the Commission in the G8 has grown in the last decades (Niemann and Huigens 2011), although the President of the European Council now also plays an important role, based on the increased activity of the European Council in this area since 2009;
- this system is largely mirrored in the G20: the Commission and European Council presidents represent the EU jointly at G20 summits, whereas at lower levels various configurations are used comprising representatives from the Commission, the rotating Presidency and/or the ECB. Since the G20 started to convene at the level of heads of state and government in the context of the global financial crisis in November 2008, the EU has established a rather strong internal coordination system for the G20. This contrasts with the situation at the G7 and G8, where EU coordination is low and mostly limited to briefing by the Commission (Wouters *et al.* 2013b).

The way the EU is present in the Gx is challenged both from inside and outside the EU (Debaere and Orbie 2013). First, smaller member states, which are not able to participate directly in the Gx, envy the privileged position of the EU4, which echoes discussions on the advantaged position of bigger member states in the IMF, World Bank or the UNSC (see above). Second, non-European countries criticize the overrepresentation of 'Europe' in the G7 and G8, arguing that the presence of four member states and the EU around a table of fewer than 10 participants no longer reflects today's global power distribution.

The EU seems to succeed in playing a major role in the Gx since it is able to contribute substantive knowledge, financial resources and the special relations some of its member states have with third countries (e.g. the ACP countries, see Chapter 9) to the Gx process (Debaere and Orbie 2013). Moreover, the EU has a strong implementation record of its G20 commitments, which has reinforced its position (Wouters *et al.* 2013b). The EU perceived the G20 as a useful venue to promote its agenda and, from 2008 on, to tackle the financial crisis. However, the financial and sovereign debt crisis in Europe resulted in a shift in the EU's role and importance within the various Gx negotiations, as this crisis dominated the Gx's agenda meeting after meeting. The Europeans were no longer part of the solution, but part of the problems that were to be tackled through the Gx. This provided the perfect context for the emerging powers and the US to get decisions agreed upon during the subsequent G20 meetings to tackle the aforementioned overrepresentation of European states in the IFIs (Wade 2011).

A final question is how the rise of the Gx relates to the EU's commitment to effective multilateralism. The answer seems to be qualified. On the one hand, multilateral processes can be reinforced or stimulated by guidance from the Gx. But on the other hand, there is also the risk that in practice the Gx takes over the role of other more inclusive multilateral fora and increasingly sidelines international organizations like the UN.

Competing Multilateralisms

An additional challenge emerging for the EU is the rising importance of other multilateral settings in which the EU is largely absent and in which competing conceptions of multilateralism are cherished (Keukeleire and Bruyninckx 2011; Keukeleire and Hooijmaaijers 2014). Figure 13.1 gives an overview of the main overlapping, partially competing or complementary, multilateral frameworks in the Southern hemisphere and the Asia-Pacific area in particular. They reflect a general shift in the international balance of power, with the centre of gravity moving from the Euro-Atlantic to the Asia-Pacific area and from the North and West to the South and East (see Mahbubani 2008, 2013).

It is beyond the scope of this book to discuss each of these 'emerging powers alliances' (Bava 2011) and variations on Asian regionalism (see Novotny and Portela 2012; Stubbs and Beeson 2012). However, three examples can help to illustrate their diverse nature as well as their potential impact on the EU (for *IBSA*, see Chapter 12). First, the *Asia-Pacific Economic Cooperation* (APEC) brings together 21 states, including major powers such as China, the US and Russia and emerging or mid-sized powers in Asia and America – accounting together for 40 per cent of the world's population, 44 per cent of world trade and 54 per cent of world GDP (Bisley 2012). Crucially, it links the US – still the largest global political, economic and military power – with the increasingly important Asian continent. A second example is the *BRICS* framework, launched in 2008 and covering four continents, which allows Brazil, Russia, India, China and South Africa to enter into regular dialogue and counter Western dominance in international financial and economic governance (in particular by preparing and influencing meetings within the G20, IMF and World Bank) (Gowan 2012) (see also the previous sections). Finally, climate change policies have been coordinated through the *BASIC* format, including Brazil, South Africa, India and China. The BASIC format was conducive to negotiating a deal at the 2009 Copenhagen climate change conference with the US and ultimately sidelining the EU (Hallding *et al.* 2011) (see Chapter 10).

On the whole, a new constellation of networks has emerged in which the EU or its member states are mostly not represented. The Europeans are involved in only two of these fora. First, the EU is a member of the ASEAN Regional Forum (ARF), established to foster consultation on political and security issues of common interest and contribute to confidence-building and preventive diplomacy in the Asia-Pacific region (Yuzawa 2012). Second, and more important for the EU, is the Asia–Europe Meeting (ASEM), initiated as an informal process of dialogue among 19 Asian countries, all EU member states, the European Commission and the ASEAN Secretariat. However, ASEM 'failed to stamp its own purpose on region-to-region relations' and fulfil initial expectations (Gilson 2012: 404; see also Doidge 2011: 113–44). As was highlighted in Chapter 12, the EU also had problems using its so-called 'strategic partnerships' with various of the emerging powers in the region to further its own interest and forge real strategic partnerships.

None of these variations on Asian regionalism and emerging power alliances is as such very influential. However, taken together, they have two major consequences for the EU and its commitment to multilateralism. First, Asian or Southern countries have clearly also made 'the choice for multilateralism'– just like the Europeans. However, it is a choice based on fundamentally different principles, in many ways resembling the American position on the issue (Keukeleire *et al.* 2011: 7–8). In terms of substance, they prioritize economic growth and development, with a

Figure 13.1   Competing constellations of power and forms of multilateralism centred around the BRICS

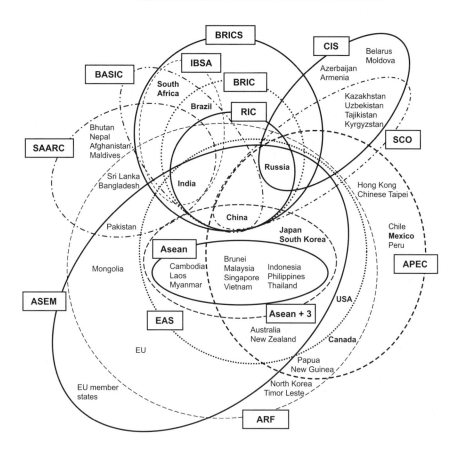

APEC: Asia-Pacific Economic Cooperation
ARF: ASEAN Regional Forum
ASEAN: Association of South East Asian Nations
ASEAN+3: ASEAN + Japan, Korea, China
ASEM: Asia-Europe Meeting
BASIC: Brazil, South Africa, India, China
BRIC: Brazil, Russia, India, China
BRICS: Brazil, Russia, India, China, South Africa
CIS: Commonwealth of Independent States

EAS: East Asia Summit
IBSA: India, Brazil, South Africa
RIC: Russia, India, China
SAARC: South Asian Association for Regional Cooperation
SCO: Shanghai Cooperation Organisation

Countries in bold are considered by the EU as 'strategic partners'

Source: Own design based on Yannick Schoensetters, Stephan Keukeleire and Hans Bruyninckx. In: Keukeleire and Bruyninckx (2011: 400).

reluctance to let economic issues be restricted by concerns that Europeans regularly emphasize, such as human rights or environmental and social protection. In terms of approach, they adopt a purely inter-governmental method, characterized by consensus decision-making, voluntary commitments and respect for national sovereignty. This contrasts with the European preference for legally binding commitments and strong international regimes. Whereas the EU had hoped at the start of the millennium that its model of 'effective multilateralism' would gradually become the global standard and that it would increasingly be a core actor within this multilateral system (see Laatikainen and Smith 2006b), the EU now sees itself gradually marginalized with regard to the way the international scene is structured.

Second, Europeans often dismiss these various fora for dialogue and cooperation as insignificant because of the often substantial differences among participating countries and the lack of binding commitments. However, looking at the agendas and outcomes of these fora, it appears that they jointly constitute a dense set of partially overlapping formal and informal networks, on all political, diplomatic and administrative levels, covering an ever-widening scope of policy areas. Taken together, they increasingly inform and impact upon national policies and positions, including in international negotiation processes where the EU feels the impact of these 'competing multilateralisms'.

Conclusion

The EU's discourse systematically highlights that the EU and multilateralism go hand in hand: effective multilateralism is one of the fundamental foreign policy choices of the EU. A more nuanced picture emerges, however, when analysing the EU's actual behaviour towards and in international organizations and regimes. In some cases, such as environmental governance, the EU manages to act as a leader or at least bridge-builder in promoting multilateralism. However, in other cases the EU has many more problems, or simply fails, both in asserting itself as a champion of multilateralism and in promoting its interests.

There are many reasons that explain the largely varied position and performance of the EU in international organizations and regimes. These include the internal convergences and divergences between the EU institutions and EU member states; the status of the member states in these organizations and fora, which member states in general do not like to see threatened; the EU's legal status in the various international organizations; and the nature of internal coordination and external representation mechanisms. More fundamentally, the EU faces a dual challenge. Fuelled by the financial and sovereign debt crisis in Europe, the EU is facing decreasing legitimacy and influence in the IFIs and the G7/8/20. Added to this is the emergence in the South and Asia-Pacific region of competing multilateral fora in which the Europeans are largely absent and in which competing views on multilateralism and global governance are cherished.

Chapter 14

Conclusions: Theorizing EU Foreign Policy

To conclude, we turn to the implications of this book's findings for both International Relations and European integration theories. This chapter aims to provide some stepping stones that can be used for a further and deeper theoretical analysis of the EU's foreign policy and the politics behind it. We consider these theoretical frameworks as lenses through which EU foreign policy and the political dynamics that drive it can be better understood and explained. None of these lenses provide 'right' or 'wrong' answers, but they do offer useful analytical insights that allow for making sense of what we empirically observe. We cannot provide a systematic overview of the vast corpus of theoretical literature. Theoretical analyses as well as summaries can be found in the works of, *inter alia*, Andreatta (2011), Irondelle *et al.* (2011), Kratochvil and Tulmets (2010); Kurowska and Breuer (2012). Neither do we present an exhaustive overview of theoretical approaches, as a result of which we do not discuss useful approaches such as foreign policy analysis (Larsen 2009), discourse analysis (Gariup 2010; Jokela 2011a), network analysis (Mérand *et al.* 2011), governmentality theory (Merlingen 2011) or critical theories (Bailey 2011; Canterbury 2010; Oikonomou 2012).

Rather, we combine our conclusions with a brief evaluation of the relevance of some main International Relations (neo-realism, neo-liberalism), European integration (liberal intergovernmentalism, neo-functionalism, new institutionalism) and constructivist approaches. As these are all large schools of thought, with different subsections, trends and interpretations, the approach taken here is necessarily generalized and selective.

We also evaluate the conceptual framework which we proposed in Chapter 1 by developing a 'structural foreign policy versus relational foreign policy' continuum. Here we assess how this conceptualization links with other theoretical approaches and to what extent these concepts can contribute to our understanding of what foreign policy is. We finish with some critical comments on the field of (EU) foreign policy analysis.

International Relations Theories

The very development of EU foreign policy over the last two decades runs counter to the (neo-)realist argument (see Bendiek 2012; Hyde-Price 2012, 2013; Rynning 2011; Wohlforth 2012) that, since foreign, security and defence policy lie at the heart of national sovereignty, states will not integrate in these fields and an international organization itself cannot have a foreign policy. As we have shown in many of the preceding chapters, the EU today has an extensive foreign policy apparatus, including a complex civilian and even military institutional set-up, and a range of civilian and military instruments. In line with neo-liberal perspectives (see Doyle 2012; Jørgensen and Aarstad 2013; Lamy 2011), the EU has proved that it can act as a relatively autonomous force which influences the behaviour of third actors outside Europe, which in some policy areas has a substantive impact on the international environment and which is an important player in the complex set of multilateral institutions. As was argued in Chapter 9, it was the EU (in conjunction with NATO) and not individual member states (even the most powerful) that played the pivotal role in one of the West's major foreign policy successes of the last decades: the sustainable transformation and stabilization of 10 Central and Eastern Europe countries and, since the late 1990s, of the Western Balkan countries. Member states also accepted the EU being involved and taking the lead in, for example, developing and implementing a policy towards Somalia, which included the fight against piracy and support for Somali combat troops (Chapter 6). Further foreign policy achievements discussed in Chapters 7 and 10, including diplomatic successes between Serbia and Kosovo and the EU's leadership attempts on environmental affairs, are testimony to the impact that an actor like the EU can have. Many of these successes were particularly pertinent given the vehement opposition of other major world powers.

However, when the agenda turned to issues of survival and the use of hard military power, neo-realist arguments started to look more convincing. EU foreign policy has been thrown into disarray in crises and wars (Iraq) or has been partially sidelined by the largest member states and/or by NATO (Libya). In these cases, the balance of power at the international level and the uneven distribution of capabilities between member states has determined the outcome and the (in)action of the EU. Moreover, Chapters 1 and 7 demonstrated that at least initially, member states saw CFSP less as a way to construct a common EU policy than as a national foreign policy tool to achieve interrelational goals by controlling their fellow member states.

Although member states gradually agreed to develop military capabilities within the EU framework, they remained averse to renouncing their sovereignty. Many were reluctant to allow the EU to do more in civilian or military crisis management than was useful for, or complementary to, their national policies, NATO and the predominance of the transatlantic security architecture in particular. In a similar vein, we saw in Chapter 13 that while member states were happy for the EU to pronounce its 'choice of multilateralism', they are not very eager to give the EU the status or representation arrangements in international fora to actually translate this statement into reality.

European Integration Theories

The development of EU foreign policy is also a matter of discussion among European integration theorists. One of the primary questions revolves around the impact of the various actors on the development and functioning of EU foreign policy. From an intergovernmentalist perspective, EU foreign policy is essentially driven by the member states, by their national interests and by intergovernmental bargains (see Eilstrup-Sangiovanni 2006; Gegout 2010; Hofmann 2012; Puetter 2012).

Member states' ability to reach 'history-making decisions' is understood as the key to the development of EU foreign, security and defence policies. As demonstrated in Chapter 2, this argument can be persuasive if we take a historical overview of the process. Member states' agreements have been crucial in driving EU foreign policy forward: from informal agreements at the outset of EPC in the early 1970s to breakthroughs on CSDP since the late 1990s. These agreements between member states were initially often informal (or political) and were then formally (or legally) codified the Treaties. Reflecting the balance of power between member states, substantive changes in sensitive issues have only proved possible once a preliminary understanding could be reached among the three most powerful member states, and between the UK and France in particular (see Chapter 8). The corollary of this is that developing a robust EU foreign policy with regard to crucial issues (such as the Libya crisis and relations with Russia and China) has been impeded by the failure of intergovernmental bargaining to find a consensus.

However, the development of EU foreign policy equally provides examples of 'history-making decisions' and grand bargains being less 'history-making' or 'grand' than they appear at first sight. Thus, while on paper it seemed that the Maastricht Treaty's CFSP was to send the EU down an exciting new foreign policy route, in fact it was the then first pillar (which we now call the EU's external action or the external dimension of internal policies) that, at least initially, remained the policy-makers' main site for foreign policy elaboration. Furthermore, the liberal intergovernmentalists' argument that the need to make concessions to the least compromising governments drives agreements towards the lowest common denominator is contested by the practice of EU foreign policy-making. Both the development of the EU foreign policy mechanism in broad terms and the EU's specific policies towards other regions, countries and issues indeed go much further than a rational assessment of member states' national interests would suggest. Certain dynamics ensure that even in the still intergovernmentally organized CFSP/CSDP, the limitations of consensus-orientated decision-making can be overcome. One explanation is the dynamic generated by institutional actors and mechanisms – both in CFSP/CSDP and in the EU's external action and the external dimension of internal policies. Another explanation is the informal division of labour and partial segmentation of EU foreign policy, with small groups of member states working together and with institutional actors to shape policy (see Chapters 4 and 13).

It is also in this context that propositions of new institutionalism in its various forms are interesting (see Breuer 2012; Elgström and Pilegaard 2008; Furness 2013; Hofmann 2012; Juncos 2011; Menon 2011b; Mérand 2012; Peters D. 2010; Petrov 2011; Thomas 2012; Weiss 2011; Wolff 2012). As new institutionalist approaches argue, the EU's expanding foreign policy institutional mechanisms clearly matter and affect the content, scope and impact of its foreign policy. Chapters 2 and 3 showed that the gradual institutionalization of CFSP/CSDP – adding to the already strong institutional framework of the other facets of the EU's foreign policy (i.e. external action and the external dimension of internal policies) – has led to new mechanisms to define, defend, promote and represent common EU interests, and to develop and implement common policies from this European perspective. Institutional frameworks, with their constituting rules and norms, provide the appropriate setting for member states to accept constraints on their behaviour – and thus to compromise – in order to pursue better their foreign policy interests. However, these and other chapters have also illuminated the fact that there are limits to this institutionalization process and that member states are often to find a balance between their national interest and their European responsibilities.

Within one specific branch within new institutionalism, principal–agent scholars have portrayed and explained the relations between various EU institutions, and more particularly between those who delegate powers (the member states in the Council) and those that represent them at the international level, such as the Commission, the EEAS, or the rotating Presidency (see da Conceição-Heldt 2011; Delreux 2011b; Dür and Elsig 2011; Kerremans 2006; Klein 2011; Niemann and Huigens 2011). Principal–agent analyses teach us something about reasons why member states-as-principals work through these common institutions in foreign policy (such as creating bargaining/market power, maximizing credibility or just making foreign policy activities more feasible). Besides, they have also helped us to understand the level of autonomy enjoyed by European representatives or negotiators at the international level vis-à-vis the member states at the EU level, which in turn contributes to our understanding of who is pulling the strings in the EU's foreign policy. Heterogeneity in member state preferences, a compelling international context that exerts pressure on the EU or a relatively low level of politicization are typical factors that contribute to a more autonomous – and thus more powerful – agent and, consequently, to member states losing control over foreign policy.

As our discussion on the 'single voice' in Chapter 13 has demonstrated, a more autonomous agent *in* the EU does not necessarily lead to a stronger influence or effectiveness *of* the EU at the international level. Assessing and measuring influence is very difficult and methodologically challenging in many subfields of political science. However, examining how the EU is 'performing' internationally may be an interesting and feasible way out (Jørgensen *et al.* 2011), as this takes into account the EU's goal achievement, relevance, efficiency and financial viability.

EU foreign policy to some extent also supports the historical institutionalists' idea that institutions create path dependencies and that historical participation in the EC/EU plays a role in the formation of national objectives. As argued in Chapter 5, participation in EU foreign policy-making leads member states to develop foreign policy objectives on issues and countries on which they previously had no policy. Chapter 6 also provides examples of this: the majority of member states would without the EU never have been involved in implementing a Strategy for the Sahel region or a Strategy for the Horn of Africa. Historical institutionalists also argue that decisions can evolve in a way that surpasses the original intention and that creates unintended consequences. Hence, as argued in Chapters 2 and 9, the Commission was able to use its 1957 Rome Treaty powers in the fields of trade and entering into contractual agreements with third countries to develop a fledgling foreign policy, even though this had not originally been foreseen. In the same sense, the EU's external action now includes crisis management instruments and activities which were initially not at all forecasted (see Chapter 6). Finally, historical institutionalism also emphasizes that institutions are 'sticky' and difficult to change. Although the EU treaties have modified and strengthened the institutional foreign policy architecture of the EU, the various difficulties and drawbacks identified in Chapters 3 and 4 demonstrate that often old habits still prevail and institutional development never starts from scratch.

This observation on incrementalism brings us to neo-functionalism, which receives surprisingly little attention in the EU foreign policy literature. According to neo-functionalist logic, EU foreign policy has at least partially been driven forwards by the internal dynamic of integration. This dynamic is based both on the impulse provided by activist non-state actors which act as policy entrepreneurs or as 'engines of integration' (such as the Commission or the EEAS) and on the mechanism of functional spillover (with measures in one policy field leading to pressure for integration and measures in other policy fields) (see Niemann and Schmitter 2009). Concerning the first point, there are clear examples of major foreign policy initiatives which would not have been adopted, or which would not have been discussed in the same way, without the Commission's entrepreneurship. Examples from Chapters 8, 10 and 11 include the EU's long-term strategies towards third countries and regions, including enlargement, and towards 'new' foreign policy challenges, such as energy supply initiatives and security related research. The same holds true for the EEAS if we look at the above mentioned strategies on the Horn of Africa and the Sahel region. But, as intergovernmentalists have taught us, this neo-functionalist argument has limits – member states have been careful to make foreign and security policy subject to an intergovernmental policy-making method and have happily risked limiting the substance of EU foreign policy output in return for confining the Commission's, HR/VP's and EEAS's pretensions.

While the entrepreneurial role of the Commission and other actors is one explanation for the increasing scope of EU foreign policy, a further reason is that the traditional realm of foreign policy is increasingly intertwined with other policy areas. Chapters 7 to 9 have provided ample illustration of this point: security policy is no longer just about soldiers, but also about training police forces and organizing rule-of-law missions, as well as about border protection and migration flows; development cooperation agreements are no longer just about fighting poverty, but also about counter-terrorism and good governance; technology and the environment are no longer just internal policy domains or areas of international cooperation on these transboundary issues, but now also foreign policy and security concerns. However, this functional spillover effect is not always inevitable – or at least it does not always lead to more integration in the classic sense. Indeed, functional spillover in foreign policy can also lead to less far-reaching coordination or cooperation – possibly between a limited number of member states – rather than expanding integration.

Constructivism: Ideas, Values and Identity

In contrast to rationalist accounts of EU foreign policy, constructivism focuses on immaterial dimensions such as ideas, values, roles and identity (see Aggestam 2013; Breuer 2012; Flockhart 2012; Jørgensen and Aarstad 2013; Kurowska and Kratochvil 2012; Meyer and Strickmann 2011; Tonra 2003; Waever 2000). These are considered not only as influencing EU foreign policy, but also as providing the constitutive elements of EU foreign policy. From this perspective, developing EU foreign policy depends not only, or not in the first place, on the creation of an effective institutional framework, on acquiring foreign policy instruments, or even on defining common interests. Rather, it hinges on the emergence – or absence – of a shared understanding among EU member states' elites and populations about what should be the EU's role in the world and about which values it should sustain, promote and defend. In Chapter 5 we thus discussed the role of socialization and related Europeanization processes even though it was argued that this should not be overstated. One of the reasons is that member states are equally subject to other socialization processes outside the EU and therefore do not necessarily converge in terms of their world-view, role conception and identity.

In various chapters we have indicated that a shared normative and cognitive framework is being gradually developed within the EU on some issues and is reflected in the values it promotes on the international stage. According to the preamble to the Treaty on European Union, member states are resolved to implement a CFSP, 'thereby reinforcing the European identity'. In Chapter 1 and throughout this book, it appeared that pursuing identity objectives was just as important as a desire to realize external objectives in the development of EU foreign policy. In Chapter 6 we showed that the EU's objectives include promoting international cooperation, developing democracy and the rule of law, and respect for human rights and fundamental freedoms. Consolidating these values within the EU and then promoting them externally are defining elements of the EU's identity.

Analysts of the EU as a normative power – an actor whose foreign policy is driven by identity and values rather than interests – can find ample evidence to support their claims in the growing role of political conditionality in agreements with third countries, in the insertion of social clauses such as labour rights or environmental clauses in multilateral agreements, and in the creation of specific instruments to promote democracy and human rights (see Chapters 6 and 9). However, the picture is not so clear-cut (see Lucarelli and Manners 2006; Sjursen 2006; Whitman 2011). While values are undoubtedly a cornerstone of EU foreign policy, the EU and its member states are just as quick to protect their narrow self-interests and geostrategic interests – the EU's policies with regard to Russia and the Gulf states being examples (see Chapter 12).

The constructivist emphasis on ideas and identities provides some insight into the main successes and failures of EU foreign policy, as discussed in Chapter 9. EU foreign policy's primary success to date relates to redefining the identity of the Central and Eastern European countries. And, at its core, the EU's current foreign policy priority in the Western Balkans is to transform the perceptions held by societies and individuals about each other, to change their identity and to alter the norms and values that sustain their actions. From this perspective, the essence of EU foreign policy is about transforming the identity of other entities and about shaping ideas held about 'the other'. Arguably, the debate about the EU's relationship with Turkey is first and foremost centred on issues of identity and values. Interests, power and institutional set-ups are not unimportant, but they nevertheless play second fiddle.

However, the four decades of cooperation in the field of foreign policy and the 25-year-old endeavour to construct a common policy have only managed to reshape national foreign policy identities to a limited extent. Despite a strengthened shared normative framework, foreign policy interventions and even some successes, differences in power and in interests remain crucial to explaining member states' foreign policy and whether a common EU foreign policy is achievable.

Structural Foreign Policy

This book presented the 'structural foreign policy versus relational foreign policy' framework as a lens through which to conceptualize foreign policy, including that of the EU. Employing this approach throughout the preceding chapters had several advantages. Most importantly, the structural foreign policy concept allows us to accentuate what is too often neglected in the analysis of foreign policy: influencing and shaping structures – defined as relatively permanent organizing principles, institutions and norms – can be the main objective of foreign policy. The concept of structural foreign policy goes beyond concepts like 'Europeanization', 'external governance' or 'diffusion' (Börzel and Risse 2012b; Lavenex and Schimmelfennig 2009b, 2010) (see Box 9.1), which are used in research on the transferral of EU rules beyond EU borders, because it firmly embeds the focus on structures within the analysis of foreign policy, which broadens its potential applicability. As Chapters 11 and 12 highlighted, the relational versus structural foreign policy conceptualization can indeed also be used as a basis for a comparative analysis of the foreign policies of the EU, US, Russia, China and middle powers such as Turkey or Saudi Arabia.

The structural foreign policy versus relational foreign policy approach also provides some explanations for the successes and failures of the EU's foreign policies. We recall here three basic features that need to be present to make structural foreign policy work and that also appeared in the preceding chapters. First, to increase its likelihood of success, structural foreign policy must be complemented by relational foreign policy that also tackles hard security issues. Conversely, relational foreign policy must be complemented by structural foreign policy. This resonates with neo-realist and neo-liberal perspectives on foreign policy. Indeed, EU structural foreign policy towards the CEECs and the Western Balkans could be a success because the military security dimension was being dealt with by NATO. But, if the EU and other international

---

> **Box 14.1**   **The interrelationship between sectors and levels: the example of rule-of-law promotion**
>
> Through its policies that focus on the promotion of rule of law in third countries, the EU provides legal, operational and financial assistance to reform or shape the judiciary in these countries, for instance through so-called 'technical assistance' or in the framework of civilian CSDP missions. This assistance for structural reforms can be situated in the 'legal sector/state level' cell in the matrix in Figure 1.2.
>
> However, achieving sustainable results also depends on the structures in other sector/level cells (see Keukeleire 2013: 68–9; Metais *et al.* 2013), such as the:
>
> - economic sector/individual level cell (e.g. the guaranteed availability of decent salaries for judges);
> - economic sector/state level cell (e.g. state revenues and the guaranteed availability of a budget to pay these salaries);
> - economic sector/global level cell (e.g. the rules imposed by the IMF on public expenditure);
> - security sector/individual level cell (e.g. guarantees for the personal security of judges); and
> - legal sector/societal level cell (e.g. 'rule of law' being considered as a legitimate principle in the society).

organizations had not provided a structural foreign policy, the results of NATO's successful intervention in the Western Balkans in the 1990s would most probably not have been sustainable. Also the corollary of this proved true: EU structural foreign policy with regard to the Palestinian territories has been a failure because no actor has been able to resolve the relational foreign policy issues at stake.

Second, a successful structural foreign policy requires the various interrelated sectors and levels being taken into account (see Figure 1.2), as the EU has successfully done in its foreign policy towards the CEECs (and in the future possibly also the Western Balkans). Conversely, not taking into account the interconnectedness between sectors and levels can explain why measures in support of structural changes do not lead to sustainable results (see Box 14.1 for the example of interrelated sectors and levels in the promotion of rule of law). Equally undermining the effectiveness and legitimacy of a structural foreign policy is a one-sided focus on some structural reforms (for instance, the need to democratize political structures) while neglecting others that can be considered as more urgent (for instance, the need to pursue economic reforms that allow for more welfare for the local population).

Third, reflecting constructivist perspectives, the extent to which a structural foreign policy also tackles immaterial factors (in addition to

---

Box 14.2   Do it yourself: how to analyse structural foreign policy

Analyses on 'structural foreign policy' are to start from research questions that reflect the two core dimensions of 'structural': structures and sustainability (see Chapter 1). Research questions should indeed focus on the extent to which a foreign policy is aimed at, and is successful in, influencing or shaping *structures* in a *sustainable* way, as well as on the factors that explain this. This can lead to several sub-questions that inquire into the various material and immaterial factors discussed in Chapter 1, which in their turn are translated in various hypotheses that are then tested through empirical research (see also the suggestions below). These sub-questions can also inquire into the interrelationship between a limited number of sections of the matrix presented in Figure 1.2 (see also Box 14.1).

An analysis of structural foreign policy can focus on and differentiate between the different stages of the policy process:

- policy objectives and agenda-setting: to what extent do the declaratory objectives point to the intention to sustainably influence structures? Through which actors and factors and through which mechanisms is the shaping of structures in specific countries or regions put on the political agenda?
- policy-making: the usual research questions with regard to the EU's foreign policy-making process can be applied to the analysis of structural foreign policy. These include, for example: which member states and EU institutional actors do promote or counter the development of a

→

---

the material factors) is critical: structures and structural changes must be seen as legitimate and they must be or become part of the belief system or identity of the people concerned in order to have sustainable effects. In Central and Eastern Europe, a large majority of the population and the elite wanted change after the end of the Cold War. While the costs associated with these changes might not have been palatable, they were accepted: not only because the EU offered a clear reward (i.e. entry into the EU), but also because the end goal was firmly rooted in the popular consciousness. The uprisings in the Arab world demonstrated that endogenous processes provided – more than expected – fertile ground for the structural changes that the EU was hoping for but that the EU's ENP itself could not induce. But the first democratic elections in the region showed that Islamic parties were seen as more legitimate and as resonating more with belief systems in Arab societies than explicitly Western-oriented parties.

Using the structural foreign policy versus relational foreign policy framework also throws up its own challenges. Because this book could only scrape the surface of the EU's often highly intricate structural foreign policies towards any given country/region, the conclusions structural foreign policy of the EU towards a specific country or region, and for what reasons? Which actors have been most influential in the policy-making process, and why? Under what circumstances do member states-as-principals choose to develop a structural foreign policy through the EU institutions-as-agents, and what level of autonomy do the Commission, the EEAS, the EU Delegations or CSDP actors in third countries enjoy in the implementation of this policy? Which (external) conditions need to be present in order to translate a particular institutional set-up into effectiveness?

- policy outputs: to what extent is the intention to influence structures reflected in making available adequate (a) policy instruments (such as diplomatic pressure, technical assistance or association agreements) (b) budgets and (c) staff (diplomats, civil servants, external agents, etc.), to implement the policy? And how can this be explained?
- policy implementation: to what extent are these instruments, budgets and staff also effectively used in practice (both in Brussels and in the third country or region) to influence structures? Which factors help to explain this?
- policy outcomes: to what extent is the intention to influence structures visible in (a) the policy results (what are the concrete results of the implementation of the policy?) (b) the effects (what are the actual effects in the third country or region?) and (c) the relevance (how relevant are these effects within the broader context in this country or region?) Under which conditions does this occur?

drawn have likewise been relatively generalized. The conceptual framework is particularly strong when applied systematically and in detail to a foreign policy and when the specific features of a third country or society can be brought into the equation. In practical terms, it can be difficult to obtain a sufficiently deep understanding of a foreign policy's structural impact on the third party. This also relates to the difficulty of analysing long-term changes, of isolating different variables and of identifying causal relations. Indeed, the difficulties in determining whether a desired change has been the result of an EU policy as distinct from other actors or factors are not inconsequential.

The previous paragraphs already spelled out elements of a future empirical and theoretical research agenda (see also Smith K. 2010b): detailed case studies of the EU's structural foreign policy towards specific countries or regions, and of the interrelationship with relational foreign policy; comparative studies of the impact of the structural foreign policy of the EU and other international actors; an analysis of the scope conditions for successful structural foreign policy; studies of the promotion and internalization of structural changes, including through insights from the external governance and diffusion literature (see Box 9.1); studies on the interaction between structural changes on the societal and state level and the implications for EU foreign policy; and the application of foreign policy analysis (FPA) on structural foreign policy (Keukeleire 2014a). As indicated in Chapter 1, the structural foreign policy framework and the matrix presented in Figure 1.2 can be used to develop more detailed, focused and in-depth research projects that analyse the foreign policy of the EU or other actors. In addition to the above-mentioned elements of a research agenda, Box 14.2 presents some further suggestions for a more detailed analysis.

The analysis of structural foreign policy also points to the need to adopt a clearer interdisciplinary approach, given the emphasis on the interrelated sectors (political, legal, social, economic, security) and levels (from the individual up to the global) and the pertinence of both material and immaterial factors. Indeed, a sound understanding of the EU's structural foreign policy means that analyses and concepts from various academic fields such as political science, economics, law, history, sociology or anthropology must be more systematically incorporated. Equally, our understanding would be heightened through greater cooperation with specialized sub-fields of IR and political science, such as globalization studies, security studies, democracy studies, development studies and, particularly, area studies. EU foreign policy analysis now too often occurs in isolation from these sub-fields, without the much needed intellectual cross-fertilization. Excellent examples of what cross-fertilization can look like are the studies on the EU's role in promoting or inhibiting democratization in the Mediterranean, incorporating insights from different research fields (Pace and Seeberg 2009; Cavatorta and Pace 2010a; Youngs 2010c).

Finally (EU) foreign policy analysts may become more conscious of the impact of what is effectively a Western academic hegemony characterized by 'Westphalian Eurocentrism', a reluctance of European scholars to deal with 'difference', and a limited input from non-Western scholars (Inayatullah and Blaney 2004; Kayaoglu 2010; Waever 1998). The limited input of Asian, Arab or African academics is problematic considering that EU foreign policy is to a large extent directed towards these continents and that, consequently, insights, concepts and approaches developed by these scholars might be indispensable for a serious assessment of Western foreign policy. The generally predominant inside-out analysis thus has to be complemented by an outside-in perspective, in which not the EU but the other region or society is the point of departure for analysing EU foreign policy and in which insights from non-Western scholars are integrated (Keukeleire 2014b) (see for example the analysis of China–EU relations in Pan 2012a). Adopting this outside-in perspective can also breathe new life into the analysis of EU foreign policy. This can help to deal with one of the major academic challenges for theorizing EU foreign policy in the twenty-first century: incorporating non-Western perspectives, and thinking about not only international relations but also foreign policy differently (see Acharya and Buzan 2010; Tickner and Blaney 2012; Tickner and Waever 2009).

References

Acharya, A. and Buzan, B. (2010) *Non-Western International Relations Theory: Perspectives on and beyond Asia* (Oxon.: Routledge).

Adebahr, C. (2009) *Learning and Change in European Foreign Policy: The Case of the EU Special Representatives* (Baden-Baden: Nomos).

— (2011) 'The comprehensive approach to crisis management in a concerted Weimar effort', *Genshagener Papiere*, 6, 1–18.

Adler, E. and Barnett, M. (eds.) (1998) *Security Communities* (Cambridge: Cambridge University Press).

Adomeit, H. (2012) 'Russia. ENP competitor' in Lannon, E. (ed.) *The European Neighbourhood Policy's Challenges* (Brussels: PIE Peter Lang), 381–409.

Aggestam, L. (2000) 'Germany' in Manners, I. and Whitman, R. (eds.) *The Foreign Policies of European Union Member States* (Manchester: Manchester University Press), 64–83.

— (ed.) (2008) 'Special issue: the EU as an ethical power', *International Affairs*, 84(1), 1–130.

— (2013) *European Foreign Policy and the Quest for a Global Role – Britain, France and Germany* (Oxon.: Routledge).

Alecu De Flers, N. (2012) *EU Foreign Policy and the Europeanization of Neutral States: Comparing Irish and Austrian Foreign Policy* (Oxon.: Routledge).

Alecu De Flers, N. and Müller, P. (2012) 'Dimensions and mechanisms of the Europeanization of member state foreign policy: state of the art and new research avenues', *Journal of European Integration*, 34(1), 19–35.

Al-Fattal Eeckelaert, R. (2013) *Transatlantic Trends in Democracy Promotion: Electoral Assistance in the Palestinian Territories* (Aldershot: Ashgate).

Allen, D. (2013) 'The EU and India: strategic partners but not a strategic partnership' in Christiansen, T., Kirchner, E. and Murray, P. B. (eds.) *The Palgrave Handbook of EU–Asia Relations* (Basingstoke: Palgrave Macmillan), 571–86.

Allen, D. and Hauri, A. (2011) 'The Euro-Arab dialogue, the Venice Declaration, and beyond: the limits of a distinct EC policy, 1974–89' in Möckli, D. and Maurer, V. (eds.) *European–American Relations and the Middle East. From Suez to Iraq* (Oxon.: Routledge), 92–107.

Allen, D. and Smith, M. (1990) 'Western Europe's presence in the contemporary international arena', *Review of International Studies*, 16(1), 19–37.

— (2012) 'Relations with the rest of the world', *Journal of Common Market Studies*, 50 (Annual Review), 162–77.

Alter, K. J. (2012) 'The global spread of European style international courts', *West European Politics*, 35(1), 135–154.

Anderson, E. A. (2010) 'It's a pirate's life for some: the development of an illegal industry in response to an unjust global power dynamic', *Indiana Journal of Global Legal Studies*, 17(2), 319–39.

Andersson, J. J. (2013) 'Defence industry and technology: a base for a more capable Europe' in Biscop, S. and Whitman, R. (eds.) *The Routledge Handbook of European Security* (Oxon.: Routledge), 105–14.

Andoura, S. (2011) 'A modern European external energy policy' in Lieb, J., Schwarzer, D. and Van Ondarza, N. (eds.) *The European Union in International Fora: Lessons for the Union's External Representation after Lisbon* (Baden-Baden: Nomos), 37–52.

— (2013) 'Energy security: a missing link between EU energy and foreign policies' in Biscop, S. and Whitman, R. (eds.) *The Routledge Handbook of European Security* (Oxon.: Routledge), 243–252.

Andreatta, F. (2011) 'The European Union's international relations: a theoretical view' in Hill, C. and Smith, M. (eds.) *International Relations and the European Union* (Oxford: Oxford University Press), 21–43.

Argomaniz, J. (2011) *The EU and Counter-Terrorism. Politics, Polity and Policies after 9/11* (Oxon.: Routledge).

— (2012) 'A rhetorical spillover? Exploring the link between the European Union Common Security and Defence Policy (CSDP) and the External Dimension in EU counterterrorism', *European Foreign Affairs Review*, 17(2/1), 35–52.

Argomaniz, J. and Rees, W. (2013) 'The EU and counter-terrorism' in Biscop, S. and Whitman, R. (eds.) *The Routledge Handbook of European Security* (Oxon.: Routledge), 225–34.

Arrébola Rodríguez, C.-A. (2011) 'From Washington Consensus to post-Washington Consensus: consequences in transition economies', *Journal on European Perspectives of the Western Balkans*, 3(1), 19–34.

Azzam, M. (2006) 'Islamism revisited', *International Affairs*, 82(6), 1119–32.

Bailes, A. J. K. and Depauw, S. (eds.) (2011) *The EU Defence Market: Balancing Effectiveness with Responsibility* (Brussels: Flemish Peace Institute).

Bailey, D. (2011) 'The European Union in the world: critical theories' in Wunderlich, J.-U. and Bailey, D. (eds.) *The European Union and Global Governance* (Oxon.: Routledge), 37–47.

Balfour, R. (2012) *Human Rights and Democracy in EU Foreign Policy. The Cases of Ukraine and Egypt* (Oxon.: Routledge).

Balfour, R., Bailes, A. J. K. and Kenna, M. (2012) 'The European External Action Service at work: how to improve EU foreign policy', *EPC Issue Paper*, 67.

Balossi-Restelli, L. M. (2011) 'Fit for what? Towards explaining Battlegroup inaction', *European Security*, 20(2), 155–84.

Baranovsky, V. and Utkin, S. (2012) 'Europe as seen from Russia', *Perspectives*, 20(2), 63–82.

Barbé, E. (2004) 'The evolution of CFSP institutions: where does democratic accountability stand?', *International Spectator*, 2, 47–60.

Barbé, E. and Herranz-Surrallés, A. (eds.) (2012) *The Challenge of Differentiation in Euro-Mediterranean Relations: Flexible Regional Cooperation or Fragmentation* (Oxon.: Routledge).

Baroncelli, E. (2013) 'The World Bank' in Jørgensen, K. E. and Laatikainen, K. V. (eds.) *Routledge Handbook on the European Union and International Institutions* (Oxon.: Routledge), 205–20.

Bartelt, S. (2012) 'ACP–EU Development Cooperation at a crossroads? One year after the second revision of the Cotonou Agreement', *European Foreign Affairs Review*, 17(1), 1–25.

Barysch, K. (2010) 'Should the Nabucco pipeline project be shelved?', *Centre for European Reform Policy Brief*.

Basu, S. (2012) 'The EU in the Human Rights Council' in Wouters, J., Bruyninckx, H., Basu, S. and Schunz, S. (eds.) *The European Union and Multilateral Governance: Assessing EU Participation in United Nations Human Rights and Environmental Fora* (Basingstoke: Palgrave), 86–102.

Baun, M. and Marek, D. (eds.) (2013) *The New Member States and the European Union: Foreign Policy and Europeanization* (Oxon.: Routledge).

Bátora, J. (2013) 'The "Mitrailleuse Effect": The EEAS as an Interstitial Organization and the Dynamics of Innovation in Diplomacy', *Journal of Common Market Studies*, 51(4), 598–613.

Bava, U. S. (2011) 'Emerging power alliances in perspective: IBSA, BRIC, BASIC' in Kornegay, F. and Masters, L. (eds.) *From BRIC to BRICS. Report on the Proceedings of the International Workshop on South Africa's Emerging Power Alliances* (Pretoria: Institute for Global Dialogue),

— (2013) 'The efficiency of the EU's External Actions and the EU–India relationship' in Telò, M. and Ponjaert, F. (eds.) *The EU's Foreign Policy: What Kind of Power and Diplomatic Action?* (Aldershot: Ashgate), 209–18.

Baylis, J. and Wirtz, J. (2007) 'Introduction' in Baylis, J., Wirtz, J., Gray, C. S. and Cohen, E. (eds.) *Strategy in the Contemporary World* (Oxford: Oxford University Press), 1–15.

Bechtel, M. M. and Schneider, G. (2010) 'Eliciting substance from "hot air": financial market responses to EU summit decisions on European defense', *International Organization*, 64(2), 199–223.

Behr, T. (2013) 'EU foreign policy and political Islam: towards a new entente in the post-Arab Spring era?', *International Spectator*, 48(1), 20–33.

Bekou, O. and Chadwick, M. (2011) 'The EU commitments to international criminal justice: achievements and possibilities' in Wetzel, J. E. (ed.) *The EU as a 'Global Player' in Human Rights?* (Oxon.: Routledge), 82–96.

Belyi, A. V. (2008) 'EU external energy policies: a paradox of integration' in Orbie, J. (ed.) *Europe's Global Role: External Policies of the European Union* (Aldershot: Ashgate), 203–216.

Bendiek, A. (2012) 'European realism in the EU's Common Foreign and Security Policy' in Cardwell, P. J. (ed.) *EU External Relations Law and Policy in the Post-Lisbon Era* (Basingstoke: Palgrave Macmillan), 35–58.

Benedetto, G. (2011) 'The European Parliament' in Wunderlich, J.-U. and Bailey, D. (eds.) *The European Union and Global Governance. A Handbook* (Oxon.: Routledge), 79–88.

Berg, C. (2012) 'Lebanon and Syria' in Peters, J. (ed.) *The European Union and the Arab Spring: Promoting Democracy and Human Rights in the Middle East* (Lanham: Lexington), 93–108.

Beyers, J. (2010) 'Conceptual and methodological challenges in the study of European socialization', *Journal of European Public Policy*, 17(6), 909–20.

Biava, A. (2011) 'The emergence of a strategic culture within the Common Security and Defence Policy', *European Foreign Affairs Review*, 16(1), 41–58.

Biava, A., Drent, M. and Herd, G. P. (2011) 'Characterizing the European Union's strategic culture: an analytical framework', *Journal of Common Market Studies*, 49(6), 1227–48.

Bicchi, F. (2006) 'Want funding? Don't mention Islam: EU democracy promotion in the Mediterranean', *CFSP Forum*, 4(2), 10–12.

— (2010) 'Dilemmas of implementation: EU democracy assistance in the Mediterranean', *Democratization*, 17(5), 976–96.

— (2011) 'The EU as a community of practice: foreign policy communications in the COREU network', *Journal of European Public Policy*, 18(8), 1115–32.

— (2012) 'The impact of the ENP on EU–North Africa relations: the good, the bad and the ugly.' in Whitman, R. and Wolff, S. (eds.) *The European Neighbourhood Policy in Perspective: Context, Implementation and Impact* (Basingstoke: Palgrave Macmillan), 206–22.

Bicchi, F. and Gillespie, R. (eds.) (2011) 'Special issue: the Union for the Mediterranean: continuity or change in Euro-Mediterranean relations? '*Mediterranean politics*, 16(1), 1–219.

Bickerton, C. J. (2010) 'Functionality in EU foreign policy: towards a new research agenda?', *Journal of European Integration*, 32(2), 213–27.

— (2011) *European Union Foreign Policy: From Effectiveness to Functionality* (Basingstoke: Palgrave Macmillan).

Bieber, F. (ed.) (2012) *EU Conditionality in the Western Balkans* (Oxon.: Routledge).

Biscop, S. (2008) 'Permanent structured cooperation and the future of the ESDP: transformation and integration', *European Foreign Affairs Review*, 13(4), 431–48.

Biscop, S. and Andersson, J. J. (eds.) (2007) *The EU and the European Security Strategy: Forging a Global Europe* (Oxon.: Routledge).

Biscop, S. and Coelmont, J. (2012) *Europe, Strategy and Armed Forces: The Making of a Distinctive Power* (Oxon.: Routledge).

— (2013) 'Military CSDP: the quest for capability' in Biscop, S. and Whitman, R. (eds.) *The Routledge Handbook of European Security* (Oxon.: Routledge), 78–90.

Biscop, S. and Whitman, R. (eds.) (2013) *The Routledge Handbook of European Security* (Oxon.: Routledge).

Bisley, N. (2012) 'APEC: Asia-Pacific Economic Cooperation' in Stubbs, R. and Beeson, M. (eds.) *Routledge Handbook of Asian Regionalism* (Oxon.: Routledge), 350–63.

Blavoukos, S. and Bourantonis, D. (2011) 'Introduction: The EU presence in international organisations' in Blavoukos, S. and Bourantonis, D. (eds.) *The EU Presence in International Organizations* (Oxon.: Routledge), 1–15.

— (2013) 'The UN Security Council reform debate' in Jørgensen, K. E. and Laatikainen, K. V. (eds.) *Routledge Handbook on the European Union and International Institutions: Performance, Policy, Power* (Oxon.: Routledge), 128–40.

Blockmans, S. (2012) 'The European External Action Service one year on: first signs of strengths and weaknesses', *CLEER working papers 2012*, 2.

Blockmans, S. and Hillion, C. (2013) 'EEAS 2.0: a legal commentary on Council Decision 2010/427/EU establishing the organisation and functioning of the European External Action Service', *SIEPS Working Paper Series*, 1.

Blockmans, S., Wouters, J. and Ruys, T. (eds.) (2010) *The European Union and Peacebuilding. Policy and Legal Aspects* (The Hague: TMC Asser Press).

Blunden, M. (2000) 'France' in Manners, I. and Whitman, R. (eds.) *The Foreign Policies of European Union Member States* (Manchester: Manchester University Press), 19–43.

Bogdani, M. (2011) *Turkey and the Dilemma of EU Accession: When Religion Meets Politics* (London: Palgrave Macmillan).

Börzel, T. (2005) 'Europeanization: how the European Union interacts with its member states' in Bulmer, S. and Lequesne, C. (eds.) *The Member States of the European Union* (New York: Oxford University Press), 45–69.

Börzel, T. A. and Risse, T. (2012a) 'From Europeanisation to diffusion: introduction', *West European Politics*, 35(1), 1–19.

— (eds.) (2012b) 'Special issue: from Europeanisation to diffusion', *West European Politics*, 35(1), 1–207.

Bosse, G. (2011) 'The EU in Georgia: towards a coherent crisis management strategy?' in Gross, E. and Juncos, A. E. (eds.) *EU Conflict Prevention and Crisis Management* (Oxon.: Routledge), 131–45.

Bossuyt, F. and Kubicek, P. (2011) 'Advancing democracy on difficult terrain: EU democracy promotion in Central Asia', *European Foreign Affairs Review*, 16(5), 639–58.

Bouchard, C., Peterson, J. and Tocci, N. (eds.) (2013) *Multilateralism in the 21st Century: Europe's Quest for Effectiveness* (Oxon.: Routledge).

Bourblanc, M. (2011) 'The EU and global environmental governance' in Wunderlich, J.-U. and Bailey, D. (eds.) *The European Union and Global Governance. A Handbook* (Oxon.: Routledge), 131–9.

Bouris, D. (2010) 'The European Union's role in the Palestinian Territory after the Oslo Accords: stillborn state-building', *Journal of Contemporary European Research*, 6(3), 376–94.

BP (British Petroleum) (2012) *BP Statistical Review of World Energy June 2012* (London: BP).

Brantner, F. and Gowan, D. (2008) 'A missed opportunity? The EU and the reform of the UN human rights architecture' in Laïdi, Z. (ed.) *EU Foreign Policy in a Globalized World. Normative Power and Social Preference* (Oxon.: Routledge), 83–103.

Bretherton, C. and Vogler, J. (2006) *The European Union as a Global Actor* (Oxon.: Routledge).

Breuer, F. (2012) 'Sociological institutionalism, socialization and Brusselization in CSDP' in Kurowska, X. and Breuer, F. (eds.) *Explaining the EU's Common Security and Defence Policy: Theory in Action* (Basingstoke: Palgrave Macmillan), 111–35.

Bromley, M. (2012) 'The review of the EU common position on arms exports: prospects for strengthened controls', *Non-Proliferation Papers*, 7.

Brosig, M. (2011) 'The emerging peace and security regime in Africa: the role of the EU', *European Foreign Affairs Review*, 16(1), 107–22.

Brummer, K. (2009) 'Imposing sanctions: the not so "normative power Europe"', *European Foreign Affairs Review*, 14(2), 191–207.

Burgat, F. (2009) 'Europe and the Arab world. The dilemma of recognising counterparts', *International Politics*, 46, 616–35.

Burke, E. (2010) 'Iraq. A new European engagement' in Youngs, R. (ed.) *The European Union and Democracy Promotion. A Critical Global Assessment* (Baltimore: John Hopkins University Press),

Buzan, B. (1993) 'Societal security, state security and internationalisation' in Waever, O., Buzan, B., Kelstrup, M. and Lemaitre, P. (eds.) *Identity, Migration and the New Security Agenda in Europe* (London: Pinter), 41–58.

Calleo, D. P. (1983) 'Early American views of NATO: then and now' in Freedman, L. (ed.) *The Troubled Alliance. Atlantic Relations in the 1980s* (London: Heinemann), 7–27.

— (1987) *Beyond American Hegemony: The Future of the Western Alliance* (New York: Basic Books).

Cameron, F. (2012) An Introduction to European Foreign Policy (Oxon.: Routledge).

Canterbury, D. C. (2010) *European Bloc Imperialism* (Leiden: Brill).

Caporaso, J. A. and Jupille, J. (1998) 'States, agency and rules: the EU in global environmental politics' in Rhodes, C. (ed.) *The European Union in the World* (Boulder, CO: Lynne Rienner), 213–31.

Carbone, M. (2011a) 'Development policy. The European Union as a multilateral and bilateral donor' in Wunderlich, J.-U. and Bailey, D. (eds.) *The European Union and Global Governance. A Handbook* (Oxon.: Routledge), 157–65.

— (2011b) 'The EU and the developing world: partnership, poverty, politicization' in Hill, C. and Smith, M. (eds.) *International Relations and the European Union* (Oxford: Oxford University Press), 324–48.

Cardwell, P. J. (2011) 'Mapping out democracy promotion in the EU's external relations', *European Foreign Affairs Review*, 16(1), 21–40.

Carlson, A. (2011) 'Moving beyond sovereignty? A brief consideration of recent changes in China's approach to international order and the emergence of the tianxia concept', *Journal of Contemporary China*, 20(68), 89–102.

Carta, C. (2012) *The European Union Diplomatic Service. Ideas, Preferences and Identities* (Oxon.: Routledge).

Carter, K. R. (2010) 'Should international relations consider rape a weapon of war?', *Politics & Gender*, 6(3), 343–71.

Casier, T. (2007) 'The clash of integration processes? The shadow effect of the enlarged EU on its eastern neighbours' in Malfliet, K., Verpoest, L. and Vinokurov, E. (eds.) *The CIS, The EU and Russia. Challenges of Integration* (Basingstoke: Palgrave MacMillan), 73–94.

— (2011) 'To adopt or not to adopt: explaining selective rule transfer under the European Neighbourhood Policy', *Journal of European Integration*, 33(1), 37–53.

— (2012) 'The European Neighborhood Policy: living up to regional ambitions?' in Bindi, F. and Angelescu, I. (eds.) *The Foreign Policy of the European Union. Assessing Europe's Role in the World* (Washington, DC: Brookings Press), 99–117.

— (2014) 'The EU and Russia: a marriage of convenience' in Smith, M., Keukeleire, S. and

Vanhoonacker, S. (eds.) *The Diplomatic System of the European Union: Evolution, Change and Challenges* (Oxon.: Routledge),

Cassarino, J. P. (2012) 'Reversing the hierarchy of priorities in the EU–Mediterranean relations' in Peters, J. (ed.) *The European Union and the Arab Spring* (Lanham, MD: Lexington Books), 1–16.

Cavatorta, F. (2009) '"Divided they stand, divided they fail": opposition politics in Morocco', *Democratization*, 16(1), 137–56.

Cavatorta, F. and Pace, M. (eds.) (2010a) 'Special issue: the post-normative turn on European Union (EU)–Middle East and North Africa (MENA) relations', *European Foreign Affairs Review*, 15(5), 581–737.

— (2010b) 'The post-normative turn in European Union (EU)–Middle East and North Africa (MENA) relations: an introduction', *European Foreign Affairs Review*, 15(5), 581–7.

Chaban, N. and Holland, M. (eds.) (2008) *The European Union and the Asia-Pacific. Media, Public and Elite Perceptions of the EU* (Oxon.: Routledge).

— (eds.) (2013) *Europe and Asia: Perceptions from Afar* (Baden-Baden: Nomos).

Chafer, T. and Cumming, G. (eds.) (2011) *From Rivalry to Partnership? New Approaches to the Challenges of Africa* (Surrey: Ashgate).

Chang, F.-C. (2011) 'European Defense Agency – motor of strengthening the EU's military capabilities', *European Foreign Affairs Review*, 16(1), 59–87.

Chaturvedi, S., Fues, T. and Sidiropoulos, E. (eds.) (2012) *Development Cooperation and Emerging Powers. New Partners or Old Patterns?* (London: Zed Books).

Chen, Z. (2012) 'Europe as a global player: a view from China', *Perspectives*, 20(2), 7–30.

— (2013) 'The efficacy of post-Lisbon Treaty EU's External Actions and China–EU strategic partnership' in Telò, M. and Ponjaert, F. (eds.) *The EU's Foreign Policy: What Kind of Power and Diplomatic Action?* (Aldershot: Ashgate), 175–88.

Chen, Z. and Song, L. (2012) 'The conceptual gap on soft power between China and Europe and its impact on bilateral relations' in Pan, Z. (ed.) *Conceptual Gaps in China–EU Relations: Global Governance, Human Rights and Strategic Partnerships* (Basingstoke: Palgrave Macmillan), 50–64.

Cherry, J. and Dobson, H. (2012) '"Seoul-searching": the 2010 G-20 Seoul Summit', *Global Governance*, 18(3), 363–81.

Cheru, F. and Obi, C. (eds.) (2010) *The Rise of China and India in Africa* (New York: Zed Books).

Christiansen, T., Kirchner, E. and Murray, P. B. (eds.) (2013) *The Palgrave Handbook of EU–Asia Relations* (Basingstoke: Palgrave Macmillan).

Cline, R. S. (1980) *World Power Trends and US Foreign Policy for the 1980s* (Boulder, CO: Westview Press).

Cloos, J., Reinesch, G., Vignes, D. and Weyland, J. (1993) *Le Traité de Maastricht. Genèse, analyse, commentaires* (Bruxelles: Emile Bruylant).

Cœuré, B. and Pisani-Ferry, J. (2007) 'The governance of the European Union's international economic relations: how many voices?' in Sapir, A. (ed.) *Fragmented Power: Europe and the Global Economy* (Brussels: Bruegel), 21–60.

Collantes-Celador, G. and Juncos, A. E. (2011) 'Security sector reform in the Western Balkans: the challenge of coherence and effectiveness' in Ekengren, M. and Simons, G. (eds.) *The Politics of Security Sector Reform. Challenges and Opportunities for the European Union's Global Role* (Farnham: Ashgate), 127–54.

Commission: see European Commission.

Cook, D. (1989) *Forging the Alliance. NATO, 1945–1950* (London: Secker & Warburg).

Coolsaet, R. (2010) 'EU counterterrorism strategy: value added or chimera?', *International Affairs*, 86(4), 857–873.

— (ed.) (2011) *Jihadi Terrorism and the Radicalisation Challenge: European and American Experiences* (Aldershot: Ashgate).

Corbett, R., Jacobs, F. and Shackleton, M. (2005) *The European Parliament* (London: John Harper).

— (2011) *The European Parliament* (London: John Harper).

Corthaut, T. and Van Eeckhoutte, D. (2012) 'Legal aspects of EU participation in global environmental governance under the UN umbrella' in Wouters, J., Bruyninckx, H., Basu, S. and Schunz, S. (eds.) *The European Union and Multilateral Governance. Assessing EU Participation in United Nations Human Rights and Environmental Fora* (Basingstoke: Palgrave Macmillan), 145–70.

Costa, O. and Jørgensen, K. E. (eds.) (2012) *The Influence of International Institutions on the EU* (New York: Palgrave Macmillan).

Cottey, A. (2013) *Security in Twenty-First Century Europe* (Basingstoke: Palgrave Macmillan).

Council: see Council of the European Union

Council of the European Union (2004) *Basic principles on the use of restrictive measures (sanctions)*, 10198/1/04 REV 1, 7 June, Europa website.

— (2005) *The European Union Counter-Terrorism Strategy*, 14469/4/05, 30 November, Europa website.

— (2006) *EU Strategy to combat illicit accumulation and trafficking of small arms and light weapons (SALW) and their ammunition*, 5319/06, 13 January, Europa website.

— (2008) *Council Common Position 2008/944/CFSP of 8 December 2008 defining common rules governing control of exports of military technology and equipment*, OJ L 335/99–103.

— (2009a) *EU guidelines: human rights and international humanitarian law*, Europa website.

— (2009b) *Joint Declaration of the Prague Eastern Partnership Summit*, 8435/09, 7 May.

— (2010a) *Council decision 2010/427/EU establishing the organisation and functioning of the European External Action Service*, OJ L 201/30, 26 July.

— (2010b) *New lines for action by the European Union in combating the proliferation of weapons of mass destruction and their delivery systems – Council conclusions*, 17078/10, 16 December, EEAS website.

— (2011a) *Main aspects and basis choices of the CFSP – 2010 – annual report from the High Representative of the European Union for Foreign Affairs and Security Policy to the European Parliament*, 12562/11, 8 July, Europa website.

— (2011b) *Council decision 2011/411/CFSP defining the statute, seat and operational rules of the European Defence Agency*, OJ L 183, 12 July.

— (2011c) *Council conclusions on a European Union Strategy for Security and Development in the Sahel*, 8030/11, 21 March.

— (2011d) *Thirteenth annual report defining common rules governing control of exports of military technology and equipment* (2011/C 382/01), OJ C 382/1–470, 30 December.

— (2011e) *EU Action Plan on combating Terrorism*, 17594/1/11, 9 December, Europa website.

— (2011f) *Council conclusions on civilian CSDP capabilities*, 21 March, Europa website.

— (2011g) *A strategic framework for the Horn of Africa*, 16858/11, 14 November.

— (2012a) *Agendas of meetings of the Council of the European Union*, Europa website.

— (2012b) *List of Council preparatory bodies*, 5269/11, Europa website.

— (2012c) *EU Diplomatic Representation in third countries – First half of 2012*, 18975/1/11, Europa website.

— (2012d) *EU Strategic Framework and Action Plan on Human Rights and Democracy*, 11855/12, 25 June, EEAS website.

— (2012e) *EU adopts Strategic Framework and Action Plan on Human Rights and Democracy*, PR 285, 25 June, EEAS website.

— (2012f) *Twelfth Progress Report on the implementation of the EU Strategy to combat illicit accumulation and trafficking of SALW and their ammunition* (2011/II), OJ C 66/24–7.

— (2012g) *EU Counter-Terrorism Strategy – Discussion Paper*, 9990/12, 23 May, Europa website.

— (2012h) *Main aspects and basis choices of the CFSP – 2011 – annual report from the High Representative of the European Union for Foreign Affairs and Security Policy to the European Parliament*, 14605/1/12, 9 October, Europa website.

— (2012i) *Council Decision 2012/173/CFSP on the activation of the EU Operations Centre for the Common Security missions and operation in the Horn of Africa*, OJ L 89/66–68, 23 March.

— (2012j) *Council conclusions on pooling and sharing of military capabilities*, 22–23 March, Europa website.

— (2013) *CFSP Budget Report – monthly update as of 31 December 2012*, 5124/13, 9 January.

Court of Justice of the European Union (2008) Joined Cases C-402/05 P and C-415/05 P: *Kadi and Al Barakaat International Foundation* v. *Council and Commission*, ECR I-6351, 3 September.

— (2010) *Case T-85/09 Kadi* v. *Commission*, ECR II-05177, 30 September.

Cremona, M. (2011) 'Coherence in European Union foreign relations law' in Koutrakos, P. (ed.) *European Foreign Policy: Legal and Political Perspectives* (Cheltenham: Edward Elgar), 55–94.

Cross, M. K. (2011) *Security Integration in Europe: How Knowledge-based Networks are Transforming the European Union* (Ann Arbor, MI: University of Michigan Press).

Crowe, B. (2005) *Foreign Minister of Europe* (London: Foreign Policy Centre).

CSDP MAP (2013) *Mission Analysis Partnership*, CSDPmap.eu.

Cuyckens, H. (2012) 'The EU and China: emerging global powers capable of balancing US hegemony and shaping a new world order' in Wouters, J., de Wilde d'Estmael, T., Defraigne, P. and Defraigne, J.-C. (eds.) *China, the European Union and the Restructuring of Global Governance* (Cheltenham: Edward Elgar), 297–310.

da Conceição-Heldt, E. (2010) 'Who controls whom? Dynamics of power delegation and agency losses in EU trade politics', *Journal of Common Market Studies*, 48(4), 1107–26.

— (2011) 'Variation in EU member states' preferences and the Commission's discretion in the Doha Round', *Journal of European Public Policy*, 18(3), 403–19.

Dai, B. (2013) 'China in EU–East Asia economic relations' in Christiansen, T., Kirchner, E. and Murray, P. B. (eds.) *The Palgrave Handbook of EU–Asia Relations* (Basingstoke: Palgrave Macmillan), 481–91.

Damro, C. (2006) 'EU–UN environmental relations: shared competence and effective multilateralism' in Smith, K. E. and Laatikainen, K. V. (eds.) *The European Union and the United Nations: Intersecting Multilateralisms* (Basingstoke: Palgrave Macmillan), 175–92.

— (2012) 'Market power Europe', *Journal of European Public Policy*, 19(5), 682–99.

Dari, E., Price, M., Van der Wal, J., Gottwald, M. and Koenig, N. (2012) *CSDP Missions and Operations: Lessons Learned Processes* (Brussels: European Parliament).

Darnis, J.-P. and Veclani, A. (2011) *Space and Security: The Use of Space in the Context of the CSDP* (Brussels: European Parliament).

Dashwood, A., Dougan, M., Rodger, B., Spaventa, E. and Wyatt, R. (2011) *Wyatt and Dashwood's European Union Law* (Oxford: Hart).

David, M. (2011) 'A less than special relationship: the UK's Russia experience', *Journal of Contemporary European Studies*, 19(2), 201–12.

David, M., Gower, J. and Haukkala, H. (eds.) (2011) 'Special issue: the European Union and Russia', *Journal of Contemporary European Studies*, 19(2), 183–272.

David, M., Gower, J. and Haukkala, H. (eds.) (2013) *National Perspectives on Russia: European Foreign Policy in the Making?* (Oxon.: Routledge).

Davies, J. (2010) 'The Aceh Monitoring Mission: securing peace and democracy' in Blockmans, S., Wouters, J. and Ruys, T. (eds.) *The European Union and Peacebuilding: policy and legal aspects* (The Hague: TMC Asser Press), 375–86.

De Baere, G. (2012) 'European integration and the rule of law in foreign policy' in Dickson, J. and Eleftheriadis, P. (eds.) *Philosophical Foundations of European Union Law* (Oxford: Oxford University Press),

De Bruycker, P. and Weyemberg, A. (2009) 'The external dimension of the European Area of Freedom, Security and Justice' in Telò, M. (ed.) *The European Union and Global Governance* (Oxon.: Routledge), 210–32.

de Jong, S. and Schunz, S. (2012) 'Coherence in European Union External Policy before and after the Lisbon Treaty: the cases of energy security and climate change', *European Foreign Affairs Review*, 17(2), 165–88.

de Jong, S., Wouters, J. and Sterkx, S. (2010) 'The 2009 Russian–Ukrainian gas dispute: lessons for European energy crisis management after Lisbon', *European Foreign Affairs Review*, 15(4), 511–38.

De Lombaerde, P. and Schulz, M. (eds.) (2010) *The EU and World Regionalism: The Makability of Regions in the 21st Century* (Aldershot: Ashgate).

de Vasconcelos, A. (2012) *Listening to Unfamiliar Voices. The Arabic Democratic Wave* (Paris: European Union Institution for Security Studies).

de Wilde d'Estmael, T. (2012) 'The EU vis-à-vis China: a question of power and coercion?' in Wouters, J., de Wilde d'Estmael, T., Defraigne, P. and Defraigne, J.-C. (eds.) *China, the European Union and the Restructuring of Global Governance* (Cheltenham: Edward Elgar), 283–96.

Debaere, P. and Orbie, J. (2013) 'The European Union's role in the G8: a principal–agent perspective' in Jørgensen, K. E. and Laatikainen, K. V. (eds.) *Routledge Handbook on the European Union and International Institutions* (Oxon.: Routledge), 311–23.

Dee, M. (2012) 'Standing together or doing the splits? Evaluating European Union performance in the nuclear Non-Proliferation Treaty review negotiations', *European Foreign Affairs Review*, 17(2), 189–212.

Defraigne, J.-C. (2012) 'China shakes the world: challenges arising from shift in the global balance of power' in Wouters, J., de Wilde d'Estmael, T., Defraigne, P. and Defraigne, J.-C. (eds.) *China, the European Union and Global Governance* (Cheltenham: Edward Elgar), 13–49.

Degrand-Guillaud, A. (2009) 'Characteristics of and recommendations for EU coordination at the UN', *European Foreign Affairs Review*, 14(4), 607–22.

Della Posta, P. and Talani, L. S. (eds.) (2011) *Europe and the Financial Crisis* (Basingstoke: Palgrave Macmillan).

Delputte, S. and Söderbaum, F. (2012) 'European aid coordination: is the Commission calling the tune?' in Gänzle, S., Grimm, S. and Makhan, D. (eds.) *The European Union and Global*

Development. An Enlightened Superpower in the Making? (Basingstoke: Palgrave Macmillan), 37–56.

Delreux, T. (2009) 'Cooperation and control in the European Union. The case of the European Union as international environmental negotiator', *Cooperation and Conflict*, 44(2), 189–208.

— (2011a) *The EU as International Environmental Negotiator* (Aldershot: Ashgate).

— (2011b) 'The relation between the European Commission and the EU member states in the transatlantic Open Skies negotiations: an analysis of their opportunities and constraints', *Journal of Transatlantic Studies*, 9(2), 113–35.

— (2012a) 'The rotating Presidency and the EU's External Representation in Environmental Affairs: the case of climate change and biodiversity negotiations', *Journal of Contemporary European Research*, 8(2), 210–27.

— (2012b) 'The EU as an actor in global environmental politics' in Jordan, A. and Adelle, C. (eds.) *Environmental Policy in the EU. Actors, Institutions and Processes* (Oxon.: Routledge), 287–305.

Delreux, T. and Kerremans, B. (2010) 'How agents weaken their principals' incentives to control: the case of EU negotiators and EU member states in multilateral negotiations', *Journal of European Integration*, 32(4), 357–74.

Delreux, T. and Van den Brande, K. (2013) 'Taking the lead: informal division of labour in the EU's external environmental policy-making', *Journal of European Public Policy*, 20(1), 113–31.

Dennison, S. and Dworkin, A. (2010) 'Towards an EU human rights strategy for a post-Western world', *ECFR Policy Brief*, 1–16.

Denoeux, G. (2002) 'The forgotten swamp: navigating political Islam', *Middle East Policy*, 9(2), 56–82.

Depauw S. (2012) 'The European Union's involvement in negotiating an Arms Trade Treaty', *Non-Proliferation Papers*, No. 23.

Develtere, P. (2012) *How Do We Help? The Free Market in Development Aid* (Leuven: Leuven University Press).

Devuyst, Y. (2012) 'The European Council and the CFSP after the Lisbon Treaty', *European Foreign Affairs Review*, 17(3), 327–50.

Devuyst, Y. and Men, J. (2012) 'Political dialogue as an instrument of EU diplomacy: the case of China' in Mahncke, D. and Gstöhl, S. (eds.) *European Union Diplomacy. Coherence, Unity and Effectiveness* (Brussels: Peter Lang), 169–94.

Diez, T. (2005) 'Constructing the self and changing others: problematising the concept of "normative power Europe"', *Journal of International Studies*, 33(3), 613–36.

Dijkstra, H. (2011) 'The role of the Council Secretariat and the European Commission in EU foreign policy' (thesis), Maastricht University.

Dijkstra, H. (2013) *Policy-Making in EU Security and Defense: An Institutional Perspective* (Basingstoke: Palgrave Macmillan).

Dimitrovova, B. (2010) 'Cultural bordering and re-bordering in the EU's neighbourhood: members, strangers or neighbours?', *Journal of Contemporary European Studies*, 18(4), 463–81.

Ding, C. (2012) 'Conceptual gaps on stability in Chinese and European contexts' in Pan, Z. (ed.) *Conceptual Gaps in China–EU Relations: Global Governance, Human Rights and Strategic Partnerships* (Basingstoke: Palgrave Macmillan), 128–40.

Dobson, A. (2009) 'Negotiating the EU–US Open Aviation Area Agreement 2007 in the context of transatlantic airline regimes since 1944', *Diplomacy & Statecraft*, 20(1), 136–60.

Doidge, M. (2011) *The European Union and Interregionalism: Patterns of Engagement* (Aldershot: Ashgate).

Doyle, M. W. (2012) 'Liberalism and foreign policy' in Smith, S., Hadfield, A. and Dunne, T. (eds.) *Foreign Policy. Theories Actors Cases* (Oxford: Oxford University Press), 54–77.

Drieskens, E. (2011) 'Ceci n'est pas une Présidence: the 2010 Belgian Presidency of the EU', *Journal of Common Market Studies*, 49(1), 91–102.

— (2012) 'What's in a name? Challenges to the creation of EU Delegations', *The Hague Journal of Diplomacy*, 7(1), 51–64.

Drieskens, E. and Bouchard, C. (2013) 'Researching the European Union at the United Nations in New York: current trends and future agendas' in Laatikainen, K. V. and Jørgensen, K. E. (eds.) *Handbook on Europe and Multilateral Institutions* (Oxon.: Routledge), 115–27.

Drieskens, E., Van Dievel, L. and Reykers, Y. (2014) 'The EU's search for effective participation at the UN General Assembly and UN Security Council' in Drieskens, E. and van Schaik, L. (eds.) *The EU and Effective Multilateralism: Internal and External Reform Practices* (Oxon.: Routledge).

Drieskens, E. and van Schaik, L. (eds.) (2014) *The EU and Effective Multilateralism: Internal and External Reform Practices* (Oxon.: Routledge).

Druláková, R., Rolenc, J. M., Travnickova, Z. and Zemanova, S. (2010) 'Assessing the effectiveness of EU sanctions policy', *Central European Journal of International and Security Studies*, 4(1), 101–22.

Duchêne, F. (1972) 'Europe's role in world peace' in Mayne, R. (ed.) *Europe Tomorrow. Sixteen Europeans Look Ahead* (London: Collins), 32–47.

— (1973) 'The European Community and the uncertainties of interdependence' in Kohnstamm, M. and Hager, W. (eds.) *A Nation Writ Large? Foreign-Policy Problems before the European Community* (Basingstoke: Macmillan), 1–21.

— (1994) *Jean Monnet: The First Statesman of Interdependence* (New York/London: Norton).

Duke, S. (1999) *The Elusive Quest for European Security: From EDC to CFSP* (Basingstoke: Palgrave Macmillan).

— (2011a) 'Consistency, coherence and European Union external action: the path to Lisbon and beyond' in Koutrakos, P. (ed.) *European Foreign Policy: Legal and Political Perspectives* (Cheltenham: Edward Elgar), 15–54.

— (2011b) 'The EU, NATO and the Lisbon Treaty: still divided within a common city', *Studia Diplomatica*, 64(2), 19–35.

— (2012) 'The European External Action Service: antidote against incoherence?', *European Foreign Affairs Review*, 17(1), 45–68.

Dür, A. (2008) 'Bargaining power and trade liberalization: European external trade policies in the 1960s', *European Journal of International Relations*, 14(4), 645–69.

— (2011) 'Fortress Europe or liberal Europe? The single market programme and EU's external policies', *Journal of European Public Policy*, 18(5), 619–35.

Dür, A. and De Bièvre, D. (2007) 'Inclusion without influence: NGOs in European trade policy', *Journal of Public Policy*, 27(1), 79–101.

Dür, A. and Elsig, M. (eds.) (2011) *The European Union's Foreign Economic Policies* (Oxon.: Routledge).

Dursun-Ozkanca, O. and Vandemoortele, A. (eds.) (2012) 'Special issue: the European Union and the security sector reform practices: challenges of implementation', *European Security*, 21(2), 139–309.

Echeverria Jesús, C. (2012) 'The ENP and the Middle East' in Whitman, R. and Wolff, S. (eds.) *The European Neighbourhood Policy in Perspective: Context, Implementation and Impact* (Basingstoke: Palgrave Macmillan), 247–58.

Eckes, C. (2012) 'EU counter-terrorist sanctions against individuals: problems and perils', *European Foreign Affairs Review*, 17(1), 113–32.

EDA (European Defence Agency) (2008) *Future trends from the Capability Development Plan*, 8 July, EDA website.

— (2011) 2010 *Defence data*, EDA website.

— (2012) *European and United States defence expenditure in 2010*, EDA website.

Edwards, J. (2011) 'The EU Defence and Security Procurement Directive', *International Security Programme Paper*, 5.

EEAS (2011a) *Report by the High Representative to the European Parliament, the Council and the Commission*, 22 December, EEAS website.

— (2011b) *CSDP – Battlegroups (factsheet)*, January, EEAS website.

— (2011c) *Common Security and Defence Policy: development of European military capabilities*, January, EEAS website.

— (2012a) *Athena*, EEAS website.

— (2012b) *Human Rights and Democracy in the World – Report on EU Action in 2011* (Brussels: European External Action Service).

— (2012c) *Instrument for Stability (IfS) – EU in action*, EEAS website.

— (2012d) *Factsheet – the activation of the EU Operations Centre*, April 16, EEAS website.

— (2013a) 2011 *Discharge to the EEAS. Answers by the High Representative/Vice President Catherine Ashton to the written questions of the Committee on Budgetary Control* (Brussels: European External Action Service).

— (2013b) *European External Action Service: graphic representation*, Europa website.

— (2013c) *CSDP operations – overview of the missions and operations of the European Union*, EEAS website.

— (2013d) *Strategy for Security and Development in the Sahel*, EEAS website.

— (2013e) *The EU fight against piracy in the Horn of Africa*, EEAS website.

— (2013f) *China*, EEAS website.

— (2013g) *Countries/territories*, EEAS website.

Eeckhout, P. (2011) *EU External Relations Law* (Oxford: Oxford University Press).

Ehrhardt, H.-G. and Petretto, K. (2012a) 'The EU, the Somalia challenge, and counter-piracy: towards a comprehensive approach?', *European Foreign Affairs Review*, 17(2), 261–84.

— (2012b) 'The EU and Somalia: counter-piracy and the question of a comprehensive approach', *Study for the Greens/European Free Alliance*, 1–50.

Eilstrup-Sangiovanni, M. (2006) *Debates on European Integration* (Basingstoke: Palgrave Macmillan).

Ekengren, M. and Simons, G. (eds.) (2011) *The Politics of Security Sector Reform. Challenges and Opportunities for the European Union's Global Role* (Aldershot: Ashgate).

Elgström, O. (2007) 'Outsider's perceptions of the European Union in international trade negotiations', *Journal of Common Market Studies*, 45(4), 949–67.

— (2009) 'Trade and aid? The negotiated construction of EU policy on economic partnership agreements', *International Politics*, 46(4), 451–68.

Elgström, O. and Frennhof Larsén, M. (2010) 'Free to trade? Commission autonomy in the Economic Partnership Agreement negotiations', *Journal of European Public Policy*, 17(2), 205–23.

Elgström, O. and Pilegaard, J. (2008) 'Imposed coherence: negotiating economic partnership agreements', *Journal of European Integration*, 30(3), 363–80.

Elsig, M. (2007) 'The EU's choice of regulatory venues for trade negotiations: a tale of agency power?', *Journal of Common Market Studies*, 45(4), 927–48.

Emerson, M. (2012) 'Do the BRICS make a bloc?', *CEPS Commentary*, 30 April, 1–7.

Emerson, M., Balfour, R., Corthaut, T., Wouters, J., Kaczynski, P. M. and Renard, T. (2011) *Upgrading the EU's Role as Global Actor: Institutions, Law and the Restructuring of European Diplomacy* (Brussels: CEPS).

Engert, S. (2010) *EU Enlargement and Socialization. Turkey and Cyprus* (Oxon.: Routledge).

Epstein, R. A. and Sedelmeier, U. (eds.) (2009) *International Influence Beyond Conditionality. Postcommunist Europe After EU Enlargement* (Oxon.: Routledge).

Erkelens, L. and Blockmans, S. (2012) 'Setting up the European External Action Service: an institutional act of balance', *CLEER working papers 2012*, 1.

ESA (2009) *Space: A Key Asset for Europe to Face Global Challenges* (Noordwijk: European Space Agency).

ESRIF (European Security Research and Innovation Forum) (2009) *ESRIF Final Report* (Brussels: ESRIF).

EU Delegation to the UN (2012) 'About the EU at the UN', Europa website.

European Commission (2003) *Wider Europe – Neighbourhood: A New Framework for Relations with our Eastern and Southern Neighbours*, COM(2003)320, 11 March.

— (2004) *Communication from the Commission – European Neighbourhood Policy – Strategy Paper*, COM(2004)373.

— (2005a) *Communication on policy coherence for Development. Accelerating progress towards attaining the Millennium Development Goals*, COM(2005)134 final, 12 April.

— (2005b) *Green Paper – Confronting demographic change: a new solidarity between the generations*, COM(2005)94, 16 March.

— (2006a) *Commission Communication. The demographic future of Europe – from challenge to opportunity*, COM(2006) 571 final, 12 October.

— (2006b) *Communication on Strengthening the European Neighbourhood Policy*, COM(2006)726, 4 December.

— (2006c) *Commission staff working documents – Overall assessment/ENP National Progress Reports/Sectoral Progress Report* SEC(2006)1504–12, 4 December.

— (2007) *Communication on the EU Code of Conduct on Division of labour in Development Policy*, COM(2007)72 final, 28 February.

— (2008) *EMU@10. Successes and challenges after ten years of Economic and Monetary Union* (Brussels: European Communities).

— (2009) *Communication on A European Security Research and Innovation Agenda – Commission's initial position on ESRIF's key findings and recommendations*, COM(2009)691 final, 21 December.

— (2010a) *Energy 2020. A strategy for competitive, sustainable and secure energy*, COM(2010) 639 final, 10 November.

— (2010b) *European Instrument for Democracy and Human Rights (EIDHR) – Strategy Paper 2011–2013*, C(2010)2432, 21 April.

— (2010c) *Commission staff working document. Policy Coherence for Development Work Programme 2010–2013. A twelve-point EU action plan in support of the Millennium Development Goals*, SEC(2010)421 final, 21 April.

— (2011a) 'Galileo: Europe launches its first satellites for smart navigation system', press release, 21 October, Europa website.

— (2011b) *Increasing the impact of EU Development Policy: An Agenda for Change*, COM(2011) 637 final, 13 November.

— (2011c) *Proposal for a regulation establishing a financing instrument for development cooperation*, COM(2011) 840 final, 7 December.

— (2011d) *Communication on security of energy supply and international cooperation – 'The EU Energy Policy: Engaging with Partners beyond Our Borders'*, COM(2011) 539 final, 7 September.

— (2011e) *Communication on the Global Approach to Migration and Mobility*, COM(2011) 743 final, 18 November.

— (2012a) *EU Accountability Report 2012 on Financing for Development*, SWD(2012) 199, Europa website.

— (2012b) *Eurobarometer 77, Spring. Public opinion in the European Union* (Brussels: European Union).

— (2012c) *Communication – The EU Strategy towards the Eradication of Trafficking in Human Beings 2012–2016*, COM(2012) 286 final, 19 June, Europa website.

— (2012d) *2011 Annual Report on the Instrument for Stability*, COM(2012) 405 final, 24 July, Europa website.

— (2012e) *Instrument for Stability*, Europa website.

— (2012f) *Annual Report 2011 – The African Peace Facility* (Brussels: European Union).

— (2012g) *Defence Package – Towards an EU Defence Equipment Policy*, Europa website.

— (2012h) *Restrictive measures (sanctions) in force*, EEAS website.

— (2012i) *European Neighbourhood Policy – Reference documents*, Europa website.

— (2013a) *EuropeAid – Work with us*, Europa website.

— (2013b) *Statistics main economic indicators*, Europa website.

— (2013c) *Speech: Transatlantic Trade and Investment Partnership: Opening free trade negotiations with the United States*, SPEECH/13/147, 21 February.

— (2013d) *List of programmes under the MFF 2014–2020 adjusted post European Council conclusions*, Ares (2013)517415.

European Commission and High Representative of the Union for Foreign Affairs and Security Policy (2011) *A partnership for democracy and shared prosperity with the Southern Mediterranean* COM(2011) 200 final, 8 March.

— (2012a) *Delivering on a new European Neighbourhood Policy*, JOIN(2012) 14 final, 15 May.

— (2012b) *Eastern Partnership: A Roadmap to the autumn 2013 Summit*, JOIN(2012) 13 final, 15 May.

European Council (2003a) *European Security Strategy – A secure Europe in a better world, 12 December*, Europa website.

— (2003b) *EU Strategy against the Proliferation of Weapons of Mass Destruction*, 12 December, Europa website.

— (2008) *Report on the Implementation of the European Security Strategy: Providing Security in a Changing World*, S407/08 11 December.

European External Action Service: *see* EEAS.

European Parliament (2010) *European Parliament legislative resolution on the proposal for a Council decision establishing the organisation and functioning of the European External Action Service*, 08029/2010 – C7–0090/2010 – 2010/0816(NLE), 8 July.

— (2011) *European Parliament resolution of 25 October 2011 on Global Economic Governance*, P7_TA(2011)0457.

European Parliament and the Council of the European Union (2010a) *Regulation (EU, EURATOM) No. 1080/2010 amending the Staff Regulations of Officials of the European Communities and the Conditions of Employment of Other Servants of those Communities*, OJ L 311/1, 24 November.

— (2010b) *Regulation (EU, EURATOM) No. 1081/2010 amending Council Regulation (EC, Euratom) No. 1605/2002 on the Financial Regulation applicable to the general budget of the European Communities, as regards the European External Action Service*, OJ L 311/9, 24 November.

European Union (2003) *Sixth China–EU Summit: Joint Press Statement*, 13424/03 (Press 298), 30 October.

— (2009) *European security and defence policy: the civilian aspects of crisis management, August*, Europa website.

— (2010) *Consolidated Treaties. Charter of Fundamental Rights* (Luxembourg: Publications Office of the European Union).

— (2011) *The Multiannual Financial Framework: The proposals on external action instruments*, Memo/11/878, 7 December.

— (2012) *Human Rights and Democracy in the World – Report on EU Action in 2011* (Brussels: European External Action Service).

Eurostat (2012a) *Statistics by theme*, Eurostat website.

— (2012b) *Energy Dependence*, Eurostat website.

— (2012c) *Statistic explained: Energy production and imports*, Eurostat website.

Faber, G. and Orbie, J. (eds.) (2007) *European Union Trade Politics and Development. 'Everything But Arms' Unravelled* (Oxon.: Routledge).

Fagan, A. (2010) *Europe's Balkan Dilemma. Paths to Civil Society or State-Building* (London: I.B. Tauris).

Faleg, G. (2013) 'Castles in the sand: Mali and the demise of the EU's Common Security and Defence Policy', *CEPS Commentary*.

Faleg, G. and Giovannini, A. (2012) 'The EU between pooling & sharing and smart defence: making a virtue of necessity?', *CEPS Special Report*, 1–22.

Falkner, R. (2007) 'The political economy of "normative power" Europe: EU environmental leadership in international biotechnology regulation', *Journal of European Public Policy*, 14(4), 507–26.

Ferreira-Pereira, L. C. and Martins, B. O. (eds.) (2012) 'Special issue: the external dimension of the European Union's counter-terrorism', *European Security*, 21(4), 459–611.

Fierro, E. (2003) *The EU's Approach to Human Rights Conditionality in Practice* (The Hague: Martinus Nijhoff).

Fioramonti, L. (2012) 'Is the EU a "Better" global player? An analysis of emerging powers' perceptions' in Renard, T. and Biscop, S. (eds.) *The EU and Emerging Powers in the 21st Century: How Europe Can Shape a New Global Order* (Farnham: Ashgate), 147–64.

Flockhart, T. (2012) 'Constructivism and foreign policy' in Smith, S., Hadfield, A. and Dunne, T. (eds.) *Foreign Policy. Theories, Actors, Cases* (Oxford: Oxford University Press), 78–93.

Foreign Ministers (2011a) *Joint Letter from the Foreign Ministers of Belgium, Estonia, Finland, France, Germany, Italy, Latvia, Lithuania, Luxembourg, the Netherlands, Poland and Sweden to the High Representative of the Union for Foreign Affairs and Security Policy and Vice President of the European Commission, Catherine Ashton*, 8 December.

— (2011b) *Non-paper on the European External Action Service from the Foreign Ministers of Belgium, Estonia, Finland, France, Germany, Italy, Latvia, Lithuania, Luxembourg, the Netherlands, Poland and Sweden*, 8 December.

Forsberg, T. (2011) 'Normative power Europe, once again: a conceptual analysis of an ideal type', *Journal of Common Market Studies*, 49(6), 1183–204.

Forster, A. (2000) 'Britain' in Manners, I. and Whitman, R. (eds.) *The Foreign Policies of European Union Member States* (Manchester: Manchester University Press), 44–63.

Freeman, D. and Geeraerts, G. (2012) 'Europe, China and expectations for human rights' in Pan, Z. (ed.) *Conceptual Gaps in China–EU Relations: Global Governance, Human Rights and Strategic Partnerships* (Basingstoke: Palgrave Macmillan), 98–112.

Freire, M. R. and Kanet, R. E. (eds.) (2012) *Russia and Its Near Neighbours* (Basingstoke: Palgrave Macmillan).

Freyburg, T., Lavenex, S., Schimmelfennig, F., Skripka, T. and Wetzel, A. (2009) 'EU promotion of democratic governance in the neighbourhood', *Journal of European Public Policy*, 16(6), 916–34.

Freyburg, T. and Richter, S. (2010) 'National identity matters: the limited impact of EU political conditionality in the Western Balkans', *Journal of European Public Policy*, 17(2), 263–81.

Friis, K. (2007) 'The referendum in Montenegro: the EU's "postmodern diplomacy"', *European Foreign Affairs Review*, 12(1), 67–88.

Fröhlich, S. (2012) *The New Geopolitics of Transatlantic Relations. Coordinated Responses to Common Dangers* (Washington, DC: Woodrow Wilson Center Press).

FRS, CNRS, RSA, SDRA, IAI and RAS (2011) *Understanding the European Space Policy. The Reference Book* (Paris: Fondation pour la recherche stratégique).

Furness, M. (2013) 'Who controls the European External Action Service? Agent autonomy in EU external policy', *European Foreign Affairs Review*, 18(1), 103–26.

Fursdon, E. (1980) *The European Defence Community: A History* (London: Macmillan).

Gänzle, S. (2012) 'Coping with the "security–development nexus": the European Union and the instrument for stability' in Gänzle, S., Grimm, S. and Makhan, D. (eds.) *The European Union and Global Development: An 'Enlightened Superpower' in the Making?* (Basingstoke: Palgrave Macmillan), 116–35.

Gänzle, S., Grimm, S. and Makhan, D. (eds.) (2012) *The European Union and Global Development. An Enlightened Superpower in the Making?* (Basingstoke: Palgrave Macmillan).

Gariup, M. (2009) *European Security Culture. Language, Theory, Policy* (Hampshire: Ashgate).

Gebhard, C. (2011) 'Coherence' in Hill, C. and Smith, M. (eds.) *International Relations and the European Union* (Oxford: Oxford University Press), 101–27.

Gegout, C. (2010) *European Foreign and Security Policy: States, Power, Institutions, and American Hegemony* (Toronto: University of Toronto Press).

Ghazaryan, N. (2012) 'The ENP and the South Caucasus: meeting expectations?' in Whitman, R. and Wolff, S. (eds.) *The European Neighbourhood Policy in Perspective: Context, Implementation and Impact* (Basingstoke: Palgrave Macmillan), 223–46.

Gilson, J. (2012) 'The Asia–Europe Meeting (ASEM)' in Stubbs, R. and Beeson, M. (eds.) *Routledge Handbook of Asian Regionalism* (Oxon.: Routledge), 394–405.

Ginsberg, R. H. (2001) *The European Union in International Politics – Baptism by Fire* (New York: Rowman & Littlefield).

Ginsberg, R. H. and Penksa, S. E. (2012) *The European Union in Global Security: The Politics of Impact* (Basingstoke: Palgrave Macmillan).

Giovannini, A., Gros, D., Ivan, P., Kaczynski, P. M. and Valiante, D. (2012) *External Representation of the Euro Area* (Brussels: European Parliament).

Giumelli, F. (2010) 'Bringing effectiveness into the debate: a guideline to evaluating the success of EU targeted sanctions', *Central European Journal of International and Security Studies*, 4(1), 81–100.

— (2011) *Coercing, Constraining and Signaling: Explaining UN and EU Sanctions after the Cold War* (Essex: ECPR Press).

Giusti, S. and Penkova, T. (2012) 'Ukraine and Belarus: floating between the European Union and Russia' in Bindi, F. and Angelescu, I. (eds.) *The Foreign Policy of the European Union. Assessing Europe's Role in the World* (Washington, DC: Brookings Press), 134–52.

Glöckler, G. and Truchlewski, Z. (2011) 'From polyphony to harmony? The external representation of EMU' in Lieb, J., Schwarzer, D. and Van Ondarza, N. (eds.) *The European Union in International Fora: Lessons for the Union's External Representation after Lisbon* (Baden-Baden: Nomos), 117–36.

Gomez, R. (2003) *Negotiating the Euro-Mediterranean Partnership: Strategic Action in EU Foreign Policy* (Aldershot: Ashgate).

Goodin, R. E. and Tilly, C. (eds.) (2006) *The Oxford Handbook of Contextual Political Analysis* (Oxford: Oxford University Press).

Gottwald, J.-C. and Duggan, N. (2012) 'Diversity, pragmatism and convergence: China, the European Union and the issue of sovereignty' in Pan, Z. (ed.) *Conceptual Gaps in China–EU Relations: Global Governance, Human Rights and Strategic Partnerships* (Basingstoke: Palgrave Macmillan), 35–49.

Gough, I., Wood, G., Barrientos, A., Bevan, P., Davis, P. and Room, G. (eds.) (2004) *Insecurity and Welfare Regimes in Asia, Africa and Latin America* (Cambridge: Cambridge University Press).

Gourlay, C. (2010) 'UN–EU cooperation in peacebuilding: natural partners?' in Blockmans, S. and Wouters, J. (eds.) *The European Union and Peacebuilding: Policy and Legal Aspects* (The Hague: TMC Asser Press), 107–40.

— (2013) 'Civilian CSDP: a tool for state-building?' in Biscop, S. and Whitman, R. (eds.) *The Routledge Handbook of European Security* (Oxon.: Routledge), 91–104.

Gowan, R. (2012) 'Asymmetrical multilateralism: The BRICS, the US, Europe and the reform of global governance (2005–2011)' in Renard, T. and Biscop, S. (eds.) *The EU and Emerging Powers in the 21st Century: How Europe Can Shape a New Global Order* (Farnham: Ashgate), 165–84.

Gowan, R. and Brantner, F. (2008) 'A Global Force for Human Rights? An Audit of European Power at the UN', *ECFR Policy Paper*, 1–74.

— (2010) 'The EU and human rights at the UN: 2010 review', *ECFR Policy Brief*, 24, 1–12.

Gower, J. and Timmins, G. (eds.) (2010) *The European Union, Russia and the Shared Neighbourhood* (Oxon.: Routledge).

Grabbe, H. (2006) *The EU's Transformative Power: Europeanization through Conditionality in Central and Eastern Europe* (Basingstoke: Palgrave Macmillan).

Grant, W. (2011) 'Global governance and the Common Agricultural Policy' in Wunderlich, J.-U. and Bailey, D. (eds.) *The European Union and Global Governance. A Handbook* (Oxon.: Routledge), 149–56.

Gratius, S. (2012) 'The new six year term in Mexico and its (un)strategic relationship with the EU', *FRIDE Policy Brief*, 84, 1–5.

Grevi, G. (2013) 'The EU strategic partnerships: process and purposes' in Telò, M. and Ponjaert, F. (eds.) *The EU's Foreign Policy: What Kind of Power and Diplomatic Action?* (Aldershot: Ashgate), 159–74.

Grevi, G., Helly, D. and Keohane, D. (eds.) (2009) *European Security and Defence Policy. The First 10 years (1999–2009)* (Paris: European Union Institute for Security Studies).

Grevi, G. and Khandekar, G. (2011) *Mapping EU Strategic Partnerships* (Madrid: FRIDE).

Griller, S. and Ziller, J. (eds.) (2008) *The Lisbon Treaty: EU Constitutionalism without A Constitutional Treaty* (Wien: Springer).

Grimm, S. and Hackenesch, C. (2012) 'European engagement with emerging actors in development: forging new partnerships?' in Gänzle, S., Grimm, S. and Makhan, D. (eds.) *The European Union and Global Development: An 'Enlightened Superpower' in the Making?* (Basingstoke: Palgrave Macmillan), 211–28.

Grip, L. (2009) 'The EU non-proliferation clause: a preliminary assessment', *SIPRI Background Paper*, November, 1–19.

Groen, L., Niemann, A. and Oberthür, S. (2012) 'The EU as a global leader? The Copenhagen and Cancun UN climate change negotiations', *Journal of Contemporary European Research*, 8(2), 173–91.

Groom, A. (2006) 'Multilateralism as a way of life in Europe' in Newman, E., Tirman, J. and Thakur, R. (eds.) *Multilateralism under Challenge? Power, International Order, and Structural Change* (Tokyo: United Nations University Press), 460–480.

Gross, E. (2009) *The Europeanization of National Foreign Policy. Continuity and Change in European Crisis Management* (Basingstoke: Palgrave Macmillan).

— (2010) 'The EU in Afghanistan: peacebuilding in a conflict setting' in Blockmans, S., Wouters, J. and Ruys, T. (eds.) *The European Union and Peacebuilding: Policy and Legal Analysis* (The Hague: TMC Asser Press), 295–312.

— (2011) 'The EU in Afghanistan: crisis management in a transatlantic setting' in Gross, E. and Juncos, A. E. (eds.) *EU Conflict Prevention and Crisis Management: Roles, Institutions and Policies* (Oxon.: Routledge), 117–30.

Gross, E. and Jian, J. (2012) 'Conceptual gaps on global governance between China and the EU' in Pan, Z. (ed.) *Conceptual Gaps in China–EU Relations: Global Governance, Human Rights and Strategic Partnerships* (Basingstoke: Palgrave Macmillan), 202–215.

Gross, E. and Juncos, A. E. (eds.) (2011) *EU Conflict Prevention and Crisis Management. Institutions, Policies and Roles* (Oxon.: Routledge).

Gstöhl, S. (2009) '"Patchwork power" Europe: the EU's representation in international institutions', *European Foreign Affairs Review*, 14(3), 385–403.

— (2012) 'EU multilateral diplomacy after Lisbon: more single European voice in the United Nations?' in Mahncke, D. and Gstöhl, S. (eds.) *European Union Diplomacy. Coherence, Unity and Effectiveness* (Brussels: Peter Lang), 143–68.

Gstöhl, S. and Lannon, E. (eds.) (2014) *The Neighbours of the European Union's Neighbours: Diplomatic and Geopolitical Dimensions beyond the European Neighbourhood Policy* (Farnham: Ashgate).

Gürsel, S. (2013) 'Turkey as a regional power, unfounded ambition or future reality?' in Kastoryano, R. (ed.) *Turkey between Nationalism and Globalization* (Oxon.: Routledge),

Guzzini, S. (1993) 'Structural power: the limits of neorealist power analysis', *International Organization*, 47(3), 443–78.

Hadfield, A. (2007) 'Janus advances? An analysis of EC development policy and the 2005 Amended Cotonou Partnership Agreement', *European Foreign Affairs Review*, 12(1), 39–66.

Hadfield, A., Manners, I. and Whitman, R. (eds.) (2014) *Foreign Policies of EU Member States* (Oxon.: Routledge).

Hafner-Burton, E. M. (2009) 'The power politics of regime complexity: human rights trade conditionality in Europe', *Perspectives on Politics*, 7(1), 33–7.

Hallding, K., Olsson, M., Atteridge, A., Vihma, A., Carson, M. and Roman, M. (2011) *Together Alone. BASIC Countries and the Climate Change Conundrum* (Copenhagen: Nordic Council of Ministers).

Halliday, F. (2005) *The Middle East in International Relations. Power, Politics and Ideology* (Cambridge: Cambridge University Press).

Halper, S. A. (2010) *The Beijing Consensus: How China's Authoritarian Model Will Dominate the Twenty-first Century* (New York: Basic Books).

Hanf, D. (2012) 'The European Neighbourhood Policy in the light of the new "Neighbourhood Clause" (Article 8 TEU)' in Lannon, E. (ed.) *The European Neighbourhood Policy's Challenges* (Brussels: PIE Peter Lang), 109–26.

Harpaz, G. (2009) 'Judicial review by the European Court of justice of UN "smart sanctions" against terror in the Kadi dispute', *European Foreign Affairs Review*, 14(1), 65–88.

Haukkala, H. (2010) *The EU–Russia Strategic Partnership. The Limits of Post-Sovereignty in International Relations* (Oxon.: Routledge).

Held, D. and McGrew, A. (eds.) (2000) *The Global Transformations Reader. An Introduction to the Globalization Debate* (Cambridge: Polity Press).

— (eds.) (2002) *Governing Globalization. Power Authority and Global Governance* (Cambridge: Polity Press).

Held, D., McGrew, A., Goldblatt, D. and Perraton, J. (eds.) (1999) *Global Transformations. Politics Economics and Culture* (Cambridge: Polity Press).

Helly, D. (2012) 'The EU–South Africa strategic partnership: changing gear?', *ESPO Policy Brief*, 7.

— (2013) 'From the Sahel to Somalia: responding to crises' in Grevi, G. and Keohane, D. (eds.) *Challenges for European Foreign Policy in 2013* (Madrid: FRIDE), 71–8.

Helwig, N., Ivan, P. and Kostanyan, H. (2013) *The New EU Foreign Policy Architecture: Reviewing the First Two Years of the EEAS* (Brussels: Centre for European Policy Studies).

Hengari, A. T. (2012) 'The European Union and global emerging powers in Africa: containment, competition or cooperation?', *South African Journal of International Affairs*, 19(1), 1–24.

High Representative of the Union for Foreign Affairs and Security Policy and European Commission (2011) *Joint Communication – A new response to a changing neighbourhood: A review of European Neighbourhood Policy*, COM(2011) 303, 25 may.

Hill, C. (1993) 'The capability–expectations gap, or conceptualizing Europe's international role', *Journal of Common Market Studies*, 31(3), 305–28.

— (1998) 'Closing the capability–expectations gap' in Peterson, J. and Sjursen, H. (eds.) *A Common Foreign Policy for Europe? Competing Visions of the CFSP* (Oxon.: Routledge), 18–38.

— (2003) *The Changing Politics of Foreign Policy* (Basingstoke: Palgrave Macmillan).

— (2011) 'The Big Three and the High Representative: dilemmas of leadership inside and outside the EU' in Blavoukos, S. and Bourantonis, D. (eds.) *The EU Presence in International Organizations* (Oxon.: Routledge), 78–95.

Hill, C. and Smith, K. (2000) *European Foreign Policy. Key Documents* (Oxon.: Routledge).

Hill, C. and Wallace, W. (1996) 'Introduction: actors and actions' in Hill, C. (ed.) *The Actors in Europe's Foreign Policy* (Oxon.: Routledge), 1–18.

Hillion, C. and Koutrakos, P. (eds.) (2010) *Mixed Agreements Revisited. The EU and Its Member States in the World* (Oxford: Hart).

Hocking, B. (2005) 'Introduction: gatekeepers and boundary-spanners – thinking about foreign ministries in the European Union' in Hocking, B. and Spence, D. (eds.) *Foreign Ministries in the European Union. Integrating diplomats* (Basingstoke: Palgrave Macmillan), 1–17.

Hoffmeister, F. (2007) 'Outsider or frontrunner? Recent developments under international and European law on the status of the European Union in international organizations and treaty bodies', *Common Market Law Review*, 44, 41–68.

— (2011) 'The European Union's Common Commercial Policy a year after Lisbon – sea change or business as usual?' in Koutrakos, P. (ed.) *The European Union's External Relations a Year after Lisbon* (The Hague: CLEER working paper 2011/3), 83–95.

Hofmann, S. C. (2011) 'Why institutional overlap matters: CSDP in the European security architecture', *Journal of Common Market Studies*, 49(1), 101–20.

— (2012) 'CSDP: approaching transgovernmentalism?' in Kurowska, X. and Breuer, F. (eds.) *Explaining the EU's Common Security and Defence Policy: Theory in Action* (Basingstoke: Palgrave Macmillan), 41–62.

Hogan, M. (1987) *The Marshall Plan: America, Britain and the Reconstruction of Western Europe, 1947–1952* (Cambridge: Cambridge University Press).

Holden, P. (2009) *In Search of Structural Power: EU Aid Policy as a Global Political Instrument* (Aldershot: Ashgate).

— (2014) 'Testing EU structural diplomacy: the challenge of change in North Africa' in Smith, M.,

Keukeleire, S. and Vanhoonacker, S. (eds.) *The Diplomatic System of the European Union: Evolution, Change and Challenges* (Oxon.: Routledge),

Holland, M. (ed.) (1997) *Common Foreign and Security Policy. The Record and Reforms* (London: Pinter).

— (2002) *The European Union and the Third World* (Basingstoke: Palgrave Macmillan).

Holland, M. and Doidge, M. (2012) *Development policy of the European Union* (Basingstoke: Palgrave Macmillan).

Holslag, J. (2011a) 'The elusive axis: assessing the EU–China Strategic Partnership', *Journal of Common Market Studies*, 49(2), 293–313.

— (ed.) (2011b) 'Special issue: China's evolving Africa Policy: the limits of "socialization"', *Journal of Current Chinese Affairs*, 40(4), 3–173.

Holsti, K. J. (1970) 'National role conceptions in the study of foreign policy', *International Studies Quarterly*, 14(3), 233–309.

— (1995) *International Politics. A Framework for Analysis* (London: Prentice Hall).

Holzinger, K. and Schimmelfennig, F. (2012) 'Differentiated integration in the European Union: many concepts, sparse theory, few data', *Journal of European Public Policy*, 19(2), 292–305.

Horký, O. and Lightfoot, S. (eds.) (2012) 'Special issue: from aid recipients to aid donors?: Development policies of Central and Eastern European states', *Perspectives on European Politics and Society*, 13(1), 1–130.

House of Lords (2012) *European Defence Capabilities: Lessons from the Past, Signposts for the Future*, 31st Report of Session 2010–12, European Union Committee, 4 May.

Howorth, J. (2000) 'Britain, France and the European Defence Initiative', *Survival*, 42(2), 22–55.

— (2001) 'European defence and the changing politics of the European Union: hanging together or hanging separately', *Journal of Common Market Studies*, 39(4), 765–89.

— (2007) *Security and Defence Policy in the European Union* (Basingstoke: Palgrave Macmillan).

— (2010) 'Sarkozy and the American mirage or why Gaullist continuity will overshadow transcendence', *European Political Science*, 9(2), 199–212.

— (2011) 'The "new faces" of Lisbon: assessing the performance of Catherine Ashton and Herman Van Rompuy on the global stage', *European Foreign Affairs Review*, 16(3), 303–23.

— (2012) 'Decision-making in security and defense policy: towards supranational inter-governmentalism?' *Cooperation and Conflict*, 47(4), 433–53.

— (2014) *Security and Defence Policy in the European Union* (Basingstoke: Palgrave Macmillan).

Huff, A. (2011) 'The role of EU defence policy in the eastern neighbourhood', *ISS Occasional Paper*, 11, 1–41.

Hughes, E. (2011) *Turkey's Accession to the European Union: The Politics of Exclusion?* (Oxon.: Routledge).

Huysmans, J. (2006) *The Politics of Insecurity: Fear, Migration and Asylum in the EU* (Oxon.: Routledge).

Hyde-Price, A. (2006) '"Normative" power Europe: a realist critique', *Journal of European Public Policy*, 13(2), 217–34.

— (2012) 'Neorealism: a structural approach to CSDP' in Kurowska, X. and Breuer, F. (eds.) *Explaining the EU's Common Security and Defence Policy: Theory in Action* (Basingstoke: Palgrave Macmillan), 16–40.

— (2013) 'Realism: a dissident voice in the study of the CSDP' in Biscop, S. and Whitman, R. (eds.) *The Routledge Handbook of European Security* (Oxon.: Routledge),

Hynek, N. (2011) 'EU crisis management after the Lisbon Treaty: civil–military coordination and the future of the EU OHQ', *European Security*, 20(1), 81–102.

Hynek, N. and Eichler, J. (2012) 'A Faustian bargain: US clients in the "New Europe" and regime change wars', *International Peacekeeping*, 19(4), 525–38.

IEA/OECD (2011) *Facts on Libya: oil and gas*, iea.org.

ILO (International Labour Organization) (2012) ILO 2012 *Global Estimate of Forced Labour – Executive Summary* (Geneva: ILO).

IMF (2012) *Factsheet. The IMF and Europe*, IMF.org.

Inayatullah, N. and Blaney, D. L. (2004) *International Relations and the Problem of Difference* (New York/London: Routledge).

Inkster, N. (2010) 'Terrorism in Europe' in Giegerich, B. (ed.) *Europe and Global Security* (Oxon.: Routledge), 79–102.

International Crisis Group (2011) 'Popular protests in North Africa and the Middle East (III): the Bahrain revolt', *Crisis Group Middle East/North Africa Report*, 105.

International Institute for Strategic Studies (IISS) (2011) *The Military Balance 2011*. (London: IISS).
— (2012) *The Military Balance 2012* (London: IISS).
— (2013) *The Military Balance 2013* (London: IISS).
Ioannides, I. and Collantes-Celador, G. (2011) 'The internal–external–security nexus and EU police/rule of law missions in the Western Balkans', *Conflict, Security & Development*, 11(4), 415–45.
Irondelle, B., Bickerton, C. J. and Menon, A. (eds.) (2011) 'Special issue: security cooperation beyond the nation state: the EU's Common Security and Defence Policy', *Journal of Common Market Studies*, 49(1), 1–190.
Irondelle, B. and Mérand, F. (2010) 'France's return to NATO: the death knell for ESDP?' *European Security*, 19(1), 29–43.
Jain, R. K. (2012) 'The European Union as a global power: Indian perceptions', *Perspectives*, 20(2), 31–44.
Jeandesboz, J. and Ragazzi, F. (2010) *Review of Security Measures in the Research Framework Programme* (Brussels: European Parliament).
Johannsen, J. (2011) *The EU's Comprehensive Approach to Crisis Management* (Baden-Baden: Nomos).
Jokela, J. (2011a) *Europeanization and Foreign Policy. State Identity in Finland and Britain* (Oxon.: Routledge).
— (2011b) 'The G-20: a pathway to effective multilateralism?', *EU Institute for Security Studies – Chaillot Papers*, 125.
Jönsson, C. (2002) 'Diplomacy, bargaining and negotiation' in Carlsnaes, W., Risse, T. and Simmons, B. A. (eds.) *Handbook of International Relations* (London: Sage), 212–34.
Jordan, A., Huitema, D., Van Asselt, H., Rayner, T. and Berkhout, F. (eds.) (2010) *Climate Change Policy in the European Union. Confronting the Dilemmas of Mitigation and Adaptation?* (Cambridge: Cambridge University Press).
Jørgensen, K. E. (1997) 'PoCo: the diplomatic republic of Europe' in Jørgensen, K. E. (ed.) *Reflective Approaches to European Governance* (London: MacMillan), 167–80.
— (2012) 'Analysing the performance of the European Union' in Jørgensen, K. E. and Laatikainen, K. (eds.) *Routledge Handbook on the European Union and International Institutions* (Oxon.: Routledge), 86–101.
Jørgensen, K. E. and Aarstad, A. K. (2012) 'Liberal, constructivist and critical studies of European security' in Biscop, S. and Whitman, R. (eds.) *The Routledge Handbook of European Security* (Oxon.: Routledge), 28–37.
Jørgensen, K. E. and Laatikainen, K. V. (eds.) (2013) *Routledge Handbook on the European Union and International Institutions: Performance, Policy, Power* (Oxon.: Routledge).
Jørgensen, K. E., Oberthür, S. and Shahin, J. (2011) 'Introduction: assessing the EU's performance in international institutions – conceptual framework and core findings', *Journal of European Integration*, 33(6), 599–620.
Jørgensen, K. E. and Wessel, R. A. (2011) 'The position of the European Union in (other) international organizations: confronting legal and political approaches' in Koutrakos, P. (ed.) *European Foreign Policy. Legal and Political Perspectives* (Cheltenham: Edward Elgar), 261–86.
Juncos, A. and Pomorska, K. (2013) '"In the face of adversity": explaining the attitudes of EEAS officials vis-à-vis the new service', *Journal of European Public Policy*, 20(9), 1332–49.
Juncos, A. E. (2011) 'The other side of EU crisis management: a sociological institutionalist analysis' in Gross, E. and Juncos, A. E. (eds.) *Conflict Prevention and Crisis Management* (Oxon.: Routledge), 84–100.
— (2012) 'Member state-building versus peacebuilding: the contradictions of EU state-building in Bosnia and Herzegovina', *East European Politics*, 28(1), 58–75.
Justaert, A. (2012) 'The implementation of EU's security sector reform policies in the DR Congo', *European Security*, 21(2), 219–35.
— (2014) 'Reform without alignment? The lack of a European structural diplomacy in the Congolese police reform' in Smith, M., Keukeleire, S. and Vanhoonacker, S. (eds.) *The Diplomatic System of the European Union: Evolution, Change and Challenges* (Oxon.: Routledge),
Justaert, A. and Keukeleire, S. (2010) 'The EU's security sector reform policies in the Democratic Republic of Congo', *European Integration Online Papers-EIoP*, 14(1).
— (2012) 'Informal governance and networks in EU foreign policy' in Christiansen, T. and Neuhold, C. (eds.) *International Handbook on Informal Governance* (Cheltenham: Edward Elgar), 558–90.
Kaczmarski, M. (2011) 'Which rules for the global order? The global dimension of the Russian–EU

relationship – the case of international crises', *Journal of Contemporary European Research*, 7(2), 159–74.

Karatnycky, A. (2005) 'Ukraine's Orange Revolution', *Foreign Affairs*, 84(2), 35–52.

Kaunert, C. and Zwolski, K. (2012) 'Somalia versus Captain "Hook": assessing the EU's security actorness in countering piracy off the Horn of Africa', *Cambridge Review of International Affairs*, iFirst, 1–20.

Kavalski, E. (2012) *Central Asia and the Rise of Normative Powers: Contextualizing the Security Governance of the European Union, China, and India* (London: Bloomsbury).

Kayaoglu, T. (2010) 'Westphalian Eurocentrism in International Relations theories', *International Studies Review*, 12(2), 193–217.

Keck, J., Vanoverbeke, D. and Waldenberger, F. (eds.) (2013) *EU–Japan Relations, 1970–2012. From Confrontation to Global Partnership* (Oxon.: Routledge).

Kelemen, D. R. (2010) 'Globalizing European Union environmental policy', *Journal of European Public Policy*, 17(3), 335–49.

Kelemen, D. R. and Vogel, D. (2010) 'Trading places: the role of the United States and the European Union in International Environmental politics', *Comparative Political Studies*, 43(4), 427–56.

Kelly, R. (2012) 'Korea–European Union relations: beyond the FTA?', *International Relations of the Asia-Pacific*, 12(1), 101–32.

Ker-Lindsay, J. (2011) 'Between "pragmatism" and "constitutionalism": EU–Russian dynamics and differences during the Kosovo status process', *Journal of Contemporary European Research*, 7(2), 175–94.

Kerremans, B. (2004a) 'The European Commission and the EU member states as actors in the WTO negotiating process: decision making between Scylla and Charibdis?' in Reinalda, B. and Verbeek, B. (eds.) *Decision Making within International Organizations* (Oxon.: Routledge), 45–58.

— (2004b) 'What went wrong in Cancun? A principal–agent view on the EU's rationale towards the Doha Development Round', *European Foreign Affairs Review*, 9(3), 363–93.

— (2006) 'Proactive policy entrepreneur or risk minimizer? A principal–agent interpretation of the EU's role in the WTO' in Elgström, O. and Smith, M. (eds.) *The European Union's Roles in International Politics. Concepts and Analysis* (Oxon.: Routledge), 172–88.

— (2011) 'The European Commission in the WTO's DDA negotiations. A tale of an agent, a single undertaking, and twenty-seven nervous principals' in Blavoukos, S. and Bourantonis, D. (eds.) *The EU Presence in International Organizations* (Oxon.: Routledge), 132–49.

Kerremans, B. and Orbie, J. (2009) 'The social dimension of European Union trade policies', *European Foreign Affairs Review*, 14(5), 629–41.

Kettell, B. (2011) *Introduction to Islamic Banking and Finance* (Chichester: Wiley).

Keukeleire, S. (1998) *Het buitenlands beleid van de Europese Unie* (Deventer: Kluwer).

— (2003) 'The European Union as a diplomatic actor: internal, traditional and structural diplomacy', *Diplomacy and Statecraft*, 14(3), 31–56.

— (2006) 'EU foreign policy and (the lack of) "political will"', *CFSP Forum*, 4(5), 11–14.

— (2008) 'The European Union as a diplomatic actor: internal, traditional and structural diplomacy' in Rees, W. and Smith, M. (eds.) *International Relations of the European Union* (London: Sage).

— (2013) 'Concluding remarks' in Metais, R., Thépaut, C. and Keukeleire, S. (eds.) *The EU's Rule of Law promotion in its Neighbourhood: A Structural Foreign Policy Analysis* (College of Europe: EU Diplomacy Paper, no. 4), 66–9.

— (2014a, forthcoming) 'Structural foreign policy: reconstituting political agency in a globalized world' (*submitted*).

— (2014b) 'Lessons for EU Diplomacy from an outside-in perspective' in Gstöhl, S. and Lannon, E. (eds.) *The Neighbours of the European Union's Neighbours: Diplomatic and Geopolitical Dimensions beyond the European Neighbourhood Policy* (Farnham: Ashgate),

Keukeleire, S. and Bruyninckx, H. (2011) 'The European Union, the BRICs and the emerging new world order' in Hill, C. and Smith, M. (eds.) *International Relations and the European Union* (Oxford: Oxford University Press), 380–403.

Keukeleire, S. and Hooijmaaijers, B. (2014) 'The BRICS and other emerging power alliances and multilateral organisations in the Asia-Pacific and the Global South: challenges for the European Union and its view on multilateralism', *Journal of Common Market Studies*, 52 (forthcoming).

Keukeleire, S. and Justaert, A. (2012) 'EU foreign policy and the challenges of structural diplomacy: comprehensiveness, coordination, alignment and learning', *DSEU Policy Paper*, 12.

Keukeleire, S., Justaert, A. and Thiers, R. (2009) 'Reappraising diplomacy: structural diplomacy and the case of the European Union', *The Hague Journal of Diplomacy*, 4(2), 143–65.

Keukeleire, S., Kalaja, A. and Çollaku, A. (2011) 'The European Union's policy on Kosovo' in Koutrakos, P. (ed.) *European Foreign Policy. Legal and Political Perspectives* (Cheltenham: Edward Elgar), 172–203.

Keukeleire, S., Keuleers, F. and Raube, K. (2014) 'Structural diplomacy of the European Union' in Smith, M., Keukeleire, S. and Vanhoonacker, S. (eds.) *The Diplomatic System of the European Union: Evolution, Change and Challenges* (Oxon.: Routledge),

Keukeleire, S. and MacNaughtan, J. (2008) *The Foreign Policy of the European Union* (Basingstoke: Palgrave Macmillan).

Keukeleire, S., Mattlin, M., Hooijmaaijers, B., Behr, T., Jokela, J., Wigell, M. and Kononenko, V. (2011) *The EU Foreign Policy towards the BRICS and Other Emerging Powers: Objectives and Strategies* (Brussels: European Parliament).

Keukeleire, S. and Metais, R. (2014) 'Structural diplomacy in action: the EU and Kosovo' in Smith, M., Keukeleire, S. and Vanhoonacker, S. (eds.) *The Diplomatic System of the European Union: Evolution, Change and Challenges* (Oxon.: Routledge).

Keukeleire, S. and Petrova, I. (2014) 'The EU, Eastern partnership and Russia', in Telò, M. (ed.), *European Union and New Regionalism: Regional Actors and Global Governance in a Post-Hegemonic Era* (Aldershot: Ashgate).

Keukeleire, S. and Raube, K. (2013) 'The security–development nexus and securitisation in the EU's policies towards developing countries', *Cambridge Review of International Affairs*, 26(4).

Keukeleire, S. and Thiers, R. (2010) 'EULEX Kosovo' in Blockmans, S., Wouters, J. and Ruys, T. (eds.) *The European Union and Peacebuilding. Policy and Legal Aspects* (The Hague: TMC Asser Press), 353–74.

Khan, I. (2009) *The Unheard Truth: Poverty and Human Rights* (New York: W. W. Norton).

Kirchner, E. (2011) 'EU contribution to and cooperation with multilateral organizations' in Blavoukos, S. and Bourantonis, D. (eds.) *The EU Presence in International Organizations* (Oxon.: Routledge), 16–32.

Kirchner, E. and Berk, C. (2010) 'European energy security co-operation: between amity and enmity', *Journal of Common Market Studies*, 48(4), 859–80.

Kirisci, K. (2012) 'Turkey's engagement with its neighborhood: a "synthetic" and multidimensional look at Turkey's foreign policy transformation', *Turkish Studies*, 13(2), 319–41.

Kissack, R. (2010) *Pursuing Effective Multilateralism. The European Union, International Organisations and the Politics of Decision Making* (Basingstoke: Palgrave Macmillan).

— (2011) 'The performance of the European Union in the International Labour Organization', *Journal of European Integration*, 33(6), 651–65.

— (2012) 'The EU in the negotiations of a UN General Assembly Resolution on a Moratorium on the Use of the Death Penalty' in Wouters, J., Bruyninckx, H., Basu, S. and Schunz, S. (eds.) *The European Union and Multilateral Governance* (Basingstoke: Palgrave),

Klein, N. (2011) 'Conceptualizing the EU as a civil–military crisis manager: institutional actors and their principals' in Gross, E. and Juncos, A. E. (eds.) *Conflict Prevention and Crisis Management* (Oxon.: Routledge), 66–83.

Klinke, I. (2007) 'The European Union's strategic non-engagement in Belarus. Challenging the hegemonic notion of the EU as a toothless value diffuser', *Perspectives*, 27, 25–43.

Knudsen, T. B. (2013) 'The responsibility to protect: European contributions in a changing world order' in Jørgensen, K. E. and Laatikainen, K. V. (eds.) *Routledge Handbook on the European Union and International Institutions: Performance, Policy, Power* (Oxon.: Routledge), 157–70.

Koops, J. A. (2011) *The European Union as an integrative power? Assessing the EU's 'Effective Multilateralism' towards NATO and the United Nations* (Brussels: VUB Press).

— (2012) 'NATO's influence on the evolution of the European Union as a security actor' in Costa, O. and Jørgensen, K. E. (eds.) *The Influence of International Institutions on the European Union* (Basingstoke: Palgrave MacMillan), 155–85.

Korosteleva, E. (ed.) (2011) 'Special issue: the Eastern Partnership initiative', *Journal of Communist Studies and Transition Politics*, 27(1), 1–141.

— (ed.) (2013) *Eastern Partnership: A New Opportunity for the Neighbours?* (Oxon.: Routledge).

Kratochvil, P. and Tulmets, E. (2010) *Constructivism and Rationalism in EU External Relations. The Case of the European Neighbourhood Policy* (Baden-Baden: Nomos).

Kulovesi, K., Morgera, E. and Muñoz, M. (2011) 'Environmental integration and multi-faceted international dimensions of EU Law: unpacking the EU's 2009 climate and energy package', *Common Market Law Review*, 48(3), 829–91.

Kurowska, X. and Breuer, F. (eds.) (2012) *Explaining the EU's Common Security and Defence Policy: Theory in Action* (Basingstoke: Palgrave Macmillan).

Kurowska, X. and Kratochvil, P. (2012) 'The social constructivist sensibility and CSDP research' in Kurowska, X. and Breuer, F. (eds.) *Explaining the EU's Common Security and Defence Policy: Theory in Action* (Basingstoke: Palgrave Macmillan), 86–110.

Kuzemko, C., Belyi, A., Goldthau, A. and Keating, M. F. (eds.) (2012) *Dynamics of Energy Governance in Europe and Russia* (Basingstoke: Palgrave Macmillan).

Laatikainen, K. V. (2010) 'Multilateral leadership at the UN after the Lisbon Treaty', *European Foreign Affairs Review*, 15(4), 475–93.

Laatikainen, K. V. and Smith, K. (2006a) 'Introduction – the European Union at the United Nations: leader, partner or failure?' in Smith, K. E. and Laatikainen, K. V. (eds.) *Intersecting Multilateralisms: The European Union and the United Nations* (Basingstoke: Palgrave Macmillan), 1–23.

— (eds.) (2006b) *Intersecting Multilateralisms: The European Union and the United Nations* (Basingstoke: Palgrave Macmillan).

Lacher, W. (2012) 'Organized crime and conflict in the Sahel–Sahara region', *Carnegie Papers*, September, 1–25.

Laenen, R. (2012) 'Russia's "vital and exclusive" national interests in the near abroad' in Freire, M. R. and Kanet, R. E. (eds.) *Russia and Its Near Neighbours* (Basingstoke: Palgrave Macmillan), 17–38.

Laïdi, Z. (ed.) (2008) *EU Foreign Policy in a Globalized World. Normative Power and Social Preferences* (Oxon.: Routledge).

Lake, D. A. (2010) 'Making America safe for the world: multilateralism and the rehabilitation of US authority', *Global Governance*, 16(4), 471–84.

Lamy, P. (2002) 'Europe's role in global governance: the way ahead'. Speech at Humboldt University, Berlin.

Lamy, S. L. (2011) 'Contemporary mainstream approaches: neo-realism and neo-liberalism' in Baylis, J., Smith, S. and Owens, P. (eds.) *The Globalization of World Politics. An Introduction to International Relations* (Oxford: Oxford University Press), 114–29.

Langton, C. (2010) 'The effects of global demographics' in Giegerich, B. (ed.) *Europe and Global Security* (London: International Institute for Strategic Studies), 59–77.

Lannon, E. (ed.) (2012) *The European Neighbourhood Policy's Challenges* (Brussels: PIE Peter Lang).

Lannon, E. and Van Elsuwege, P. (2012) 'The Eastern Partnership. Prospects of a new regional dimension within the European Neighbourhood Policy' in Lannon, E. (ed.) *The European Neighbourhood Policy's Challenges* (Brussels: PIE Peter Lang).

Larik, J. and Weiler, Q. (2011) 'Going naval in troubled waters: the EU, China and the fight against piracy off the coast of Somalia' in Men, J. and Barton, B. (eds.) *China and the European Union: Partners or Competitors in Africa?* (Hampshire: Ashgate), 81–104.

Larsen, H. (2009) 'A distinct FPA for Europe? Towards a comprehensive framework for analysing the foreign policy of EU member states', *European Journal of International Relations*, 15(3), 537–66.

Larsen, H. B. L. (2012) 'The Russo-Georgian war and beyond: towards a European great power concert', *European Security*, 21(1), 102–21.

Latouche, S. (1996) *The Westernization of the World* (Cambridge: Polity Press).

Laursen, F. and Vanhoonacker, S. (eds.) (1992) *The Intergovernmental Conference on Political Union. Institutional Reforms, New Policies and International Identity of the European Union* (Maastricht: EIPA and Martinus Nijhoff).

Lavenex, S. (2004) 'EU external governance in "wider Europe"', *Journal of European Public Policy*, 11(4), 680–700.

— (2006) 'EU immigration policies between supranational integration and intergovernmental venue-shopping', *EUSA Review*, 19(3).

— (2011) 'Concentric circles of flexible European integration: a typology of EU external governance relations', *Comparative European Politics*, 9(3), 372–93.

Lavenex, S. and Schimmelfennig, F. (eds.) (2009a) 'Special issue: European Union external governance', *Journal of European Public Policy*, 16(6), 791–949.

— (2009b) 'EU rules beyond EU borders: theorizing external governance in European politics', *Journal of European Public Policy*, 16(6), 791–812.

— (eds.) (2010) *EU External Governance. Projecting EU Rules beyond Membership* (Oxon.: Routledge).

— (eds.) (2012) *Democracy Promotion in the EU's Neighbourhood: From Leverage to Governance?* (Oxon.: Routledge).

Lavenex, S. and Wichmann, N. (2009) 'The External governance of EU internal security', *Journal of European Integration*, 31(1), 83–102.

Lehne, S. (2012) 'Kosovo and Serbia. Toward a normal relationship', *Carnegie Policy Outlook*, March.

Lenaerts, K. and Van Nuffel, P. (2011) *European Union Law* (London: Sweet & Maxwell).

Li, A. and Liu, H. (2013) *China and Africa in a Global Context*. Articles, chapters and reviews published by PKUCAS members (Beijing: Center for African Studies – Peking University).

Lindstrom, G. (2007) 'Enter the EU Battlegroups', *EU Institute for Security Studies – Chaillot Papers*, 97.

Liqun, Z. (2010) 'China's foreign policy debates', *Chaillot paper*, 121.

Lirong, L. (2011) 'The EU and China's engagement in Africa: the dilemma of socialisation', *ISS Occasional Paper*, 93.

Liu, H. (2012) 'Africa's emerging endogenous dynamics and new thoughts on Sino-African cooperation' in Jisi, W. (ed.) *China International Strategy Review 2012* (Beijing: Center for International and Strategic Studies), 210–30.

Lokongo, A. R. (2012) 'The distorted democracy in Africa: examining the cases of South Africa, Libya and Ivory Coast', *International Critical Thought*, 2(2), 209–27.

Lord, C. (2011) 'Legitimate and democratic? The EU's international role' in Hill, C. and Smith, M. (eds.) *International Relations and the European Union* (Oxford: Oxford University Press), 128–48.

Lucarelli, S. and Fioramonti, L. (eds.) (2010) *External Perceptions of the European Union as a Global Actor* (Oxon.: Routledge).

Lucarelli, S. and Manners, I. (eds.) (2006) *Values and Principles in European Union Foreign Policy* (Oxon.: Routledge).

Lucarelli, S., Van Langenhove, L. and Wouters, J. (eds.) (2013) *The EU and Multilateral Security Governance* (Oxon.: Routledge).

Lütz, S. and Kranke, M. (2011) 'Paradox of weakness in crisis lending: how the European Commission prevails over the IMF', paper presented at ISA Annual Conference, Montreal.

Macaj, G. (2011) 'The "one voice" monologues: a critique of the EU's diplomatic outreach at the UN Human Rights Council', paper presented at doctoral workshop 'EU as a Global Actor', Paris.

McInnes, C. and Lee, K. (2006) 'Health, security and foreign policy', *Review of International Studies*, 32, 5–23.

MacKenzie, A. (2010) 'The European Union's increasing role in foreign policy counterterrorism', *Journal of Contemporary European Research*, 6(2), 147–63.

Macmillan, C. (2010) 'Privileged partnership, open ended accession negotiations and the securitisation of Turkey's EU accession process', *Journal of Contemporary European Studies*, 18(4), 447–62.

Magen, A., Risse, T. and McFaul, M. A. (eds.) (2009) *Promoting Democracy and the Rule of Law: American and European Strategies* (Basingstoke: Palgrave Macmillan).

Mahbubani, K. (2008) *The New Asian Hemisphere. The Irresistible Shift of Global Power to the East* (New York: Public Affairs).

— (2013) *The Great Convergence. Asia, the West, and the Logic of One World* (New York: Public Affairs).

Mahncke, D. and Gstöhl, S. (eds.) (2012) *European Union Diplomacy. Coherence, Unity and Effectiveness* (Brussels: Peter Lang).

Major, C. and Mölling, C. (2011) 'EU Battlegroups: what contribution to European defence?', *SWP Research Paper*, 8.

Malfliet, K., Verpoest, L. and Vinokurov, E. (eds.) (2007) *The CIS, The EU and Russia. Challenges of Integration* (Basingstoke: Palgrave Macmillan).

Mangala, J. (ed.) (2013), *Africa and the European Union. A Strategic Partnership* (Basingstoke: Palgrave Macmillan).

Manners, I. (2002) 'Normative power Europe: a contradiction in terms?' *Journal of Common Market Studies*, 40(2), 235–58.

— (2006) 'Normative power Europe reconsidered: beyond the crossroads', *Journal of European Public Policy*, 13(2), 182–99.

— (2012) 'The European Union's normative power in global politics' in Zimmermann, H. and Dür, A. (eds.) *Key Controversies in European Integration* (Basingstoke: Palgrave Macmillan), 192–9.

Manners, I. and Whitman, R. (2000a) 'Conclusion' in Manners, I. and Whitman, R. (eds.) *The Foreign Policies of European Union Member States* (Manchester: Manchester University Press), 243–73.

— (eds.) (2000b) *The Foreign Policies of European Union Member States* (Manchester: Manchester University Press).

Marangoni, A. (2013) 'Coordination of external policies: feudal fiefdoms to coordinate.

Organisational and procedural frameworks of consistency within the European Commission' in Boening, A., Kremer, J. and van Loon, A. (eds.) *Global Power Europe Vol. 1* (Berlin: Springer-Verlag), 37–54.

March, J. and Olsen, J. (1989) *Rediscovering Institutions. The Organizational Basics of Politics* (New York: Free Press).

Maresceau, M. and Lannon, E. (eds.) (2001) *The EU's Enlargement and Mediterranean Strategies. A Comparative Analysis* (Basingstoke: Palgrave Macmillan).

Marsh, S. and Rees, W. (2012) *The European Union in the Security of Europe. From Cold War to Terror War* (Oxon.: Routledge).

Marshall, G. (1947) *The Marshall Plan Speech*, America.gov.

Martin, I. (2012) 'The European Neighbourhood Policy response to the socio-economic challenges in the Arab Mediterranean partner "countries"' in Lannon, E. (ed.) *The European Neighbourhood Policy's Challenges* (Brussels: PIE Peter Lang), 225–48.

Martinelli, M. (2010) 'Strengthening security, building peace: the EU in the Democratic Republic of Congo' in Blockmans, S., Wouters, J. and Ruys, T. (eds.) *The European Union and Peacebuilding. Policy and Legal Aspects* (The Hague: TMC Asser Press), 221–48.

Mattelaer, A. (2013) *The Politico-Military Dynamics of European Crisis Response Operations* (Basingstoke: Palgrave Macmillan).

Mayer, H. (2013) 'The challenge of coherence and consistency in EU foreign policy' in Telò, M. and Ponjaert, F. (eds.) *The EU's Foreign Policy: What Kind of Power and Diplomatic Action?* (Aldershot: Ashgate), 105–18.

Mayer, H. and Zielonka, J. (eds.) (2012) 'Special issue: Europe as a global power: views from the outside', *Perspectives*, 20(2), 1–128.

Mbangu, L. (2005) 'Recent cases of Article 96 consultations', *ECDPM Discussion Paper*, 64.

Meijer, H. L. E. (2010) 'Post-Cold War trends in the European defence industry: implications for transatlantic industrial relations', *Journal of Contemporary European Studies*, 18(1), 63–77.

Men, J. (2011) 'Between human rights and sovereignty – an examination of EU–China political relations', *European Law Journal*, 17(4), 534–50.

Men, J. and Balducci, G. (2010) *Prospects and Challenges for EU–China Relations in the 21st Century: The Partnership and Cooperation Agreement* (Brussels: Peter Lang).

Men, J. and Barton, B. (eds.) (2011) *China and the European Union: Partners or competitors in Africa?* (Hampshire: Ashgate).

Menon, A. (2011a) 'European defence policy from Lisbon to Libya', *Survival*, 53(3), 75–90.

— (2011b) 'Power, institutions and the CSDP: the promises of institutionalist theory', *Journal of Common Market Studies*, 49(1), 83–100.

Mérand, F. (2012) 'Bricolage: a sociologic approach to the making of CSDP' in Kurowska, X. and Breuer, F. (eds.) *Explaining the EU's Common Security and Defence Policy: Theory in Action* (Basingstoke: Palgrave Macmillan), 136–61.

Mérand, F., Hofmann, S. C. and Irondelle, B. (2011) 'Governance and state power: a network analysis of European security', *Journal of Common Market Studies*, 49(1), 121–47.

Merket, H. (2012) 'The European External Action Service and the nexus between CFSP/CSDP and development cooperation', *European Foreign Affairs Review*, 17(4), 625–52.

Merlingen, M. (2011) 'From governance to governmentality in CSDP: towards a Foucauldian research agenda', *Journal of Common Market Studies*, 49(1), 149–69.

— (2012) *EU Security Policy: What It Is, How It Works, Why It Matters* (Boulder, CO: Lynne Rienner).

— (2013) 'The CSDP in the Western Balkans: from experimental pilot to security governance' in Biscop, S. and Whitman, R. (eds.) *The Routledge Handbook of European Security* (Oxon.: Routledge), 145–58.

Metais, R., Thépaut, C. and Keukeleire, S. (2013) 'The EU's rule of law promotion in its neighbourhood: a structural foreign policy analysis', *EU Diplomacy Paper*, 4, College of Europe, 1–73.

Meunier, S. (2005) *Trading Voices. The European Union in International Commercial Negotiations* (Princeton, NJ: Princeton University Press).

Meunier, S. and Nicolaïdis, K. (2005) 'The European Union as a trade power' in Hill, C. and Smith, M. (eds.) *International Relations and the European Union* (Oxford: Oxford University Press), 247–69.

— (2006) 'The European Union as a conflicted trade power', *Journal of European Public Policy*, 13(6), 906–25.

— (2011) 'The European Union as a trade power' in Hill, C. and Smith, M. (eds.) *International Relations and the European Union* (Oxford: Oxford University Press), 275–98.

Meyer, C. O. (2004) 'Theorising European strategic culture. Between convergence and the persistence of national diversity', *CEPS Working Document*, 204, 25.

— (2007) *The Quest for a European Strategic Culture: Changing Norms on Security and Defence in the European Union* (Basingstoke: Palgrave Macmillan).

— (2013) 'European strategic culture: taking stock and looking ahead' in Biscop, S. and Whitman, R. (eds.) *The Routledge Handbook on European Security* (Oxon.: Routledge),

Meyer, C. O. and Strickmann, E. (2011) 'Solidifying constructivism: how material and ideational factors interact in European defence', *Journal of Common Market Studies*, 49(1), 61–81.

Michel, L. (2013) 'NATO and the United States: working together with the EU to strengthen Euro-Atlantic security' in Biscop, S. and Whitman, R. (eds.) *The Routledge Handbook of European Security* (Oxon.: Routledge), 255–69.

Migdal, J. S. (1988) *Strong Societies and Weak States: State-Society Relations and State Capabilities in the Third World* (Princeton, NJ: Princeton University Press).

— (2001) *State in Society: Studying How States and Societies Transform and Constitute One Another* (Cambridge: Cambridge University Press).

Ministry of External Affairs India (2012) *Media Note on the informal meeting of BRICS leaders ahead of G20 Summit in Los Cabos*, mea.gov.in.

Missiroli, A. (2010) 'The new EU "foreign policy" system after Lisbon: a work in progress', *European Foreign Affairs Review*, 15(4), 427–52.

Möckli, D. and Maurer, V. (eds.) (2011) *European–American Relations and the Middle East. From Suez to Iraq* (Oxon.: Routledge).

Mölling, C. and Brune, S.-C. (2011) *The Impact of the Financial Crisis on European Defence* (Brussels: European Parliament).

Monar, J. (2010) 'The rejection of the EU–US SWIFT Interim Agreement by the European Parliament: a historic vote and its implications', *European Foreign Affairs Review*, 15(2), 143–51.

Monar, J. and Wessels, W. (2001) *The European Union after the Amsterdam Treaty* (London: Continuum).

Monnet, J. (2003) 'A ferment of change' in Nelsen, B. F. and Stubb, A. (eds.) *The European Union. Readings on the Theory and Practice of European Integration* (Basingstoke: Palgrave Macmillan), 19–26.

Morlino, L. and Sadurski, W. (eds.) (2010) *Democratization and the European Union. Comparing Central and Eastern European Post-Communist Countries* (Oxon.: Routledge).

Moumoutzis, K. (2011) 'Still fashionable yet useless? Addressing problems with research on the Europeanization of foreign policy', *Journal of Common Market Studies*, 49(3), 607–29.

Mügge, D. (2011) 'The European presence in global financial governance: a principal–agent perspective', *Journal of European Public Policy*, 18(3), 383–402.

Müller, P. (2012) *EU Foreign Policymaking and the Middle East Conflict. The Europeanization of National Foreign Policy* (Oxon.: Routledge).

Müller, P. and Spencer, C. (2011) 'From Madrid to Camp David: Europe, the US, and the Middle East peace process in the 1990s' in Möckli, D. and Maurer, V. (eds.) *European–American Relations and the Middle East. From Suez to Iraq* (Oxon.: Routledge), 108–23.

Müller-Brandeck-Bocquet, G. (2006) *The Future of European Foreign, Security and Defence Policy after Enlargement* (Baden-Baden: Nomos Verlag).

Müller-Brandeck-Bocquet, G. and Rüger, C. (eds.) (2011) *The High Representative for the EU Foreign and Security Policy – Review and Prospects* (Baden-Baden: Nomos Verlag).

Murinson, A. (2012) 'Turkish foreign policy in the twenty-first century', *Mideast Security and Policy Studies*, 91, 31.

Murphy, J. (2008) *The World Bank and Global Managerialism* (Oxon.: Routledge).

Murray, P. and Rees, N. (eds.) (2010) 'Special issue: European and Asian regionalism: form and function', *International Politics*, 47(3–4), 269–449.

Musu, C. (2011) 'The Middle East Quartet: a new role for Europe?' in Mockli, D. and Mauer, V. (eds.) *European–American Relations and the Middle East. From Suez to Iraq* (Oxon.: Routledge), 124–38.

— (2013) 'Europe, the southern neighbourhood and the Middle East: struggling for coherence' in Biscop, S. and Whitman, R. (eds.) *The Routledge Handbook of European Security* (Oxon.: Routledge), 170–8.

Nakamura, H. (2013) 'The efficiency of European External Action and the institutional evolution of EU–Japan political relations' in Telò, M. and Ponjaert, F. (eds.) *The EU's Foreign Policy: What Kind of Power and Diplomatic Action?* (Aldershot: Ashgate), 176–88.

Nicolaïdis, K. and Whitman, R. (eds.) (2013) 'Special issue on Normative Power Europe', *Cooperation and Conflict*, 48(2).

Niemann, A. and Huigens, J. (2011) 'The European Union's role in the G8: a principal–agent perspective', *Journal of European Public Policy*, 18(3), 420–42.

Niemann, A. and Schmitter, P. (2009) 'Neofunctionalism' in Wiener, A. and Diez, T. (eds.) *European Integration Theory* (New York: Oxford University Press), 45–66.

Nonneman, G. (2011) 'Europe, the US, and the Gulf after the Cold War' in Möckli, D. and Maurer, V. (eds.) *European–American Relations and the Middle East. From Suez to Iraq* (Oxon.: Routledge), 203–19.

Norheim-Martinsen, P. M. (2010) 'Managing the civil–military interface in the EU: creating an organisation fit for purpose', *European Integration online Papers*, 14(10).

— (2013) *The European Union and Military Force. Governance and Strategy* (Cambridge: Cambridge University Press).

Nousios, P., Overbeek, H. and Tsolakis, A. (eds.) (2012) *Globalisation and European Integration* (Oxon.: Routledge).

Noutcheva, G. (2009) 'Fake, partial and imposed compliance: the limits of the EU's normative power in the Western Balkans', *Journal of European Public Policy*, 16(7), 1065–84.

— (2012) *European Foreign Policy and the Challenges of Balkan Accession. Conditionality, Legitimacy and Compliance* (Oxon.: Routledge).

Noutcheva, G. and Aydin-Dzigit, S. (2012) 'Lost in Europeanisation: the Western Balkans and Turkey', *West European Politics*, 35(1), 59–78.

Novotny, D. and Portela, C. (eds.) (2012) *EU–ASEAN Relations in the 21st Century: Strategic Partnership in the Making* (Basingstoke: Palgrave Macmillan).

Nugent, N. and Saurugger, S. (2002) 'Organizational structuring: the case of the European Commission and its external policy responsibilities', *Journal of European Public Policy*, 9(3), 345–64.

Nuttall, S. (1992) *European Political Co-operation* (Oxford: Clarendon Press).

— (1997) 'Two decades of EPC performance' in Regelsberger, E., De Schoutheete De Tervarent, P. and Wessels, W. (eds.) *Foreign Policy of the European Union. From EPC to CFSP and beyond* (Boulder, CO: Lynne Rienner), 19–39.

— (2000) *European Foreign Policy* (Oxford: Oxford University Press).

Oberthür, S. and Pallemaerts, M. (eds.) (2010) *The New Climate Policies of the European Union* (Brussels: Institute for European Studies).

Oberthür, S. and Roche Kelly, C. (2008) 'EU leadership in international climate policy: achievements and challenges', *International Spectator*, 45(3), 35–50.

OECD (2013) 'Long-term growth scenarios', *OECD Economics Department Working Papers*, No. 1000, 1–91.

OECD/DAC High Level Forum (2005) *Paris Declaration on Aid Effectiveness: Ownership, Harmonisation, Alignment, Results and Mutual Accountability*, Paris.

Oikonomou, I. (2012) 'A historical materialist approach to CSDP' in Kurowska, X. and Breuer, F. (eds.) *Explaining the EU's Common Security and Defence Policy: Theory in Action* (Basingstoke: Palgrave Macmillan), 162–87.

Ojanen, H. (2000) 'Participation and influence: Finland, Sweden and the post-Amsterdam development of the CFSP', *ISS Occasional Paper*, 11, 1–26.

Oksamytna, K. (2011) 'The European Union Training Mission in Somalia and the limits of liberal peacebuilding', *International Spectator*, 46(4), 97–113.

Olsen, G. R. and Pilegaard, J. (2005) 'The costs of Non-Europe? Denmark and the Common Security and Defence Policy', *European Security*, 14(3), 339–60.

Olsen, J. P. (2002) 'The many faces of Europeanization', *Journal of Common Market Studies*, 40(5), 921–52.

O'Neill, M. (2012) *The Evolving EU Counter-Terrorism Legal Framework* (Oxon.: Routledge).

Orbie, J. (2006) 'Civilian power Europe. Review of the original and current debates', *Cooperation and Conflict*, 41(1), 123–8.

— (2012) 'The EU's role in development: a full-fledged development actor or eclipsed by superpower temptations?' in Gänzle, S., Grimm, S. and Makhan, D. (eds.) *The European Union and Global Development. An Enlightened Superpower in the Making?* (Basingstoke: Palgrave Macmillan), 17–36.

Pace, M. (2010) 'Interrogating the European Union's democracy promotion agenda: discursive configurations of "democracy" from the Middle East', *European Foreign Affairs Review*, 15, 611–28.

Pace, M. and Seeberg, P. (eds.) (2009) *The European Union's Democratization Agenda in the Mediterranean* (Oxon.: Routledge).

Pan, Z. (ed.) (2012a) *Conceptual Gaps in China–EU Relations: Global Governance, Human Rights and Strategic Partnerships* (Basingstoke: Palgrave Macmillan).

— (2012b) 'Introduction: exploring the conceptual gaps in China–EU relations' in Pan, Z. (ed.) *Conceptual Gaps in China–EU Relations: Global Governance, Human Rights and Strategic Partnerships* (Basingstoke: Palgrave Macmillan), 1–18.

— (2012c) 'Sovereignty in China–EU relations: the conceptual gap and its implications' in Pan, Z. (ed.) *Conceptual Gaps in China–EU Relations: Global Governance, Human Rights and Strategic Partnerships* (Basingstoke: Palgrave Macmillan), 19–34.

Pant, H. V. (2011) 'Iran and the bomb. Washington, the EU, and Iranian nuclear ambitions' in Möckli, D. and Maurer, V. (eds.) *European–American Relations and the Middle East. From Suez to Iraq* (Oxon.: Routledge), 220–34.

Papadimitriou, D. and Petrov, P. (2012) 'Whose rule, whose law? Contested statehood, external leverage and the European Union's rule of law mission in Kosovo', *Journal of Common Market Studies*, 50(5), 746–63.

Parker, C. F. and Karlsson, C. (2010) 'Climate change and the European Union's leadership moment: an inconvenient truth?' *Journal of Common Market Studies*, 48(4), 923–43.

Passos, R. (2011) 'The European Union's external relations a year after Lisbon: a first evaluation from the European Parliament' in Koutrakos, P. (ed.) *The European Union's External Relations: A Year after Lisbon* (The Hague: CLEER working paper 2011/3), 49–56.

Patrick, S. (2010) 'Irresponsible stakeholders? The difficulty of integrating rising powers', *Foreign Affairs*, 89(6), 44–53.

Patten, C. (2005) *Not Quite the Diplomat. Home Truths about World Affairs* (London: Allen Lane).

Pavese, C. and Torney, D. (2012) 'The contribution of the European Union to global climate change governance: explaining the conditions for EU actorness', *Revista Brasileira de Política Internacional*, 55, 125–43.

Pech, L. (2012) 'Rule of law as a guiding principle of the European Union's external action', *CLEER working paper*, 3, 1–56.

Peers, S. (2011) *EU Justice and Home Affairs Law* (Oxford: Oxford University Press).

Peters, D. (2010) *Constrained Balancing: The EU's Security Policy* (Basingstoke: Palgrave Macmillan).

Peters, D., Wagner, C. and Deitelhoff, N. (2010) 'Parliaments and European security policy. Mapping the parliamentary field', *European Integration online Papers*, 14(1).

Peters, J. (ed.) (2012a) *The European Union and the Arab Spring: Promoting Democracy and Human Rights in the Middle East* (Lanham, MD: Lexington).

— (2012b) 'Introduction: Europe and the challenge of the Arab Spring' in Peters, J. (ed.) *The European Union and the Arab Spring: Promoting Democracy and Human Rights in the Middle East* (Lanham, MD: Lexington), xi–xxi.

Petrov, P. (2011) 'Introducing governance arrangements for EU conflict prevention and crisis management operations: a historical institutionalist perspective' in Gross, E. and Juncos, A. E. (eds.) *Conflict Prevention and Crisis Management* (Oxon.: Routledge), 49–65.

Petrov, P., Pomorska, K. and Vanhoonacker, S. (eds.) (2012) 'Special issue: the emerging EU diplomatic system', *The Hague Journal of Diplomacy*, 7(1).

Pew Research Center (2011) 'China seen overtaking US as global superpower: 23-nation Pew Global Attitudes Survey', *Survey Report*, July, 1–157.

Piana, C. (2002) 'The EU's decision-making process in the Common Foreign and Security Policy: the case of the former Yugoslav Republic of Macedonia', *European Foreign Affairs Review*, 7, 209–26.

PIIA (Polish Institute of International Affairs) (2012) 'The EU external representation in the area of shared competences', January.

Pijpers, A., Regelsberger, E. and Wessels, W. (eds.) (1988) *European Political Cooperation in the 1980s* (Dordrecht: Martinus Nijhoff).

Pinfari, M. (2012) 'Tunisia and Libya' in Peters, J. (ed.) *The European Union and the Arab Spring: Promoting Democracy and Human Rights in the Middle East* (Lanham, MD: Lexington), 33–48.

Pirani, S. (2012) 'Russo-Ukrainian gas wars and the call on transit governance' in Kuzemko, C., Belyi, A. V., Goldthau, A. and Keating, M. F. (eds.) *Dynamics of Energy Governance in Europe and Russia* (Basingstoke: Palgrave Macmillan), 169–88.

Piris, J.-C. (2012) *The Future of Europe. Towards a Two-Speed EU?* (Cambridge: Cambridge University Press).

Poletti, A. (2012) *The European Union and Multilateral Trade Governance: The Politics of the Doha Round* (Oxon.: Routledge).

Poletti, A. and De Bièvre, D. (2013) 'The political science of European trade policy: a literature review with a research outlook', *Comparative European Politics*, online.

Pollack, M. (2012) 'Living in a material world: a critique of "normative power Europe"' in Zimmermann, H. and Dür, A. (eds.) *Key Controversies in European Integration* (Basingstoke: Palgrave Macmillan), 199–204.

Pollak, J. and Slominski, P. (2009) 'Experimentalist but not accountable governance? The role of Frontex in managing the EU's external borders', *West European Politics*, 32(5), 904–24.

Popescu, N. (2009) 'EU and the eastern neighbourhood: reluctant involvement in conflict resolution', *European Foreign Affairs Review*, 14(4), 457–77.

— (2011) *EU Foreign Policy and Post-Soviet Conflicts. Stealth Intervention* (Oxon.: Routledge).

Portela, C. (2010) *European Union Sanctions and Foreign Policy. When and Why Do They Work?* (Oxon.: Routledge).

Portela, C. and Raube, K. (2012) 'The EU polity and foreign policy coherence', *Journal of Contemporary European Research*, 8(1), 3–20.

Posch, A. (2009) 'The *Kadi* case: rethinking the relationship between EU law and international law?', *Columbia Journal of European Law Online* 15(1).

Posch, W. (2013) 'The EU and Iran' in Biscop, S. and Whitman, R. (eds.) *The Routledge Handbook of European security* (Oxon.: Routledge), 179–88.

Puetter, U. (2011) 'The Council. How the member states agree on Europe's external policies' in Wunderlich, J.-U. and Bailey, D. (eds.) *The European Union and Global Governance. A Handbook* (Oxon.: Routledge), 89–98.

— (2012) 'The latest attempt at institutional engineering: the treaty of Lisbon and deliberative inter-governmentalism in EU Foreign and Security Policy Coordination' in Cardwell, P. J. (ed.) *EU External Relations Law and Policy in the Post-Lisbon Era* (Basingstoke: Palgrave Macmillan), 17–34.

Qin, Y. (2011) 'Rule, rules, and relations: towards a synthetic approach to governance', *Chinese Journal of International Politics*, 4(2), 117–45.

Quille, G. (2013) 'The EU and non-proliferation of weapons of mass destruction' in Biscop, S. and Whitman, R. (eds.) *The Routledge Handbook of European Security* (Oxon.: Routledge), 235–42.

Radaelli, C. M. and Exadaktylos, T. (2010) 'New directions in Europeanization research' in Egan, M., Nugent, N. and Paterson, W. E. (eds.) *Research Agendas in EU Studies. Stalking the Elephant* (Basingstoke: Palgrave Macmillan), 189–215.

Radchuk, T. (2011) 'Contested neighbourhood, or how to reconcile the differences', *Journal of Communist Studies and Transition Politics*, 27(1), 22–49.

Rahman, S. A. (2009) 'Secularism and modernity. Alienation and the renewal of values in political Islam', *Journal of Islamic Law and Culture*, 11(1), 38–51.

Ramo, J. C. (2004) *The Beijing Consensus* (London: Foreign Policy Centre).

Raube, K. (2012) 'The European External Action Service and the European Parliament', *The Hague Journal of Diplomacy*, 7, 65–80.

Redmond, J. (ed.) (1992) *The External Relations of the European Community: The International Response to 1992* (New York: St Martin's Press).

Rees, W. (2011) 'The External face of internal security' in Hill, C. and Smith, M. (eds.) *International Relations and the European Union* (New York: Oxford University Press), 226–45.

Regelsberger, E., de Schoutheete de Tervarent, P. and Wessels, W. (eds.) (1997) *Foreign Policy of the European Union. From EPC to CFSP and beyond* (Boulder, CO: Lynne Rienner).

Renard, T. (2011) 'The treachery of strategies: a call for true EU strategic partnerships', *Egmont Paper* 45.

Renard, T. and Biscop, S. (eds.) (2012) *The EU and Emerging Powers in the 21st Century: How Europe Can Shape a New Global Order* (Farnham: Ashgate).

Rhode, B. (2010) 'WMD proliferation' in Giegerich, B. (ed.) *Europe and Global security* (Oxon.: Routledge), 149–76.

Ricci, A. (ed.) (2010) *Making the difference? What works in response to crises and security threats – The debate continues* (Luxembourg: Office for Official Publications of the European Communities).

Richter, S. and Leininger, J. (2012) 'Flexible and unbureaucratic democracy promotion by the EU? SWP Comments', *SWP Comments*, 26, 1–8.

Riddervold, M. and Sjursen, H. (2012) 'Playing into the hands of the Commission? The case of EU coordination in the ILO' in Costa, O. and Jørgensen, K. E. (eds.) *The Influence of International Institutions on the EU. When Multilateralism Hits Brussels* (Basingstoke: Palgrave Macmillan), 42–57.

Rijpma, J. (2012) 'Hybrid agentification in the Area of Freedom, Security and Justice and its inherent tensions: the case of Frontex' in Busuioc, M., Groenleer, M. L. P. and Trondal, J. (eds.) *The Agency*

Phenomenon in the European Union. Emergence, Institutionalisation and Everyday Decision-making (Manchester: Manchester University Press), 84–102.

Riley, A., Alex, B. and Rauscher, D. (2012) *EU Energy Roadmap 2050: EU External Policies for Future Energy Security* (Brussels: European Parliament).

Roberts, H. (2011) 'Logics of Jihadi violence in North Africa' in Coolsaet, R. (ed.) *Jihadi Terrorism and the Radicalisation Challenge: European and American Experiences* (Aldershot: Ashgate), 27–43.

Rosamond, B. (2002) *Theories of European Integration* (Basingstoke: Macmillan).

Ruano, L. (2012) *The Europeanization of National Foreign Policies towards Latin America* (Oxon.: Routledge).

Rubin, B. (ed.) (2013) *Islamic Political and Social Movements* (Oxon.: Routledge).

Rupnik, J. (ed.) (2011) 'The Western Balkans and the EU: "the hour of Europe"', *Chaillot Paper*, 126.

Rutten, M. (2001) 'From St-Malo to Nice. European defence: core documents', *Chaillot paper*, 47.

Rynning, S. (2011) 'Realism and the Common Security and Defence Policy', *Journal of Common Market Studies*, 49(1), 23–42.

Sadik, G. (2012) 'Magic blend or dangerous mix? Exploring the role of religion in transforming Turkish foreign policy from a theoretical perspective', *Turkish Studies*, 13(3), 293–317.

Saferworld, InterAfrica Group and Africa Peace Forum (2005) *Strengthening civil society participation and promoting conflict prevention under the Cotonou Partnership Agreement*. Report of a regional meeting on lessons learned in the Horn of Africa.

Saivetz, C. R. (2012) 'The ties that bind? Russia's evolving relations with its neighbors', *Communist and Post-Communist Studies*, 45(3–4), 401–12.

Saraiva, M. G. (2012) 'Brazil's strategies and partnerships: the place of the European Union', *Perspectives*, 20(2), 45–62.

Sasse, G. (2012) 'The ENP and the EU's eastern neighbours: Ukraine and Moldova as test cases' in Whitman, R. and Wolff, S. (eds.) *The European Neighbourhood Policy in Perspective: Context, Implementation and Impact* (Basingstoke: Palgrave Macmillan), 181–205.

Sautenet, A. (2012) 'The EU's strategic partnerships with emerging powers: institutional, legal, economic and political perspectives' in Renard, T. and Biscop, S. (eds.) *The EU and Emerging Powers in the 21st Century: How Europe Can Shape a New Global Order* (Farnham: Ashgate), 123–46.

Sautter, G. (2012) 'The financing of Common Foreign and Security Policy' in Blanke, H.-J. and Mangiameli, S. (eds.) *The European Union after Lisbon: Constitutional Basis, Economic Order and External Action* (Berlin: Springer), 567–82.

Scheffran, J., Brzoska, M., Brauch, H., Link, P. and Schilling, J. (eds.) (2012) *Climate Change, Human Security and Violent Conflict. Challenges for Societal Stability* (Heidelberg: Springer).

Scheipers, S. and Sicurelli, D. (2008) 'Empowering Africa: normative power in EU–Africa relations', *Journal of European Public Policy*, 15(4), 607–23.

Schimmelfennig, F. (2008) 'EU political accession conditionality after the 2004 enlargement: consistency and effectiveness', *Journal of European Public Policy*, 15(6), 918–37.

— (2011) 'EU membership negotiations with Turkey: entrapped again' in Thomas, D. C. (ed.) *Making EU Foreign Policy. National Preferences, European Norms and Common Policies* (Basingstoke: Palgrave Macmillan), 111–30.

Schimmelfennig, F. and Scholtz, H. (2008) 'EU democracy promotion in the European neighbourhood: political conditionality, economic development and transnational exchange', *European Union Politics*, 9(2), 187–215.

Schimmelfennig, F. and Sedelmeier, U. (2004) 'Governance by conditionality: EU rule transfer to the candidate countries of Central and Eastern Europe', *Journal of European Public Policy*, 11(4), 661–79.

— (eds.) (2005) *The Europeanization of Central and Eastern Europe* (Ithaca, NY: Cornell University Press).

Schimmelfennig, F. and Wagner, W. (eds.) (2004) 'Special issue – external governance in the European Union', *Journal of European Public Policy*, 11(4), 657–758.

Schmidt, P. and Zyla, B. (eds.) (2013) *European Security Policy and Strategic Culture* (Oxon.: Routledge).

Schrijver, N. (2009) 'The EU's common development cooperation policy' in Telò, M. (ed.) *The European Union and Global Governance* (Oxon.: Routledge), 176–91.

Schulz, M. (2012) 'Palestine' in Peters, J. (ed.) *The European Union and the Arab Spring: Promoting Democracy and Human Rights in the Middle East* (Lanham, MD: Lexington), 65–76.

Schumacher, T. (2012) 'Gulf Cooperation Council Countries and Yemen' in Peters, J. (ed.) *The*

European Union and the Arab Spring: Promoting Democracy and Human Rights in the Middle East (Lanham, MD: Lexington), 109–26.

— (2014) 'The EU and democracy promotion: readjusting to the Arab Spring" in Sadiki, L. (ed.) *Routledge Handbook of the Arab Spring: Rethinking Democratization* (Oxon.: Routledge),

Schuman, R. (1950) *Declaration of 9 May 1950*, Europa website.

Schunz, S. (2011) 'The European Union's representation in global climate governance: lessons from the past, prospects for the future' in Schwarzer, D., Lieb, J. and Von Ondarza, N. (eds.) *The EU in International Fora – Lessons for the Union's External Representation* (Baden-Baden: Nomos), 53–67.

Scott, D. (2013) 'Multilateralism, multipolarity, and beyond ...? EU–China understandings of the international system', *International Relations*, 27(1), 30–51.

Sedelmeier, U. (2012) 'Is Europeanisation through conditionality sustainable? Lock-in of institutional change after EU accession', *West European Politics*, 35(1), 20–38.

Sedra, M. (2011) 'Security sector reform in sub-Saharan Africa: a new playground' in Ekengren, M. and Simons, G. (eds.) *The Politics of Security Sector Reform. Challenges and Opportunities for the European Union's Global Role* (Aldershot: Ashgate), 229–42.

Sen, A. (2011) 'Quality of life: India vs. China', *New York Review of Books*, 58(8).

Sepos, A. (2010) 'Foreign and security policies: "trilateral" Europe?' in Dyson, K. and Sepos, A. (eds.) *Which Europe? The Politics of Differentiated Integration* (Basingstoke: Palgrave Macmillan),

Serra, N. and Stiglitz, J. (eds.) (2008) *The Washington Consensus Reconsidered. Towards a New Global Governance* (Oxford: Oxford University Press).

Servent, A. R. and MacKenzie, A. (2012) 'The European Parliament as a "norm taker"? EU–US relations after the SWIFT Agreement', *European Foreign Affairs Review*, 17(2/1), 71–86.

Shambaugh, D. and Xiao, R. (2012) 'China: the conflicted rising power' in Nau, H. R. and Ollapally, D. M. (eds.) *Worldviews of Aspiring Powers: Domestic Foreign Policy Debates in China, India, Iran, Japan, and Russia* (Oxford: Oxford University Press), 36–72.

Sicurelli, D. (2010) *The European Union's Africa Policies. Norms, Interests and Impact* (Hampshire: Ashgate).

Simao, L. (2011) 'EU–South Caucasus relations: do good governance and security go together?' *Political Perspectives*, 5(2), 33–57.

Simón, L. and Mattelaer, A. (2011) 'EUnity of command: the planning and conduct of CSDP operations', *Egmont Paper*, 41, 1–26.

Simón, L., Mattelaer, A. and Hadfield, A. (2011) *A Coherent EU Strategy for the Sahel* (Brussels: European Parliament).

Sinkkonen, T. (2011) 'A security dilemma on the boundary line: an EU perspective to Georgian–Russian confrontation after the 2008 war', *Southeast European and Black Sea Studies*, 11(3), 265–78.

SIPRI (Stockholm International Peace Research Institute) (2012) *SIPRI Arms Transfers Database*, sipri.org.

Sjøstedt, G. (1977) *The External Role of the European Community* (Farnborough: Saxon House).

Sjursen, H. (ed.) (2006) 'Special issue: what kind of power? European foreign policy in perspective', *Journal of European Public Policy*, 13(2), 167–327.

— (ed.) (2011) 'Special issue: the EU's Common Foreign and Security Policy: the quest for democracy', *Journal of European Public Policy*, 18(8), 1069–1207.

Skidmore, D. (2011) 'The Obama presidency and US foreign policy: where's the multilateralism?' *International Studies Perspectives*, 13(1), 43–64.

Smith, K. (2003) *European Union Foreign Policy in a Changing World* (Cambridge: Polity Press).

— (2006) 'The European Union, human rights and the United Nations' in Smith, K. E. and Laatikainen, K. V. (eds.) *Intersecting Multilateralisms: The European Union and the United Nations* (Basingstoke: Palgrave Macmillan), 154–74.

— (2008) *European Union Foreign Policy in a Changing World* (Cambridge: Polity Press).

— (2010a) 'The European Union at the Human Rights Council: speaking with one voice but having little influence', *Journal of European Public Policy*, 17(2), 224–41.

— (2010b) 'The European Union in the world: future research agendas' in Egan, M., Nugent, N. and Paterson, W. E. (eds.) *Research Agendas in EU Studies* (Basingstoke: Palgrave Macmillan), 329–53.

— (2011) 'Enlargement, the neighbourhood, and European order' in Hill, C. and Smith, M. (eds.) *International Relations and the European Union* (New York: Oxford University Press), 299–323.

Smith, M. (1997) 'The Commission and external relations' in Edwards, G. and Spence, D. (eds.) *The European Commission* (Essex: Longman), 262–302.

— (2013) 'Beyond the comfort zone: internal crisis and external challenge in the European Union's response to rising powers', *International Affairs*, 89(3), 653–71.

Smith, M. and Steffenson, R. (2011) 'The EU and the United States' in Hill, C. and Smith, M. (eds.) *International Relations and the European Union* (New York: Oxford University Press), 404–31.

Smith, M. E. (2001) 'Diplomacy by decree: the legalization of EU foreign policy', *Journal of Common Market Studies*, 39(1), 79–104.

— (2011) 'The European Union, the USA and global governance' in Wunderlich, J. and Bailey, D. (eds.) *The European Union and Global Governance. A Handbook* (Oxon.: Routledge), 264–273.

— (2013a) 'Symposium: building the European External Action Service' *Journal of European Public Policy*, 20(9), 1299–1367.

— (2013b) 'The European External Action Service and the security–development nexus: organizing for effectiveness or incoherence?' *Journal of European Public Policy*, iFirst.

Smith Stegen, K. (2011) 'Deconstructing the "energy weapon": Russia's threat to Europe as a case study', *Energy policy*, 39, 6505–13.

Socor, V. (2012) 'Post-Nabucco era in Caspian pipeline business and politics', *Eurasia Daily Monitor*, 9(24).

Söderberg, M. (ed.) (2012) 'Special issue: EU–Japan relations', *Japan Forum*, 24(3), 249–382.

Solonenko, I. (2012) 'European Neighbourhood Policy implementation in Ukraine. Local context matters' in Lannon, E. (ed.) *The European Neighbourhood Policy's Challenges* (Brussels: PIE Peter Lang), 345–80.

Song, X. (2013) 'Security and the role of China' in Christiansen, T., Kirchner, E. and Murray, P. B. (eds.) *The Palgrave Handbook of EU–Asia Relations* (Basingstoke: Palgrave Macmillan), 471–480.

Sourd, R. (2005) 'L'Union et l'Afrique subsaharienne: quel partenariat?', *ISS Occasional Paper*, 58.

Spence, D. (2011) 'Prospects and advantages of EU security sector reform' in Ekengren, M. and Simons, G. (eds.) *The Politics of Security Sector Reform* (Aldershot: Ashgate), 93–100.

— (2012) 'The early days of the European External Action Service: a practitioner's view', *The Hague Journal of Diplomacy*, 7(1), 115–34.

Spence, D. and Fluri, P. (eds.) (2008) *The European Union and Security Sector Reform* (London: John Harper).

Sperling, J. (2011) 'The European Union and NATO: subordinate partner, cooperative pillar, competing pole?' in Blavoukos, S. and Bourantonis, D. (eds.) *The EU Presence in International Organizations* (Oxon.: Routledge), 33–60.

Stacey, J. (2010) *Integrating Europe. Informal Politics and Institutional Change* (New York: Oxford University Press).

Stahl, B. (2011) 'Perverted conditionality: the Stabilisation and Association Agreement between the European Union and Serbia', *European Foreign Affairs Review*, 16(4), 465–87.

Statewatch (2009) *NeoConOpticon. The EU Security–Industrial Complex* (London: Statewatch and Transnational Institute).

Stepak, A. and Whitlark, R. (2012) 'The battle over America's foreign policy doctrine', *Survival*, 54(5), 45–66.

Stephen, M. D. (2012) 'Rising regional powers and international institutions: the foreign policy orientations of India, Brazil and South Africa', *Global Society*, 26(3), 289–309.

Sterckx, S. (2008) 'The external dimension of EU asylum and migration policy: expanding fortress Europe?' in Orbie, J. (ed.) *Europe's Global Role. External Policies of the European Union* (Aldershot: Ashgate), 117–38.

Stern, M. and Öjendal, J. (2010) 'Mapping the security–development nexus: conflict, complexity, cacophony, convergence?' *Security Dialogue*, 41(1), 5–29.

Stewart, S. (2011) 'EU democracy promotion in the eastern neighbourhood: one template, multiple approaches', *European Foreign Affairs Review*, 16(5), 607–21.

Stocchetti, M. (2010) 'The development dimension of disillusion? The EU's development policy goals and the Economic Partnership Agreements' in Nganghoh-Hodu, Y. and Matambalya, F. A. S. T. (eds.) *Trade Relations between the EU and Africa* (Oxon.: Routledge), 40–58.

Storey, A. (2006) 'Normative power Europe? Economic Partnership Agreements and Africa', *Journal of Contemporary African Studies*, 24(3), 331–46.

Strange, S. (1994) *States and Markets* (London: Pinter).

Stubbs, R. and Beeson, M. (2012) *Routledge Handbook of Asian Regionalism* (Oxon.: Routledge).

Stumbaum, M.-B. U. and Xiong, W. (2012) 'Conceptual differences of strategic partnership in EU–China relations' in Pan, Z. (ed.) *Conceptual Gaps in China–EU Relations: Global*

Governance, Human Rights and Strategic Partnerships (Basingstoke: Palgrave Macmillan), 156–72.

Szabo, E. M. (2011) 'Background vocals: what role for the rotating presidency in the EU's external relations post-Lisbon?' *EU Diplomacy Paper*, 5.

Tanaka, T. (2013) 'EU–Japan relations' in Christiansen, T., Kirchner, E. and Murray, P. B. (eds.) *The Palgrave Handbook of EU–Asia Relations* (Basingstoke: Palgrave Macmillan), 509–20.

Taylor, I. (2011) 'The EU's perceptions and interests towards China's rising influence on human rights in Africa' in Men, J. and Barton, B. (eds.) *China and the European Union in Africa: Partners or Competitors?* (Farnham: Ashgate), 127–46.

Telò, M. (2006) *Europe: A Civilian Power? European Union, Global Governance, World Order* (Basingstoke: Palgrave Macmillan).

— (ed.) (2009) *The European Union and Global Governance* (Oxon.: Routledge).

— (ed.) (2014) *European Union and New Regionalism: Regional Actors and Global Governance in a Post-Hegemonic Era* (Aldershot: Ashgate).

Telò, M. and Ponjaert, F. (eds.) (2013) *The EU's Foreign Policy: What Kind of Power and Diplomatic Action?* (Aldershot: Ashgate).

Thépaut, C. (2011) 'Can the EU pressure dictators? Reforming ENP conditionality after the Arab Spring', *EU Diplomacy Paper*, 6.

— (2012) *Comprendre l'Islam politique dans les sociétés Arabes Méditerranéennes: Défis et Perspectives pour la Politique Etrangère de l'UE*. Rapport de la conférence internationale, Chaire TOTAL sur la Politique étrangère de l'UE, Collège d'Europe, Bruges, 24 février.

Thépaut, C. and Keukeleire, S. (2012) 'Structural competition in Arab Mediterranean societies: Islamist parties and European foreign policy after the Arab uprisings'. Paper presented at the KFG workshop 'Europe and the Arab Region Post January 2011', Berlin, 8–9 June.

Thomas, D. (2012) 'Still punching below its weight? Coherence and effectiveness in European Union foreign policy', *Journal of Common Market Studies*, 50(3), 457–74.

Thym, D. (2006) 'Beyond Parliament's reach? The role of the European Parliament in the CFSP', *European Foreign Affairs Review*, 11(1), 109–27.

Tickner, A. B. and Blaney, D. L. (eds.) (2012) *Thinking International Relations Differently* (Oxon.: Routledge).

Tickner, A. B. and Waever, O. (eds.) (2009) *International Relations Scholarship around the World* (London/New York: Routledge).

Timmins, G. (2011) 'German–Russian bilateral relations and EU policy on Russia: between normalisation and the "multilateral reflex"', *Journal of Contemporary European Studies*, 19(2), 189–99.

Tocci, N. (2013) 'The Middle East Quartet and (in)effective multilateralism', *Middle East Journal*, 67(1), 29–44.

Tocci, N., Maestri, E., Özel, S. and Güvenç, S. (2012) *Ideational and Material Power in the Mediterranean: The Role of Turkey and the Gulf Cooperation Council* (Washington, DC: German Marshall Fund).

Toje, A. (2008) 'The European Union as a small power, or conceptualizing Europe's strategic actorness', *European Integration*, 30(2), 199–215.

Tömmel, I. and Verdun, A. (eds.) (2009) *Innovative Governance in the European Union. The Politics of Multilevel Policymaking* (London: Lynne Rienner).

Tonra, B. (2003) 'Constructing the Common Foreign and Security policy: the utility of a cognitive approach', *Journal of Common Market Studies*, 41(4), 731–56.

— (2012) 'Identity construction through the ENP: borders and boundaries, insiders and outsiders' in Whitman, R. and Wolff, S. (eds.) *The European Neighbourhood Policy in Perspective: Context, Implementation and Impact* (Basingstoke: Palgrave Macmillan), 51–72.

Trauner, F. and Carrapiço, H. (2012) 'The external dimension of EU Justice and Home Affairs after the Lisbon Treaty', *European Foreign Affairs Review*, 17(2/1), 1–18.

Tsebelis, G. (1994) 'The power of the European Parliament as a conditional agenda setter', *American Political Science Review*, 88(1), 128–42.

Turner, B. S. (ed.) (2010) *The Routledge International Handbook of Globalization Studies* (Oxon.: Routledge).

Ugur, M. (2010) 'Open-ended membership prospect and commitment credibility: explaining the deadlock in EU–Turkey accession negotiations', *Journal of Common Market Studies*, 48(4), 967–91.

UN (2012a) *The Millennium Development Goals Report 2012* (New York: United Nations).

— (2012b) *General Assembly Votes Overwhelmingly to Accord Palestine 'Non-Member Observer State' Status in United Nations*, UN.org.

UN Department of Economic and Social Affairs (2011) 'World population prospects: the 2010 revision', *Working Paper* ESA/P/WP. 220, 1–142.

UNAIDS/WHO (2009) *AIDS Epidemic Update: December 2009*, UNAIDS/09.36E / JC1700E.

UNDP (2011) *Human Development Report 2011. Sustainability and Equity: A Better Future for All* (New York: UNDP).

UNHCR (2012) *Mediterranean takes record as most deadly stretch of water for refugees and migrants in 2011*, UN Refugee Agency Briefing Notes, 31 January, unhcr.org.

United Nations (2013) *UN Data. Gross Domestic Product (current US$)*, data.un.org.

Usul, A. R. (2010) *Democracy in Turkey: The Impact of EU Political Conditionality* (Oxon.: Routledge).

Vaïsse, J. and Kundnani, H. (eds.) (2012) *European Foreign Policy Scorecard 2012* (London: European Council on Foreign Relations).

Van Elsuwege, P. (2010) 'EU External Action after the collapse of the Pillar Structure: in search of a new balance between delimitation and consistency', *Common Market Law Review*, 47(4), 987–1019.

— (2012) 'Variable Geometry in the European Neighbourhood Policy. The principle of differentiation and its consequences' in Lannon, E. (ed.) *The European Neighbourhood Policy's Challenges* (Brussels: PIE Peter Lang), 59–84.

Van Hüllen, V. (2012) 'Europeanisation through cooperation? EU democracy promotion in Morocco and Tunisia', *West European Politics*, 35(1), 117–34.

van Schaik, L. (2011) 'The EU's performance in the World Health Organization: internal cramps after the "Lisbon cure"', *Journal of European Integration*, 33(6), 699–713.

— (2013) *EU Effectiveness and Unity in Multilateral Negotiations: More than the Sum of Its Parts?* (Basingstoke: Palgrave Macmillan).

van Schaik, L. and Schunz, S. (2012) 'Explaining EU activism and impact in global climate politics: is the Union a norm- or interest-driven actor?' *Journal of Common Market Studies*, 50(1), 169–86.

Van Vooren, B. (2011) 'A legal–institutional perspective on the European External Action Service', *Common Market Law Review*, 48(2), 475–502.

Van Vooren, B., Blockmans, S. and Wouters, J. (eds.) (2013) *The EU's Role in Global Governance* (Oxford: Oxford University Press).

Vanhoonacker, S., Dijkstra, H. and Maurer, A. (eds.) (2010) 'Special issue: understanding the role of bureaucracy in the European Security and Defence Policy: the state of the art', *European Integration Online Papers*, 14 (Special Issue 1).

Vanhoonacker, S. and Pomorska, K. (2013) 'The European External Action Service and agenda-setting in European foreign policy', *Journal of European Public Policy*, 20(9), 1316–31.

Veclani, A., Darnis, J.-P. and Miranda, V. (2011) *The Galileo programme: management and financial lessons learned for future space systems paid out of the EU budget* (Brussels: European Parliament).

Verdun, A. (2011) 'The EU and the global political economy' in Hill, C. and Smith, M. (eds.) *International Relations and the European Union* (Oxford: Oxford University Press), 246–274.

Versluys, H. (2008) 'European Union humanitarian aid: lifesaver or political tool?' in Orbie, J. (ed.) *Europe's Global Role. External Policies of the European Union* (Aldershot: Ashgate), 91–115.

Vieira, M. A. and Alden, C. (2011) 'India, Brazil and South Africa (IBSA): South–South cooperation and the paradox of regional leadership', *Global Governance*, 17, 507–28.

Vogler, J. (2011) 'The challenge of the environment, energy, and climate change' in Hill, C. and Smith, M. (eds.) *International Relations and the European Union* (Oxford: Oxford University Press), 349–79.

Vogler, J. and Stephan, H. (2007) 'The European Union in global environmental governance: leadership in the making?' *International Environmental Agreements*, 7(4), 389–413.

Vončina, T. (2011) 'Speaking with one voice: statements and declarations as an instrument of the EU's Common Foreign and Security Policy', *European Foreign Affairs Review*, 16(2), 169–86.

Wade, R. H. (2011) 'Emerging world order? From multipolarity to multilateralism in the G20, the World Bank, and the IMF', *Politics and Society*, 39(3), 347–78.

Waever, O. (1993) 'Societal security: the concept' in Waever, O., Buzan, B., Kelstrup, M. and Lemaitre, P. (eds.) *Identity, Migration and the New Security Agenda in Europe* (London: Pinter), 17–27.

— (1998) 'The sociology of a not so international discipline: American and European developments in international relations', *International Organization*, 52(4), 687–727.

— (2000) 'The EU as a security actor: reflections from a pessimistic constructivist on post-sovereign security orders' in Kelstrup, M. and Williams, M. C. (eds.) *International Relations Theory and the Politics of European Integration. Power, Security and Community* (Oxon.: Routledge), 250–94.

Wagner Givens, J. (2011) 'The Beijing Consensus is neither: China as a non-ideological challenge to international norms', *St Antony's International Review*, 6(2), 10–25.

Wallace, H. (2000) 'The policy process; a moving pendulum' in Wallace, H. and Wallace, W. (eds.) *Policy-Making in the European Union* (Oxford: Oxford University Press), 39–64.

— (2005) 'An institutional anatomy and five policy modes' in Wallace, H., Wallace, W. and Pollack, M. A. (eds.) *Policy-Making in the European Union* (Oxford: Oxford University Press), 49–90.

Wang, Y. (2012) 'China and the EU in global governance: seeking harmony in identities' in Wouters, J., de Wilde d'Estmael, T., Defraigne, P. and Defraigne, J.-C. (eds.) *China, the European Union and Global Governance* (Cheltenham: Edward Elgar), 50–61.

Warleigh-Lack, A., Robinson, N. and Rosamond, B. (eds.) (2011) *New Regionalism and the European Union: Dialogues, Comparisons and New Research Directions* (Oxon.: Routledge).

Weil, S. and Jing, Y. (2012) 'The EU and China's perspective of democracy and their impact on China–EU relations' in Pan, Z. (ed.) *Conceptual Gaps in China–EU Relations: Global Governance, Human Rights and Strategic Partnerships* (Basingstoke: Palgrave Macmillan), 113–27.

Weinhardt, C. (2011) 'The EU as a friend of the developing world? Self portrayal and outside perceptions in the negotiations of EPA's' in Lieb, J., Schwarzer, D. and Van Ondarza, N. (eds.) *The European Union in International Fora: Lessons for the Union's External Representation after Lisbon* (Baden-Baden: Nomos), 99–114.

Weiss, M. (2011) *Transaction Costs and Security Institutions: Unravelling the ESDP* (Basingstoke: Palgrave Macmillan).

Wendt, A. (1999) *Social Theory of International Politics* (Cambridge: Cambridge University Press).

Wessel, R. A. (2011a) 'The EU as a party to international agreements: shared competences, mixed responsibilities' in Dashwood, A. and Maresceau, M. (eds.) *Law and Practice of EU External Relations. Salient Features of a Changing Landscape* (Cambridge: Cambridge University Press), 152–87.

— (2011b) 'The legal framework for the participation of the European Union in international institutions', *Journal of European Integration*, 33(6), 621–35.

Wessel, R. A., Marin, L. and Matera, C. (2011) 'The external dimension of the EU's Area of Freedom, Security and Justice' in Eckes, C. and Konstadinides, T. (eds.) *Crime within the Area of Freedom, Security and Justice: A European Public Order* (Cambridge: Cambridge University Press), 272–300.

Wetzel, A. and Orbie, J. (eds.) (2011) 'Special issue: promoting embedded democracy? Researching the substance of EU democracy promotion', *European Foreign Affairs Review*, 16(5), 565–734.

Wetzel, J. E. (ed.) (2011) *The EU as a 'Global Player' in Human Rights?* (Oxon.: Routledge).

Whitman, R. (2010) 'Muscles from Brussels. The demise of civilian power Europe?' in Elgström, O. and Smith, M. (eds.) *The European Union's Roles in International Politics* (Oxon.: Routledge), 101–17.

— (ed.) (2011) *Normative Power Europe: Empirical and Theoretical Perspectives* (London: Palgrave Macmillan).

Whitman, R. and Juncos, A. (2012) 'The Arab Spring, the eurozone crisis and the neighbourhood: a region in flux', *Journal of Common Market Studies*, 50(2), 147–61.

Whitman, R. and Rodt, A. (2012) 'EU–Brazil relations: a strategic partnership?' *European Foreign Affairs Review*, 17(1), 27–44.

Whitman, R. and Wolff, S. (2012a) 'Much ado about nothing? The European Neighbourhood Policy in context' in Whitman, R. and Wolff, S. (eds.) *The European Neighbourhood Policy in Perspective: Context, Implementation and Impact* (Basingstoke: Palgrave Macmillan), 3–28.

— (eds.) (2012b) *The European Neighbourhood Policy in Perspective. Context, Implementation and Impact* (Basingstoke: Palgrave Macmillan).

Wight, C. (2006) *Agents, Structures and International Relations: Politics as Ontology* (Cambridge: Cambridge University Press).

Wisniewski, E. (2013) 'The influence of the European Parliament on the European External Action Service', *European Foreign Affairs Review*, 18(1), 81–102.

Wissenbach, U. (2013) 'The EU and the two Koreas – one strategic partner, one strategic liability' in Christiansen, T., Kirchner, E. and Murray, P. B. (eds.) *The Palgrave Handbook of EU–Asia Relations* (Basingstoke: Palgrave Macmillan), 521–37.

Wittebrood, C. and Gadrey, C. (2010) 'The European Union and peacebuilding: the case of Chad' in

Blockmans, S., Wouters, J. and Ruys, T. (eds.) *The European Union and Peacebuilding: Policy and Legal Aspects* (The Hague: TMC Asser Press), 249–68.

Wohlforth, W. C. (2012) 'Realism and foreign policy' in Smith, S., Hadfield, A. and Dunne, T. (eds.) *Foreign Policy. Theories Actors Cases* (Oxford: Oxford University Press), 35–53.

Wolff, S. (2012) *The Mediterranean Dimension of the European Union's Internal Security* (Basingstoke: Palgrave Macmillan).

Wong, R. (2011) 'The Europeanization of foreign policy' in Hill, C. and Smith, M. (eds.) *International Relations and the European Union* (Oxford: Oxford University Press), 149–70.

Wong, R. and Hill, C. (eds.) (2011) *National and European Foreign Policies: Towards Europeanization* (Oxon.: Routledge).

Wouters, J., Bruyninckx, H., Basu, S. and Schunz, S. (eds.) (2012a) *The European Union and Multilateral Governance: Assessing EU Participation in United Nations Human Rights and Environmental Fora* (Basingstoke: Palgrave Macmillan).

Wouters, J. and Burnay, M. (2012) 'China and the European Union in the World Trade Organization: living apart together?' in Wouters, J., de Wilde d'Estmael, T., Defraigne, P. and Defraigne, J.-C. (eds.) *China, the European Union and the Restructuring of Global Governance* (Cheltenham: Edward Elgar), 79–97.

Wouters, J., De Baere, G., Van Vooren, B., Raube, K., Odermatt, J., Ramopoulos, T., Van den Sanden, T. and Tanghe, Y. (2013a) *The Organisation and Functioning of the European External Action Service: Achievements, Challenges and Opportunities* (Brussels: European Parliament).

Wouters, J., de Wilde d'Estmael, T., Defraigne, P. and Defraigne, J.-C. (eds.) (2012b) *China, the European Union and the Restructuring of Global Governance* (Cheltenham: Edward Elgar).

Wouters, J., Odermatt, J. and Ramopoulos, T. (2011) 'The status of the European Union at the United Nations after the General Assembly Resolution of 3 May 2011', *Global Governance Opinions*, July.

Wouters, J. and Raube, K. (2012) 'Seeking CSDP accountability through interparliamentary scrutiny', *International Spectator*, 47(4), 149–63.

Wouters, J. and Van Kerckhoven, S. (2013) 'The International Monetary Fund' in Jørgensen, K. E. and Laatikainen, K. V. (eds.) *Routledge Handbook on the European Union and International Institutions* (Oxon.: Routledge), 221–33.

Wouters, J., van Kerckhoven, S. and Odermatt, J. (2013b) 'The EU at the G20 and the G20's impact on the EU' in Van Vooren, B., Blockmans, S. and Wouters, J. (eds.) *The EU's Role in Global Governance: The Legal Dimension* (Oxford: Oxford University Press), 259–70.

WTO (World Trade Organization) (2012) *WTO Trade Profiles*, stat.wto.org.

Wu, C.-H. (2012) 'Beyond European conditionality and Chinese non-interference: articulating EU–China–Africa trilateral relations' in Wouters, J., de Wilde d'Estmael, T., Defraigne, P. and Defraigne, J.-C. (eds.) *China, the European Union and Global Governance* (Cheltenham: Edward Elgar), 106–24.

Wunderlich, J.-U. and Bailey, D. (eds.) (2011) *The European Union and Global Governance* (Oxon.: Routledge).

Wurzel, R. and Connelly, J. (eds.) (2010) *The European Union as a Leader in International Climate Change Politics* (Oxon.: Routledge).

Young, A. and Peterson, J. (2006) 'The EU and the new trade politics', *Journal of European Public Policy*, 13(6), 795–814.

Young, A. R. (2011) 'The rise (and fall?) of the EU's performance in the multilateral trading system', *Journal of European Integration*, 33(6), 715–29.

Youngs, R. (2009) *Energy Security. Europe's New Foreign Policy Challenge* (Oxon.: Routledge).

— (2010a) 'Introduction: idealism at bay' in Youngs, R. (ed.) *The European Union and Democracy Promotion: A Critical Global Assessment* (Baltimore, MD: Johns Hopkins University Press), 1–15.

— (ed.) (2010b) *The European Union and Democracy Promotion: A Critical Global Assessment* (Baltimore, MD: Johns Hopkins University Press).

— (2010c) *The EU's Role in World Politics. A Retreat from Liberal Internationalism* (Oxon.: Routledge).

Yuzawa, T. (2012) 'The ASEAN regional forum. Challenges and prospects' in Stubbs, R. and Beeson, M. (eds.) *Routledge Handbook of Asian Regionalism* (Oxon.: Routledge), 338–49.

Zaborowski, M. (2011) 'How to renew transatlantic relations in the 21st century', *International Spectator*, 46(1), 101–13.

Zhang, C. (2012) 'The conceptual gap on human rights in China–Europe relations' in Pan, Z. (ed.) *Conceptual Gaps in China–EU Relations: Global Governance, Human Rights and Strategic Partnerships* (Basingstoke: Palgrave Macmillan), 83–97.

Zhang, Q. (2010) *China's Diplomacy* (Beijing: China Intercontinental Press).

Zhang, X. (2012) 'Multipolarity and multilateralism as international norms: the Chinese and European perspectives' in Pan, Z. (ed.) *Conceptual Gaps in China–EU Relations: Global Governance, Human Rights and Strategic Partnerships* (Basingstoke: Palgrave Macmillan), 173–86.

Zielonka, J. (2011) 'America and Europe: two contrasting or parallel empires', *Journal of Political Power*, 4(3), 337–54.

Zito, A. (2005) 'The European Union as an environmental leader in a global environment', *Globalizations*, 2(3), 363–75.

Zwolski, K. (2011) 'The External dimension of the EU's non-proliferation policy: overcoming inter-institutional competition', *European Foreign Affairs Review*, 16(3), 325–40.

Index

Note: page numbers in **bold** are major entries.

369